WAGES AND EMPLOYMENT IN AFRICA

The Making of Modern Africa

Series Editors: Abebe Zegeye and John Higginson

Gender, Family and Work in Tanzania
Edited by Colin Creighton and C.K. Omari

Contesting Forestry in West Africa
Edited by Reginald Cline-Cole and Clare Madge

Electoral Territoriality in Southern Africa
Stephen Rule

Community Health Needs in South Africa
Ntombenhle Protasia Khoti Torkington

Consolidation of Democracy in Africa
A view from the South
Edited by Hussein Solomon and Ian Liebenberg

Ghana in Search of Development
The challenge of governance, economic management and institution building
Dan-Bright S. Dzorgbo

Regional and Local Economic Development in South Africa
The experience of the Eastern Cape
Etienne Louis Nel

Agrarian Economy, State and Society in Contemporary Tanzania
Edited by Peter G. Forster and Sam Maghimbi

Entrepreneurial Ethics and Trust
Cultural foundations and networks in the Nigerian plastic industry
Yakubu Zakaria

Growth or Stagnation? South Africa Heading for the Year 2000
Mats Lundahl

Wages and Employment in Africa

DIPAK MAZUMDAR WITH ATA MAZAHERI
University of Toronto, Canada

Ashgate

Published by
Ashgate Publishing Limited
Gower House
Croft Road
Aldershot
Hampshire GU11 3HR
England

Ashgate Publishing Company
131 Main Street
Burlington, VT 05401-5600 USA

Ashgate website: http://www.ashgate.com

British Library Cataloguing in Publication Data
Mazumdar, Dipak, 1932-
Wages and employment in Africa. - (The making of modern Africa)
1. Labor market - Africa 2. Wages - Africa
I. Title II. Mazaheri, Ata
331.1'096

Library of Congress Control Number: 2001096526

ISBN 0 7546 1911 7

Printed and bound in Great Britain by
Antony Rowe Ltd, Chippenham, Wiltshire

Contents

Part IV: Impact of Wage Decline

Part V: The Structure of Labor Markets in African Manufacturing

Part VI: Conclusions

List of Figures

List of Tables

Plan of the Book

This book, despite its length, is a selective treatment of some aspects of employment and labor markets in sub-Saharan Africa. A wide view of labor markets is taken — they include not only labor working for wages but also those pursuing their livelihood through self-employment in the agricultural and service and the informal manufacturing sectors. Wage employment is largely confined to the so-called formal sector of the economy, consisting of government employment — both government services and state enterprises — and private enterprises employing more than a few workers. The formal sector is expected to follow more contractually specified labor practices and is subject to detailed labor legislation and/or institutionally determined working conditions. Although a small part of the economy in terms of employment, the formal sector is much more important as a proportion of the monetized part of the GDP, and for setting critical trends in the economy.

Furthermore, in Africa more than in other regions, research is driven by the availability of data. Labor market data are relatively more plentiful for the wage sector, though the gap in statistical knowledge of the non-wage economy is being increasingly filled by household surveys conducted under the auspices of the World Bank in recent years.

The book begins with a thorough treatment of the trends in employment and labor earnings in the formal wage sector. In the introductory chapter of Part I we try to indicate the quantitative importance of different segments of the African labor markets, before examining in some detail the institutional influences which might have impacted on the working of the formal labor markets of this region. Part II analyzes labor market trends in the formal sector, largely relying on the data for the manufacturing sector — the statistics, which have been most systematically collected for several sub-Saharan countries. The time series generally extend from the early seventies to the early nineties. We try to bring out the salient features of the African wage sector, in the context of both the development earlier in the post-independence decade of the sixties, and the experience of other regions of the world.

There is generally a significant time lag in the public availability of labor market data for SSA countries. Thus, our story generally ends in the mid-nineties, though an attempt has been made to update some of the data wherever possible. Many of the trends identified in the analysis have been continued in more recent years, and some other issues, notably the impact of AIDS on the labor market, are beginning to emerge as important concerns. It is felt that the analysis of developments of a quarter of a century before the mid-nineties would serve as the basis for the assessment of developments of the most recent decade, when adequate data become available.

The African story of the period covered has been that of declining per capita income. Real earnings in the manufacturing sector have also generally experienced a declining trend as our detailed analysis shows. Nevertheless, and perhaps because of it, employment growth in formal manufacturing has been positive — more so than in many other regions of the world. The informal parts of the urban economy have, however, grown much faster in terms of numbers employed. The massive rural-to-urban migration would suggest that in spite of the wage decline in the formal sector earnings remain higher in the urban economy to attract the migrants. We need to know how the gap in earnings between the formal and the informal sectors within the urban economy, and the earnings difference between the rural and the urban sectors — once thought to have been huge — have changed over time. Important conceptual and statistical problems arise in this type of comparison, because, among other factors, of the prevalence of different types of migration involving all or parts of a rural household. We need to consider the relative family sizes and their earner-dependent ratios in different sectors in order to come to a reasonable judgment of the extent of the difference in income levels of family members. At the same time the interrelationship between income differentials, rural-urban migration and the incidence of poverty are central topics in any analysis of African economies. Part III of this book is devoted to theses issues. After a thorough discussion of conceptual issues, the study relies on intensive case studies, making use of household survey data — two (Kenya and Ghana) in much detail and three (Zambia, Sierra Leone and Cote d'Ivoire) in a more capsule form — to throw empirical light on the extent of the rural-urban earnings gap. The countries are selected to represent both Eastern and Western Africa, and possible differences in the nature of rural-urban links between the two regions are noted.

Another important issue turns round the question: has the trend decline in wages in African manufacturing increases the external competitiveness of African manufacturing. This group of issues is examined in Part III with the help of a case study of Kenya — for which long time-series of relevant variables are available.

Finally, in Part IV we return to labor in African manufacturing. The availability of a rich data set generated by special enterprise surveys in seven countries under the auspices of the Research Program in Enterprise Development (RPED) of the World Bank enables us to study in detail the earnings and other labor variables in terms of the characteristics of different types of industrial firms.

Acknowledgements

The work was started when the principal author had an appointment as labor specialist in the Office of the Chief Economist of the Africa Region of the World Bank in Washington D.C. After his retirement from this position the work has been supported by the unit for the Research Program in Enterprise Development (RPED) of the World Bank. Our thanks are due to the head of the unit, Mr. Tyler Biggs, who not only gave us the permission to use the RPED data sets for the analysis reported in the book, but also provided the necessary financial and infrastructure support for the work to proceed. Mr. Biggs has been responsible for organizing the RPED surveys. He put together almost single-handedly the organization and financial resources needed to carry through the ambitious project of data generation in the African manufacturing sector. Our thanks are due to his staff, particularly Manju Shah — who manages the RPED data set, Melanie Mbuyi, the program officer, and A. Robinson who typed the first complete version of the manuscript.

A number of research assistants had worked on the material other than the RPED data set. The most important among them was Tilahun Temesgen of the World Bank. His dedication and care in the handling of rather difficult data sets have been invaluable in bringing the analysis to a conclusion.

Part I:
Introduction

1 Labor Markets and their Development in sub-Saharan Africa

Peasant farming dominates the economies of sub-Saharan Africa, as in other developing countries. Thus, self-employment accounts for the major part of the labor market. The self-employed, however, have become an increasingly important part of the labor market outside the farming sector. This is partly because of the growing importance of off-farm activities of peasant households, but more importantly because of the large expansion of the 'informal sector' which has accompanied the high rate of urbanization. The urban informal economy is host to a variety of petty businesses, often single entrepreneurs working on their own, with some help, on a regular or part-time basis, from family members. Such businesses are found largely in the sales and service sectors, but also include simple manufacturing. The 'informal' sector is generally defined to also include some wage-workers, often employed in small enterprises — who are outside the purview of regular regulations or do not participate any formal employment contract. But the proportion of such workers is typically small. Employment for wages is provided by larger firms and by the public sector, the latter, in recent years, growing into a major actor in the market for wage labor, particularly in the urban areas.

The structure of the labor market can be illustrated by data collected from household surveys in Ghana between 1987 and 1992 (three rounds of the so-called General Living Standard Survey-GLSS), a source which will figure prominently in our subsequent analysis in several chapters.

The table shows that public sector employment accounts for nearly half of total wage employment in these years. The public sector has become a major provider of jobs in the formal sector as African governments expanded the civil service dramatically in recent years. Publicly owned commercial enterprises, sometimes operated jointly with the private sector, are also important sources of formal employment, but as Table 1.1 shows the contribution of such enterprises is typically small compared to administration and services (although in some countries the parastatals would be undoubtedly more important in wage employment).

Table 1.1 Distribution of Labor Force by Types of Employment

Percentages	*1987-8*	*1988-9*	*1991-2*
Wage Employees	17.3	18.1	15.3
Government	*8.0*	*7.7*	*7.7*
State Enterprises	*1.9*	*1.1*	*1.1*
Private	*7.4*	*6.5*	*6.5*
Farmer	58.7	56.6	56.6
Non-agricultural self-employment	19.5	23.5	23.5
Unpaid family	2.2	1.3	1.3
Unemployed	2.2	3.2	3.2
Total	100	100	100
Sample size	6076	6259	8021

Source: Teal (2000), Table 1, p.9.

The observed unemployment rate is seen to be very low in Ghana. Other surveys in sub-Saharan Africa report much higher rates. Of course, in economies dominated by the self-employed the recording of the unemployed is a hazy task at best, and much depends on the way surveys questions are formulated and administered. But even if we confine ourselves to the *urban* sector, where active search for jobs have more meaning with a larger incidence of wage employment, the unemployment rate was 2.1 percent in Ghana, rising to 5.8 percent in 1991-2. This contrasts with 8.2 percent in urban Kenya reported by a household survey in 1978, and 11.7 percent in 1986 (see Chapter 9 for details of the survey). Inter-country differences could be real to a significant extent. Much depends on the nature of the informal sector, which dominates the urban labor market, the ease of entry into it, and its perception by the job seekers and their families. A recent analysis of the labor market in Ethiopia throws out suggestive points on this issue.

Table 1.2 gives the data on labor allocation based on the household surveys conducted in urban areas. The very high rate of unemployment in urban Ethiopia is balanced by the comparatively lower proportion of labor in gainful self-employment. In urban Ghana in 1991 the self-employed comprised no less than 55 percent of the labor force. The implication is clear that in economies with a relatively underdeveloped informal sector of small businesses (petty trade, manufacturing and repair), the marginal return from work in the informal sector is too low — and below the reservation price of the unemployed. The educational level of the unemployed was found to be well above that of the self-employed in Ethiopia (only 15 percent of the unemployed had less than primary education in 1997 compared to 39 percent of the self-employed). The unemployed also seemed to come from better-off households and most of them reported that their main source of support while unemployed was help from the families. Their job preference was overwhelmingly directed towards the pubic sector (ibid, table 2), emphasizing the value the job-seekers attached to queuing rather than search in the private sector.

Table 1.2 Unemployment and Employment for Men in Urban Ethiopia, 1994-97 (Percentages of the Labor Force)

	1994	*1997*
Unemployment	33.8	27.7
Public Sector	26.4	29.3
Private sector	21.0	25.0
Self-employment	18.8	18.0

Source: Ethiopian Urban household Survey. Reported in Table 1, Krishnan (2000).

The contrast between Ghana and Ethiopia underlines a major point of the inter-country difference between the structure of labor markets in sub-Saharan Africa. The relative development of earnings opportunity in the informal, and particularly the self-employed sector in urban areas, is a crucial aspect of these differences. The informal sector will be an important part of the discussion on the formation of earnings in the urban economy in our detailed case studies of Kenya and Ghana in Part III.

Labor Market Trends

Developments in labor markets in Africa have been propelled by the high rate of growth of population and the labor force in recent decades. Table 1.3 gives the relevant data for the principal SSA countries figuring in this book.

Table 1.3 Growth Rate of Labor Force (Percentage per annum)

Country	*Population 1999(Millions)*	*Labor Force 1999(Millions)*	*1970-80*	*1980-90*	*1990-99*
Kenya	30.0	15	3.6	3.7	3.3
Tanzania	32.9	17	2.8	3.3	2.6
Zambia	9.9	4	2.8	2.8	2.9
Zimbabwe	11.9	5	2.8	3.5	2.2
Ghana	18.9	9	2.4	3.3	2.7
Cote d'Ivoire	14.7	6	2.5	3.0	3.2
Cameroon	14.7	6	1.5	2.3	3.0

Source: World Development Report.

The high and, in some countries, accelerating growth of the labor force has been accompanied by a net and sometimes substantial increase in the urban population. Table 1.4 gives the relevant figures.

Table 1.4 Level and Rate of Urbanization

Country	*Urban Population as Percent of Total*			*Average Annual Growth Rate*		*Population in Capital City (Percent of Urban)*	*Population in ≥ 1 million centers as percent urban*	
	1970	1993	1999	1970-80	1980-93	1990	1970	1995
Kenya	10	26	32	8.1	7.0	27	45	28
Tanzania	7	23	32	11.0	6.5	31	43	25
Zambia	30	42	40	5.9	3.8	29	0	31
Zimbabwe	17	31	35	5.8	5.6	30	0	0
Ghana	29	35	38	2.9	4.2	22	8	10
Côte d'Ivoire	27	42	46	6.4	5.2	45	37	45
Cameroon	20	43	48	7.1	5.3	17	22	40

Source: World Development Report, 1995, Table 31; 2000, Table 1.

It is important to note the high rate of urbanization continued into the eighties in spite of the fact that the rate of growth of GDP per capita had fallen to a level close to zero or even negative. Of course, the countries of sub-Saharan Africa span a wide range of income levels and degrees of urbanization. But it can be seen from Tables 1.4 and 1.5 (below) that this rather peculiar phenomenon was widespread. The only exception might be Ghana, which showed moderate rates of urban growth. The structural adjustment program had been initiated early in the eighties, and Ghana, as we shall see in detail in Chapter 10 (part III), had successfully raised relative incomes in the rural sector by the end of the decade.

Table 1.5 GNP per capita and Growth Rates of GDP

Country	*GNP per capita (1999 dollars)*	*GNP per capita (1999 PPP dollars)*	*Growth Rate of GDP*		
			1970-81	1980-90	1990-99
Kenya	360	975	5.8	4.2	2.2
Tanzania	240	478	5.1	2.8	3.1
Zambia	320	686	8.4	1.0	1.0
Zimbabwe	520	2470	1.8	3.6	2.4
Ghana	390	1793	-0.2	3.0	4.3
Cote d'Ivoire	710	1546	6.2	0.7	3.7
Cameroon	580	1444	6.3	3.4	1.3
SSA	500	1450			
USA	30,600	30,600			

Source: World Development Report, various years.

The rate of urbanization in SSA, as elsewhere in the developing world, has been driven partly by push and partly by pull factors. It is true that the rate of agricultural growth, although not dismal, has not been all that much higher than population growth in most of SSA, so that the pressure of population on land has clearly been an element in the urban drift.

But this pressure has been supplemented by powerful pull factors attracting migrants from the rural to the urban labor markets. The public sector has taken the lead in the creation of jobs in the modern sector in most African economies, and the urban bias in this type of employment is quite strong. The increase in schooling in the SSA has shifted job-seekers preference for modern sector jobs, disproportionately located in urban areas, and the growing importance of such jobs has been an important element in the rural-to-urban migration. During periods of difficulties in recent years, and sometimes declining GDP, the public sector has sought to protect and even increase employment in the modern wage sector. Job security in public employment has been an important element in the desire for job seekers to seek a foothold in this sector.

Wage Employment in sub-Saharan Africa

We begin our discussion of wage and employment trends in SSA in Part II with the segment of the labor market in which workers are employed for wages. Much of the data compiled on wages pertain to the formal sector, but it would be inappropriate to equate wage workers with formal sector workers. If we theorize that the formal sector is one where conditions of wage and employment are established by formal rules, then wage workers employed on a casual day-to-day contract will be outside the formal sector — such workers can be found in sizeable numbers in agriculture (largely but not exclusively outside plantations), and also in a variety of urban occupations, e.g. transport and construction. Furthermore, workers employed in enterprises below a certain size (e.g., less than 5 workers) are generally considered to be in the informal sector, because their conditions for employment are less formalized.

Table 1.6 provides data, covering four periods for the number of wage workers in selected African countries over the decade and a half ending in 1990. Since a great deal of our discussion in subsequent parts of the book is on the formal manufacturing sector, data on employment in this sector is also included in Table 1.6. Between 1975 and 1980 total wage employment increased by 14.7 percent. However, the next five years saw a sharp decline in growth, which increased by only 5.4 percent. Nevertheless, wage employment appeared to have recovered in Sub-Saharan Africa as a whole during the second half of the eighties, when it rebounded with an increase of 14.9 percent.

This statement might come as a surprise to many people who have shared the common perception that the formal wage sector in sub-Saharan Africa has been uniformly characterized by declining employment trends in the last decades. Dabelan (2001) complains that the above result might be 'biased upward' because the sample includes Botswana and Mauritius, two countries that saw rapid growth during parts of the period. He cited the cases of Zambia (which is in the sample) and Ghana (which is not in the sample) where there has been a decline in wage employment in the decade of the eighties. No doubt there are large variations in the growth rates of formal employment in these decades as between countries, but it is not correct to state that the dominant feature of African employment in the formal sector was a substantial decline in the eighties. As can be seen from Table 1.6 employment increased, albeit slowly, in two of the largest formal sectors of the continent — Kenya and Zimbabwe.

Table 1.6 Wage Employment in Selected African Countries 1975-90

Country	*Total wage employment (thousands)*				*Manufacturing wage employment (thousands)*			
	1975	1980	1985	1990*	1975	1980	1985	1990
1. Benin	33.1	66.2	80.8	51.2	1.15	6.45	8.34	
2. Botswana	57.3	83.4	117.2	209.0	3.85	5.60	9.90	24.30
3. Burundi	28.5	38.2	44.7	47.3	2.67	3.93	5.59	7.02
4. Côte d'Ivoire	340.9	470.2	415.5	385.0				
5. Gambia	18.8	29.6	24.1	31.3	2.30		1.38	
6. Kenya	819.1	1,005.8	1,174.4	1,409.0	100.70	141.30	158.80	178.70
7. Malawi	276.83	370.4	394.6	473.4		39.65	46.17	51.41
8. Mauritius	168.6	197.1	209.5	278.8	22.52	36.36	62.95	107.79
9. Niger	20.5	26.0	22.5	25.2				
10. Seychelles	13.8	17.9	18.2	23.5	0.58	1.10	1.06	2.60
11. Sierra Leone	61.8	69.9	69.4	70.2	5.84	7.43	8.14	
12. Swaziland	64.6	75.1	72.8	91.3	9.00	9.25	10.60	
13. Zambia	393.5	379.3	361.5	359.6	44.33	47.76	48.49	50.90
14. Zimbabwe	1,050.2	1,009.9	1,039.4	1,192.2	156.00	159.40	169.60	195.30
Total	3,347.3	3,839.0	4,044.6	4,647.0	348.94	458.23	531.03	618.02
with data for 1980 and 1975					346.64	418.58		
with data for 1985 and 1980						458.23	529.65	
with data for 1990 and 1985							502.56	618.02
Ratio of current year to Five Years Earlier **		1.147	1.054	1.149		1.208	1.156	1.230

*Data for Gambia, Swaziland and Zambia are for 1989 and for Sierra Leone, it is for 1988) ** Ratios are calculated for totals of countries that have data for both the periods.

Sources: Vandemoortele, 'Labor market informalization in Sub Saharan Africa' in Standing and Tokman (Ed.) 'Towards Social Adjustment: Labor market issues in structural Adjustment', Table 6 P.91, ILO Geneva 1991; ILO Yearbook of Labor Statistics 1992.

Time series data reported from another source, the UNIDO, discussed in a later section, confirms the point about a mean positive growth of formal employment in Sub-Saharan Africa (SSA), though not in all countries. A second reason for the popular perception of the decline in employment in SSA in the eighties has been the remarkable growth in labor absorption in the informal sector of the urban economies. The rate of urbanization in SSA has been very high, as we have seen. Indeed, the World Bank estimates the rate of urbanization in SSA in the period 1980-93 to have been 4.3 percent per annum (World Development Report 1995), higher than any other region in the world, and the rate was obviously higher in some countries. Thus, most of the increase in employment in the urban economy seems to have been in the informal sector, giving the impression that employment in the urban formal sector had actually been declining.[1]

The data available to us ends in 1990. But it is possible to piece together some data on growth rates in the nineties at least for some of the countries covered by the Bank's RPED Surveys. This has been done by Dabalen. The data are reproduced in Table 1.7.

Table 1.7 Employment Growth in the 1990s in Selected Countries (Percentage)

Industry	*Cameroon 1991-1995*	*Ghana 1991-95*	*Kenya 1990-94*	*Tanzania 1993-96*	*Zimbabwe 1991-94*
Food	-20	39		8	-0.6
Wood	16	-6		5	26.4
Furniture		12			
Textiles	0	7		-6	3.3
Garments					10.3
Metal	-18	12		-3	-14.1
All Firms	-14	16	12.5	2.9	3.5

Source: Dabelan (2001). Original sources are various as detailed in Dabelan.

The growth rates vary by country and industry. But apart from Cameroon, the growth in employment in all the countries was moderately positive. Ghana and Kenya led the way with annual growth rates of 3-4 percent while Zimbabwe had a growth rate of just 1 percent per annum. Another important fact pin-pointed in Table 1.6 is that manufacturing wage employment during this period accounted for no more than around 12

[1]House, Ikiara and McCormick found that between 1980 and 1985 self-employment in Kenya grew at 8 percent per annum, compared to 3.5 percent for the formal wage sector.

percent of total wage employment. A significant part of this small part of the workforce would be public employees. Public sector employment has been extremely important in Africa. According to a report, around 1980, on international comparison, the share of public sector employees in non-agricultural wage employment was the highest in Africa (54 percent), followed by Asia (36 percent), Latin America (27 percent), and the OECD countries (24 percent) (Heller and Tait 1984). It is, however, very likely that the share of the public sector in total wage employment has decreased in the decade of the eighties since many governments were faced with fiscal constraints — but adequate data for a recent year are unavailable. Also it should be noted that the share of the public sector in employment is probably less in manufacturing than in services.

There are large variations in the extent of wage employment among countries in Africa — Table 1.8 provides the data for some selected countries in 1990. Notably while the majority have only a small proportion of their labor force in wage employment, a few have a very substantial proportion — Botswana, Mauritius, Swaziland and Zimbabwe. In addition, the figures show the proportion of wage employment to the labor force for 1980 for the same countries for which data were available for 1990. Evidently, the growth of wage employment in the decade as a whole did not keep up with the growth of the labor force — a reversal of the trend observed in the decade of the seventies.

Given this perspective on the nature and extent of wage employment in SSA we can now focus our attention on the study of wages and the trends in wages over the decades of the seventies and eighties. The delay in the availability of African statistics preclude the analysis of the trends in the nineties. We have tried, however, to include some material on the first half of the nineties as available. Our two major sources of information are the data collected annually by the ILO and UNIDO — the latter confined to the manufacturing sector. The sources of the data also are quite different simply because various agencies within the national statistical departments are responsible for producing these returns for both UN organizations. The ILO data, as pointed out above, are confined to employment and wages, while the UNIDO data include returns on outputs, inputs and value added as well. It is likely that the organizations which participate in the regular industrial censuses (or sample surveys) will have a higher cut-off point in terms of size. However, the surveys conducted for the ILO (usually carried out by the Ministry of Labor) in the countries concerned do not include small firms in the informal sector.

Table 1.8 Importance of Wage Employment in Sub-Saharan Africa in 1990

Country	*Labor Force (Thousands)*	*Wage Employment (Thousands)*	*Share (%)*
Benin	2,194.7	51.2	2.33
Botswana	445.6	209.0	46.90
Burkina Faso	4,167.1	150.1	3.60
Burundi	2,819.9	47.3	1.68
Côte d'Ivoire	4,598.6	385.0	8.37
Gambia, The	329.3	31.3	9.50
Ghana	5,686.3	214.9	3.78
Kenya	10,011.2	1,409.0	14.07
Malawi	3,494.9	473.4	13.55
Mauritius	439.8	278.8	63.39
Mozambique	8,437.4	201.6	2.39
Niger	3,619.0	25.2	0.70
Senegal	3,191.9	130.1	4.08
Sierra Leone	1,437.6	70.2	4.88
Swaziland	306.4	91.3	29.80
Togo	1,396.3	63.9	4.58
Zambia	2,643.7	359.6	13.60
Zimbabwe	3,920.9	1,192.2	30.41
Total	59,140.7	5,384.1	9.10
Memo: Totals and ratio of these countries in 1980	42,277.0	5,192.1	12.28

Source: Wage employment from ILO: Yearbook of Labor Statistics. Labor force from World Bank: Social Indicators of Development, 1993. Data for 1980 from Jan Vandemoortele in Standing and Tokman (Ed.), 'Towards Social Adjustment: Labor Market Issues in Structural Adjustment.' Table 7 P. 93. ILO, Geneva 1991.

Before coming to this analysis of trends in employment and wages in the formal sector in Part II, we look briefly in Chapter 2 at the major institutional factors, which have impinged on the sector in the countries of the region.

2 Labor Market Institutions in Africa

This chapter will review the principal channels through which institutional interventions have affected employment and wages in the formal wage sector in Africa, with particular attention to the countries discussed in this book. In recent African economic history, there have been four major areas of institutional influence on the labor market. These are:

- Minimum wage legislation
- Public sector employment
- Job security legislation and other methods of protecting employment
- Unions and their role in the determination of wages and employment

We shall assess the importance of each of these factors in an historical context. In this chapter and particularly sections 3 and 4 we refer to the data generated by the RPED Survey of the World Bank. This is a sample survey of manufacturing enterprises and their workers in a number of African countries, carried out in three years of the mid-nineties. A discussion of the nature of the surveys and the methodology employed is to be found in the Appendix.

The Impact of Minimum Wage Legislation

We will see in Part II that African countries followed a policy of wage increase in the fifties and the sixties, using basically minimum wages and arbitration by government sponsored wage boards as an instrument. We reproduce data presented by A.D. Smith in particular, which shows the unique experience in Africa of real wage increases at rates of four to five times of per capita GDP.

It will, however, be emphasized in the discussion that it would be extremely naive to brand this period of unprecedented wage increase as one, which was being driven solely, or mainly by unthinking political pressures working on or with the state. Smith was quick to point out that there was a major economic objective behind the state-supported policies for raising wages. This was the desire to change the labor system from one dependant on the migrant labor system to one making use of stabilized labor, settled in the urban location.

Apart from the productivity augmentation factor, there were serious discussions based on equity in favor of the high wage policy. Migrant labor, working only in urban industry in a temporary capacity, was not in a position to acquire the skills necessary to move up in the occupation hierarchy. Consequently, skilled labor was recruited largely from expatriates and non-African sources and it benefited from monopoly rents, which led to a highly skewed distribution of earnings in the industrial sector. The political realities of this Colonial system of administration no doubt exaggerated this phenomenon. It would be reasonable to assume that the newly independent governments were induced to change this labor system.[2]

The failure to recognize the economic factors behind the institutionally driven wage increase induced many commentators to diagnose a serious 'disequilibrium' or 'distortion' in the urban formal sector of African countries. This point will be extensively discussed in Chapter 6 of Part III, where we use we hope to show how exaggerated the idea of a grossly inflated formal sector wage was in the context of the African economic system. It seems clear, given the analysis of the issues in that chapter, that the equilibrium real wage difference in favor of stable urban labor was significantly smaller than Turner's numbers suggest — even at the time when relative urban wages reached their peak around 1970.

The Post-1970 Experience

The high wage policy in African countries more or less ended by the mid- or end-sixties. In many countries, as the economies were threatened with budget deficits and inflationary trends, the emphasis shifted to income policies to restrain wage increase (see, for example, the discussion on the Kenyan legislation in the seventies in Mazumdar 1993). In fact, over the last three decades minimum wages have failed to maintain their levels in real terms in most of Africa, and some countries have experienced a substantial decline.

One study of minimum wages has given the following figures for three

[2] Indeed, in a well-known text on development, Professor Hla Myint described this maldistribution of the surplus created by modern technology as the crucial problem of 'underdevelopment'.

African countries:

Table 2.1 Trends in Real Minimum Wages in Selected Countries (1980=100)

Country	*1970*	*1975*	*1980*	*1985*	*1990*
Côte d'Ivoire	104	114	100	84	NA
Ghana	415	509	100	144	114
Kenya	119	121	100	68	NA

Source: Squire and Suthiwart-Narueput (1997).

Sahn (1992) gave some indication of trends in real minimum wages, basing himself on the data for a large number of African countries culled together by Starr (1987). Unfortunately, the material gives the story only to 1986, but Starr's summary is reproduced in Figure 2.1 for the light it throws on the substantial decline in the real value of minimum wages, which took place in Africa across the board in the period between 1970 and 1976.

Table 2.2 gives the minimum wage for the manufacturing sector of Ghana.

Table 2.2 Earnings by Firm Size, Average Earnings in the Public Sector and the Minimum Wage, 1992-94

Earnings (monthly, in cedis)	*Wave 1 (1992)*	*Wave 2 (1993)*	*Wave 3 (1994)*
Large (100+)	41,420	48,876	56,849
Medium (30-100)	31,820	38,392	41,017
Small (5-29)	17,943	25,098	26,682
Micro (<5)	13,419	13,161	14,264
All	25,696	33,272	36,215
Average Earnings in the Public Sector	62,687		
Minimum Wage	13,617		

Source: The data for the manufacturing enterprises are generated by the RPED surveys and are taken from the analysis of F. Teal (1996), Table 3, p. 971. The average public sector earnings for 1991 are taken from SSER 1994, Table 8.14, p. 153. They have been blown up by 80 percent in the across-the-board wage increase granted to public employees in July 1992. The figure for the minimum wage is from the same source, adjusted by the cost-of-living index for Accra.

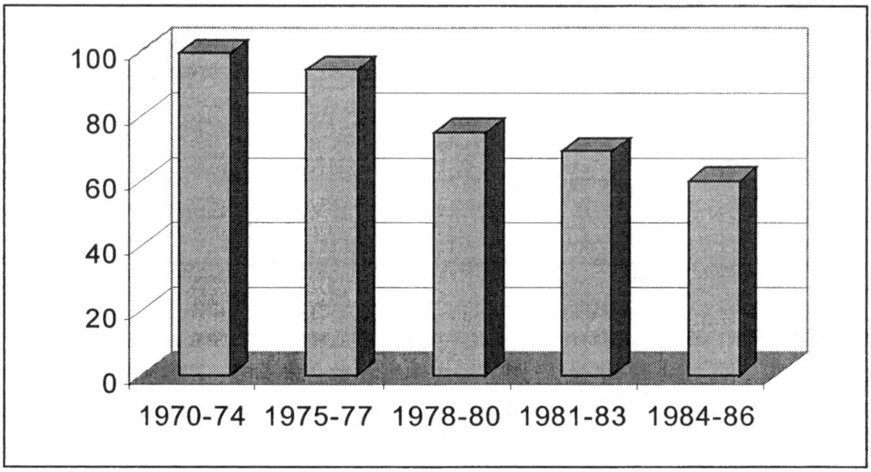

Figure 2.1 Trends in Real Official Minimum Wage Indices in sub-Saharan Africa (1970=100)

It does seem that the minimum wage is on par with the wage levels on *micro* enterprises in Ghana. However, the wage levels in larger firms and in the public sector are well above the minimum wage level. This result is consistent with the answers obtained in the RPED surveys to questionnaires addressed to employers on the ranking of different kinds of legal constraints affecting them in their production and labor deployment decisions (see below pp. 26-28).

The Role of the Public Sector

The Experience of the Sixties and the Seventies

Formal Sector Employment A striking feature of employment growth in the developing countries since the Second World War has been the large role played by the public sector. By definition, public sector jobs belong to the formal sector. The public sector has therefore been instrumental in expanding the formal urban labor market in many developing countries, including those in Africa.

A well-known study in the eighties by Heller and Taite (1983) brought together data from 23 developing countries. It showed the public sector in these countries account for 44 percent of total non-agricultural employment. This contrasts with the corresponding figure of 24 percent of the 14 industrialized countries in the sample (Table 1, p.7). In some developing countries, the proportion of non-agricultural employment in the public sector was much higher. Ghana, Tanzania, and Zambia, for example, along with India had a ratio more than 70 percent.

In the first three decades of the post war world, the public sector increased its importance even in advanced countries. According to Musgrave and Musgrave (1980, pp. 142-49) today's industrialized countries experienced, a gradual increase in the relative size of public sector employment at the same rate as their per capita income grew. Nevertheless, data brought together by Knight and Sabot (1988) showed that in the 14 developing countries for which data was available, including four countries in sub-Saharan Africa, public sector employment expanded much faster in the sixties and the seventies. The data for the African countries are presented below in Table 2.3 along with the mean of the sample of 14 countries.

Table 2.3 Growth of Wage Employment in the Public and the Private Sectors in Selected Countries

		Average growth (% per year)		
Country	Period	Public	Private	Total
Ghana	1960-78	3.4	-5.9	-0.6
Kenya	1963-81	6.4	2.0	3.7
Tanzania	1962-76	6.1	-3.8	1.6
Zambia	1966-80	7.2	-6.2	0.9
Unweighted mean of 14 countries		5.5	0.3	2.4

Source: Knight and Sabot (1988) Table 1.

These dramatic figures reveal that in the four African countries the public sector was responsible for whatever employment growth took place in the formal sector in the sixties and the seventies. With the persistent decline in the fiscal position of governments in the subsequent decades, and the insistence of foreign aid agencies on 'structural adjustment' programs of reform, governments in Africa became increasingly aware of the need to reign in their public expenditure programs. But they have been often unable to resist the strong pressure to expand employment in the face of the rapid increase in the number of job-seekers, and the poor performance of the formal private sector. The case of Kenya discussed in detail in Part III illustrates the trend. The growth rate of public employment in the seventies was 5.8 percent per annum compared to 2.3 percent for the formal private sector. In the next decade the two rates came much closer together, but at

4.4 percent the public sector rate was still significantly higher than the private sector (3.1 percent). The public sector protected its employment growth by letting real wages fall at a higher rate than the private sector — a decline of 2.5 percent per annum against 1.1 percent in the latter.

Interpreting the Public-Private Wage Differential

Wage determination in the public sector is an administrative decision. It is subject to two constraints: first is the budget constraint. It determines the wage bill, which the authorities are able to finance without risking macro-economic instability. Secondly, given the wage bill the public sector is faced with a trade-off between the level of the average wage per worker and the volume of employment in this sector. In fact, the relationship between the two elements is governed by a rectangular hyperbola the area under which measures the wage bill. The point at which point of the hyperbola the public sector opts to rest is determined by their welfare function determining the relative weight they attach to the wage level on the one hand, and the volume of employment it can offer on the other. It is easy to see that economic concerns are not the only factors entering the values of the welfare function. Social and political concerns would be of equal or more importance.

This formulation probably contrasts with a likely situation in economies where the public sector is a small part of the wage labor market. In such economies, which might represent the case of some advanced countries, the public sector is a price taker. The wage level will be determined by the earnings of labor of equivalent quality and grade in the private sector. Thus, public sector employment is determined residually in terms of the budget constraint.

However, in most developing countries, and certainly in Africa, in the most general case the public sector employment is so large that where it locates on the (given) rectangular hyperbola will surely affect both the wage level and employment in the private sector. It can do so directly by altering the demand and/or the supply curves of labor in the private sector. It can also affect it indirectly by acting as a 'wage leader' to private firms.

Even though in the 'African' case it is likely to be the private sector rather than the public which would be acting more like a price taker, we should generally not expect to see a significant wage gap in the two sub-sectors, if we accurately control for labor quality. As a profit maximizer private firms will set the wage which reflects the marginal supply price of labor, and the latter is given by the administered price set in the public sector for labor of equivalent quality. If a public-private sector gap is still observed it might be because of one of three reasons: (i) if wage levels are changing significantly over a period of time, there might be persistent lags in the adjustment of wages in the private sector to the administered public wage; (ii) there might be queuing for jobs and rationing in the public sector, so that the actual wage in the private sector is equated to the public sector wage only after discounting the latter by the probability of obtaining employment in it; and (iii) the quality of labor is not properly captured in all its elements by the characteristics of labor we are able to observe and measure. With respect to the last point, it might be noted that in the private sector employers would try to base their wages having regard to efficiency wage consideration — so as to minimize the cost of an unit of labor effort — and this might be higher than the wage per man in the public sector. The productivity or efficiency of labor is unobserved in many lines of activity of the public sector, and in any case they might not be interested in minimizing the efficiency cost of labor in the absence of profit-maximizing goals.

The Experience of the Sixties In the fifties and the sixties the public sector in Africa generally used wage policy in this sector to supplement the tool of minimum wages in the private sector to increase African wage levels throughout the modern sector. In most countries, three was a premium in wages paid in the public sector. Lindauer and Sabot (1983) found that the premium (controlling for measurable characteristics of labor) was 11 percent for the public sector in Tanzania in 1971 and 29 percent for the parastatal sector. The higher wages for the parastatals was a common phenomenon — at that time, as it is in more recent years.

Lindauer (1991) surveyed the situation in a number of African countries and found that parastatals (or public enterprises — PEs) were different from private enterprises as well as the civil service in wage policies. 'For private establishments, firm profitability determines long-run survival. The same cannot be said of PEs. Their frequent ability to pass on losses on to the government treasury removes some of the discipline of the market place in conditioning factor-pricing decisions... In setting wages, PEs may also be less constrained relative to government employees. Unlike individual ministries, most PEs earn revenues which can facilitate payment of wages and other benefits which exceed market rates. In contrast, centralized salary grading systems condition civil service pay and make it difficult for individual ministries to exceed government wage scales.' (p.835).

Employment and Wages After the Early Seventies The high wage policies petered out in most countries by the end of the sixties or early seventies. By then African economies had become burdened with severe budget deficit problems which implied that the public sector had to be reigned in terms of wage escalation or employment expansion or both. There was growing concern as well of the low growth of formal sector employment. Therefore, the policy makers were beginning to pay serious attention to the argument that the rapid increase in real wages might indeed have been one of the causes of the stagnation of employment growth particularly in the private sector.

A set of studies on pay and employment policies in the government sector in a number of African countries in the mid-eighties documented the basic trends over the previous 15 years (Lindauer, Meesook and Subsaeng). The sample included Ghana, Malawi, Sudan, and Tanzania. Basic real salaries were eroded by inflation in the face of infrequent salary adjustments that did not keep pace with price increases. The rate of decline in real salaries were much more than that of per capita GDP. Table 2.4 reproduces some of the figures for a basic middle grade of administrative staff.

Table 2.4 Trends in Real Basic Starting Salaries in the Public Sector 1975-83 (percent per annum)

Country	*Real Salary*	*Real GDP per capita*
Ghana	-26.9	-4.8
Malawi	-3.7	1.2
Nigeria	-11.4	-2.1
Senegal	-2.1	-2.6
Sierra Leone	-6.8	0.2
Sudan	-13.5	-5.2
Uganda	-33.3	-3.2

Source: Lindauer et al., Table 3, p.8.

For the sample as a whole, official non-wage benefits do not appear to have grown in response to the declining real salaries. If anything, many of them decreased in response to increasingly severe fiscal constraints.

There has been a tremendous compression of the pay structure as governments have tried to protect the real wages of the unskilled at the expense of the more skilled. In many cases, the differential in pay for the higher skills became out of line with the differentials in the private sector. In Ghana in 1985, for example, the ratio of basic compensation from top to bottom was about 10:1 in the private sector and 2:1 in the civil service (see World Bank 1985, p.139).

The private-public sector wage differential has narrowed over the period. While the State opted in favor of job retention in the employment, real wage trade off as economic decline continued, and allowed public sector wages to fall drastically, private sector wages were to some extent protected at the lower end by the necessity of ensuring a minimum level of worker efficiency. Thus, the premium that existed in many countries for the public sector fell substantially.

In contrast, employment in the public sector has consistently increased more than in the private sector in every country except Uganda. The government has been unable to resist the political pressures to provide jobs in an environment, which has seen a shrinking employment situation in the private formal sector.

The Post-Adjustment Experience The adjustment programs initiated in some sub-Saharan economies in the last decade or so have generally recognized the urgent need to reduce the size of public sector employment, both to promote efficient use of labor, and the more educated labor at that, and to manage the fiscal problems of theses economies more prudently. It is increasingly recognized that governments trying to do too many things end up by doing very little. The large wage bill of public sector workers has a social marginal productivity close to zero. While being officially on the payroll as civil servants, many of these workers have little to do on their assigned jobs, and often pursue other activities for financial gain (Lindauer and Nunberg 1994). Sahn, Dorosh and Younger write in their survey of the problem: 'These government expenditures, while technically pertaining to the various ministries and state-run enterprises are actually no more than transfer payments. As such, there are no beneficiaries other than the workers who receive the salaries'(p. 64).

Shan *et al* use household surveys to identify the income class of households which include public sector employees and the income they get from their employment. In all the four surveys studied (Cote d'Ivoire, Ghana, Mozambique (Maputo) and Guinea (Conarky), it is found that the households with public employees are more likely to be in the middle and upper quintiles of the per capita expenditure distribution, contrasted with those in self-employment or even in the private wage sector. The conclusion one draws from these data is that expenditure on public sector salaries is regressive. It is also on a sufficiently generous scale (in spite of the trend decline in public wages through the seventies and eighties mentioned above) to ensure that the recipients are better of than the population as a whole. Furthermore, the household survey data provided by Sahn et al show a clear urban bias in public sector employment, with the capital city being most favored, and also women are seen to be less likely to benefit from such employment than men.

Given the bias of the public wage sector, it is easy to understand that powerful vested interests will have been built up over the years, which will hinder reform. In spite of the widespread recognition of the economic burden imposed on African economies by an over expanded public sector, governments have been reluctant to undergo a sustained program of retrenchment. In the few countries, which have initiated such programs, implementation has been spotty. Public sector employees have often succeeded in stifling the layoffs or extracting lucrative compensations making retrenchment too costly to pursue. (Kingsbury, 1992, and Karp-Todaro, 1991). In some cases the fiscal gains of retrenchment have been reversed by renewed hiring after the start of the program. Mills and Sahn (1993) estimate that about half of the reduction of public sector employees in Guinea were offset by hiring of new civil servants. The comparable figure in Ghana was one-quarter (de Merode 1994). Lastly, while we have seen that public sector employees are generally in a higher income group than those in the private sector, there is a persistent concern among policy makers and donors alike that these households might easily slip into the low income groups if they are retrenched, adding to the economic and social problems of poverty. But this last point immediately brings us to a consideration of the 'true' wage gap between the public and private sectors, taking into account the 'quality' of labor drawn into the respective sectors.

Review of Studies of the Public-Private Wage Gap

While the large employment in the public sector (including parastatal enterprises) most likely is an important distortionary factor in the allocation of employment, particularly in the formal sector, it is not clear that a large wage differential for labor of equivalent quality still exists in favor of the public sector. One recent study for Ghana found that, controlling for human capital and locational factors public sector workers earned 55 percent more in 1987, but that the premium had dropped to 24 percent in 1991 (quoted in Canagarajah and Mazumdar 1997, table 3.4, p.14).

We have already commented on the fact that wages in parastatals have been generally even higher than other parts of the public sector. The RPED surveys provide materials, which enable us to measure the net difference in favor of parastatals in the countries surveyed. Our results, based on estimated earnings functions are presented in Table 2.5 (see Chapter 14 for details). These figures suggest that even in 1992-94 substantial wage premium existed in favor of parastatals — including those operating jointly with private owners — except perhaps in the case of Kenya.

Table 2.5 Coefficients of Ownership Dummies in Extended Earnings Regression

	Cameroon	*Côte d'Ivoire.*	*Ghana*	*Kenya*	*Tanzania*	*Zambia*	*Zimbabwe*
Foreign	0.25**	0.29**	0.24	0.22**	-0.15	0.28**	0.38**
Private-Foreign	0.05	0.31**	0.16**	0.08*	0.03	0.20**	0.19**
State- Private	0.16**	0.11	0.40**	-0.16	0.37*	0.34**	0.13
State	-0.16	0.77**	0.03	-0.72**	-0.09	0.21**	0.57**
Number of Observations	1712	1250	1613	2405	1246	2169	1907
Adjusted R^2	0.5171	0.4725	0.2271	0.3498	0.2847	0.3625	0.3880

Source: Own analysis of RPED data. See Chapter 13.

The studies referred to so far estimate the equations in the two sectors by standard OLS procedures. The validity of this procedure depends crucially on the assumption that employees are randomly distributed (with respect to their unobservable wage-determining characteristics) between the two sectors. But when sizable wage differentials exist the sample of workers employed in each sector are selected, not randomized. Potential employees will queue up for the 'preferred' sector and a selection process will determine who will obtain employment in the two sectors. In this case the selection process may lead to biases in the estimates of the parameters of the earnings functions, depending on whether the characteristics that have an impact on both the wage level and the selection process are in any way correlated.

Some authors have tried to 'correct' for this selectivity bias by estimating more elaborate models, which include an equation to determine the choice of the sector in which employment is found. One such attempt is by van der Graag and Vijverberg (1988) using the LSMS survey (1985) data for Cote d'Ivoire. They conclude: 'Though OLS estimates based on sector-specific samples show much higher wage rates in the public sector, our estimates—taking the selection process into account — do not show such dominance of public wage offers over private ones' (p.251). Wage offers (i.e., marginal wage rates which include the probability of being selected in a particular sector) are estimated to be higher in the *private* sector for low educational levels, but lower for high educational levels with 10 or more years of schooling (exactly the opposite of what is found in the estimates of earnings *conditional* upon a worker being employed in the public or the private sector).

What explains the queuing for public sector jobs if wage offers are found to be close together in the two sectors? Van der Graag and Vijverberg suggest that there are other factors, which make a public job preferable to a private one. These include job security, working hours which permit moonlighting, fringe benefits as well as the ability to command authority over other sections of society, and the additional resources, which such power might command.

Broadly, similar results were reached by Mengiastae in a more recent study of the labor market in Ethiopia based on the survey of 1994. The analysis rejected the absence of job rationing in favor of a partial queue for public sector jobs. 'The queue is largely due to the expectation of large public sector wage premiums the mean of which is estimated at 11 percent if we ignore returns to unobservable worker characteristics and at the hefty figure of 40 percent otherwise. But there is more to the length or the composition of the queue than the expectation of higher public sector wages'. The author found that, after controlling for individual differences in the expected public sector wage premium, the worker's family background was the single most important determinant of his sector preference. In particular, the worker was much more likely to be in the queue if his father's occupation were farming than if were a second generation urban dweller. The suggestion is strong that the influx of rural job seekers into the urban labor market is fuelled by the strong desire to land a public sector job, regardless of the wage premium at a point of time.

Finally, it should be emphasized that in the discussion so far we have been concentrating on the difference in earnings between the private and public wage labor markets. But most of wage employment in the private sector is in the 'formal' part of the urban labor market, whereas much of private employment in urban areas is in the informal sector where self-employment predominates. The difference in earnings between public sector employment and informal self-employment could be huge, particularly when comparisons are made for choices at the margin. This is brought out in studies, which have looked at the experience of workers who were retrenched from public sector jobs after the enactment of structural adjustment reforms. Alderman et al (1995) and Younger (1996) examine the case of Ghana, while Mills and Sahn (1995,1996) discuss the experience of Conakry, Guinea. The retrenched workers surveyed by Alderman et al mostly came from the lower echelons of the civil service: 80 percent of them had held unskilled jobs. The researchers found that while 85 percent of the retrenched had found another job at the time of the survey, their average earnings had dropped by 48 percent. The decline was not due to reduced returns to measurable human capital, but rather it appears that the whole earnings function had shifted down. There was, however, considerable heterogeneity in the group. The few who had found work in the wage sector had fared reasonably well, but the remainder suffered large decreases in earnings. For the underemployed farmers, earnings had all but disappeared.

It is tempting to conclude from the evidence that retrenched workers had a downward shift in the earnings function that they lost the rental premium, which they had enjoyed in public employment. This is indeed what Alderman et al and Younger conclude from their analysis. But the really large difference in earnings seems to be between the wage and the self-employed sectors. This is to be expected in the labor markets of developing countries where the efficiency wage mechanism, quite apart from any institutional influence, establishes a bottom for wage employees, in so far as no employer would offer a wage below the threshold at which efficiency begins to decline proportionately more than the wage. No such threshold holding up a minimum wage, of course exist for people working for themselves. Furthermore, the self-employed might be willing to start with very low earnings if they have expectations of enhanced earnings from their entrepreneurial initiatives, particularly at a later age if and when they are established.

The Impact of Job Security Laws and Practices

The government's impact on the labor market in African countries in the years after independence was felt not just through the direct action on wage levels, but also through laws to protect the security of tenure of workers employed in the formal sector. Typically such laws required that workers could be laid off only after employers had gone through a costly and time consuming procedure of approvals from regulatory bodies set up and controlled by the government. The fact that in many countries employers could avoid the impact of such legislation by employing a portion of the labor force as 'temporaries' without a long-term contract, or that in some cases separation was permitted if employers and employees agreed voluntary on the separation, did not imply that the legislation had not increased the cost of employing labor. In the former case the cost of skill formation would increase, and in the latter voluntary separation typically involved a lump sum payment to the worker. In a much quoted exercise Fallon and Lucas (1991) estimated a dynamic demand function for labor in which the impact of job security laws could be picked up by a dummy representing the date of enactment of the legislation. In an application to the time series on employment in a large number of industries in Zimbabwe, the authors purported to show that the cumulative effect of the job security legislation was large — implying a 'net' reduction of employment in manufacturing as whole of around 25 percent. But, as the authors themselves recognized, the dummy variable might be picking up not just the impact of the legislation but also of other concurrent changes after this date, e.g., the emigration of a large part of the European skilled labor force.

In more recent years Zimbabwe, along with many other African economies, have sought to liberalize the regulation of labor markets as part of the structural adjustment package. One way of assessing if this has worked in the desired direction is to analyze the responses of employers to questions addressed to employers in the set of firm surveys undertaken by RPED.

Evidence from RPED Surveys

The RPED had a series of questions addressed to the employers directed to evaluating the constraints on production and employment decisions. Table 2.6 tabulates the answers to key questions designed to gauge the effect of various restrictions affecting: (a) overall size of the workforce in the firm; and (b) the proportion of workers hired as 'permanent'. The latter determines the part of the labor costs that is viewed by management as part of their 'fixed costs'. The regulations considered are: (i) minimum wages; (ii) the cost and difficulties of laying off permanent workers; (iii) restrictions on hiring ; (iv) legal or institutionally imposed limits on hiring temporary or casual workers; and (v) permission required by law for hiring foreign workers. Two sets of statistics are presented: first, the percentage of firms indicating that it affected their hiring decision severely: and second (in parenthesis) an average score for each group of respondents which indicates the severity of the perceived regulation.

Two conclusions immediately emerge from a quick overview of the results in the Table. First, as is to be expected the effect of minimum wages is the least burdensome for the employers of all the restrictions considered. Secondly, the impact of existing labor restrictions on hiring decisions seems to be the most severe for employers in Zambia and Zimbabwe among the seven countries surveyed. Note that, as explained in the footnotes to Table 2.6 the scores given in the parentheses measure in different ways the severity of the impact. In the case of minimum wages a score approaching the maximum 3 indicates that the impact is most severe, while for the impact of hiring regulations it is the score approaching the minimum 1 which would imply the largest impact. Of the four regulations, mentioned 'restrictions on layoffs and layout benefit requirements' seem to have been the most biting. Even then, the proportion of firms recognizing it as an effective 'distortion' was in the highest case — Zimbabwe — only 38 percent of the overall sample. Turning to differences by size groups, as far as minimum wages are concerned, it is interesting to note that it is not the micro, but the small firms, which seemed to be most affected by them. Nevertheless, even for the two most severely affected countries on this point, the percentage of firms complaining was only around 30 percent.

Other regulations affecting hiring and firing of workers became, as one would expect, more 'distortionary' as the enterprise size increased, but it is highly suggestive that in nearly all cases the largest size-group was not reporting the biggest incidence. 'Medium' and 'large' firms were the most affected, and even in the worst case — Zimbabwe — only just about half of these categories reported that laws relating to layoffs had an impact on their hiring decisions. The second country in terms of the severity of the impact was Kenya — with 35 percent of the large firms saying they would increase their hiring of permanent workers if layoff regulations were removed, and the average score approaching 2.

Table 2.6 Effect of Changes in Specific Regulations on Hiring Workers

	Cameroon	*Côte d'Ivoire*	*Kenya*	*Tanzania*	*Zambia*	*Zimbabwe*
Min. wage reduced slightly[2]						
Overall	5.8 (1.08)	12.9 (1.16)	13.8 (1.2)	9.4 (1.13)	3.5 (1.04)	19.2 (1.28)
No of firms responding	172	186	210	117	202	193
By firm size						
Micro	5.7 (1.08)	0.0 (1.06)	10.2 1.14)	12.5 (1.21)	1.7 (1.02)	22.7 (1.30)
Small	0.0 (1.06)	6.2 (1.26)	20.0 (2.39)	10.4 (1.13)	7.5 (1.09)	30.2 (1.47)
Medium	5.3 (1.11)	2.5 (1.18)	19.6 (1.32)	10.3 (1.14)	0.0 (1.00)	16.4 (1.23)
Large	0.0 (1.1)	0.0 (1.14)	0.0 (1.00)	0.0 (1.00)	7.1 (1.07)	12.6 (1.19)
Very Large	0.0 (1.0)	0.0 (1.00)	0.0 (2.52)	0.0 (1.00)	0.0 (1.00)	12.5 (1.21)
Removal of the following:[3]						
1. Layoff requirements						
Overall	15.0 (2.61)	9.4 (2.81)	23.7 (2.52)	4.0 (2.88)	14.4 (2.66)	38.1 (2.18)
No of firms responding	153	181	186	199	202	189
By firm size						
Micro	7.5 (2.78)	1.9 (1.98)	14.9 (2.70)	0.0 (1.21)	6.7 (2.85)	14.6 (2.66)
Small	21.2 (2.52)	17.7 (2.65)	30.4 (2.39)	5.3 (2.88)	13.4 (2.69)	45.2 (2.10)
Medium	9.1 (2.67)	10.3 (2.77)	27.5 (2.43)	6.1 (2.76)	21.6 (2.51)	47.5 (1.97)
Large	30.0 (2.20)	0.0 (3.00)	35.7 (2.29)	16.3 (2.67)	28.6 (2.43)	46.9 (2.00)
Very Large	0.0 (3.0)	8.3 (2.83)	12.5 (2.75)	9.1 (2.46)	10.0 (2.50)	22.2 (2.25)
2. Hiring restrictions:						
Overall			14.5 (2.71)	0.0 (3.00)	2.0 (2.95)	20.0 (2.54)
No of firms responding			166	195	202	175
By firm size						
Micro			11.9 (2.76)	0.0 (3.00)	0.0 (2.98)	9.5 (2.79)
Small			15.8 (2.68)	0.0 (3.99)	1.5 (2.97)	25.9 (2.48)
Medium			14.6 (2.71)	0.0 (3.00)	5.9 (1.80)	22.8 (2.44)
Large			21.4 (2.57)	0.0 (3.00)	0.0 (3.00)	14.8 (2.67)
Very Large			14.3 (2.71)	0.0 (3.00)	0.0 (3.00)	31.8 (2.27)

Table 2.6(cont'd) Effect of Changes in Specific Regulations on Hiring Workers

	Cameroon	*Côte d'Ivoire*	*Kenya*	*Tanzania*	*Zambia*	*Zimbabwe*
3. Limits on Temp. hiring						
Overall			16.2 (2.64)	0.0 (2.98)	7.9 (2.78)	20.7 (2.50)
No of firms responding			185	196	202	169
By firm size						
Micro			10.4 (2.78)	0.0 (3.00)	0.0 (2.95)	12.2 (1.73)
Small			21.7 (2.52)	0.0 (2.99)	6.0 (2.82)	33.3 (2.30)
Medium			20.0 (2.54)	0.0 (3.00)	21.6 (2.03)	25.0 (2.35)
Large			21.4 (2.57)	0.0 (2.83)	14.3 (2.86)	11.1 (2.70)
Very Large			12.5 (2.88)	0.0 (2.90)	10.0 (2.80)	22.7 (2.46)
4. Permit foreign labor						
Overall	11.1 (1.89)	2.8 (1.97)		11.5 (1.89)	15.3 (1.85)	30.9 (1.69)
No of firms responding	171	176		200	202	178
By firm size						
Micro	6.0 (1.94)	2.0 (1.98)		0.0 (2.00)	5.0 (1.95)	12.8 (1.87)
Small	11.8 (1.88)	1.6 (1.98)		16.0 (1.84	17.9 (1.82)	17.9 (1.82)
Medium	16.2 (1.84)	2.6 (1.97)		27.3 (1.73)	19.6 (1.80)	30.5 (1.70)
Large	18.2 (1.82)	7.1 (1.93)		16.7 (1.83)	21.4 (1.79)	43.3 (1.57)
Very Large	0.0 (2.0)	8.3 (1.92)		9.1 (1.91)	30.0 (1.70)	63.6 (1.36)

Note 1: The numbers outside parentheses indicate percentage of firms that would hire more if the corresponding labor regulations are removed whereas the numbers inside parentheses are average scores for the proposed questions.

Note 2: Firms are asked what they would do if the minimum wage were reduced slightly. There were given three options N*o change*, *Hiring slightly more workers*, and *Hiring many more workers*. The score 1-3 is attributed to each option respectively.

Note 3: Questions1-3 have three optional answers with corresponding scores of 1-3. *Increase the number of permanent workers*, *Decrease the number of permanent workers*, and M*aintain the number of permanent workers*. Question 4 has two optional answers, *If entry and work permits for foreign labor were removed, would you hire more foreign workers*? Yes with score 1 and no with score 2.

Table 2.6.1 Severity of Following Regulations on Raising Cost, Decreasing Revenue, or Constraining Activities in Ghana

	Overall	*Micro*	*Small*	*Medium*	*Large*	*Very Large*
Minimum Wage Legislation	8.9 (1.28)	0.0 (1.00)	0.0 (1.00)	7.8 (1.32)	20.0 (1.57)	25.0 (1.88)
Layoff Restrictions	8.7 (1.29)	0.0 (1.00)	0.0 (1.00)	9.5 (1.33)	15.6 (1.56)	42.9 (2.43)
Hiring Restrictions	1.1 (1.04)	0.0 (1.00)	0.0 (1.00)	0.0 (1.02)	0.0 (1.06)	12.5 (1.25)
Limit on Temporary Hiring	0.0 (1.03)	0.0 (1.00)	0.0 (1.00)	0.0 (1.02)	0.0 (1.09)	0.0 (1.13)

Note: The numbers outside parentheses indicate percentage of firms claiming the regulation to severely affect their decision-making. The numbers in parentheses stand for the average score reported for each question. The scores range from one to five for which one is *not a problem* and five is a *severe problem*. Based on this score range, scores 3 to 5 are considered severe and are chosen to calculated the percentages.

The surveys had another question seeking to evaluate the impact of the layoff regulations on enterprise decision. Employers were asked if rules on layoffs, whether originating with the government or trade unions, impeded flexibility in the sense of preventing the firms from temporarily reducing production if necessary. They were also asked to evaluate the severity of this problem and that of the financial costs of layoff in this regard. The summary of the responses is given in Table 2.7.

Government regulations regarding layoffs increasing costs of short-run flexibility seemed to have been most important for Zimbabwe for practically all sizes of firms ranging from the small to the very large. This was followed in ranking by Kenya (medium and large) and Tanzania (very large only). Other countries reported little trouble with this particular problem. Trade Union rules were recognized as important in three countries — Kenya, Tanzania and Zimbabwe. The first two joined Zimbabwe even more decidedly, and was accompanied by Zambia, in recognizing the 'high financial costs of layoffs' as contributing to inflexibility. The last factor in fact scored the highest point in the severity of obstacles in the four-anglophone countries, followed by government regulations only in Zimbabwe. Evidently, firms find it costly to temporarily lay-off their firm-specific labor force even without the direct recognition of government or trade union regulations. This type of labor practice might, however, have originated historically in regulations, which cast their shadow on firm operations even after the rules themselves had been formally relaxed.

Table 2.7 Severity of the Impact of Existing Regulations on Temporary Reduction in Production[1]

	Cameroon[2]	*Côte d'Ivoire*[2]	*Kenya*	*Tanzania*	*Zambia*	*Zimbabwe*
Trade union rules						
Regarding layoffs						
Overall	8.5 (1.36)	12.7 (1.40)	33.1 (2.05)	22.0 (1.73)	17.8 (1.6)	32.4 (1.98)
No of firms responding	224	299	465	476	540	500
By firm size						
Micro	6.3 (1.22)	0.0 (1.05)	11.1 (1.38)	11.6 (1.37)	4.1 (1.1)	17.9 (2.54)
Small	8.3 (1.42)	14.5 (1.46)	34.8 (2.09)	21.6 (1.72)	13.8 (1.5)	38.0 (2.23)
Medium	10.4 (1.48)	16.9 (1.54)	47.1 (2.40)	32.9 (2.07)	32.6 (2.0)	39.7 (2.16)
Large	15.8 (1.42)	17.2 (1.48)	53.5 (2.78)	43.7 (2.50)	34.4 (2.2)	26.9 (1.96)
Very Large	10.0 (1.10)	21.7 (1.52)	52.9 (3.0)	44.5 (2.96)	42.3 (2.5)	35.7 (2.68)
Government rules						
Regarding layoffs						
Overall	13.2 (1.48)	11.7 (1.41)	27.0 (1.86)	15.1 (1.48)	11.4 (1.4)	35.4 (2.07)
No of firms responding	235	290	467	478	552	509
By firm size						
Micro	8.6 (1.32)	3.0 (1.08)	11.1 (1.36)	9.2 (1.25)	5.5 (1.2)	17.2 (1.55)
Small	14.0 (1.54)	14.2 (1.49)	21.8 (1.70)	13.7 (1.47)	10.3 (1.4)	21.2 (2.01)
Medium	20.0 (1.66)	16.0 (1.50)	42.1 (2.26)	19.7 (1.61)	17.8 (1.6)	45.5 (2.37)
Large	11.1 (1.45)	7.1 (1.39)	42.5 (2.43)	12.5 (1.57)	18.7 (1.5)	29.5 (1.89)
Very Large	9.1 (1.36)	12.5 (1.33)	47.1 (2.80)	44.5 (2.82)	19.2 (1.7)	45.6 (2.43)

Table 2.7 (Cont'd) Severity of the Existing Regulations on Temporary Reduction in Production

	Cameroon[2]	*Côte d I'voire*[2]	*Kenya*	*Tanzania*	*Zambia*	*Zimbabwe*
High Financial cost of layoffs						
Overall		21.5 (1.73)	36.8 (2.16)	38.1 (2.26)	51.5 (2.7)	35.2 (2.12)
No of firms responding		293	348	475	361	483
By firm size						
Medium		12.3 (1.42)	13.9 (1.51)	23.1 (1.78)	32.8 (2.1)	19.5 (1.67)
Small		16.0 (1.58)	39.4 (2.15)	40.7 (2.30)	47.3 (2.5)	32.9 (2.10)
Medium		30.0 (1.99)	53.1 (2.68)	42.7 (2.41)	70.9 (3.3)	34.4 (2.11)
Large		25.0 (1.75)	50.0 (2.53)	87.5 (3.94)	75.0 (3.5)	41.2 (2.2)
Very Large		41.7 (2.29)	69.2 (2.39)	78.2 (3.96	71.2 (3.5)	52.9 (2.64)

Note 1: The numbers outside parentheses indicate percentage of firms claiming the regulation to severely affect their decision-making. The numbers in parentheses stand for the average score reported for each question. The scores range from one to five for which one is *no obstacle* and five is a *very severe obstacle*. Based on this score range, scores 3 to 5 are considered severe and are chosen to calculated the percentages.
Note 2: For these two countries, the range of score is from 1 to 7 for which scores 1-5 is similar to other countries, score six is *no opinion* and score seven is *not applicable*. For the purpose of this table, score six is dropped and score seven is taken equivalent to score one.

Table 2.7.1 Severity of the Existing Regulations on Temporary Reduction in Production in Ghana

	Overall	*Micro*	*Small*	*Medium*	*Large*	*Very Large*
Trade union rules Regarding layoffs	1.2 (1.04)	0.0 (1.15)	0.0 (1.0)	0.0 (1.0)	3.0 (1.15)	0.0 (1.0)
Government rules Regarding layoffs	2.9 (1.1)	0.0 (1.0)	3.6 (1.07)	4.1 (1.14)	3.0 (1.09)	0.0 (1.0)
High financial cost of layoffs	0.6 (1.03)	0.0 (1.0)	0.0 (1.0)	1.4 (1.06)	0.0 (1.03)	0.0 (1.0)

Lastly, an attempt was made in the surveys to place the rigidities due labor regulations in the context of other problems of non-labor regulations affecting the flexibility of business operations. Employers were asked to indicate how government restrictions on transfer of assets or the legal process of bankruptcy and liquidation ranked as problems in *closing down a business* relative to labor issues emanating from the government or trade unions. The employers could base their replies on their past experience or knowledge about others. The data are given in Table 2.8.

It is seen that all the anglophone countries in Table 2.8 ‘the cost of firing workers’ was clearly the most important — and even more so for large firms. Zimbabwe was the only one reporting that government restriction on firing workers was also quite important — about 40 percent of the firms indicating this to be a significant issue with a score of 2.8 out of a maximum of 5. Trade union restrictions on dismissal were adjudged less important, although of grater importance than restrictions on selling or bankruptcy.

A very surprising aspect of the data obtained from the surveys was that the two francophone countries — Côte d'Ivoire and Cameroon — systematically gave very low scores to all the problems mentioned in the questionnaires, labor as well as non-labor. In the absence of further information about systematic bias in the survey results on this point for the francophone countries, we can only conclude that, contrary to common assumptions, labor regulations had less distortionary effects on manufacturing firms than in some of the other countries.

Table 2.8 Severity of the Impact of Existing Regulations in Closing-down a Business[1]

	Cameroon	*Côte d'Ivoire*[2]	*Kenya*	*Tanzania*	*Zambia*	*Zimbabwe*
Govt. restrictions on on selling/transfer						
Overall	3.0 (1.2)	3.7 (1.2)	11.7 (1.4)	13.5 (1.4)	8.0 (1.3)	30.5 (2.0)
No of firms responding	165	353	437	469	522	174
By firm size						
Micro	2.7 (1.1)	0.9 (1.0)	2.9 (1.1)	7.6 (1.2)	1.2 (1.2)	8.3 (1.3)
Small	3.3 (1.2)	4.3 (1.2)	11.2 (1.4)	13.2 (1.5)	4.9 (1.2)	20.0 (1.8)
Medium	3.7 (1.1)	6.9 (1.2)	15.8 (1.5)	15.3 (1.5)	16.2 (1.5)	38.6 (2.2)
Large	7.7 (1.2)	3.4 (1.1)	23.7 (1.9)	33.3 (2.1)	16.7 (1.5)	35.7 (2.2)
Very Large	0.0 (1.0)	4.5 (1.2)	33.3 (2.1)	45.0 (2.7)	18.0 (2.0)	42.2 (2.7)
Govt. restrictions on firing workers						
Overall		4.3 (1.2)	33.4 (2.1)	19.1 (1.6)	19.4 (1.6)	52.0 (2.8)
No of firms responding		349	332	194	201	175
By firm size						
Micro		4.5 (1.2)	13.8(1.4)	1.4 (1.1)	6.7 (1.2)	19.4 (2.4)
Small		6.1 (1.2)	32.6 (2.1)	24.3 (1.6)	20.5 (1.6)	45.2 (2.7)
Medium		8.6 (1.6)	48.4 (2.4)	6.2 (1.7)	30.0 (1.9)	66.1 (3.3)
Large		16.7 (1.6)	53.3 (3.0)	16.7 (2.0)	24.3 (14.2)	62.1 (2.9)
Very Large		22.7 (1.6)	53.8 (3.2)	54.5 (3.0)	40.0 (2.4)	73.9 (3.)

Table 2.8 (Cont'd) Severity of the Impact of Existing Regulations in Closing-down a Business

	Cameroon	*Côte d'Ivoire*[2]	*Kenya*	*Tanzania*	*Zambia*	*Zimbabwe*
Legal process of bankruptcy						
Overall	4.1 (1.2)	4.3 (1.2)	19.7 (1.6)	18.5 (1.6)	9.8 (1.3)	26.7 (1.9)
No of firms responding	169	345	417	460	523	158
By firm size						
Micro	3.3 (1.2)	2.7 (1.1)	17.1 (1.5)	13.6 (1.4)	3.5 (1.1)	17.1 (1.5)
Small	3.3 (1.2)	3.5 (1.2)	44.3 (2.4)	20.3 (1.6)	9.3 (1.4)	19.2 (1.7)
Medium	6.9 (1.2)	5.6 (1.2)	62.8 (2.9)	15.9 (1.5)	16,5 (1.5)	36.0 (2.0)
Large	7.7 (1.2)	10.7 (1.3)	66.7 (3.1)	31.2 (2.0)	10.0 (1.4)	25.9 (1.8)
Very Large	0.0 (1.0)	10.0 (1.4)	69.2 (3.6)	52.5 (2.4)	24.0 (1.8)	40.0 (2.4)
Cost of firing Workers						
Overall		8.3 (1.3)	42.5 (2.4)	50.0 (2.7)	57.2 (2.9)	59.1 (2.7)
No of firms responding		349	322	194	201	181
By firm size						
Micro		7.8 (1.3)	15.7 (1.5)	22.5 (1.8)	41.7 (2.5)	13.2 (1.5)
Small		7.0 (1.2)	44.3 (2.4)	59.5 (3.1)	49.3 (2.7)	38.7 (2.3)
Medium		5.0 (1.4)	62.8 (2.9)	56.3 (3.3)	70.0 (3.5)	74.1 (3.3)
Large		10.7 (1.3)	66.7 (3.1)	100.0 (4.2)	50.0 (3.0)	41.3 (3.0)
Very Large		14.3 (1.4)	69.2 (3.6)	72.7 (4.2)	50.0 (2.8)	78.3 (3.3)
Trade union restrictions on firing workers						
Overall		7.1 (1.2)	38.4 (2.2)	31.4 (2.1)	23.4 (1.9)	34.5 (2.1)
No of firms responding		350	328	194	201	171
By firm size						
Micro		1.8 (1.1)	10.1 (1.5)	4.2 (1.2)	5.0 (1.2)	11.4 (1.3)
Small		7.9 (1.3)	47.7 (2.4)	36.5 (2.2)	19.4 (1.7)	40.0 (2.3)
Medium		6.9 (1.3)	51.1 (2.5)	50.0 (2.9)	40.0 (2.4)	46.1 (2.5)
Large		7.1 (1.5)	63.3 (3.2)	100.0 (3.5)	42.9 (2.6)	34.5 (2.1)
Very Large		17.4 (1.5)	69.2 (3.6)	63.6 (3.5)	56.0 (3.1)	33.3 (2.2)

Note 1 and Note 2: See Table 2.7

Unions

The RPED data contain information on the degree of unionization in the firms surveyed. The information is given at two places. First, in the questionnaire administered to management, the respondents were asked if the enterprise had unions. Secondly, the sample of workers who were interviewed were asked if they belonged to unions. The data obtained on these points are given in the following two tables. Unionism is clearly more important in Zimbabwe than in any of the other countries of the Survey. This is true whether we look at the management data responding to unionization in their firms, or workers' indication whether or not they belonged to a union. Again, the francophone countries seem to be not what the popular image about them is. The incidence of unionism seems to be lower in these countries than in the anglophone ones.

There is a clear correlation between unionism and firm size in all countries. A very large proportion of large and very large firms are unionized, according to the managers, and this is true also of medium firms in all the anglophone countries. However, if the workers' responses are to be believed, unionism is by no means universal even in the largest firms, except perhaps in Tanzania. The sets of information provided by the managers and the workers are not necessarily inconsistent. In the manager's response, a unionized firm is one in which some, not all workers belong to unions.

Table 2.9 Percent of Firms Unionized

	Cameroon	*Côte d' Ivoire*	*Ghana*	*Kenya*	*Tanzania*	*Zambia*	*Zimbabwe*
Overall	31.4	23.4	29.7	43.6	39.3	41.2	67.5
By firm size							
Micro	5.3	2.8	2.3	4.5	10.6	2.4	89.7
Small	24.8	22.7	24.5	51.9	42.2	39.3	46.5
Medium	66.1	40.5	81.4	77.0	80.3	824	92.0
Large	87.2	43.8	87.9	88.1	93.88	93.9	96.0
Very Large	80.0	58.0	66.7	94.4	100.0	96.2	93.2
By Ownership structure							
Private	19.7	13.2	17.9	38.8	29.3	36.1	56.7
Private Foreign	62.9	21.5	42.9	69.2	82.6	88.9	92.9
Private & foreign, Joint	56.5	44.9	76.6	81.0	63.6	90.9	95.5
State & Private, Joint	68.5	57.1	64.3	85.7	81.8	100	90.0
State	80.0	50.0	78.3	100.0	88.7	85.7	100.0

Table 2.10 Percent of Workers Unionized

	Cameroon	*Côte d'Ivoire*	*Ghana*	*Kenya*	*Tanzania*	*Zambia*	*Zimbabwe*
Overall	19.9	20.5	26.7	31.5	35.1	33.1	41.8
By firm size							
Micro	2.7	2.8	1.7	3.1	9.1	1.9	16.1
Small	18.0	20.8	21.5	41.3	35.8	32.4	31.2
Medium	43.8	34.2	74.3	55.7	71.9	63.8	58.8
Large	49.2	40.0	80.7	60.1	91.3	70.9	53.1
Very Large	32.5	48.3	49.4	71.9	98.5	65.7	57.4
By Ownership structure							
Private	13.3	11.9	14.9	28.7	24.8	29.1	33.7
Private Foreign	35.7	19.1	49.3	43.8	74.2	64.5	47.3
Private-foreign, Joint	50.4	40.3	71.0	47.3	57.8	80.0	42.6
State-Private, Joint	39.0	28.6	61.9	77.0	87.1	70.8	34.9
State	49.8	56.0	40.7	90.0	80.5	68.8	35.0

The presence of unions need not necessarily augment earnings. In advanced countries it has been maintained that much depends on the welfare function of unions — if they are interested more in the 'insiders' who are already in the workforce than in the interest of potential job-seekers. In any event, the presence of unions is expected to ensure a more effective collective bargaining within the firm or enterprise. In many African countries, however, collective bargaining involving only workers and their employers is rather rare, particularly at the firm level. Boards in which the government participates along with representatives of workers and employers more generally take wage decisions. Velenchik confirms this for Zimbabwe, but suggests that 'union firms participate in different collective bargaining institutions from non-union firms, so the presence of a union indicates a different institutional environment, and may generate different wage agreements' (1997: p.320). Whether or not there are clearly distinguished collective bargaining authorities, if there is compensation decisions taken by tripartite bodies at all, the presence of unions can be expected to provide a more articulate and effective case for wage bargaining on behalf of those firms in which unions have a strong presence.

While the *potential* for a union effect on wages exist, it is another thing to maintain that this effect is significant. Empirical examination of this effect is rendered difficult because of the close relation already noted between enterprise size and unionism. As we shall see in much greater detail in later chapters (14 and 15, in particular) wages in African manufacturing increase strongly with the size of the enterprise. It is, however clear that unionism is *not* the driving factor behind the phenomenon of wages increasing with size. If this were so, we would find a much stronger size-earnings relationship in unionized firms. Velenchik, however, looking at the first wave of the Zimbabwe survey found that 'if we restrict our attention to the 1265 workers in union firms, the coefficient of ln(size) is 0.147 with a standard error of 0.025, which is slightly smaller than that estimated for the whole sample'(p.322). At the same time, the union dummy was insignificant when it was introduced into the earnings function along with size. The author also tried to see if the introduction of interaction factors between unions and firm size in the earnings function suggested any effect of unions on particular size groups. The result showed 'that unionization does generate some of the size effect in the medium size class, but this effect is not large'.

Conclusions

Our conclusion from the review of institutional influences on labor markets in Africa is that the public sector does play a decisive role in most African economies, but its impact in the last decade has been more because of its large share of urban employment than of its role in forging a significant public-private wage gap in the formal sector. The public sector has been the main provider of new jobs in the urban labor market, and seems to have been increasingly important in this role as real wages in the formal sector drifted downwards after the mid-seventies. This factor might have been one of the basic factors in the large flux of labor into the urban areas — which in fact swelled the relative size of the informal sector in the urban labor market in many African economies.

Compared to the impact of the public sector job creation, the impact of the other institutional factors reviewed in this chapter has probably been minor in recent decades. The minimum wage legislations, which had been of such importance in the sixties, have largely lost their critical importance in shaping wage levels. Judging from the responses of firm managers, the importance of job security legislation and of unions in inflating labor costs in the formal sector have probably been exaggerated.

Part II: Wage and Employment Trends in the Formal Sector

3 Trends in Manufacturing Wages in the Sixties

In 1967, A.D. Smith, using available ILO data, reviewed the trends in real wage levels in developing countries during the period 1956-64. However, his analysis was confined to the manufacturing sector 'to cover as many countries as possible on a comparable basis' (Smith, p.3). Smith summarized his results as follows:

> The most striking feature of the wage league given in Table 1 (reproduced here in Table 2.1) is the tendency of the thirty-one countries to fall into regional groupings. Four of the first fourteen countries at the head of the table are African, and as many as five of the following six countries are in Central America and the Caribbean. At the other end of the table, Far Eastern countries occupy the last four places; while four of the next five places are occupied by countries of South America. (Smith, pp. 6-7).

Smith also included available statistics on the annual growth rate of consumer prices in addition to the real GDP per capita in the tables for individual countries. The experience of the four African countries stood at as being altogether different from that of the countries in other regions — the growth rate of real wage in these countries was 4 to 5 times higher than their GDP per capita. In other regions, only two countries — Colombia and Dominican Republic had a similarly high rate of increase in real wages, which actually exceeded their GDP per capita. All the other countries in America and Asia witnessed a real wage increase close to or even below their per capita GDP growth rate.

Smith further noted: 'Whilst both the country and time coverage is limited, observers of the African scene believe that large increases in real wages are not confined to a small number of African countries nor to the periods for which changes are measured in the table' (Smith, p.31). He singled out two basic reasons for the inflation of real wages in Africa during this period. The first was the important role played by the State, which was influenced by and actively supported the Trade Unions, and the second was the economic reasons for changing the prevalent migrant labor system.

Table 3.1 Trends in Manufacturing Real Wages in Developing Countries, 1956 to 1964 (Annual Average Rates of Change in Percentage)

	Region	*Money Wages*	*Consumer Prices*	*Real Wages*
Tanzania (Tanganyika)	A.	13.5	1.1	12.3
Nigeria	A.	11.9 (a)	2.4 (a)	9.3 (a)
Southern Rhodesia	A.	11.8 (b)	2.4 (b)	9.1 (b)
Dominican Republic	C.A.	10.8	1.8	8.8
Zambia	A.	9.7	1.4	8.1
Colombia	S.A.	20.7	12.4	7.4
Panama	C.A.	7.1 (c)	0.2 (c)	6.9 (c)
Trinidad and Tobago	C.A.	9.5	2.6	6.8
Jamaica	C.A.	9.5 (d)	3.3 (d)	6.0 (d)
Mexico	C.A.	9.4	3.7	5.5
Puerto Rico	C.A.	8.0	2.6	5.3
Ceylon	F.E.	6.0	1.4	4.5
Kenya	A.	5.5 (e)	1.6 (e)	3.8 (e)
Nicaragua	C.A.	3.0	0.2	2.8
China (Taiwan)	F.E.	9.0	6.1	2.7
Barbados	C.A	4.3 (f)	1.5 (f)	2.7 (f)
Honduras	C.A.	3.6 (g)	1.4 (g)	2.3 (g)
Pakistan	F.E.	5.1	2.9	2.2
South Vietnam	F.E.	5.2	3.0	2.1
Chile	S.A.	28.8 (e)	26.2 (e)	1.9 (e)
Guatemala	C.A.	1.9	0.0	1.9
Ghana	A.	6.3	4.6	1.6
Brazil	S.A.	45.0	43.0	1.6
Peru	S.A.	10.3 (d)	8.5 (d)	1.6 (d)
Ecuador	S.A.	4.7 (h)	3.0 (h)	1.6 (h)
Argentina	S.A.	35.0	33.0	1.4
Costa Rica	C.A.	2.9 (c)	2.1 (c)	0.8 (c)
Burma	F.E.	0.6	0.3	0.4
South Korea	F.E.	10.9	10.6	0.2
India	F.E.	2.9	4.7	-1.7
Philippines	F.E.	3.3	5.4	-2.0

Notes: Regions: A.: Africa; C.A.: Central America/Caribbean; S.A.: South America; F.E.: Far East. (a) 1956-60; (b) 1961-64; (c) 1956-63; (d) 1957-64; (e) 1960-64; (f) 1959-64; (g) 1953-60; (h) 1958-64.

Source: Smith (1969), Table 1, p. 44. The original source of the data is the I.LO. Yearbooks of Labor Statistics.

The State was instrumental in bringing about wage changes in Africa not only because it was a major and — in many countries — the dominant employer, but also because the State freely exercised legislative procedures i.e. minimum wages, and wage awards in arbitration. The fact that trade unions brought pressure to bear on these young governments for adopting a high wage policy must be seen in the context of the recent attainment of independence of these countries which were quite willing to accede to the demands of pressure groups. Only a small number of people from African countries were employed at that time in the formal wage sector — this fact might have been instrumental in enabling African labor to be organized easily.

It would, however, be extremely naive to ignore this period of unprecedented wage increase as one, which was being driven solely or mainly by unthinking political pressures. Smith was quick to point out that there was a major economic objective behind the state-supported policies for raising wages. This was the desire to change the labor system from one dependant on the migrant labor system to one making use of stabilized labor, settled in the urban location. Observers of Africa had long argued that the wage level in towns was high enough to attract only temporary migrants who considered their rural farm as the principal source of their life-time income. Therefore, families were left in the rural areas to carry out agricultural work in the absence of the single individuals (usually males) who were hired to work in towns for short spans of time. This type of labor system was judged to have been responsible for the low productivity of African labor in industry. Several high level official Commissions, appointed by the Colonial government, had endorsed this conclusion even before the dawn of independence (see Chapter 7 in Part II below for further details). Since the impact of high wages on productivity would only be felt after a time lapse, and furthermore would be forthcoming only if all employees had to pay higher wages in order to attract stable migrants, a strong case could be made for the State to implement a high wage policy through minimum wage legislation.

Apart from the productivity augmentation factor, there were serious discussions based on equity in favor of the high wage policy. Migrant labor, working only in urban industry in a temporary capacity, was not in a position to acquire the skills necessary to move up in the occupation hierarchy. As a result, skilled labor was recruited largely from expatriates and non-African sources and it benefited from monopoly rents, which led to a highly skewed distribution of earnings in the industrial sector. The political realities of this Colonial system of administration no doubt exaggerated this phenomenon. It would be reasonable to assume that the newly independent governments were induced to change this labor system.[3]

[3]Indeed in a well-known text on development, Professor Hla Myint described this maldistribution of the surplus created by modern technology as the crucial problem of 'underdevelopment'.

4 Wage Trends in Recent Decades

Real Wage Trends in The Seventies and The Eighties

We now extend Smith's early work to the last two decades using a larger sample of countries reported by the ILO. The time series covering the seventies and the eighties are not complete for all the countries, which have reported the relevant statistics. We have therefore calculated the annual growth rates of money wages and consumer prices in the manufacturing sector — for as many countries and for as long a period as possible. From these figures, we derived the growth rates of real wages for the countries and periods concerned.[4] These results for Africa, America and Asia are listed separately in Table 4.1. The growth rates are reported for five-yearly periods starting around 1969, as well as for the two decades in their entirety. The time frame for all available series are also reported in the tables for each sample country. The reader should focus attention on the time period when the growth rate of wages for a particular country is studied. For most countries, however, the series extend from sometime around the early seventies to the late eighties. For a few, data exist for only the more recent decade.

The annual rate of change of real wage over the two decades was strongly positive in Asia (around 3 percent per annum), but negative in Africa and South America, with a larger negative value in Africa. The data for the Africa region are graphed in Figure 4.1.

[4] The growth rates are calculated as exponential rates by regression for each time period. The growth rate of real wage is found by subtracting the growth rate of the consumer price index from that of money wages.

Table 4.1 Growth Rates of Real Wages in Manufacturing (Annual Percentage Change)

	69-75	*75-81*	*81-86*	*86-91*	*69-81*	*81-91*	*Whole series*	*Series Over (Years)*
AFRICA								
Botswana			5.36	-1.48		1.77	1.53	79-91
Burundi		-1.64	-1.83				-0.93	73-87
Egypt	-1.90	5.85	-1.47		1.22		1.72	69-87
Gambia			-6.68				-6.35	78-87
Ghana		-23.99	19.91				-3.10	75-88
Kenya	-2.03	-1.13	-3.12	0.82	-2.11	-0.63	-1.79	69-90
Malawi	-2.68	-2.14	-7.65	-5.99	-3.18	-6.25	-3.56	69-90
Mauritius			1.57	7.77		4.40	3.91	80-91
Sierra Leone	-0.41	-3.40	-23.07		-3.64		-10.09	69-87
South Africa		3.65	-0.15	0.91		-0.04	1.30	74-91
Swaziland		3.71	-0.77		3.63		1.79	72-87
Zimbabwe	4.33	1.94	-2.69	1.45	2.32	-1.40	1.33	70-89
AVERAGE	-0.54	-1.91	-1.72	0.58	-0.29	-0.36	-1.19	
AMERICA								
Argentina			5.66	-6.28		-1.55	-1.55	82-90
Canada	3.23	0.60	-0.32	0.03	2.34	-0.29	0.81	69-91
Chile			9.29	3.37		4.71	6.97	78-91
Colombia			3.35	-0.09		1.97	2.15	80-89
Costa Rica			6.10	0.80		3.94	1.77	78-91
Dominican Republic	-2.94	-4.27	-6.72		-1.46		-2.20	69-85
El Salvador			-9.39	-18.56		-15.74	-10.86	78-90
Guatemala	-6.25	3.41	-9.80		-3.12		-1.99	69-85
Honduras		3.08	-8.73	-3.91		-7.66	0.84	73-89
Mexico	1.88	-0.27	-20.28	7.34	1.72	-5.99	-3.19	69-91
Panama	-0.92	-1.55	3.42		-0.83		-0.28	69-85
Peru	5.51	-5.45	-6.25	-33.23	-2.10	-7.79	-4.21	69-89
Puerto Rico	-0.37	3.04	2.57	-0.17	1.47	1.16	1.53	69-91
United States	0.76	-0.50	0.20	-1.61	0.31	-0.72	-0.27	69-91
MINIMUM	-6.25	-5.45	-20.28	-33.23	-3.12	-15.74	-10.86	
MAXIMUM	5.51	3.41	9.29	7.34	1.72	4.71	6.97	
AVERAGE (excluding U.S. and Canada)	-0.51	-0.29	-2.57	-5.64	-0.72	-2.99	-0.92	
ASIA								
India	-7.41	6.31	-2.11		2.12		1.25	69-86
Korea, Republic of	6.49	9.33	6.77	11.21	8.97	8.77	7.86	69-91
Pakistan	3.82	1.30	3.34		2.86		1.75	69-88
Philippines			-1.76				-0.39	78-87
Sri Lanka	1.22	0.73	4.30	0.66	3.34	2.45	1.66	69-90
Thailand			10.99	1.02		5.06	5.50	80-90
MINIMUM	-7.41	0.73	-2.11	-8.54	2.12	-0.14	-0.39	
MAXIMUM	6.59	9.33	10.99	11.21	8.97	8.77	7.86	
AVERAGE	1.03	4.42	3.59	4.30	4.32	5.42	2.94	

Source: ILO data. *Note:* Incomplete Series, see 'Series Over' Column for Details.

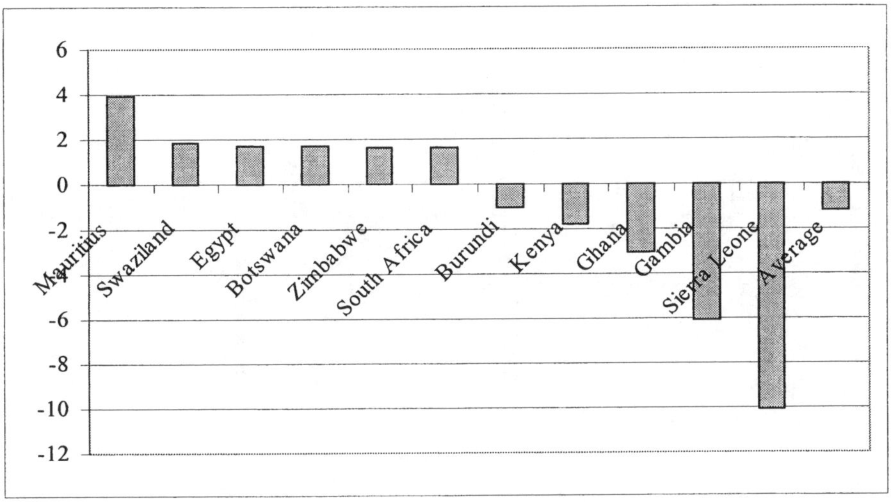

Figure 4.1 Average Annual Growth of Real Manufacturing Wages in Africa (1969-91)

Interestingly, Figure 4.1 for Africa, shows that the countries, which experienced positive trends in real wages for the period as a whole, four out of a total of six are in the southern part of the entire continent. Mauritius, of course, is exceptional among Sub-Saharan African countries in that it had a high record of manufacturing growth in the eighties and in the series as a whole. This is reflected in the positive trend in real wages in this sector. Egypt had a wage boom in the period 1975-81 — the growth rate being as high as 6 percent per annum. Hence we record a positive trend for the period as a whole although real wages were more or less constant during the eighties.

Figure 4.2 graphs separately the rates of growth of real wages — for four five-yearly periods — in the African countries sampled. However, this sample is not really large enough to pin-point differences in the 'average' experience of African countries within the four periods, if indeed such differences did exist. The small positive value for the rate of growth in the 1986-91 periods for the simple average, coming after negative values for the three earlier periods, ought to be interpreted with caution. The facts are that three specific countries — Kenya, South Africa and Zimbabwe, recovered to some extent, from their earlier losses in real wages during 1986-91. Mauritius continued its positive trend in real wages but at an accelerated rate.

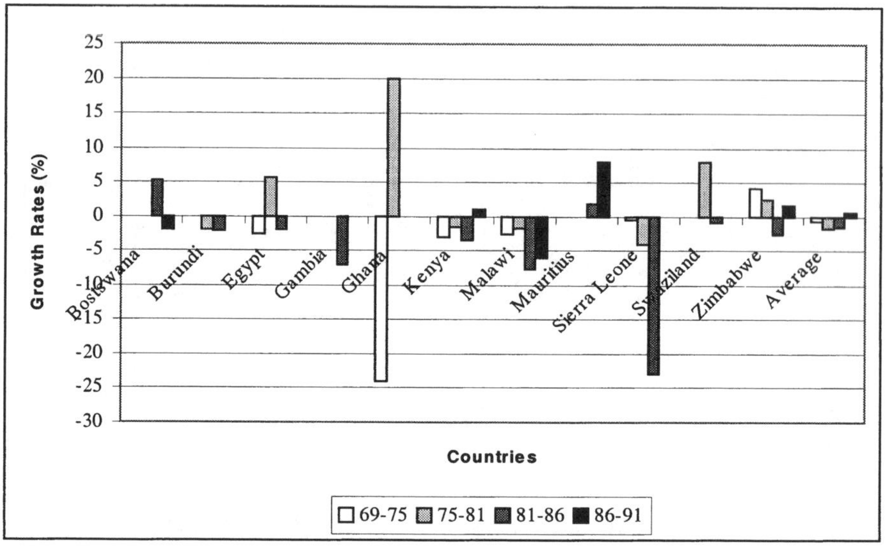

Figure 4.2 Detailed Growth of Real Manufacturing Wages in Africa (1969-91)

In his earlier study of the sixties, A.D. Smith had tried to explain — in a general fashion — the inter-country variations in the real wage changes in the manufacturing sector using a few economy-wide variables. He singled out the growth of per capita GDP and the rate of inflation as the two critical variables. The former presumably is a proxy for the supply price of labor, hence other things being equal real wages in a particular sector could be expected to move in the same direction as GDP per capita. The inflation rate is expected to be a significant explanatory variable because of inertia in the wage setting process. If wages are set autonomously by market forces there will be a lapse in the adjustment of money wages to unanticipated inflation. When institutional determination of wages is the more prevalent mode, public or other authorities may find it beneficial to whittle away real wages more easily by holding money wage increases below the rate of price increase, rather than initiating wage cuts — Smith did not investigate the problems econometrically. But his visual perception of the data suggested that such a mechanism was indeed significant in explaining inter-country variations in South America (Smith, p.12).

In this chapter, we have tried to estimate the suggested model for changes in the money wage rate on the basis of the ILO data. The exercise was carried out separately for each of the three regions — Africa, South

America and Asia.[5] Observations were obtained by pooling cross-section data for the countries in the region with time series data for the growth rates of the relevant variables. For each variable, the growth rates are the exponential rates for each of the four 5-yearly time periods depicted above. The specified model is:

$$w = c + br + cg + e$$

Where: w = Rate of growth of money wages in manufacturing;
r = Rate of inflation as measured by the Consumer Price Index;
g = Rate of growth of GDP per capita (in money terms);
e = error term.

The results are given in Table 4.2.

Table 4.2 Coefficients of Estimated Regression Equations Explaining Growth Rates of Money Wages (1969-91)

	Constant	*r*	*g*	*Adjusted R^2*
Africa	1.93 (0.61)	0.67 (5.87)	0.35 (0.94)	0.53
Latin America	-6.54 (-0.25)	0.98 (32.82)	1.45 (2.43)	0.98
Asia	-1.38 (-0.39)	0.96 (3.70)	0.83 (2.57)	0.41

Note: t-statistics are in parenthesis. See text for definition of variables.

When interpreting these results it should be noted that a coefficient of the value of unity for 'r' implies that there is full compensation for inflation in the determination of money wages in the manufacturing sector. Similarly, a coefficient of unity for 'g' means that real wages in manufacturing are barely keeping pace with the rate of growth of real GDP per capita.[6]

The African countries in the periods considered, suffered from real wage erosion in the sense that compensation for the rate of inflation was only two-thirds, after controlling for changes in the GDP per capita. This result contrasts significantly with the experience of countries in Latin America and Asia where compensation for inflationary price increase seemed almost complete. In addition, it is pertinent to note that the

[5] The lists of countries that are considered under each classification are shown in Appendix A, Part III. The Appendix shows the groupings according to both ILO and UNIDO. Note, however that, data may not necessarily cover all the countries of the groupings in each time period.

[6] The assumption here is that the price indices for consumers and producers are changing at the same rate.

coefficient for 'g' for Africa, although positive, is non-significant unlike those for the other regions. This result implies that manufacturing wages in Africa were divorced from changes in the supply price of labor, as measured by the per capita level of national product. This was unique for Africa among all the developing countries.

Latin America shows strong evidence of being dominated by the inflationary process, as evidenced by the high value of R^2 of the estimated equation — standing alone among the three regions, it has a significant negative constant term. This implies that in the absence of inflation of a minimum amount real wage would fall, ceteris paribus. The sample of Asian countries shows an interesting case of 'wage repression' in the estimated equation. Although money wages increased with GDP per capita, a coefficient for 'g' of only 0.83 imply that wages in manufacturing, in real terms, have increased at a rate 17 percent below that of GDP per capita.

The Decade of the Nineties: An Update

Most recent data available from the ILO Yearbook of Labor Statistics enable us to indicate the pattern of wage changes in recent years. These figures are presented in Table 4.3. They show that while real wage growth had slowed down in Asia, it was still positive. Several countries in Latin America had registered a transition from negative to positive real wage growth, so that the average for the sample was slightly positive. But Africa continues to register strongly negative trend in real wages (with the continuing exception of Mauritius). Again, the rapid rate of inflation was the proximate cause of the declining trend.

Table 4.3 Growth in Real Wages Since 1988 (Annual Percentage)

	Growth in nominal wage	*Growth in CPI*	*Real wage growth*	*Data available*
Africa				
Botswana	8	11	-4	88-97
Egypt	9	12	-3	88-95
Ghana	16	22	-6	88-91
Kenya	9	17	-8	88-91,97
Malawi	7	27	-20	88-95
Mauritius	13	8	5	88.97
South Africa	14	13	1	88.93
Zambia	17	24	-7	88.90
Average			-5	
Latin America				
Argentina	23	18	5	90.96
Chile	15	13	2	88-92
Columbia	24	23	1	88-95
Costa Rica	19	17	2	88-97
Dominican Rep.	18	19	-2	88-95
El Salvador	12	13	-1	88-96
Guatemala	16	15	0	88-97
Mexico	16	18	-2	88-92
Panama	6	1	5	88-94
Puerto Rico	4	4	0	
Average			0.6	
Asia				
India	3	10	-7	88-95
South Korea	13	6	7	88-97
Pakistan	7	5	1	88-90
Philippines	11	11	1	88-95
Sri Lanka	12	11	1	88-97
Thailand	8	5	3	89-97
Average			1.5	

Source: International Labor Office (ILO), Yearbook of Labor Statistics, various Years.

5 Trends in Wages, Wage Shares and Value Added in Manufacturing

The last two chapters were based on the data on wage and price trends collected by the ILO from their regional offices, and published in their Yearbook of Labor Statistics. The ILO series do not include information on trends in output (value added) or in employment from the same sample of firms which provide the data on wages. This gap is filled by the data set maintained by the United Nations Industrial Development Organization (UNIDO), which also provides information for a much larger sample of countries than is available in the ILO data analyzed in Chapter 4. In this chapter we start with a descriptive account of the trends in wages and other relevant variables as revealed by the statistics collected by the UNIDO. The sources of the data are the censuses and/or sample surveys of manufacturing establishments in the relevant countries. They are usually collected from establishments registered with the Statistical Offices of the national governments. The coverage of the data sets is therefore limited to registered establishments or the manufacturing units in the formal sector. Time series data are generally available from the seventies with some missing values, mainly for the more recent years for particular countries.

Trends in the Seventies and the Eighties in Africa and Other Regions

To set the African scene in perspective, we must first set out the average values of the annual percentage growth rates of the three variables mentioned earlier for all available countries within the four regions of the world. (See Table 4.1). At a first glance at this table, it appears that African countries as a group did not fair too badly in terms of the growth rate of manufacturing output when compared to other regions in the last two decades. The median (and mean) rates of growth of real value added in manufacturing decreased in the eighties when compared to the level attained in the seventies but not by a large amount. It is common knowledge that the countries of East Asia had a median growth rate, which was very high — greatly exceeding Africa's. But the growth rate in Africa was significantly higher than in OECD countries in both decades and higher than in Latin America during the eighties. The problem with African manufacturing growth is more appropriately addressed in the figures of growth of labor productivity — the growth rate was strikingly negative in the seventies while other regions experienced high median rates of positive growth.

Table 5.1 Annual Percentage Growth Rates

	Real Value Added		*Employment*		*Real Earnings per Worker*		*Labor Productivity Col. (1) - Col. (2)*	
Region	1971-80	1981-92	1971-80	1981-92	1971-80	1981-92	1971-80	1981-92
Medians								
SSA	3.54	2.88	5.95	2.23	-0.56	-0.81	-2.41	0.57
LAC	5.81	1.39	2.45	0.19	1.14	-0.77	3.36	1.20
ESA	10.05	10.42	6.87	5.42	2.76	4.72	3.18	5.00
OECD	2.92	2.09	-0.54	-0.90	2.64	1.23	3.46	2.99
Means								
SSA	5.14	2.97	5.09	3.00	1.74	-0.64	0.05	-0.03
LAC	5.58	0.99	2.72	0.21	1.74	-1.10	2.86	0.78
ESA	10.14	7.80	7.55	4.68	3.37	7.33	2.59	3.12
OECD	2.82	2.29	-0.40	-0.73	2.44	1.23	3.22	3.02

Source: UNIDO Data (see Appendix A, Part III for details).

The African scene reflected the widespread effects of over-manning and excessive job creation, particularly in the public sector. However, the situation improved in the eighties as the rate of growth of employment fell relative to that of output. Nevertheless, the median rate of productivity growth was only marginally higher than that of Latin America but well below that of East Asia and the OECD countries. Productivity growth is, of course, inversely related to employment growth. However an economy's ability to sustain an increase in real wages is constrained by this factor — there is clearly a trade-off in this sense between employment growth and real wage growth. The African countries as a group tilted towards the employment growth option — strongly in the seventies, and less so in the eighties. The result was a squeezing of non-wage income in the seventies, for although real wage had a negative growth, the rate of decline of labor productivity was so much greater. This trend was reversed in the eighties as real earnings continued to fall while productivity recovered.

Different countries within a particular region experienced great variations in growth rates. The summary statistical measures showing the variability within each region are given in Appendix B.2 at the end of this chapter. Notably, the variability of growth rates among individual countries (as measured by the standard deviation) was low for OECD countries, for all the variables. As far as the other regions are concerned, the variability for all three variables was generally higher for SSA compared to LAC, but interestingly not so with respect to EAS.

Table 5.2 set out the distribution of countries in Sub-Saharan Africa (SSA) in terms of the growth rates of real value added, employment and real earnings per worker respectively. For each variable, the growth rate is given separately for the two decades. The coverage varies for the different variables. More countries have growth rates of value added than of employment, with fewer countries with usable data on growth rates of real earnings per worker.[7]

[7] It should also be mentioned that observations for all years within each decade might not have been available. Countries which had less than five yearly observations reported in any one decade were rejected. All growth rates are exponential rates and are calculated by the regression method.

Table 5.2 Distribution of Growth Rates of Manufacturing in Sub-Saharan Africa

(a) Value-added deflated								
				1971-1980				
	$r<6$	$-6<r<-4$	$-4<r<-2$	$-2<r<0$	$0<r<2$	$2<r<4$	$4<r<6$	$6<r$
			Sierra Leone	Ghana	Senegal	Burkina Faso	Liberia	Botswana
			Benin		Somalia	Burundi	Nigeria	Cameroon
					Togo	Ethiopia	Swaziland	Kenya
					Zambia	Malawi		Mauritius
						Sudan		Rwanda
							Tanzania	Seychelles
						Zimbabwe		
Total N=24								
				1981-1992				
	$r<6$	$-6<r<-4$	$-4<r<-2$	$-2<r<0$	$0<r<2$	$2<r<4$	$4<r<6$	$6<r$
		Liberia	Gambia	Cameroon	Ethiopia	Burkina Faso	Chad	Benin
		Seychelles	Somalia	Gabon	Rwanda	Guinea	Comoros	Burundi
				Nigeria	Tanzania	Guinea-Bissau	Ghana	Botswana
				Sierra Leone	Zaire	Namibia	Kenya	Congo
						Swaziland	Malawi	Lesotho
						Togo	Senegal	Mauritius
						Zambia	Sudan	Uganda
						Zimbabwe		
Total N=34								

Table 5.2 (cont'd.) Distribution of Growth Rates of Manufacturing in Sub-Saharan Africa

(b) Employment							
				1971-1980			
$r<6$	$-6<r<-4$	$-4<r<-2$	$-2<r<0$	$0<r<2$	$2<r<4$	$4<r<6$	$6<r$
Central African Republic				Madagascar	Zambia	Ethiopia	Botswana
				Zimbabwe		Burundi	Kenya
				Ghana		Sierra Leone	Mauritius
				Tanzania			Swaziland
							Senegal
Total N=14							
				1981-1992			
$r<6$	$-6<r<-4$	$-4<r<-2$	$-2<r<0$	$0<r<2$	$2<r<4$	$4<r<6$	$6<r$
Central African Republic		Ghana	Cameroon	Madagascar	Ethiopia		Botswana
Togo				Malawi	Kenya		Benin
				South Africa	Senegal		Burundi
				Tanzania	Swaziland		Mauritius
				Zambia			
				Zimbabwe			
Total N=20							

Table 5.2 (cont'd.) Distribution of Growth Rates of Manufacturing in Sub-Saharan Africa

(c) Real Earnings

1971-1980

$r<6$	$-6<r<-4$	$-4<r<-2$	$-2<r<0$	$0<r<2$	$2<r<4$	$4<r<6$	$6<r$
Tanzania	Ethiopia	Kenya Zambia	Madagascar	Mauritius Zimbabwe	Botswana Swaziland		
Total N=9							

1981-1992

$r<6$	$-6<r<-4$	$-4<r<-2$	$-2<r<0$	$0<r<2$	$2<r<4$	$4<r<6$	$6<r$
Madagascar	Botswana	Cameroon	Congo	Central African Republic			Ghana
Nigeria	Burkina Faso	Malawi	Ethiopia	Liberia			Seychelles
Tanzania			Kenya Senegal Swaziland Zambia	Mauritius Niger Zimbabwe			
Total N=20							

It appears that the majority of countries had a positive rate of growth of real value added of manufacturing in both decades with a shift in the distribution to the left in the eighties as more countries suffered from low or negative growth rates. There was also a similar shift to the left in employment and in real wages.

A striking observation reflected in the tables is that while a majority of SSA countries in both the decades had positive growth rates in value added and employment, real wages in a majority of these countries suffered from negative trends.

The Trade-off between Wage Growth and Employment Growth

Employment growth in manufacturing is obviously limited by the rate of growth of output or value added. However, given the growth rate of output, there are three important elements which determine the value of the employment elasticity; (i) the trend in the share of wages, i.e., the rate of growth of the wage bill relative to value added in current prices facing the producer, (ii) the relative rates of increase in the producer and consumer price indices — which determines the value of the wage bill for the workers and (ii) the trade off between employment increase and real wage increase. We shall now elaborate the importance of each of these elements in an intuitive way. The algebraic formulation of the relationships between these variables is spelled out in the next section.

The Share of Wages

The share of wages in value added in neo-classical theory is determined by the technological factor of the production function. In alternative theories like that of Kalecki it is the mark-up price above costs which the producer is able to charge — or the 'degree of monopoly' in the market — which determines how much of output is available for distribution to labor. Whatever the importance of these factors it is likely that the share of wages would change only slowly over time. One point to note, however, in this connection is that, as will be borne out in the statistical analysis in the next section, the rate of inflation in an economy is an important determinant of the trend in the share of wages. Intuitively, it can be seen that indexation of wages to price increases can never be perfect. In economies in which the rate of inflation is high, the increase in wages lags behind prices, leading to a trend decline in the share of wages in current prices.

Given the growth of the wage bill in current prices its value in real terms from the point of view of the workers is determined by change in the ratio of producer prices to consumer prices. This ratio is sometimes called the 'domestic real exchange rate' (DRER), because the consumer goods are typically non-tradables and producer goods are more likely to be tradeables. If the DRER declines over time, then less of the wage bill cake is available to workers in real terms. It is easy to see that in an economy with a high rate of inflation, workers suffer in two ways: the value of the wage bill in current (producer) prices is reduced over time because of the lag of wage adjustment to price increase. Additionally, during inflationary spirals consumer prices are prone to increase faster than producer prices.[8] Both these effects are combined in the 'price effect' calculated in the algebraic decomposition given earlier.

The Employment-Wage Trade-off

The increase in the wage bill can be used to support either increase of employment at the going wage or increase in the real average earnings of workers. There is thus a clear trade-off between employment growth and wage growth. Alternative theories of wage determination are possible to account for the causal mechanism underlying the trade-off. In the neo-classical models of labor markets the causal mechanism runs from wages to employment. Real wage growth is determined first by the trends in the supply price of labor (alternative earnings), and employment growth responds to it through an inverse functional relationship. The extent of the trade-off is determined by the properties of the production function — more specifically by the elasticity of substitution between labor and other co-operant factors, principally capital and management. In the alternative neo-Keynesian version the causality runs more the other way. Labor market institutions, public policy and the macro-environment determine how the available cake is to be shared between employment growth and wage growth.

Two important points have been stressed in the literature, which emphasizes the autonomous determination of wages. First, we have the concern with the strength of 'insider' power. The insiders are those who are already in employment. They lean towards increasing their real wages at the expense of increasing the employment of more workers who are on the

[8] This is because as mentioned producer goods are more likely to be tradables whose international prices are tied to the world market. The domestic prices of such goods will depend on the exchange rate, and during a sustained inflationary period, the rate of devaluation is likely to lag behind the rate of inflation.

outside as job seekers. Labor laws in some countries might strengthen the 'insider' power either by supporting unions directly in the interest of industrial peace, or more commonly by instituting job security legislation, which helps to create a permanent elite workforce.

A second strand of research has stressed the point that the supply price of labor is never really given to the employer in a particular firm, as is purported to be the case in textbook models of competitive firms. The serious flaw in this formulation is that it fails to recognize that, even after we have controlled for the measurable human capital attributes like education, training and experience, labor has two dimensions to its supply — the number of workers and the flow of efficiency units per worker. The latter is not simply the hours of work per day or week, but also the intensity of work per hour. The supply of efficiency units per worker is generally a positive function of the wage per worker, increasing as the wage increases. Thus, the employer, responding to an increased demand for labor, has the option of hiring more bodies of workers at the going wage or getting more efficiency units per worker by increasing the wage of the existing workforce. The optimum combination of strategy for a profit-maximizing firm is to select that combination where the marginal cost of hiring extra workers just equals the marginal cost of getting additional efficiency units per worker by increasing wages. The former includes the cost of supervising a larger body of workers, and would increase if the supply of effective supervisors were limited. Institutional factors like job security legislation would also increase the cost of hiring more workers. Thus the wage offered by the average firm — even to its new, unskilled recruit — is a variable subject to management decisions in which the institutional environment plays a big role. It should also be remembered that the choice between the two strategies of increasing the supply of labor units will vary with the size of the firms apart from other attributes. Thus the outcome for an average firm depends also on the structure of industry.

Both the strands of research — insider power and efficiency wage — are merged together in the idea of internal labor markets specific to the firm. Manufacturing firms develop a labor system in which the stable core of workers enjoys lifetime employment in exchange for attachment to the individual firm. This system, which seems to have been most completely developed in the Japanese manufacturing industry, depends on the cooperation of enterprise-based unions with management. Recruitment of new workers tales place mostly at the entry level, at a young school-leaving age, and demand for experienced and skilled workers are sought to be made from the ranks of the firm-specific workforce through internal training. Furthermore, new recruitment is made only for perceived long-term growth of employment. Short-term fluctuations of employment are taken care of either by the employment of casual non-tenured workers, or by the system of outsourcing in which some components of the final manufactured product are subcontracted to smaller firms. The larger enterprises with the internal labor markets would have a bias towards increase in earnings rather than employment as a means of increasing the input of labor in response to an increase in demand.

The discussion so far has not mentioned technical progress, and hence concentrated on the wage-employment trade off at a point of time. In a dynamic setting we must allow not only for changes in the strength of the factors governing the trade-off (e.g., the institutional influence of trade unions or government), but also technological progress affecting the production process. Generally we would expect technical progress to increase the skill levels demanded of labor. This would lead to an outward shift of the wage-efficiency function so that mangers would be more inclined to meet a given increase in labor demand through raising wages rather than hiring more workers. The optimum wage, at which managers are indifferent between raising wages or hiring extra hands, increases. Such changes also might be brought about by economic polices which have an effect on the efficiency with which co-operant factors are used in the manufacturing firm. In the recent history of the manufacturing industry in India economic liberalization has eased the bottlenecks in the supply of essential inputs which had been responsible for the low utilization of capacity in the manufacturing firms. As it has become easier for Indian managers to increase the utilization of machines in their plants, they have been more inclined to increase the number of hours supplied by a typical worker, and have been willing to pay a higher wage per man to elicit the extra hours contributed by each. This is one hypothesis which has been advanced to explain the phenomenon of 'jobless growth' noticed in Indian industry in the eighties (Bhalotra 1998).

In the next section we present a decomposition exercise which allows us to compare the trade-off between employment growth and wage growth, given the growth rate of value added in manufacturing, and the other factors discussed in this section. The detailed explanation of the tradeoff achieved within each region can, of course, only be worked out through intensive country-specific research. However, a comparison of the outcome as between broad regions of the world is of some interest. It shows how the fruits of growth in manufacturing are shared out between 'insiders' and those outside the employed labor-force in this sector.

A Quantitative Analysis of the Wage-Employment Trade-off

The statistical methodology suggested below allows us to decompose the factors affecting real wage growth rate for any period and country into the various elements discussed in 5.3: the rate of growth of rat output; the trend share of wages; the rate of employment growth; and the relative price effect. Important differences between countries and regions are noticed in terms of these variables. The results of the statistical analysis allow us to form a quantitative idea of the differences in the employment-wage trade off, after we have controlled for the other factors in the exercise. We utilize for this purpose the UNIDO data set which provides time series on wages (average earnings per worker), value added, and employment in the manufacturing industries of a number of countries. These data are supplemented by time series of the manufacturing value added deflator (i.e. the producer price index for manufacturing sector) and of the consumer price index which are available in the World Tables.

Methodology

Define the following variables:

w = real wage (average earnings per worker)

S_W = wage bill (in current prices)

V = value added (in current prices)

v = value added (in constant prices)

L = employment

P_p = index of producer prices

P_c = index of consumer prices

To define the relationship defining the movement of the wage bill with respect to value added over time we specify the following equation:

$$S_w = V^{\alpha} \quad (1)$$

α - is a technological and behavioral parameter which is assumed to remain constant over the period under consideration. However, it can take any positive value and would generally vary from one economy to another depending on the factors determining the share of wages over time. If it has a value of unity, the share of wages remains constant.

A variable written with a dot on top (·) represents rate of change of the variable concerned.

Note that from (1)

$$\dot{S}_w / S_w = \alpha \dot{v} / v = \alpha(\dot{v} / v + \dot{P}_p / P_p)$$

We can then write the equation for the real wage growth as:

$$\dot{w} / w = \dot{S}_w / S_w - \dot{L} / L - \dot{P}_c / P_c$$

$$= \alpha(\dot{v} / v + \dot{P}_p / P_p) - \dot{L} / L - \dot{P}_c / P_c \qquad (2)$$

$$= \alpha \dot{v} / v - \dot{L} / L + \alpha \dot{P}_p / P_p - \dot{P}_c / P_c \qquad (2a)$$

= Output Effect + Employment Effect + Price Effect

The equation 2(a) allows us to breakdown the rate of change of real wage into three elements. As shown the first term measures the output effect — the part of the real wage increase that could be ascribed to real growth in value added — given the value of the parameter determining the course of the share of wages. The second term can be called the 'employment effect': it expresses the already established idea that given the growth in the wage bill, the smaller is the increase in real wage per worker the higher the employment growth. The last term shows the impact on real wage growth of changes the price levels facing producers and consumers over time. It is really composed of two distinct elements. The last term in equation (2a) could be re-written as:

$$(\alpha + 1)\dot{P}_p / P_p + (\dot{P}_p / P_p - \dot{P}_c / P_c) \qquad (3)$$

The first term in (3) could be called the 'wage share effect' of price changes over time. If α < 1 the share of wages in net output falls over time in current prices in accordance with equation (1). In this case the first term in (3) is negative, showing that a certain part of the real output growth, as measured by this term, is not available for the growth of the real wage bill. The second term is the rate of change in the ratio of producer to consumer prices or the so-called 'domestic real exchange rate' (DRER). One can intuitively grasp its importance by considering the case of an inflationary economy in which the exchange rate depreciation lags behind the rate of inflation — a common enough scenario in developing countries. In this case the consumer price level which affects the real value of workers' wages, increases faster than producer prices which are tied to international prices of traded goods. Thus the second term in (3) is also negative implying that a portion of the real output growth is used to keep the wage bill growing at the same real rate. Both these 'price effects', if negative, can be thought of as 'leakages' from the real output growth — which decreases the rate of growth of the portion available for supporting employment or real wage growth.

All the variables in equation (2a) can be calculated directly from the UNIDO data set. There are, however, two alternative ways of dealing with α, the parameter determining the share of wages. The first method is to treat the equation essentially as an identity since all the variables can be quantified empirically except for the coefficient 'a'. We could then, for any specified time period, plug in the growth rates of the different variables in the equation, including the actual growth rate of real wages, and then solve for 'a'. A second approach would be to estimate econometrically the time series data on value added and the wage bill — assuming a functional form relating to the two variables as in the equation (1) — thereby predicting the value for the growth trend of real wages. To the extent that our estimate contains an error term the predicted value will differ from the actual value.

Results based on the first approach only are presented in what follows. Although the equation is an identity, it has an economic content, laying out as it does the existence of a trade-off between real wage growth and employment growth. The rate of growth of value added — after allowing for the DRER effect and the value of the parameter α — determines the trade off between employment growth and wage growth. The higher the employment effect *ceteris paribus* the lower the wage growth. Alternative theories of wage determination are possible to account for the causal mechanism underlying the trade-off. In the neo-classical models of labor markets the causal mechanism runs from wages to employment. Real wage growth is determined first by the trends in the supply price of labor (alternative earnings), and employment growth responds to it through an inverse functional relationship. In the alternative neo-Keynesian version the causality runs more the other way. Labor market institutions, public policy and the macro-environment determines how the available cake is to be shared between employment growth and wage growth. In this chapter we do not propose to sort out the validity of the two alternative views of wage determination. The final outcome is probably the result of a combination of both sets of factors highlighted by the two theories. For our present discussion suffice it to note that the regions studied show widely different outcomes and clearly labor market institutions are at least partly responsible for these differences.

The Empirical Results for Four Regions

Results based on using equation 2(b) as an identity are presented in Table 5.3. Four large regions of the world are considered. The area of the post-war 'miracle growth', the region of East Asia (ESA) including China is highlighted in this table, along with OECD countries, Latin America and the Caribbean (LAC), and Sub-Saharan Africa (SSA).

As could be expected the region with the smallest proportion of its countries figuring in our sample is sub-Saharan Africa. There are numerous gaps in the data set. The decision was taken to include only those countries which had data for most years for all the variables included in our decomposition exercise.[9] The countries included in this exercise are given in Appendix II.4. Nevertheless, we believe that the regional results represent the trends in not only the sample countries, but for a large part of the region not represented by country observations. The detailed study of two countries — Ghana and Kenya using national data sources, reveal a pattern not dissimilar to that emerging for the SSA region in this chapter (Chapter 8 and 9).

---

[9]This is the major reason why the data on growth rates of wages, employment and value added given in Table 4. 5 differ from those given in Table 4.4 with a much larger sample of countries. But although the magnitudes differ in detail the basic trends are the same.

Table 5.3 Decomposition of Effects on the Growth Rate of Real Wage

Period/Region	*Real Wage Growth*	*Output Effect*	*Employment Effect (-)*	*a*	P_P/P_P	P_C/P_C	*Price Effect*
1971-80							
East Asia (ESA)	5.32	11.47	5.77	1.07	6.78	7.61	−0.41
OECD	1.72	3.27	-0.23	0.99	7.66	9.37	−1.78
LA & Caribbean (LAC)	−2.13	1.83	-0.64	0.97	129.99	130.51	−4.60
Sub-Saharan Africa (SSA)	−3.44	2.34	4.45	0.85	12.94	12.29	−1.33
1981-92							
East Asia (ESA)	5.17	12.04	4.36	1.09	4.69	7.61	−2.53
OECD	1.35	3.03	-0.31	0.80	2.17	3.74	−1.99
LA & Caribbean (LAC)	−3.13	1.77	−0.78	0.97	52.80	56.86	−5.68
Sub-Saharan Africa (SSA)	−4.36	3.66	3.59	0.87	9.71	12.86	−4.43

Source: UNIDO data and price indices from World Tables. See text for definition of variables. See Appendix B.3 for details of the sample of countries making up each region.

Notes: * The growth rates are weighted by ratios of average exchange rates and average real value added figures of each country in the sample for each region. ** Figures may not add up due to rounding.

The data given in Table 5.3 reiterate the point already made that the manufacturing sector of the SSA region had quite a respectable growth rate of value added in both periods. Note that the column showing figures for the 'output effect' in the table is the growth rate of real value added multiplied by the parameter α — which had a value of less than unity in both periods.

The results for the ESA region confirms the point made many time in recent discussions of growth in the world economy — that this region led the world in its rate of growth, particularly in manufacturing by a wide margin. Even allowing for the variations in the value of α shown in column 5, the figures in column 3 show the extent of the disparity between ESA and the other regions in both periods. The labor market outcomes — giving the different proportions in which that the fruits of output growth were shared between employment growth and real wage growth — were markedly different as between the four regions. But before coming to this topic we should draw attention to one important result revealed by the statistical analysis, and that is the importance of the price factor in determining the portion of the output growth that was ultimately available for supporting employment or wage growth.

The Price Effect

All regions in both periods suffered from a negative price effect. But the *magnitude* of the negative effect was much more important in some regions than in others. LAC had very large negative price effects, which more than wiped out the modest output growth in both periods. In the seventies, the adverse movement of DRER contributed modestly to this state of affairs, as the consumer price index increased at a faster rate than the producer prices. But the more important reason for the large negative price effect was the high rate of inflation in this region. It is seen from the data presented that in both periods the share of wages in current prices fell modestly at the rate of 0.03 percent. But applied to the inflation rate of nearly 130 percent in the first period, this added up to a substantial rate of 'leakage' from the real output growth which could sustain the growth in the wage bill (cf. equation 3 above). In the second period the rate of inflation moderated somewhat to a level of around 50 percent, but the favorable effect from this slow-down was more than offset by a much larger DRER effect.

SSA suffered from an adverse price effect as well — much more so in the second period, when it came close to the LAC figure. But this increase in the negative price effect for SSA is seen to be due entirely to the enhanced DRER effect, with consumer prices running ahead of producer prices.

Compared to the LAC and SSA regions, both EAS and OECD had a much smaller 'leakage' due to the price effect. Given the modest inflation rate, the negative 'wage share effect' was not important except for OECD in the eighties, when there was a significant downward trend in the share of wages. The negative price effect for these regions were mostly due to the adverse DRER effect.

As a final comment it is useful to recall the point mentioned earlier that in inflationary conditions it is normal to expect that the DRER effect would be negative, as the depreciation of the exchange rate lags behind the rate of domestic inflation, so that the consumer price index (dominated by non-tradable) increase faster than the producer price index (with a larger weight of tradable). However, it is now seen from the data presented in Table 5.6 that even in regions with moderate inflation like EAS and OECD, the DRER trends were significantly negative in both the decades. Evidently the worldwide negative trend in the prices of manufactured goods had a pervasive effect on most countries. This topic deserves more detailed research.

Labor Market Outcomes

Given the real output growth, net of the price effect, the labor market shares out the potential gains partly in the form of employment increase and partly as increase in real earnings per worker. It is seen from Table 5.3 that the regions varied enormously in the proportions in which the output gain was divided. East Asia, in both periods, distributed the fruits of output growth almost equally between employment and wage growth. This implies that wages increased at roughly the same rate as labor productivity, and given the high rate of growth of output, the increase in wage was considerable. This type of labor market outcome is consistent with much discussion of wage setting institutions in East Asian countries. The study of Korea can be cited as an example. It has been maintained that profit sharing principles are ingrained in the wage formation process of Korean manufacturing. A substantial portion of workers' remuneration, perhaps as much as a third, are given in the form of productivity and profit related bonuses. An econometric model of wage determination strongly supported the hypothesis that wages seemed to be significantly determined by a 'target wage' based on productivity growth of a previous period (Mazumdar 1993; cf. also Amsden 1990).

Sub-Saharan Africa and the OECD regions appear from the results shown in Table 5.3 to have been at opposite ends of the spectrum of employment-wage growth trade-off in both decades. In the seventies the growth rate of manufacturing value added, although lower than that of the OECD and the East Asia regions, was somewhat higher than that of LAC. The negative 'price effect', however was much less than in LAC. Nevertheless, net of the price effect the wage bill in real terms grew at a rate barely exceeding 1 percent per annum. Yet, employment growth was at a substantial rate of over 4.4 percent. The only way the manufacturing sector of this region could accommodate this rate of employment growth was by a massive decline in real wage at the rate of 3.4 percent per annum. In the next decade, the manufacturing sector of SSA seemed to have recovered a lot, registering a rate of growth of output averaging 4.4 percent per annum over the period. But unfortunately the negative trends in the price effect nullified much of this enhanced growth. Net of the price effect output growth could not sustain the combined wage and employment growth at any higher level. Thus as employment growth continued to be high, although slackening a little from the value of the seventies, the SSA region as a whole experienced a decline in real wage at a rate even greater than what was witnessed in the previous decade. This experience of massive decline in real wage has already been noted for many individual countries in Africa in the discussion above. It is now seen that the more important cause of the wage decline was not so much the stagnation of manufacturing output as the phenomenon of 'labor retention' on the part of African employers in the formal sector, reinforced in the later decade by the adverse price effect facing manufacturing. A large proportion of manufacturing enterprises in the large-scale (as opposed to the informal) manufacturing sector have been state-owned or joint State-private ventures. The pressure to provide employment in this sector has been strong, and has increased as the decline in the economy shrank earnings and employment opportunities in other sectors. Although the UNIDO data set for SSA is imperfect, and number of countries which could be included in the sample is small, the over-all pattern is consistent with the conclusions of other case studies.

Turning to OECD countries, whose data reported to the UNIDO, are of the highest quality in the sample, output growth in this region as a whole has been modest, well below that of East Asia, but not as low as LAC in both periods, and SSA in the first. But the labor market trade-off is exactly the opposite of what was seen in Sub-Saharan Africa. These economies as a whole preferred to realize their gains in output over time in the form of real wage enhancement rather than employment growth. In fact the results show that the real wage growth was high enough — given the modest output growth — to actually result in a declining trend in employment in both periods. This story is again consistent with much discussion of the power of the 'insiders' in OECD industrial firms.

LAC had the lowest growth rate of output of all four regions in both periods. To make matters worse the price effect exerted a substantial negative trend, which could only be accommodated by declining trends in both real wage per worker and employment. Our results bring out the important point that this region took out the adverse effect of the declining 'pie' more on wages than employment both in the seventies and the eighties — thus showing some of the characteristics of SSA in labor retention.

Conclusions

This part of the book has explored the data collected by international agencies over a long period of time on wages in the formal sector of the reporting countries. The following is an incomplete list of some of the more important conclusions.

A review of the data on manufacturing wages in the files of the ILO shows the difference in the trends of real wages in African countries in the first 15 or 20 years after independence and the next 15-20 years. An early study of the period 1956-64 showed that the African countries in the sample were set quite apart from the countries of the other regions in experiencing a remarkably high growth rate of real wages per annum — of the order of 4 or 5 times the annual rate of growth of GDP per capita, even though the latter was positive in this period. The primary objective of this extraordinary wage increase — propelled by periodic hikes in minimum wages — was a change in the labor system: from one based on unstable circulatory labor to one making use of settled rural-to-urban migrants. A secondary reason was the desire to reduce the wide disparities in the wages of high and low paid workers inherited from the colonial wage system.

The peak of the wage inflation was reached in the late sixties for most countries, and in the early seventies for some. Both the ILO and the UNIDO data sets suggest that the real wage trends for a majority of African countries have been negative over the last two decades. Because of the variability of country experiences — and perhaps more importantly for the available series not being complete for the whole of the period for many countries — it is impossible to give an accurate statistical summary measure of the trend in real wages for the Africa region compared to other parts of the world. The best summary picture is probably what is reported in Table 5.1: the median trend in real wage change in SSA countries was — 0.56 percent per annum it the decade of the seventies, and 0.81 in the eighties. The sample of countries included in this table is quite large, and included some like Mauritius and Botswana, which had significant increases in wages. However, when we used a more restricted sample of countries (to achieve completeness of coverage for all the time series needed) and derived weighted average of the trend rate, the negative trend growth rate was much higher. In any event, it is clear from all the data sources, and different statistical treatments, that the negative wage trend was more substantial for the SSA region than for Latin America — the other region which recorded negative real wage growth, particularly in the eighties. This picture contrasts sharply with the experience of East Asian countries, where the positive wage trend was higher in the eighties. Even the OECD countries had a reduced but positive growth of real wage in the eighties, compared to the previous decade.

Our regression analysis of changes in average wages from a limited sample of countries in the different regions suggests that failure to compensate for inflationary increases in prices was the major mechanism of real wage decline (Table 4.2). This is what distinguished the experience of Africa over the last two decades from that of either Latin America or Asia. It was interesting to see that in the cross country experience the influence of per capita GDP growth on wage changes over time was not statistically significant for Africa (unlike the other regions).

The UNIDO data set allowed us to explore the relationships between the growth rates in real wages, value added, employment and domestic real exchange rate (DRER) within the manufacturing sector of the countries in the different regions. A model was proposed which allows one to decompose the determinants of the change in real wage growth over time into several components: those due to change in value added; due to change in employment; and due to change in the DRER. Our results show that a major determinant of the real wage decline in SSA countries in the seventies was the large growth rate of employment relative to the sluggish growth in manufacturing value added. In the eighties the rate of growth of value added recovered and employment growth slackened somewhat, but the strong negative movement of the DRER (due to consumption prices increasing faster than producer prices) was the major cause of real wage decline. Contrasts with the experience of other regions are suggested in the detailed analysis in the text.

The adverse DRER movement (from the point of view of the negative real wage trend) in SSA in the eighties is partly a consequence of domestic inflation, and partly of the declining barter terms of trade. But it follows from the large values of the employment effect that retention of labor is at least an important cause of real wage decline. SSA economies as a group, in this interpretation, showed rigidity in adjusting employment to value added changes, but demonstrated remarkable downward flexibility of wages.

Appendices to Part II

Appendix II.1: Methodology for Preparing Regional Averages of Time Trends of Variables

The UNIDO data set provides time series for the variables used in this study for the period 1971-92 for individual countries of each region. This data set is available in the diskettes made available by the World Bank under the title of 'STARS: World Tables 1994'. We needed to construct regional averages of exponential growth rates of each of the variables from the country level data. The weighting factor for the growth rates of value added, wage bill and producer and consumer prices was the relative size of the economy in the region measured in dollar values. Thus to calculate the growth rate of real value added for the region the following steps are involved:

- First the value added series is deflated by the producer price index for manufacturing, available in the UNIDO data set, and exponential growth rates for the periods 1971-80 and 1981-92 are calculated for each country. In doing this part of the exercise, countries with less than 4 observations in each period were dropped.
- After calculating the growth rates, the average value added deflated and the average exchange rates Local currency per dollar) for each period were used for weighting to adjust for differences in the size of the economy and exchange rate fluctuations. To find the averages we took the figures for 1st, middle and last years of each period for each variable (i.e., the average value added deflated and average exchange rates for the years 1971, 1976 and 1980 were used for the period 1971-80, and we used the observations for 1981, 1986 and 1992 for the next period.
- The ratio between the average value added and average exchange rate is then used as a weighting factor to value the figures of growth rates in terms of a common currency. The weighted growth rate for each country would then be the growth rate for each country multiplied by the corresponding weighting factor.
- Finally, the weighted average for each period is calculated as the ratio

between the sum of the weighted country level growth rates in the region and the regional sum of the weighting factors.

For calculating the growth rate of employment growth, a different weighting scheme was adopted. Unlike the other variables, the average employment in each country (instead of value added and exchange rate) was used as the weighting factor. However, due to data insufficiency, we had to stick to the value added weights for the growth rates of employment for East Asia and Latin America.

Table IIA.1 Statistics for the Average Growth Rates of Manufacturing in SSA, EAS, OECD and LAC (1971-80 and 1981-92)

	SSA		*East Asia*		*OECD*		*LAC*	
Value added deflated								
	1971-80	1981-92	1971-80	1981-92	1971-80	1981-92	1971-80	1981-92
Observations	24	34	8	10	14	17	26	32
1st Quartile	1.90	0.43	6.37	2.44	1.99	1.02	2.65	-0.33
Median	3.54	2.88	10.05	10.42	2.92	2.09	5.81	1.39
3rd Quartile	6.66	4.68	12.25	11.85	3.25	3.08	7.57	3.13
Mean	5.14	2.97	10.14	7.80	2.82	2.29	5.58	0.99
Skewness	1.50	0.09	0.49	-0.38	0.40	0.69	1.41	-1.13
Standard Dev.	5.91	4.00	4.04	5.49	1.89	1.63	4.87	3.33
Maximum	22.01	11.96	16.71	14.86	6.38	5.88	22.48	6.41
Minimum	-3.66	-5.25	5.80	0.09	-0.18	0.14	-2.97	-8.24
Employment								
	1971-80	1981-92	1971-80	1981-92	1971-80	1981-92	1971-80	1981-92
Observations	10	21	9	9	14	16	16	16
1st Quartile	3.38	0.27	4.75	3.29	-1.20	-1.39	-0.25	-1.59
Median	5.95	2.23	6.87	5.42	-0.54	-0.90	2.45	0.19
3rd Quartile	8.10	5.12	11.13	5.64	0.41	-0.21	4.99	1.69
Mean	5.09	3.00	7.55	4.68	-0.40	-0.73	2.72	0.21
Skewness	-1.24	0.79	-0.21	0.48	0.29	0.61	0.17	-0.36
Standard Dev.	5.63	4.99	4.02	3.27	1.50	1.18	4.29	3.38
Maximum	12.40	16.50	12.53	11.19	2.82	1.49	9.97	5.33
Minimum	-7.78	-6.74	2.09	-0.45	-3.30	-2.37	-4.61	-6.61
Real Wages								
	1971-80	1981-92	1971-80	1981-92	1971-80	1981-92	1971-80	1981-92
Observations	9	21	8	9	14	17	15	15
1st Quartile	-2.28	-3.63	2.00	3.84	2.11	0.63	-0.62	-2.89
Median	-0.56	-0.81	2.76	4.72	2.64	1.23	1.14	-0.77
3rd Quartile	2.20	0.67	5.02	6.19	3.11	2.00	3.68	1.17
Mean	1.74	-0.64	3.37	7.33	2.44	1.23	1.74	-1.10
Skewness	1.46	0.61	0.23	2.44	-0.76	-0.44	0.56	-0.20
Standard Dev.	6.41	6.53	4.21	10.64	1.22	1.06	3.05	3.64
Maximum	14.94	16.78	10.56	34.35	4.33	2.91	8.03	4.61
Minimum	-4.03	-13.56	-3.34	-3.42	-0.09	-0.68	-2.83	-7.42

Source: Based on the UNIDO data (see Appendix B.3 for details).

Appendix II.2 Countries and their Regional Groupings: ILO and UNIDO Data Sources

ILO

The ILO series include the following countries:

Africa – Botswana; Burundi, Egypt, Gambia, Ghana, Kenya, Malawi, Sierra Leone, South Africa, Swaziland, Zimbabwe
America – Argentina, Chile, Colombia, Costa Rica, Dominican Republic, El Salvador, Guatemala, Honduras, Mexico, Panama, Peru, Puerto Rico
Asia – India, Rep. of Korea, Pakistan, Philippines, Sri Lanka, Thailand

UNIDO

The UNIDO sample includes the following countries:
Sub-Saharan Africa (SSA) – Botswana; Burkina Faso Cameroon, Central African Republic, Congo, Côte d'Ivoire, Ethiopia, Gambia, Ghana, Kenya, Liberia, Madagascar, Malawi, Mauritius, Niger, Nigeria, Senegal, Seychelles, Swaziland, Tanzania, Zambia, Zimbabwe
East Asia (ESA) – China, Fiji, Indonesia, Rep. of Korea, Malaysia, Philippines, Thailand, Tonga, Papua New Guinea
Latin America and the Caribbean (LAC) – Argentina, Barbados, Bolivia, Brazil, Chile, Colombia, Ecuador, Honduras, Jamaica, Mexico, Panama, Suriname, Trinidad and Tobago, Uruguay, Venezuela
OECD – Australia, Austria, Belgium, Canada, Denmark, France, Finland, Germany, Iceland, Italy, Japan, Luxembourg, New Zealand, Norway, Spain, Sweden, United States

Note: Available data for each decade may not necessarily cover all the countries in that group.

Appendix II.3 Countries Included in the Decomposition Exercise

It was decided that for the decomposition exercise presented in section 4.4 above we should include only those countries in each region which had time series available for all the variables used in the analysis. Thus the sample of countries used differ somewhat from those mentioned in Appendix B.3.

Table IIA.2 The Country Sample for Each Region

Sub-Saharan Africa	East Asia	OECD	Latin America & Caribbean
Botswana	China	Australia	Argentina
Ethiopia	Fiji	Austria	Barbados
Kenya	Indonesia	Belgium	Bolivia
Mauritius	South Korea	Canada	Chile
Swaziland	Malaysia	Denmark	Colombia
Tanzania	Philippines	France	Ecuador
Zambia	Thailand	Finland	Honduras
Zimbabwe	Tonga	Germany	Jamaica
	Papua New Guinea	Iceland	Mexico
		Italy	Panama
		Japan	Surinam
		Luxembourg	Trinidad and Tobago
		New Zealand	Uruguay
		Norway	Venezuela
		Spain	
		Sweden	
		United States	

Part III:
The Rural-Urban Wage-Gap in Africa

6 The Theory of Rural-Urban Wage Gap in Africa

The general picture of declining wages in the urban formal sector raises the issue of the rural-urban wage gap, which has figured so prominently in the discussion of urban labor markets in Africa. Does this decline imply that the large wage gap in favor of the urban formal sector tended to shrink and disappear after the wage inflation of the sixties?

Before coming to the empirical evidence on this point, we address some of the key issues, which have to be addressed conceptually in the study of the evolution of rural-urban differentials in earnings.

The African Wage Story — The Stereotype

The stereotype of African economies with large and growing rural-urban income differentials was established early in the development literature soon after these countries gained independence. In fact the two different aspects of this stereotype — often confused — ought to be kept separate because they refer to different responses to the political economy of post-colonial Africa.[10] The first is the large disparity in the levels of income or GDP per capita generated in the urban and rural economies, and the second, is the high urban wage relative to the alternative earnings of labor in the rural areas. The former is the direct outcome of decisions affecting investment, public expenditure and taxation, which impinge differentially on the urban and rural sectors. The latter has to do more specifically with the functioning of labor markets, and institutional influences affecting the wage structure in the urban, more specifically, the urban formal sector. The existence of the first phenomenon might be a necessary condition for the second, but certainly is not a sufficient condition. At the same time the non-existence of the second does not imply the absence of the first condition.

Although these are separate issues, a great deal of writing and policy

[10] This is one of the reasons for the confusing parts of the argument in Jamal and Weeks (1993) in their otherwise excellent effort.

analysis have veered towards the rural-urban wage gap issue even when ostensibly discussing the wider problems of development in the urban and rural sectors. As Jamal and Weeks wrote:

> The crucial 'price distortion' in Sub-Saharan African countries was the unskilled urban wage. If not the cause of all imbalances in the economy, it came to be viewed as at least the most fundamental distortion. On the production side it induced capital-intensive techniques, which were inefficient in and of themselves and retarded the growth of employment, while on the other side of the labor market it was the main cause of rural-to-urban migration, which provoked a variety of ills. (Jamal and Weeks, p.48).

There were several distinct elements emphasized by different commentators, which contributed to the building of this stereotype. It might be useful to separate these elements at this stage so as to facilitate our subsequent evaluation of the stereotype empirically and its subsequent evolution.[11]

Firstly, there was the rapid increase in formal sector wages which was experienced by a number of countries before the mid-70s already discussed in Part II. It is quite apparent that ignoring the economic and institutional reasons for this wage increase may have led a number of observers to adopt too simplistic an analysis of the economic implications of the wage increase. Even when the declining trend in wages in the formal sector became apparent — and as documented in the last part was continuous and substantial in many countries — the established idea of distorted labor markets favoring the urban sector seemed to have remained unshaken.[12]

Secondly, in order to establish that a labor aristocracy was unfolding in the formal sector, commentators had to pinpoint the institutional basis for the formation of the aristocracy as various authors stressed different points. The sudden access to power of unions, particularly in the more urbanized countries like Zambia, Ghana and Nigeria, may have triggered the need for the emerging politicians to comply with requests by urban unions in an

---

[11] These paragraphs draw heavily on Jamal and Weeks 1993, Chapter 3.

[12] Jamal and Weeks quotes the following passage from the World Bank Country Report on Kenya (1983):
'The [present] policy of wage restraint should probably be maintained for the foreseeable future. First, labor markets are not in equilibrium, as there is considerable gap between wages earned in the modern or formal sector and those available in [the urban informal sector] for comparable skill levels. Second, in so far as wage restraint moderates increases in domestic prices, this policy has beneficial effects on rural real incomes. Thus this policy effectively redistributes income from urban to rural households' (Quoted by Jamal and Weeks, p.31).

effort to strengthen their fragile power base (Leys 1971). Also stressed was the importance of public sector in total employment in the formal sector, coupled with the exercise of wage leadership by the public sector in the urban labor market (Kilby 1969). Jamal and Weeks make an interesting point that the 'judgment that wage earners represented a privileged and perhaps parasitic class was endorsed by observers across the political spectrum.' (p.44). There was a short step from the neo-classical economist's concerns about the excessive rural-urban wage gap and with the Marxist diagnosis that the African workers' conservatism in the formal sector was due to his privileged position relative to other groups (Arrighi and Saul 1968).

Thirdly, some writers stressed their concern over the inappropriate technology choice as a determinant in the creation of 'enclaves' wherein workers enjoyed inflated wages. Thus Stewart (1972) argued that technology and factor proportions are product specific given the fact that products are not too sensitive to changes in factor proportions. The poor consumed labor intensive products while the rich consumed capital intensive products of Western origin. Given the wide income inequality engendered by the development process in Sub-Saharan Africa, capital intensive enclaves were created in which labor productivity was high. Labor employed in this sector therefore was able to share in this high productivity generated by inappropriately high capital intensity — because profits were high and the share of total labor costs was low. In this analysis the causation ran, not from high wages to inappropriately high capital intensive techniques — as in standard neo-classical analysis — but in reverse instead, starting with a product composition determined by the distribution of income. A similar view is implicit in the well-known ILO Kenya Employment Report (1972).

Fourthly, the Harris-Todaro model — said to be based on East African experience in the late sixties — stressed a probabilistic migration function in which rural-to-urban migrants responded not to actual wage difference but to the probable lifetime income stream. Migrants were compensated for a waiting period by a higher income stream after they had secured jobs in the formal sector. The prediction for such a model was that high formal sector wages induced excessive migration, which added to over-urbanization problems while draining the rural economy of potentially productive prime age workers.[13] Migrants flocked the ranks of workers in the urban informal sector consequently its relative earnings were depressed.

Lastly, the concept of a high lifetime earnings stream *à la* Harris-Todaro was tied to the assumption that once a person got a job in the formal sector, it was for a lifetime. Public sector employment rules and labor legislation governing employment conditions in the large scale private sector assured security of tenure.

It is surprising to find that very little of the various elements discussed above have been supported by detailed, or even not so detailed empirical evidence. The point on which there is most evidence is the gap in labor earnings between the rural and the urban formal sector. We shall therefore begin the review of the empirical material with a critique of this evidence using Zambia pinpointed in the literature as a striking example of the excessive wage gap.

The Case of Zambia: Evidence on the Rural-Urban Wage Gap in Africa

The diagnosis of the Zambian economy — one afflicted by the problem of the wage gap — resulting from two ILO/JASPA missions (1977 and 1981) and two reports based on the wage policy by J.W. Turner sponsored by the ILO (1969 and 1978). Turner in his initial report noticed the rapid increase in real wages, at an annual double digit rate over the preceding five years (see section A of this paper). Over the entire period in the second half of the sixties, the total increase in real wages was nearly two-thirds. As nothing like this was perceived for the income of farmers in the rural sector, Turner's quick conclusion was that 'a very wide gap had developed between the standard of life of the urban Zambian employees and that of Zambian villagers' (ILO 1969, p.10). Table 6.1 sets out two estimates — one by Turner and the other by the World Bank — on the rural-urban earnings gap around 1970. Both estimates are reproduced from Jamal and Weeks. The earnings gap between farmers and mine workers — a privileged group in the urban labor market — was much larger than shown in the table, estimated by Turner to be around 9:1. Many commentators

[13] There was a contradiction in the model in so far as expected wages were a function of the wage level and the probability of employment. As wages increased and employment growth decreased, it is not clear that the value of the probability term would necessarily increase: rather it would depend on the elasticity of the negative function relating wage to employment growth. For a critique of this and other aspects of the model see Mazumdar (1989).

have taken the Zambian statistics as shown in Table 6.1 at face value without discerning the many underlying assumptions. We will now examine the major issues, some of them mentioned by Jamal and Weeks, which needs to be raised before accepting the figures in the table at their face value.

Table 6.1 Zambia: Measures of the Rural-Urban Gap, Two Selected Years

	Ratio	*Wage earners*	*Farmers*	*Basis*
1.Wage Earner / peasant	4.9	713	145	Wage compared to peasant family income
2. Minimum wage / agricultural value added per worker	3.5	400	114	Wage compared to output per agricultural. worker

Source: Jamal and Weeks (1993), Table V.5, p. 126. Original Sources are:(1) from ILO 1969, p. 11. (2) from World Bank 1987a.

- It should be noted that data on wage earnings in the urban formal sector are collected from the Statistical Office, which obtains its returns from registered establishments. However, the earnings data relating to farmers have to be estimated indirectly from other sources. Turner's estimates — using the National Accounts — were derived from totaling the income originating from this sector then dividing it by the total estimated number of farm households. It is not clear that subsistence income was adequately covered in the national account estimates. Also excluded were the numbers on off-farm income, an important component of rural household income. Furthermore, there is a serious problem about prices i.e., the national accounts evaluate farm income at farm gate prices which are not used by urban wage earners to purchase food. If we reevaluate the farmer's income using the urban retail prices for food the value of the wage gap would be reduced significantly. Obviously, there is the wider issue of the difference in the cost of living between time and country. Higher cost of housing and transport in the urban sector, are among other important reasons for a substantially higher cost of living at existing prices in the town. It is, however, clear that the estimates shown in Table 6.1 might have exaggerated the extent of the wage gap by failing to adjust for the differences in the cost of living.
- The comparison of average incomes for farmers and wage earners implicitly assumes that the distribution of earnings in the relevant range of incomes for the two groups are not very different. However, if the

groups being compared are the small-holders in rural areas and all wage and salary earners in the urban formal sector — as in Turner's numbers — then it is fairly apparent that the comparison will be weighted in favor of the urban workers whose average earnings are augmented by highly paid employees. The World Bank numbers for comparing the minimum wage with average farm income might be more appropriate on the assumption that the skill levels of workers near the minimum wage level are more comparable to the levels of small-holder farmers. In any event in the absence of any information on this crucial point the quantification of the wage gap by Turner and similar commentators are highly debatable.

- The comparison of the average worker's earnings in rural and urban areas implicitly assumes that the dependent-earner ratio of a typical household is the same in country and town. In so far as the dependent-earner ratio is higher in town — typically because of the smaller scope for the employment of women and children in income producing work in the town — the wage gap is exaggerated if we wish to compare income levels of mature households in the two sectors.

This point brings us to an important issue, which casts some doubt on the alarming hypothesis of Turner. He found the rural-urban wage gap to be near 'dangerous' levels in Zambia because, as we have seen, the real wages in the urban formal sector workers had increased in the sixties at a rate several times higher than agricultural production per capita. But he neglected to consider the factors behind the wage increase: the decision to increase the minimum wage in order to change the labor system from migrating to stable labor. This led Turner to exaggerate what might be called the 'equilibrium' wage differential between the rural and the urban sectors based on the migration of family migrants. It is possible that the inflation of wages in Zambia had overshot the mark needed to attract stable family migrants, but this is a question which Turner or the ILO/JASPA missions failed to pursue. The relationship between different types of rural-urban migrants and the determination of the equilibrium wage in the urban labor market is discussed in more detail in the next section.

Conceptual Issues in the Comparison of Rural and Urban Earnings

What measure of rural income should we consider when comparing rural income to urban wages? Using the wage rate per unit of time (day or hour) is clearly inappropriate. Urban workers, particularly in the formal sector, would generally have around-the-year employment whereas wage-workers in agriculture often work part-time. The hours worked on a family farm by an average active member are uncertain and difficult to measure.

A first step in tackling this issue is to compare earnings per worker (or earners) in the two sectors over an extended period of time, e.g. one year. But while an 'earner' may be easy to define in the case of a rural wage employee, a worker in a family farm, in which almost everybody contributes some hours to economic work from a very early age, can only be defined by some arbitrary standard. Furthermore, a measure of income which is appropriate to approximate the supply price of labor from the rural areas depends very much on: (i) the type of migration and; (ii) the different life cycle effects affecting the earning strength of the family in the two sectors. Let us consider each of these two points in turn.

Type of Migration and the Supply Price of Labor

Two distinct types of migrants workers are typically attracted to the urban labor markets from the rural areas in developing countries: individual migrants who work in urban areas while their families stay behind and family migrants who move with their families or even if starting off single, eventually want to settle in town with their families. The former type is generally dominated by short-period or circulatory migrants. They generally spend a part of their working life in town, whether for a season or for longer periods, but continue to have a stake in the rural economic life. Some individual migrants adopt a commuter life-style over an extended period of time, firmly committed to urban work but with their families staying behind in the villages. Generally, however, permanent migrants to the urban areas are dominated by family migrants.

The supply price (or alternative earnings) of individual migrants is different from that of family migrants. If we assume full employment of labor in agriculture and identical employment opportunities for members of a family in both rural and urban areas then no difference in the supply prices of the two groups exists, except for the higher difference cost of living due to housing cost in urban areas. Adjusting for this loss of income due to the departure of the migrant in either form will be equal to the income per-earner, and this will give the supply price. It is the prevalence of disguised unemployment and the difference in employment opportunities in rural and urban labor markets, which causes the supply prices of the two types to be different.[14]

Disguised unemployment implies that, although practically all adults contribute in some form to the economic activity of the rural household the intensity of employment is less than full-time for nearly all members of the family. In this case, the withdrawal of one earner from the family labor force will lead to a loss of income much less than the average income per-earner, because his labor can at least be partly replaced by the labor of other members. Here the supply price of the individual migrant will be different from the average income per-earner and will be dependent on the individual's welfare function, particularly if the individual is interested in maximizing his own welfare or that of his family.

- An individual welfare maximizer will migrate to an urban area so long as his welfare is higher than his share in the family pot of the rural household. Thus, his supply price is the income *per capita* of the family; or if one makes allowance for different age groups among family members, the income *per adult equivalent unit (AEU)* of the family.
- A family income maximizer will, however, be willing to migrate as long as his income in town is greater than his *marginal contribution* to the income of the rural household. For a range of families this magnitude could be less than the income per capita (or income per adult equivalent unit). For such households what the family loses due to the departure of the individual migrant *qua* producer is more than compensated for by his withdrawal *qua* consumer. Thus his supply price is his *marginal contribution(MP).*

This magnitude might be greater or less than the *per capita* income of the family depending on the degree of underemployment in the family farm or business. When the incidence of underemployment is severe, MP could indeed be lower than the per capita income of the family.

Now consider the supply price of the migrant who settles or plans to settle in towns, with his family. In this case the migrant gives up his income in the rural areas. His supply price will therefore be the *income per family* in the rural labor market. There are two reasons why this might be higher than the income per earner. First, if the land market in the rural areas is imperfect or non-existent, the family migrant is not able to get the full value of his land through sale or rental at the time of migration. We must

[14]The analysis given here was first made in one of my earliest papers, see Mazumdar(1959), Cf. also Mazumdar (1983).

therefore add to the current earnings of the household the discount value of the benefits flowing from the possession of the land other than the current flow of incomes. The most important value, though hard to quantify, is that of a social safety net which possession of the land confers. Secondly, and more quantifiably, the family would need to be compensated for the fall in its earnings strength (earner-dependent ratio) when it moves into town. Specifically, earners in the rural family farm would certainly include most of the adult women and some of the children, while opportunities for gainful work are much more limited for these groups in the urban labor market. For both these reasons the supply price of family migrants as given by the income *per family* is higher than the income *per earner.*

We then have various levels of the supply prices of different categories of migrants. This is summarized and portrayed in Figure 6.1

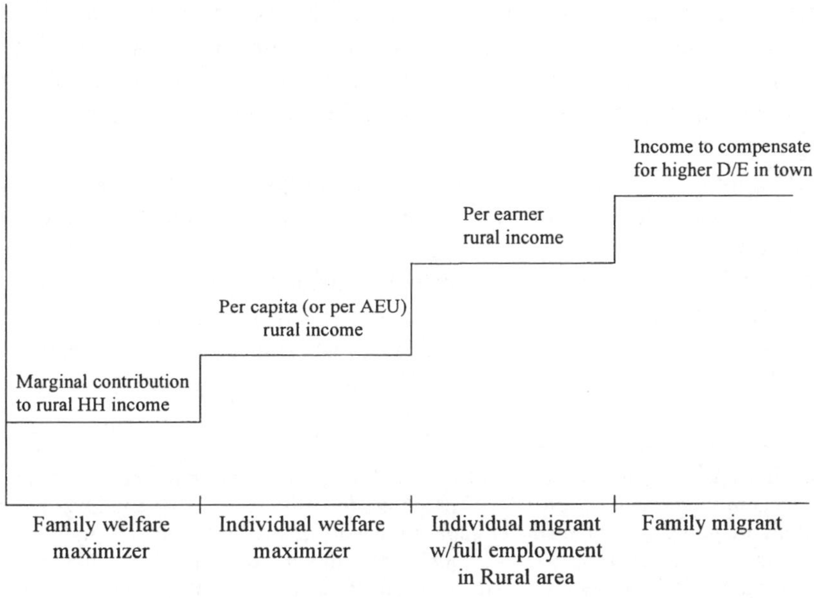

Figure 6.1 Supply Price of Different Types of Migrants from Rural to Urban Areas

In such a situation, if the demand prices for the various types of migrants from the point of view of the urban employer were the same, family migrants would not figure in the urban labor market at all as long as there is a plentiful supply of individual migrants with relatively low supply prices. This was indeed the case in pre-Independence East African countries as well as in other parts of Africa. A labor force composed entirely of individual migrants, however, tends to be highly unstable in terms of attachment to urban jobs. The resulting higher rates of labor turnover could lead to lower productivity particularly as more sophisticated industries develop. Given the difference in the productivity of unstable (individual) and stable (family) migrants, employers might be induced to set wages at a high enough level to attract family migrants to the urban labor force in the expectation that the higher wage per worker will be more than compensated for by higher efficiency of labor.[15]

Since a transition from a labor system based on unstable circulatory migrants to one with stabilized family migrants is initially a costly investment, requires the concerted action of a large group of employers, and indeed may not be fully understood by individual employers used to stereotypes about the work ethics of migrants,[16] private decisions might not be sufficient to achieve this transition. As we shall see in more detail in the discussion of the Kenya case in the next chapter this was indeed the motivation for state action to raise formal sector wages through minimum wage legislation. It achieved the desired goal of stabilizing the labor force working in the formal sector.

In other parts of the developing world this type of 'high wage' policy may have come about through the action of profit maximizing employers acting in concert.[17]

We conclude that there are different measures of the rural-urban earnings gap, and a judgment as to the more appropriate one cannot be made without an understanding of the types of migrants which are in the labor market and in what proportions. We shall take this point into account

---

[15]It is not necessary for this argument to be valid that all individual migrants are unstable and that all family migrants are unstable. The point would be valid if the employer has to attract family migrants with their higher supply price at the margin to achieve the desired degree of stability of labor. In general we could expect that there would be a monotonically increasing degree of labor stability as the portion of family migrants in the labor force increases, and so will there be an increasing marginal supply price of labor. It is possible to visualize a profit maximizing equilibrium point (with a particular wage level and a particular proportion of family migrants in the labor force) where the saving in wage cost through increased labor efficiency is balanced by the increase in the wage per worker.

[16]In East Africa the perception of white employers was dominated by the perception of a supposedly 'backward bending supply curve of effort' of African workers. It was hypothesized that the African rural-to-urban migrant had the need for a fixed amount of cash income. If the daily wage rate were increased all that will happen is that the worker would reduce the number of days of work needed to achieve his fixed target of cash earnings.

[17]See the case of the Bombay Labor market discussed in Mazumdar (1973).

in our analysis of the empirical data in the Kenyan case study.

The Life Cycle Effect in Rural and Urban Areas

The discussion so far has taken place as though we are considering the relative earnings of workers in the two sectors at a specific and comparable points in their life cycles. But changes in income over the life cycle might be different for rural and urban workers. For individuals the age earning profiles might be shaped differently, or if the usual concave profile held in both areas the slopes might be different. For families, the income per capita or per AEU could be further affected by the variations in the ratio of dependents to earners over the life cycle of the head or the principal earner. The 'age profile' of this ratio will be different in the two sectors not only because of different demographic and economic factors, but also because the urban profile in particular would be affected by the pattern of migration. For normal nuclear families we can expect to see a bell-shaped distribution of the dependent-earner ratio (D/E). The ratio rises with age, peaking at roughly 40-45 years when children begin to leave home and form their own households. (Figure 6.2). The exact age when the D/E ratio starts to decline will also be affected by the age at which mothers begin to reenter the labor force after being absent during the birth and early years of the children. Thus, although the age-earning profiles of individual earners normally begin to turn downwards in the 45-50 age group, in the normal nuclear (and probably Western pattern), the age profile of *income per AEU of the family* will not show the same decline or any decline at all compared to the individual earner's age-earnings profile.

The age profile for households in rural areas of developing countries will almost certainly differ from the 'Western' type economies, if for no other reason than that the incidence of joint families is much greater in the former. On the one hand, grown children entering the labor market tend to stay longer with their parents, lowering the D/E ratio of this age-group. On the other hand, if the elderly are being supported by younger earners, the downturn in the D/E ratio observed for nuclear families may not occur.

In the urban labor market, the predominance of young migrants either as single earner families or as earning couples without children implies that, for an extended length of the age distribution at the lower end, there will be a large proportion of families with zero D/E ratios. Thus we can expect to see the age profile of the D/E ratio to be flat at a low value for the younger ages, and only beginning to rise after 30-35 years (Figure 6.2).

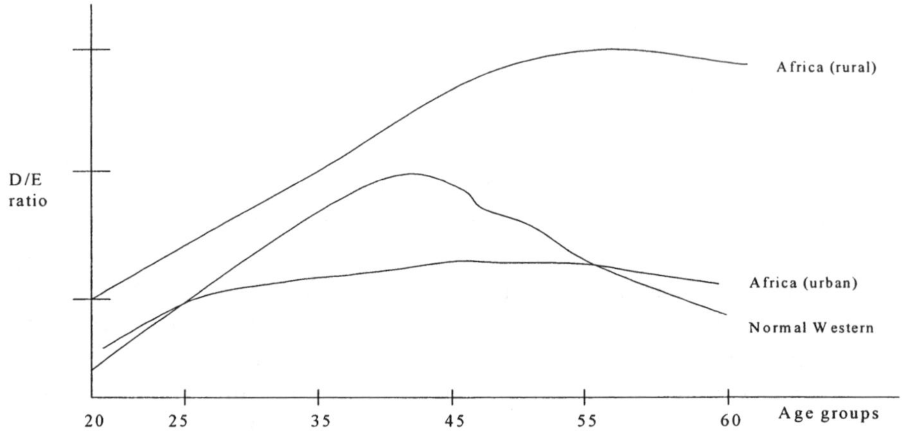

Figure 6.2 Expected Life-Cycle Patterns of D/E Ratio

Two points emerge which should be emphasized for examination of the rural-urban wage gap. First, the comparison of mean income per AEU of rural and urban households could be heavily influenced by the actual age distribution, migration patterns, and D/E ratios observed in the two areas. It will almost certainly exaggerate the economic gain a stable family can make by moving from the rural to the urban sector if it were to stay in town for a long period. Secondly, to assess the likely economic gain for such a family we have to examine in a fairly detailed way, what the D/E ratio for a mature family is likely to be in town compared to the rural areas.

The Implications of Changes in the Rural Terms of Trade

Before leaving this discussion on conceptual aspects of the evaluation of rural-urban earnings differences, we ought to examine another important issue relating to the change in relative prices of agricultural products. In recent years, African economies have witnessed dramatic changes in their internal terms of trade between agricultural and non-agricultural products. These changes partly resulted from fluctuations in external terms of trade, and partly from the impact of domestic policies relating to inflation and the pricing policies of marketing boards, in particular. We have also witnessed substantial movements of money and real wages in the formal sector of the urban economy. Therefore, one has to be careful in interpreting the implications of these changes for the difference in the real wage of urban formal sector workers on the one hand, and the real income of various types of groups in the agricultural sector, which supply labor to the urban economy.

A distinction ought to be made between cash and food crops from the inception. If there is a relative change in the price of cash crops then the cost of living is unaffected for the urban and rural workers. The only change, *ceteris paribus*, is on the standard of living of farmers producing cash crops if they are in the relevant group of potential rural-to-urban migrants. Some small-holders no doubt produce cash crops and are potential migrants but their relative incomes are affected to an extent depending on the importance of the cash crops in their total income. It is, however, clear that big farmers who have a larger proportion of their total output in cash crops would be more affected.

When the relative price of food crops changes, net sellers and buyers of food are affected in opposite ways. For example, a relative increase in the price of food crops would hurt urban workers, agricultural laborers, and small farmers who have to buy a portion of their food. But subsistence farmers who grow most of their own food will not be affected, while those farmers who grow enough to sell substantial parts of their output would benefit from the change in terms of trade.

This represents the caseof rural-to-urban migrants who do not dispose of their agricultural holdings in the course of their urban residence. In this sense the analysis would apply more appropriately to temporary migrants who work only part-time, or during part of their working life in town, without foregoing their relationship with the rural farm.

If migrants are free to dispose of their rural farms during or soon after migration, the supply price would be severely affected by changes in rural terms of trade, even if they were considered subsistence farmers. In the case of Kenya, the data discussed by Jamal and Weeks show that real wages in the urban formal sector fell significantly in the 1970s and 1980s, but the agricultural sector terms of trade had a large upward swing, between 1970 and 1978, but subsequently fell to the same level as in the early 1970s, by the end of the decade (J-W Tables 4.8, 4.9 and Figures 4.2 and 4.3, pp.62-5). According to their calculations, in 1970 a subsistence farmer who produced and consumed all his food stuff, had to produce 7.8 tons of maize per year to attain an income equal to the minimum wage. In 1988, 3.8 tons would have sufficed. It follows therefore, other things being equal, that in 1988, a subsistence farmer would be less than half as willing to sell his farm and take up a permanent urban job as in 1970.

The hypothetical situation portrayed here however, is likely to be unrealistic. Even if rural-to-urban migrants are more permanent in the sense of having at least the nuclear family members in town, and working for much of their life in the urban labor market, it is doubtful that they would sever all ties with their rural farm. To begin with the rural sector provides them with old age and sickness insurance through the support system which is not available in town. Moreover, the migrant would be able to capitalize on his income stream from his rural farm only if the market for land is developed sufficiently — such markets are ill-formed in African rural economies. Therefore, a 'permanent' rural-to-urban migrant would most likely spend the best part of his working life in town, only returning to the rural farm for vacation, illnesses and retirement. The Jamal-Weeks example therefore exaggerates the impact of rural terms of trade changes on the supply price of migrants.

Urbanization and the Growth of the Informal Sector

The last point which needs to be stressed by way of concluding this section is that in some countries, in spite of the fall in urban wage, and the slowdown in formal sector employment growth, urbanization and the rate of rural-to-urban migration seems to have decelerated only marginally in the last decade. Of the three East African countries discussed in the next chapters, in Zambia the average annual growth rate of the urban population decreased from 6.6 percent in 1965-80 to 6.2 percent in 1980-90, while in Tanzania the respective percentages were 11.3 and 10.5 (World Bank 1992, Table 31, p.278). Admittedly these are figures of gross urbanization. With rapid population growth, some rural locations would automatically be pushed into urban categories. Also a larger proportion of urban populations might, in the more recent decade, be temporary migrants. But it is clear that it is the continued growth of the urban informal sector, which has sustained the urbanization process. We can quote a dramatic passage from Jamal (1993 p.16):

> Around independence Tanzania was only 5.7 percent urbanized and had a negligible informal sector — under ten percent of the urban labor force — mostly one would guess engaged in selling produce in the urban markets and men in selling consumer goods in part-urban areas. The towns themselves were fairly 'orderly' and 'formal'. By the mid-1970s with urbanization still at 10 percent, the informal sector had crept up to one-third of the urban labor force, and by 1980, with 16 percent urbanization to over 50 percent, and by 1990 with much higher urbanization (33 percent according to the World Bank)... to over 80 percent. These are epochal trends, never before witnessed, in the sense that never in history did such massive urbanization occur without a concomitant increasing formal sector employment.

It will be recalled from the brief reference above to the non-formal urban sector in Zambia that in spite of the fall in wages, and also some fall in employment in the formal sector, the urban labor force increased by 50 percent in the period 1975-88. A large proportion of this increase must have been accommodated in the urban informal sector. It has also been suggested that it appears from consumption survey data that incomes of households in the informal sector were 30 percent lower than in the formal sector (Loxley, p.54, quoting the Prices and Income Commission of 1987). This result can be reconciled with the evidence of the large fall in real wage only on the assumption that there has been a significant realignment of the urban household economic activities. It is likely that more household members are contributing to the household income pool and also that a typical household would straddle several sectors, some part of labor time being devoted to the urban informal as well as the rural sector. We do not have too much evidence on the nature and extent of this kind of labor market adjustment. Traditional household expenditure surveys are inadequate to provide detailed information on multiple occupations of different types of earners in the household. If some or all income earners in a family are reestablishing older patterns of economic activity, in which they divide their working life between urban and rural sectors, then the concept of the household itself has to change from the one typically adopted in household surveys. A household is no longer defined as confined to those found under the same roof or sharing the same kitchen, but as those who are tied to each other in terms of mutual economic dependency. Such households, at a point in time, might indeed be split geographically between urban and rural areas. It is a challenge both to economists and statisticians implementing household surveys to come up with definitions and methodologies of surveys, which will provide information on the labor market activities of this type of household straddling several sectors.

Another important question on which answers are needed but not yet available, is what has been the impact of the fall in formal sector wage on labor productivity. If urban households have been forced by the decline in wages to revert, at least partly, to the old system of migratory labor, then we are back to the world of the Carpenter Commission and its concerns about the impact of labor instability on productivity. It is possible that the urban informal sector has developed so much in the years since the Carpenter Commission produced its report, that a household could cope with the falling formal sector wage by devoting more of the labor time of its members to the informal sector in the urban economy, rather than split its time between urban and rural areas. In this case the fall in wages will not lead to a significantly higher incidence of circulatory migrants and high labor turnover in the urban formal sector. But such thoughts remain at the moment as hypotheses. Case studies are needed to throw light on the impact of real wage decline on labor turnover and productivity, as well as on the labor market adjustments of households.

Some of these questions are treated in the Kenya case study reported below in Chapter 7. In Chapter 9 we shift our attention to West Africa. The Ghana case study reported here reveals a somewhat different type of rural-urban earnings disparity than found in the East African countries. The much smaller 'wage gap' observed in Ghana is associated with different types of rural-urban migration. A less detailed treatment of the rural-urban earnings gap in a few other countries are reported in Chapter 9, based on available secondary sources. Before coming to the country studies we present a picture of the rural-urban wage gap, pulling together the material on the earnings of wage labor given in the ILO sources. The wage labor sector in African economies is not large, and refers mostly to plantation labor. Nevertheless, the difference in the earnings of this group and the earnings in the urban formal sector might be of interest as an introduction to the detailed country studies to follow.

Appendix to Chapter 6

The Jamal-Weeks Methodology of Evaluating the Rural-Urban Wage Gap: A Critique

To analyze some of the difficulties experienced in comparing rural and urban earnings — Jamal and Weeks (J-W hereafter) — propose a simple method of evaluating the wage gap. As mentioned, the measure of rural production in the national accounts could be a serious under-estimate due to lack of knowledge on subsistence production. J-W therefore assumes that 'the average farmer in Zambia produced at least sufficient calories for the family'. The 1974 ILO/JASPA mission to Zambia calculated the cost of a diet of minimum subsistence based on a calorie requirement of 2,060 per capita as suggested by the 1974 FAO Nutrition Survey. The mission also assumed that 'food items should not account for more than 75 percent of the total expenditure (of the family)' (ILO/JASPA, 1977, pp.301-2). J-W then tried to evaluate this basket for an average rural family of 4.9 members at prices of food items prevailing in urban areas — this procedure eliminated the difficulty of price differences between rural and urban areas. On this basis, the total farm income in 1968 came to K366 per annum, which was well above double the number quoted by Turner, and reproduced in Table 5.1. 'The gap falls to 1:1.9, a far cry from the ratio of 1:4.9 that so offended Turner' (Jamal and Weeks, p.127).

However, the J-W procedure is not entirely persuasive. In the absence of detailed budget surveys we have no idea whether the relevant rural group which supplies labor to the town the marginal farmers and agricultural laborers, did meet the minimum calorie requirement. It is almost certain that since a significant proportion of the typical family of farmers would be small children, the calculation of total calorie requirement on the basis of 2,064 calories per capita would be an overestimate. It is also questionable whether or not food accounts for no more than 75 percent of the total rural household budget at the level of income for marginal farmers.

Apparently in an effort to correct the Turner-type estimate of the earnings gap J-W has gone too far. We could nevertheless agree with J-W that 'given that the average wage earner (in town) did not at most times enjoy an aristocratic living standard, a gap of 4.9 — or average farm income of only 20 percent of the average wage — (as estimated by Turner) could practically not exist for it would mean physical starvation for the farmer' (J-W, p.127).

If this were true in 1970, when minimum wages in real terms were probably at their maximum, then the gap fell to significantly lower levels in more recent years. Real average earnings of formal sector workers started to fall after 1980, and in 1988 was estimated at half that of 1975 (Loxley, 1990, Table 2.7, p.22). Hence, in the absence of evidence of dramatic falls in rural standards of living we may conclude that rural-urban earnings differentials have narrowed.[18]

---

[18]This point is examined further below in this part.

7 The Ratio of the Earnings of Wage Labor in Agriculture and Manufacturing

Before coming to the country case studies on the difference in the levels in earnings between rural and urban areas based on household surveys, we can have a brief look at published material on the earnings of wage labor. The proportion of workers employed on daily or monthly wages is not a substantial part of the labor force in Africa. They are mostly confined to labor working in plantations. But data for such workers have been regularly published in the ILO Yearbook of Labor Statistics for few countries. It is of some interest to bring together the time series of average earnings of workers in manufacturing and in agriculture for the African countries, which are available. From these time series we can construct the ratio of earnings showing the trends in the wage gap between agriculture and formal manufacturing. This gives some idea of the extent of the wage gap between the rural and urban labor markets. The data are presented in Table 7.1. For comparative purposes we also include the data on the earnings ratio for several Asian countries in the table. However, it must be remembered that the use of wage labor is much more prevalent in peasant agriculture in Asia and some of the wage data for Asian agriculture might refer to daily labor used in the peasant small-holding sector.

There are several points on the table which attract attention. First, as is to be expected, all countries — in Asia as well as in Africa — show a significant wage gap in favor of manufacturing. This gap partly reflects the fact that the skill content of manufacturing labor is likely to be higher than in agriculture, even if agriculture represents formally organized activities like plantations.

Table 7.1 Ratio of Average Earnings in Manufacturing to Agriculture (1980 to Latest)

	1980-82	*1983-85*	*1986-88*	*1989*	*1990*	*1991*	*1992*	*1993*	*1994*	*1995*	*1996*
Africa											
Botswana	2.95	3.11	3.22	2.67	2.38	2.65	2.49	2.78	2.23	2.37	–
Ghana	1.49	1.61	1.82	1.88	2.15	?	–	–	–	–	
Kenya	2.95	3.09	2.80	2.82	2.82	2.71	–	–	–	–	
Malawi	3.81	3.35	4.25	3.96	4.36	3.51	–	–	–	–	
Zimbabwe	4.53	3.99	4.23	4.41	4.35	4.66	6.55	5.09	5.43	6.45	
Asia											
China											
India	2.50	2.41	1.96	–	–	–					
Philippines	–	2.99	3.10	3.17	3.25	3.22	3.18	–	–	–	
Korea	1.30	1.40	1.55	1.59	1.43	–	–	–	–	–	
Sri Lanka	1.67	1.86	1.88	1.66	1.66	1.95	1.56	1.63	1.79	1.83	1.91

Source: International Labor Organization (ILO). Yearbook of Labor Statistics, Annual. Geneva.

Secondly, there seems to be very wide differences in the value of the ratio among African countries. It ranges from under 2 for most of the period in countries like Ghana to around 4 in Malawi and over 5 in recent years in Zimbabwe. Kenya and Botswana are countries in the intermediate range of the ratio — between 2 and 3.

Thirdly, the comparison with Asian countries, even from this limited sample is quite useful. With the exception of Ghana mentioned above the wage gap in African countries does seem to be higher relative to Asian countries. It is likely that the countries of East Asia have the lowest wage gap. The fact that the Philippines have a wage gap twice the size of Korea only draws attention to the fact that in this, as in any other respects, the Philippines are an exception to the general pattern of East Asian economies. However, even the two South Asian countries, which have somewhat higher wage gaps in favor of manufacturing, have lower values of the ratio than the African countries in the sample (other than Ghana) and of course considerably lower than Malawi and Zimbabwe.

Finally, none of the series for the African countries show any pronounced trend over the eighties, except for Botswana, which has a significant downward trend. This is surprising in view of the evidence presented above on wage decline in the manufacturing sector of many African countries. This finding only underlines the point that it is probably impossible to make generalizations which are even approximately valid for African economies as a whole.

Limitations of Comparison of Wage Earnings

The comparison of the earnings of wage earners in the rural and urban areas of Africa, and for that matter in most developing countries, give a very limited picture of the rural-urban earnings gap. The wage sector in the rural areas is a very small part of the rural areas, and the problem is compounded in sub-Saharan Africa by the fact that much of the wage labor in agriculture is employed in plantations which are in fact the 'formal' sector of the rural labor market. The predominant form of employment in the rural economy is own-account workers in farms. Since the income accruing to the family farm is most likely pooled together, it is difficult to separate out the individual earnings of each household member contributing to the earning strength of the family. The only way of getting at the earnings level of this large segment of the labor force is to consider the total family income — a statistic, which can be only collected by household surveys. We can, then, consider the *average* income per earner or per capita of rural households, as seems relevant in terms of the discussion in Chapter 6.

An added difficulty is that rural family income is not strictly labor income, but includes income accruing to capital and land owned by the family. Conceptually, economists would argue, comparison needs to be made between the labor earnings of rural and urban workers, since it is always possible for the former to sell off the land and capital they own if they are contemplating moving to wage employment in the urban areas. This textbook argument, of course, loses its significance if the market for land is limited in rural economies, as indeed is the case in much of Africa. This is specially so in the smallholder sector of the rural economy as distinguished from plantations. When an individual from a low income household in the peasant economy weighs the gains and costs of migrating to the urban wage sector, with or without his family, he will consider in his calculations, not the estimated sales price of the farm, but the costs of losing his rights to the land. Thus, the relevant comparison is between wage income in town with the income from the farm household, after adjusting for the relative earning strength of the family in town.

Such comparisons have become easier in recent years as data from Household Economic Surveys become available. In the following chapters we provide a few case studies of particular countries based on the comparison of household incomes in rural and urban areas.

8 The Evolution of Labor Markets and the Rural-Urban Earnings Gap in Kenya

Introduction

This chapter analyzes the major aspects of changes in Kenya's labor markets during the decades of the seventies and the eighties. The term 'labor markets' is used widely to include wage labor — sometimes referred to as 'paid labor' — as well as self-employed workers in the urban and the rural sectors.

There are four broad phases in Kenya's economic performance, which could be distinguished over the two decades. The rate of growth was rather low in the first half of the 1970s — under 4 percent — as the economy smarted under a terms of trade decline of 22 percent during the period 1972-75. However, it got a boost with the coffee boom of 1976-77, which sustained real growth until about 1981, in spite of the second oil shock and a partial loss of the gains from the terms of trade lift of 1976-77. Nevertheless, this period also saw a sharp fiscal expansion so often associated with short-run external windfalls, and continued well after the windfalls had ceased. By FY81, the budget deficit increased to 10 percent of GDP, inflation rate reached double digits, and the current account deficit increased to 14 percent of GDP. The third phase, 1981-84, was a period in which the economy stabilized successfully, but at a considerable cost in terms of growth and consumption. Real growth rate was augmented in the last half of the 1980s, as economic management deviated from the contractionary policies of 1982-84. Some of the steps, which were successful in stabilizing the economy during the previous period unfortunately were reversed. Budget deficits, inflation rates, and negative current external balance resumed their upward trends.

Although the real growth rate of GDP in Kenya in these two decades was quite respectable, in spite of the underlying problems of budget deficits etc., perhaps the most striking feature of labor market developments has been the persistent decline in real wages in the formal sector — in both the private and the public sub-sectors. The next section explores the supply and demand situations in Kenya's labor market over time, and examines the changing mechanisms of the formal sector wage determination.

Labor Market Developments

The Supply of Labor

The growth rate of population in Kenya has been estimated as follows (World Bank 1983,1993):

Table 8.1 Population Growth Rates in Kenya

1960-70	*1970-80*	*1980-90*
3.18 percent	3.91 percent	3.80 percent

The growth rate of the labor force has differed from these rates because of changing age composition and in age specific participation rates. Using data provided by the World Bank in 1983, Fallon reported a decline in PRs between 1960 and 1980. The figures showed that the labor force growth was lower than the population growth rate — 2.67 percent in the 1960s and 3.21 percent in the 1970s. Fallon suggests that the decline in male PRs over the 20-year period (from 53.3 percent to 47.8 percent) was due to a fall in share of 2 percent in the 15-64 years age group, and a sharp rise in the enrollment rates in *secondary* education. The decline in female PRs from 27.8 percent to 23.8 percent may have resulted from (a) an increase in family incomes, but more importantly, (b) from urbanization.

The Labor Force Surveys of the late eighties-for urban areas (1986) and for rural areas (1988)-report a reversal with a large increase in PRs, especially important for urban females.[19] The aggregate PR for this group rose to 55.8 percent from 38.8 percent. However, the aggregate PR for urban males remained practically unchanged at around 83 percent, while the aggregate PR for rural male increased by 4 percent. The 1977-8 survey used the previous *day* as the reference period while both the urban and rural surveys of the late 1980s used the previous *week*. The effect of the change in reference week undoubtedly explains part of the increase in participation

[19]The data by age groups are given in Milne (1990) Table 4, p.21. The high PR for rural females compared to the urban ones should be noted. The definition of participation is quite liberal. In the 1988-9 survey it is one of working one hour in the past *week*.

rate. Nevertheless, it is unlikely that this is the major explanation of the very large increase of female urban PRs of 17 percentage points. The working hypothesis is that the increased female PRs may indicate the need to supplement household income in the face of falling urban wages and income. In any event, the net result is that the rate of growth of the labor force was higher than the population growth for the 1980s, offsetting the slight decline in the growth rate of the latter.

The Absorption of Labor

Fallon (1985), using several sources, provided a table of the distribution of the labor force in 1980 between the 'modern' (or formal) and the informal sectors, separately for the rural and the urban areas. This is reproduced in Table 8.2. In this classification Fallon equated modern (formal) sector employment with wage employment. The informal sector workers were household workers or the self-employed.[20]

The peculiarity of the Kenyan labor markets is revealed in the data. The modern (formal) sector is not the exclusive preserve of the urban labor market. Because of the importance of the plantation sector in Kenyan agriculture in 1980 the absolute size of the formal sector employment was larger in the rural than in the urban labor market. But as a proportion of the total labor force in each sector, the formal was only 10 percent of the total in the rural areas, and 74 percent in the urban.

---

[20]We know, of course, that the distinction between the formal and the informal sectors does not exactly coincide with that between the wage employees and the self-employed. Some highly educated professionals, with protected earnings, should be properly included in the *formal* sector, while wage employees in small enterprises i.e., below a certain size, belong to the *informal* sector because they are generally outside the purview of formal wage setting processes (Mazumdar 1976). Both sets of consideration affect mostly the urban labor market. However, as far as the latter point is concerned the Kenyan official data on wage employment has a lower cut-off point for the size of enterprise which reports wage employment, and it is safe to assume that only a small proportion of wage employees in informal sector enterprises would be wrongly classified in the formal sector. Probably they would just about offset the highly educated professionals (estimated to be 3 percent of the urban labor force at this date) who are misclassified as belonging to the informal sector.

Table 8.2 Employment by Broad Urban and Rural Sectors (1980)

	No. (000s)	*Percentage*
Rural		
Modern Sector	544	10.9
Small Scale Agriculture	2899	58.0
Pastoralists	424	8.5
Non-Farm Activities	1135	22.7
Total	5002	100
Urban		
Modern Sector	501	74.9
Urban Informal	168	25.1
Total	669	100

Note: Calculated from the Report of the Presidential Committee on Unemployment(1982/3) and Livingston (1981) Table 10.23.
Source: Fallon, Table 3, p. 44.

How did the two sectors fare in the absorption of the labor force in the two decades? We have reasonably sound data on the time series of the formal (wage) sector employment as collected by the Statistics Department. The series are presented by industry. Wage employment in agriculture remained virtually constant over the two decades.[21] As far as all non-agricultural wage employment is concerned, it grew at an annual rate of 5.5 percent in the decade of the 1970s, but the growth rate declined to 4.2 percent in the next decade. Taken the two decades together the annualized growth rate was 4.7 percent. Most of the non-agricultural wage employment would be located in the urban sector. Thus, we can judge the importance of the informal urban sector in labor absorption by comparing the rate of growth of urban population in Kenya with these figures of modern sector employment growth. According to the *World Development Report* 1992 (p. 278) the former growth rate in the period 1980-90 was 7.9 percent, which was only slightly lower than the average growth rate of 8.1 percent in the period 1965-80. The Kenyan labor market experience has thus been no different from that of many African economies. Massive rural-urban migration is implied by the rate of urban population growth of more than twice the rate of growth of total population — and the formal sector employment growth in the urban economy, although significant, was

[21] *Historical Economic Data for Kenya* (Ministry of Planning and National Development), December 1991, Table 10. All statistical time series used in this work are from this source, and will henceforth be referred to as MPND 1991.

only able to absorb a fraction of the job seekers in these labor markets. These figures are consistent with the estimate of the Central Bureau of Statistics (Kenya) that employment in the informal sector grew at 14 percent per annum in 1990 and 1991.[22]

Not all of the increased labor force in the urban economy, not absorbed by the formal wage sector, would be employed in the informal sector. Some of them would swell the volume of unemployment. Comparing the data from the two labor force surveys of 1978 and 1986, it is apparent that although there was undoubtedly an increase in the rate of unemployment, it was not massive. The overall rate of unemployment increased from 8.2 percent of the labor force in 1978 to 11.7 percent in 1986. However, there was clear evidence of 'educational downgrading' of the unemployed. There seems to have been a major shift in the pattern of unemployment by education, since in 1986 we observe a large increase in the unemployment rates for males with lower levels of education, low secondary and even primary (See Mazumdar 1993, Table II.6). Evidently the urban labor market in Kenya had moved to a more pervasive surplus labor situation by 1986 compared to the earlier situation when the incidence of excessive supply.

In spite of the strong growth of rural-to-urban migrants, the rural sector was called upon to absorb a portion of the labor force growth. The predominance of males in the rural-to-urban migration stream was reflected in the fact that in 1991 females in the rural labor force exceeded the male number by around 25 percent (World Bank 1993, Table 3.8). The Rural Labor Force Survey of 1986 also showed that own-farm activities accounted for only 60 percent of rural economic activity. Other non-farm activities included: (a) water and firewood fetching — an extremely time-consuming activity carried out predominantly by females, accounting for 30 percent of their labor time, but 18 percent of total; (b) wage employment which was predominantly a male activity accounting for 16 percent of the total rural work; and (c) non-farm profit making activity, which was also more male than female, adding up to 7 percent of rural activity (World Bank 1993, Table 3.9). The picture of the growing slackness in the labor market, which has emerged so far should be reflected in downward pressures on real labor earnings over the two decades. We now turn to an analysis of evidence on this point in the next section. The statistics on wages are collected from registered firms in both agriculture (plantations) and non-agriculture, and hence represent the course of earnings in the formal sector. This is followed by an examination of the evidence on the

---

[22]Quoted in World Bank (1993), p.35.

formal-informal earnings gap in the urban labor markets. Finally, in last section we turn to a discussion of the rural-urban earnings gap, taking into account the different supply prices of types of different types of rural-to-urban migrants, as discussed in Chapter 6 above.

Wages in the Formal Sector

Trends in Real Earnings

Trends in real average earnings per wage employee are available from the annual returns of the modern sector. The annual rate of change of real wages, employment and GDP for the different macro-economic phases identified in the Introduction are shown in Table 8.3. It is apparent from an inspection of the table that real wage changes have some relationship to the rate of growth of GDP in the different phases but hardly any relationship with the varying growth rates of employment. We could conclude from this that the real wage movements in the formal sector over this period had been influenced more by changes in the supply side of the labor market than by the demand side. The percentage rate of change in GDP in the different periods (with labor force growth rates being relatively stable) is expected to be related to the rates of change of the supply-price of labor. A second important point emerging from the table is that, in all phases of the cycles, the real wage declined relative to the GDP per capita or per worker. In the two phases — the early seventies and the early eighties — when GDP growth just kept pace with the growth of the labor force or fell below it, the decline in the real wage was massive. In the other two phases when GDP increased faster than the labor force, real wage in the public sector still declined, *albeit* at a slower rate, and was more or less stagnant in the private sector.

Two points emerging from these data need to be particularly noticed. First, it is seen that the real wage level declined in the public sector at a rate two-and-a-half times of that in the private sector. Secondly, although real wage declined throughout the wage bill increased at a significant rate in both sectors. The elasticity of employment with respect to wages was well above unity (in fact close to 2) in both sectors. It is to be expected that the elasticity would be somewhat lower in the private sector since the importance of the operant factor — capital — is likely to be more important in the private sector which does not include the very large civil service component. The growth in the wage bill at 2 percent per annum over the two decades underlines the limited success of the government in controlling public sector expansion in spite of the large rate of decline in real wages. The evidence of employment expansion in both sectors is consistent with the finding in Part II of this work that Kenya — along with many other African economies — elected to give much greater weightage to employment in the employment-wage growth trade of in its labor market outcomes.[23]

Table 8.3 Real Wage and Employment Growth (Annual Average) (Percent)

	73-75	*76-81*	*82-84*	*85-90*
GDP (at 1982 prices)	3.32	6.13	1.88	5.02
Wage Employment				
Total All	4.40	3.62	3.46	3.67
All Private	3.27	1.51	3.44	2.89
All Private Non-Agriculture	6.13	3.85	3.14	3.42
All Public	6.06	6.32	3.49	4.47
Real Wage				
All Private	-4.46	0.99	-6.45	-0.64
All Public	-4.61	-1.22	-8.05	-2.62

Note: Real wage is derived form nominal average wage and weighted Nairobi CPI based on the income groups. The Lower income group has a weight of 0.768, the middle income group has 0.209, and the upper income group has 0.023 weights.

In the two decades under consideration the rates of change in employment and real wage in the formal sector were as follows:[24]

[23]See Mazumdar (1994) for evidence for the outcomes in the Africa region compared to other regions.

[24]The original data are from MNDP (1991).

Table 8.4 Rates of Change in Employment and Average Real Wages

	1972-81	*1981-90*	*1972-90*
Private Sector			
Employment	0.023	0.031	0.024
Average Real Wage	-0.006	-0.011	-0.012
Public Sector			
Employment	0.058	0.044	0.051
Average Real Wage	-0.024	-0.025	-0.029

We shall now turn to an analysis of the causes and consequences of the real wage decline in the formal sector of Kenya. In order to explore the reasons for the wage decline we need to know the institutional factors affecting wage determination in this sector. This is the subject of the next sub-section.

Wage Determination in the Formal Sector

Institutional influence on wage determination could come either through unions or the government. In Kenya the trade union movement grew quite rapidly after independence. In the early nineties it was estimated that a third of the employees in the formal sector were unionized (World Bank 1992). However, the government has for a long time tried to control industrial unrest with the Trade Disputes Act of 1964 and 1965. Further amendments were made in 1969 and 1975 resulting essentially in the outlawing of the strike action in Kenya. Most strikes are wildcat actions, which are ineffective since scab labor is readily available. This situation has been strengthened further by the Trade Disputes Act of 1980. Collective bargaining occurs in most unionized sectors and the registered contracts apply to the whole workforce including non-members. Unsettled disputes could be referred to the Industrial Court where the decision is final and binding. The few studies done to assess the influence of wages on union membership have concluded that this influence is insignificant (Cf. Rempel and House, 1978).

Unlike Trade Unions the impact of government labor market policies have been of substantial importance to wages and employment matters in the formal sector. To begin with, we have already seen that the public sector is a large employer in the formal sector, and its importance has tended to increase in the last two decades. As such it has a direct impact on the formal labor market, through the wages it sets and the conditions of employment of the labor it recruits. But apart from that the State has sought to regulate wages and employment contracts in the private sector through active labor legislation. Two important milestones in this interventionist process have been Minimum Wages to be followed by Incomes policies supported by 'tripartite' agreements.

The Policy of Minimum Wage Increase Following the recommendations of several Commissions, the policy of minimum wages was vigorously pursued during 1954-63. The Carpenter Report of 1954, in particular, suggested a 250 percent increase in wages as part of an effort to stabilize labor in the city. Kenya along with many urban areas of Eastern and Southern Africa was totally dependent on temporary migrants. These migrants were either absent from their rural homes for only part of their working lives or were dividing their time between the urban and rural markets. The high turnover of labor, resulting from this pattern of migration, was perceived to be a major cause of low labor productivity in urban industry. A very enlightening illustration of the economic cost of unstable labor was revealed in a report on 'Native Repetitive Work' carried out in a Dunlop factory in Durban.[25] The expected work period in a factory for a native was nine months, with three months in the Kraal. However about 25 percent of these natives left before the end of a 3 month periods, and another 18 percent left within a 3-6 month period. It was said 'even when the first native returns to his employer he will have lost dexterity at his particular job' and would, therefore, require retraining. In summing up the various sources of loss of productivity, the study found that the native who proved responsive to industrial work would have a productivity of around 81 percent of the normal productivity — of a European worker — if he worked round the year. However, because of the short length of service, the average responsive worker attained only 45 percent of his normal productivity. Moreover, the prevalence of nomadism prevented a selection of the stable core of native workers composed of a more responsive type. Even if the same worker returned to industrial work after a period of absence in the kraal, he was reported to have lost much of his skill and needed to be retrained. The productivity of all native workers selected by interviews and used over time was only 29 percent of normal productivity. The quantitative significance of this loss in productivity in the migratory labor system (falling from 81 percent to 29 percent) is quite dramatic.

Several observers covering this period of time maintained that apart from the quantifiable loss in productivity, migratoriness made it difficult to

[25]University of Natal (1950).

achieve any long-term goal. Hence, it was difficult to assemble a motivated and efficient urban working class. For example, Boris Grossman (1953), in addressing labor productivity in what was then Southern Rhodesia, pointed out that 'settled labor is more efficient because if it is really settled, it has something to work for beyond immediate needs and because the danger of unemployment provides an incentive'. Settlement means giving the African 'security of tenure in the urban areas or the opportunity of belonging to an established system'. He concluded that: 'Industry has probably done as much as it can, under existing conditions, to increase productivity. Only when he (the African worker) is given the opportunity of using his money to further worthwhile ends, or what to him are worthwhile ends, will he adopt a more worthwhile attitude towards his work in order to achieve his object'.[26]

The Carpenter Commission shared in the prevalent view of the urgency of creating a stable labor force in the modern sector. It felt that the existing wage would sustain only a single migrant staying in town without his family.[27] Hence the recommendation for a large increase in African wages. The government wage policy until the mid sixties reflected this recommendation, and formal sector wages were increased almost every year through hikes in the minimum wage. According to one estimate real wages of unskilled manual workers in non-agricultural activities (in the formal sector) increased at the annual rate of 6.7 percent per annum, several times the rate of per capita growth of GDP, which increased at the annual rate of 1.7 percent in real terms.[28] Collier and Lal found that after allowing for a cost of living premium of 60 percent in town the Nairobi minimum wage as well as the average earnings of workers in the formal sector were more or less in par with the earnings of African workers in agricultural estates in 1949, but by 1967 the gap was between 2.5 and 3 times.[29]

The Era of Incomes Policy The high wage policy pursued through the policy of increasing minimum wages came to an end in the mid sixties as concern grew about the consequences of wage increase in the formal sector. No attempt seems to have been made by analysts to find out if in fact wages in the formal sector had been pushed above the levels sufficient to meet the original objective of creating a stabilized labor force. But it was

[26]Similar views are expressed in another article on the subject. See P. de Bricy (1955).

[27]See section 7.5 below for a more thorough analysis of this point.

[28]Fallon(1985) Table 15, p.55.

[29]Collier and Lal, Table 6.24,p.212.

surmised — without any reference to the household composition of recent rural-urban migrants — that wages were too high in the formal sector relative to the supply price of the desired type of rural-to-urban migrants simply because they had risen at a substantially higher rate than rural per capita income. The fact that the original level of formal sector wages was deemed to have been too low *vis-a-vis* rural incomes to attract stable migrants to urban jobs was simply lost sight of.

The incomes policies introduced in the late 1960s have consisted of a set of guidelines, which are enforced by the Industrial Court. The basis of the guidelines has shifted over the years from productivity increase (early 1970s) to indexing to the cost of living series (1975), to indexing with full compensation only for the lowest wage earners (1976 and 1979). The Industrial Court looks at the wage increases implicit in the collective agreements registered by law.

Observers have maintained that income policy guidelines have had little impact on the actual yearly changes in wages. Collier and Lal (p.167) suggest that the evidence for this is twofold. First, the policy 'guidelines' were changed from year to year, moving in line with market conditions; for example, the guidelines were substantially liberalized during the coffee boom. Second, and most important, the actual bargains concluded bear little relation to the guidelines, sometimes exceeding them, almost invariably falling below them, and in aggregate usually being only one half to three quarters of the maximum permitted increase.[30] We can, therefore, conclude that the fall in real wage since its peak in the mid 1960s was a market based rather than an institutionally determined phenomenon. The downward trend was clearly helped by the weakening of union's bargaining power through legislative measures, such as those against strikes, discussed earlier in the section. However, the growing slackness in the urban labor market is evident in the discussion above — the rate of rural-to-urban migration well in excess of the rate of employment growth in the formal sector, the increase in the rate of open urban unemployment, and the finding that the incidence of unemployment was no longer disproportionately high for the educated groups (Mazumdar 1993, pp5-6).

It is arguable that the policy of high wages adopted in the post-Carpenter era had overshot its mark of creating a stabilized labor force. This can be seen from the data on turnover rates for different years compiled by Collier and Lal (p.180) and reproduced in Table 8.5, which shows that the drastic reduction in the turnover rates of the early 1950s had been achieved by the wage hikes as early as 1957. Although in 1968 wages

---

[30]See the data given in Table 6.5, Collier and Lal, p.167.

were higher, the 'quit rates' of those with less than 3 years of service fell even further, the rates for those with more than 7 years' service increased significantly. Collier and Lal argued that this was the result of the compression of the wage scale by seniority, which the policy of minimum wages produced. If the high wage policies had established a wage level higher than the supply price of stable labor by the end of the 1960s, it stands to reason that the real wages would fall once the policy had been abandoned.

Table 8.5 Estimated Quit Rates among Nairobi African Wage Earners

Length of service (years)[a]	*1953*[b]	*1957*[c]	*1968*[d]
< 0	0.48	0.15	0.12
1-2	0.38	0.22	0.10
2-3	0.37	0.20	0.13
4-5	0.21	0.06	0.15
5-6	0.27	0.07	0.09
6-7	0.25	0.07	0.09
7-8	0.17	0.07	0.14
8-9	0.20	0.08	0.17
9-10	0.25	0.09	0.20

Notes:

a: Quit rates are estimated from distribution of the labor force by years of experience. The quit rate for those with experience t_1 to t_2 is estimated as the percentage of the labor force with at least t_1 experience minus the percentage with at least t_2 experience divided by the percentage with at least t_1 experience.

b: Carpenter Survey.

c: Forrester Survey.

d: Thias and Carnoy Survey.

Source: Collier and Lal (1980), Table 6.7, Page 180.

We do not at the moment have turnover data for more recent periods. It would be interesting to see, when such data becomes available, if the downward trend in real wages has increased the instability of labor in a significant way. We have attempted, however, to provide some tentative inferences from data, on the size and composition of households in following section. It would also be interesting to see whether, and how far, the downward trend in real wages in the formal sector has affected the differential in earnings — between the formal and informal sector — in the urban economy on the one hand, and the rural and the urban sectors on the other. We attempt to do this in the next two sections respectively, using the

Labor Force Survey data.

The Earnings Gap between the Formal and the Informal Sectors in Urban Kenya

The course of earnings in the formal sector tells only part of the story of the trend in the urban economy as a whole. As we have seen the informal sector has been a growing part of the urban labor market. No systematic record of earnings over time in this sub-sector exists. We have to piece together the evidence from a variety of sources. First, we establish in the following subsection a measure of the formal-informal differential at the date of the Urban Labor Force Survey, and the factors accounting for this difference. In the following sub-section we come to some judgment about the trend in this differential over the period of the wage decline in Kenya's formal sector. The stage is then set for the comparison of levels of earnings in the urban and rural sectors.

The Formal-Informal Earnings Gap around 1986

In this section we will be using the 1986 Urban Labor Force Survey to answer the question whether after nearly two decades of falling real wages in the formal sector, and growing urbanization, the urban labor market had become sufficiently integrated so that workers earned roughly the same amount in the two sectors, after allowing for the significant differences in the characteristics and skills of the labor force?

Table 8.6 Overall Distribution of 1986 ULFS Sample

	Employees		*Self-employed*	
	Males	Females	Males	Females
Percent of total	59.7	11.8	18.7	9.8
No. in sample	1738	343	543	286

First, we should note that the ULFS allows us to distinguish between the two sectors only in terms of one criterion — i.e. is the individual worker self-employed or a paid employee? This means that the wage workers in small establishments are absorbed in the formal sector, while some professionals with protected earnings are included with the self-employed in the informal sector. Nevertheless we feel that the effect of such misallocation of labor at the margin will be small. The ULFS sample was distributed between the two categories as shown in Table 8.6.

The major characteristics of the four groups are given in Table 8.7. There are some differences in the industrial composition of the two types of workers — rather similar for males and females at this level of aggregation. More of the wage employees are found in the manufacturing and transport sectors. But the biggest difference is in the sub-categories of the tertiary sector. Employees are more pronounced in the finance/social, community and personal service group, while the self-employed have the biggest concentration in trade related activities.

Educationally, the self-employed are worse off, females more so than males. However, post primary education is important for both groups. The self-employed show 10 percentage points less in post-primary education as compared with the employees. Both the male and female self-employed workers are older than the employees. The importance of the under 30 age group in the distribution of female employees is particularly striking. This finding contradicts the characterization of the informal sector as a point of entry for young job seekers in the urban market.

Another observation which is contrary to the stereotype of the informal sector is found in the distribution of migrants to the urban market by the period of residence. Because the self-employed are older, the proportion of migrants on a long-term basis is larger among the self-employed of both sexes. By contrast, recent migrants with less than a year's service are found more among the employees, particularly the females. Evidently a good many of the self-employed are in this sector for a long-term career.

Table 8.7 Characteristics of Employees and Self-Employed, Males and Females, 1986 (Percentage Distribution by Age Groups)

	Male Employees	*Female Employees*	*Male Self-Employed*	*Female Self-Employed*
I. Age (%)				
Under 30	41.5	57.3	29.7	41.3
30-40	33.2	29.5	30.9	31.8
40-49	17.2	10.3	31.5	14.3
50+	8.1	2.9	20.4	12.5
Mean	33.8	29.6	38.7	34.5
II. Marital Status				
% married	77.8	45.5	84.3	66.1
III. Period of Residence (%)				
Natives	5.8	14.3	4.4	5.4
≤ 1	6.7	11.6	3.3	7.1
2-4	12.7	22.1	17.1	15.4
5-9	21.3	18.5	22.2	27.6
10-19	24.9	24.1	28.4	26.2
20+	13.6	9.0	24.7	14.3
IV. Education (%)				
None	8.6	16.9	15.2	31.8
St. 1-4 (primary)	8.1	7.5	11.3	12.5
St. 5-8 (primary)	32.5	26.6	35.1	38.1
Form 1-2	11.0	9.0	10.7	7.6
Form 3-4	26.5	31.0	18.5	10.0
Form 5-6	4.8	3.4	1.1	-
College	4.1	8.3	2.7	-
University	4.4	4.8	5.4	-
V. Industry (%)				
Agr./forestry	5.1	7.0	11.7	17.8
Mining & Mfg.	16.7	6.6	10.8	3.5
Elec., water/constr.	11.8	2.0	9.4	0.3
Wholesale/retail	5.8	4.8	46.4	64.3
Transportation/ Communication	18.5	7.4	3.2	0.3
Finance/Community & Social Services	41.8	72.2	18.7	13.6
VI. Location (%)				
Nairobi	47.2	30.3	42.6	25.9
Other Towns	52.8	69.7	57.4	74.1

Source: Own computations from ULFS 1986.

The earnings distribution for the two groups are given separately for males and females in Figures 8.1 and 8.2 respectively.

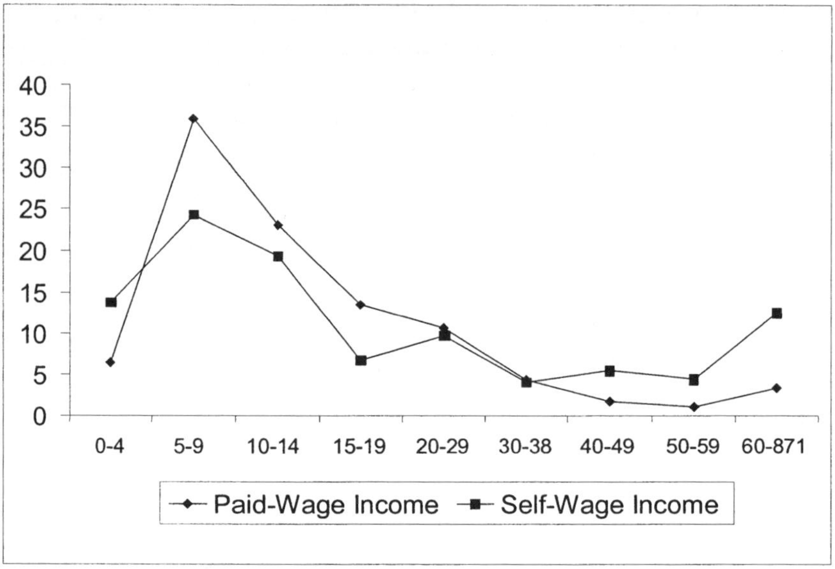

Figure 8.1 Distribution of Earnings for Male Paid-Wage and Self-Wage Earners

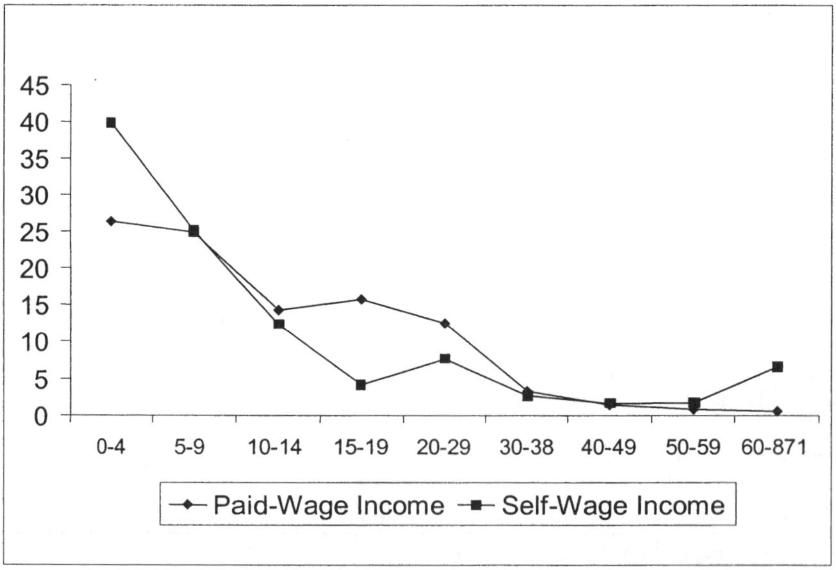

Figure 8.2 Distribution of Earnings for Female Paid-Wage and Self-Wage Earners

While the mode of the earnings distribution appears to be the same for the employees and the self-employed of both sexes, there is a larger percentage of workers in the middle range income among employees than among the self-employed. On the other hand, a somewhat larger proportion of male employees can be found in the lowest income group. Interestingly, when we look at the high income ranges we find a larger proportion of the self-employed than the employees especially when we concentrate on the non-white collar labor market by excluding those from the sample with college/university education.

Clearly there is great diversity of earnings in the formal and the informal sectors. Simple comparisons of statistical measures are not meaningful; therefore we have to control for the major factors determining earnings. Earnings functions were estimated for the two sectors separately. The explanatory variable included were: age; age-squared; eight levels of education,[31] industry, type of employment,[32] and location (Nairobi and Other towns). As expected the proportion of the variance in earnings explained is larger for the employees. The adjusted R-squared respectively for employees and the self-employed are: 0.42 and 0.22 for males; and 0.66 and 0.11 for the females.

A great deal of interest attaches to the relative returns to age and education. The values of the coefficients of these variables in the earnings function were as presented in Table 8.8. The major difference in the relative returns which stands out from this table is for males — while the earnings function with respect to age is of the usual concave type as far as male employees are concerned, it is flat for the self-employed. This difference is, however, not found in the case of females: both employees and the self-employed show a concave function, though it is much flatter than for the male employees. Turning to the returns to education, there is a difference only at the lower end of the spectrum, and then again only for the males. Those with a few years of primary education show no higher earnings than those with no education, as far as the self-employed are concerned, but the wage employees have a positive incremental return from all levels of primary education, as indeed do females of both categories. Otherwise it is interesting to note that the pattern of returns to successive levels of education is not very different for the employees and the self-employed.

---

[31] The education levels considered are: ED1. Primary 1 to 4 yrs; ED2. Primary 5-8 yrs; ED3. Secondary 1-2 yrs; ED4. Secondary 3-4 yrs; ED5. Secondary 6 yrs; ED6. College; ED7. University. The base for this set of dummies was No Edcation.

[32] Dummies for Full Time (base), part-time, casual and seasonal.

The interpretation of the difference in the coefficient of age in the earnings functions for males could have alternative interpretations. It might suggest a flatter age-earning profile for the self-employed, but it may also partly be due to the fact (which is documented below) that the downward trend in earnings in the urban labor markets of Kenya over time affected the employees more than the self-employed. The earnings functions fitted to the cross-section sample in 1986 partly reflect the fact that the wage scales of succeeding cohorts have shifted downward.

Table 8.8 Values of Coefficients of Human Capital Variables in Earnings Functions, 1986

Variables	*Males*		*Females*	
	Employees	**Self-employed**	**Employees**	**Self-employed**
Age	0.59 (0.16)	0.03 (0.03)	0.11 (0.13)	0.11 (0.04)
Age-squared	-0.0006 (00009)	-0.0002 (0.0003)	-0.001 (0.0002)	-0.001 (0.0004)
ED 1	0.12 (0.07)	-0.15 (0.24)	0.27 (0.11)	0.23 (0.25)
ED 2	0.36 (0.06)	0.31 (0.20)	0.52 (0.09)	0.71 (0.20)
ED 3	0.50 (0.07)	0.61 (0.25)	0.83 (0.11)	0.86 (0.32)
ED 4	0.77 (0.06)	0.88 (0.22)	1.29 (0.09)	1.38 (0.29)
ED 5	1.20 (0.09)	1.22 (0.62)	1.59 (0.15)	Few observations
ED 6	1.32 (0.09)	1.51 (0.41)	1.48 (0.11)	-ditto-
ED 7	1.94 (0.09)	1.83 (0.33)	2.30 (0.10)	-ditto-

Source: Urban Labor Force Survey 1986. Own estimates of earnings functions.

It might be argued that we are mixing up white-collar workers with blue-collar ones in considering the whole sample for either employment mode. We ran the regressions for the earnings functions were run excluding the workers with post secondary education from the sample. Surprisingly the results were practically the same.

The returns to education, we have seen do not differ much for the two groups, but employees increase their earnings with age, while the self-employed do not. The mean age of the self-employed at 38.7 is quite a bit higher than that of the employees at 33.5. Thus, it can be safely assumed that employees with same levels of education might start at lower earnings but soon catch up with age.

Returns to human capital are of course not the only variables determining earnings of the two groups. Employees and the self-employed also differ in terms of their distribution by industry and by location of the labor market.

We can use the regression equations to throw some light on the differences in earnings between the employees and the self-employed, taking all factors into account, separately for males and females. The fitted earnings functions for the *employees* are used to decompose the observed difference in predicted earnings into its two components — that part due to the difference in characteristics, and the other due to differences in returns to characteristics. The first line of Table 8.9 gives the predicted value for the employees *minus* the predicted value of the self-employed, using their separate earnings functions, and the mean values of the explanatory variables for each group separately. The second line gives the difference in the predicted value of the log of earnings, in the hypothetical situation if both groups had their different characteristics rewarded according to the same earnings function, i.e., of the employees. While the first line gives the total predicted difference as calculated from the estimated earnings functions, the second line gives that part of the difference which can be accounted for by the returns to the characteristics of the two groups. The remainder of the difference in total predicted earnings is then attributable to the difference in the *returns to the characteristics* of the two groups.[33]

Table 8.9 Predicted Difference in log of Earnings between Employees and the Self-Employed

	Males	*Females*
With own characteristics	0.837	0.141
With the characteristics of the self-employed	0.772	–0.166

As far as the males are concerned the predicted earnings of paid employees are higher by about 85 percent. The major part of this is accounted for by the economically better characteristics of the employees. The residual difference of log 0.065 (0.837 *minus* 0.772) can be attributed to differences in returns to attribute i.e., the difference in the coefficients of the earnings functions). The earnings pattern of the females is quite different. The mean earnings of female *employees* are higher by only about 14 percent compared to the self-employed. Furthermore, by contrast with the case of male workers, a great deal of the difference is due to the difference in the coefficients of the earnings functions of the two groups. The second line of the Table 8.10 shows that if male and female self-employed had the same characteristics, the earnings of the self-employed

[33] If We and Ws are the earnings of the employees and the self-employed respectively; the returns (regression coefficients) are denoted by βs with the appropriate subscripts; and the charcaterustics are the X's with the subscripts, then we have:

$$We - Ws = \beta e(Xe - Xs) + (\beta e - \beta s)Xs$$

The first term on the right hand side measures the part of the wage gap that is attributable to differences in endowments, and the second term is the part attributable to differences in the returns to these endowments.

would have been actually *higher* by 16 percent. Thus the difference in returns to characteristics pulls down the self-employed earnings by as much as 30 percent.

Changes in the Formal-Informal Sector Earnings Gap over Time

Detailed data, such as provided by the ULFS, does not exist from earlier dates to provide an assessment of the change in the formal-informal earnings differential. We have to draw upon whatever scattered data might exist in order to form a judgment on the probable course of the earnings gap. The famous ILO Employment mission (1972) produced a table on average income per worker in different sectors for the year 1969. The gross difference in the level of earnings between the formal and the informal sectors was enormous (7 times or more). The data was, of course quite close to the period when formal sector wages had been pushed up to their peak levels. However, probably the data base for this statistic was very weak.

In the mid-1977, an important survey, with a stringent definition of the informal sector was undertaken in Nairobi by House. Enterprises were classified as belonging to the informal sector if they operated out of a temporary structure or no structure at all.(House 1981, p.358). The survey collected data on the net weekly incomes accruing to business heads, 'after accounting for all expenses'. The *average* incomes of business heads in manufacturing, trade and services were found to be 295, 401 and 236 K.Sh. per week respectively. These levels of earnings were very reasonable, considering that the minimum wage in Nairobi at the time was 81 K. Sh. per week, and the *average* earnings in the formal non-agricultural sector (for Kenya as a whole) was 308 K.Sh. Evidently, since the ILO report of 1969, there had been substantial improvements in the relative income of the informal sector.

Unfortunately, House did not give the distribution of incomes for his sample, but he was careful to point out that there were great variations in the incomes of different types of businesses and that concentrating on a summary measure such as the mean was not sufficient. House, however, divided his sample into three groups — the lowest income group-characterized as the 'community of the poor', earned less than the weekly minimum wage and contained 43 percent of the sample. Another group, comprising of 31 percent of the sample whose earnings were high enough in that the per capita income of their households exceeded the 1977 average per capita income of Kenya (around 200 K. Sh. per week). In between two groups was the residual group which displayed some of the characteristics of both the 'stagnant' and the 'dynamic' groups. From these data we can infer that the *median* income of the business heads in the informal sector was around 110 K.Sh.

House's survey also enumerated more than 500 wage employees — over half of this sample were regular employees working for the owners of informal sector businesses and no fewer than 34 percent were 'apprentices' were paid a small cash wage. The rest of the sample (about 12 percent) were casuals whose earnings were on par with the regulars but who had no guarantee of working continuously for a complete month. House did however give the distribution of weekly earnings for the employees in the small businesses. (Table 12, p.364). The *median* earnings of this group was 82 K.Sh. — just about the same as the Nairobi Minimum wage and only 50 percent below the median of the incomes of business heads.

House's definition of informal sector workers included those working for wages in informal sector businesses. For the formal sector we have the statistics regularly collected by the Department of Statistics from 'registered' businesses. This data set provides us with a figure of *Average (mean)* earnings per wage employee in the non-agricultural sector.

For easy reference, all the relevant statistics are brought together in Table 8.10.

Table 8.10 Earnings in Kenya, 1977 (K. Shillings per week)

Nairobi Minimum Wage	Average Earnings in Non-agr. Formal Sector	Mean Wages/Income in Informal Sector		Median Income in Informal Sector	
		Employees	Business Heads[1]	Employees	Business Heads
81	308	93	295	82	110
			401		
			236		

Note: [1]The income data are for manufacturing, trade and services respectively.
Source: For formal sector earnings, Kenya (1991), 'Historical Data.' For informal sector earnings and Nairobi Minimum Wage, House (1981).

Mean wages of informal sector employees were nearly one quarter of the formal sector workers, although some of the difference would be accounted for differences in age, education etc. if we had this information. Business heads in the informal sector did much better, but the importance of the segment of high earnings among them in pulling up the mean is indicated by the fact that the *median* of the income distribution of this group was nearly a third of the average formal sector earnings (It could be expected that among wage earners the ratio of the average earnings would be markedly smaller since there will be a smaller segment of individuals with very high incomes).

It is not possible to fit earnings functions to the data presented by House. Thus, the results from the ULFS 86 discussed earlier are not strictly comparable to the House data. However, we can try to form some judgment about the change in the differential over the eight-year period by looking at 'gross' figures of earnings. It will be recalled that in our analysis of the 1986 ULFS we were able to distinguish only the self-employed component of the informal sector — the employees in the small business sector were not separately recorded. Thus, the House figures of business heads for 1977 are roughly comparable to the reported earnings of the self-employed in the UFLS. The relevant statistics are presented in Table 8.11.

Comparing Table 8.11 with 8.10 one gets the strong impression that the there has been a significant decline in the formal-informal earnings ratio. In 1977 the mean income of business heads (self-employed) in manufacturing was somewhat less than mean formal sector earnings, but in 1986 it was higher than the latter. In sales (trade) the mean self-employed income was on par with formal sector average earnings: in 1986 it was 50 percent higher.

Table 8.11 Earnings of the Self-Employed and of Formal Sector Wage Employees, 1986 (K. Shillings per Month)

	Mean	*Median*	*First Quadrile*
All Self-Employed	3,450	1,000	500
Sales Workers	3,023	982	495
Manufacturing Workers	2,447	1,104	700
Average Earnings Formal Private Sector, Non-Agr.	2,185	N.A.	N.A.

The ratio of *mean* formal wages to the *median* earnings of the self-employed (business heads) in the 1977 House survey was around 3, while in the 1986 UFLS it had fallen to 2.

The squeezing of the formal-informal earnings differential, which accompanied the decline in real wages in the formal sector is not entirely an obvious or anticipated outcome, remembering that the rate of labor absorption was much faster in the *urban informal* sector.

The shrinking of the differential is one way in which the urban economy coped with the declining earnings and massive rural-to-urban migration. Another way was the readjustment of the relationship with the rural areas which migrant families had to undertake. This is revealed in the next section where we consider the evolution of the rural-urban wage gap.

The Rural-Urban Earnings Gap

This section on the extent of the gap in earnings between the rural and the urban labor markets will use the conceptual framework developed in Chapter 6. Rural income, which is the alternative earnings of migrants from the rural to the urban areas, can be expected to approximate the supply price of labor in the urban labor market. The extent of the gap between rural income and the urban wage is an important statistic to consider when assessing whether or not urban wages are too high. However, as discussed at length in Chapter 6 the relevant rural and urban incomes to consider in this assessment vary a lot with the type of rural-to-urban migration we are considering. The pattern of such migration will be reflected in the household compositions of workers in the two areas. However, before we come to an analysis of the rural-urban earnings gap based on households as observations, we should look at the available data on the earnings of individual workers in the two sectors. Clearly this is possible only for wage employees. For family farms or businesses earnings of all workers in the household would be generally pooled together and will be reported as the income of the household head. We begin by studying the wage differential between workers in agriculture and in non-agriculture, as reported by the Statistics Division of the Ministry of Labor. Although a small proportion of agricultural wage employees may be found within the administrative boundaries of towns, this demarcation will closely approximate the division between the urban and rural labor markets.

Comparison of the Earnings of Wage Labor

The Statistics Department data refer to the formal sector in both sectors. In agriculture the statistics cover wage labor employed mostly in estates, and the data reported for non-agriculture are the earnings of workers in enterprises above a certain size which are covered by the Department Data are available only on average earnings, i.e., wage bill divided by total employment so that we cannot correct for differences in skill composition in the two sectors. Furthermore, the statistics only give us the wage income of an average individual worker, so that we cannot take into account any of the issues of household composition to be discussed below. Nevertheless it is very useful to examine these data. They are probably the most accurately reported of all the statistics that will be examined on this topic. Secondly, the earnings series are available over a long period of time, and since they have been continuously collected by the same official body, they are reliable for comparison of trends over time. The two ratios, that of average earnings of workers in private non-agriculture to those in private agriculture and that of the average earnings in public non-agriculture to the latter had the following average values at the beginning and the end of the period:

Table 8.12 Ratio of Average Earnings of Private and Public Non-Agriculture to Agricultural Workers

	1972-74	*1988-90*
Private Non-agr/Agr.	4.03	3.41
Public Non-agr/Agr.	4.12	3.32

In spite of the clear downward trend, the persistence at the end of the period of a large earnings differential in favor of workers in the formal non-agricultural sectors is at first glance rather surprising. As indicated in the Introduction above, real wages in the formal non-agriculture sector fell continuously through this period, more so in the public than in the private sector. However, income per capita in the farm sector seems to have had a clearly positive, even if low, rate of growth. Two important factors should be taken into consideration, which might have a bearing on this issue. We have used the ratio of money earnings per worker in both sectors to looking at the trend in the ratios because we do not have a separate cost of living index for the agricultural or rural sector. It is, however, possible that the cost of living appropriate to agricultural workers has moved in a different way from that affecting urban workers, which implies that the difference in the cost of living between rural and urban areas has changed significantly over time. No detailed calculation of the difference in cost-of-living between town and country is available. Collier and Lal mentions a figure of 60 percent as the premium needed to compensate for the higher cost of living in town in the early eighties(Collier and Lal, p.212).

Secondly, institutional and technical developments in the farm sector might have reduced the earnings of small holders and agricultural workers relative to the per capita income in the farm sector. Both these issues deserve fuller investigation than is possible here. (A few pertinent points will be made later.)

One important omission should be noted before we leave this section.

The differential in earnings between the formal agricultural and non-agricultural sectors does not correct for differences in the characteristics of workers — in particular differences in the human capital attributes, which affect earnings. We are not yet in a position to use relevant data to shed light on this issue. Until more appropriate data are available we can only surmise that the 'net' earnings differential will be smaller than what is shown here principally because there are more skilled and educated people in the non-agricultural workforce.

Migration and Household Composition in Kenya — Urban and Rural

We now turn to the rural-urban comparison of incomes on the basis of household surveys. We have two sets of survey data covering the urban sector — one for 1977-8 and the other for 1986. For the rural areas, the 1977-8 was conducted in both sectors. But the rural household survey of the eighties was conducted only in 1988, which is, however, a year close enough to the 1986 urban survey. In this sub-section we will examine the household composition in the urban and rural areas in Kenya with a view toward shedding light on some of the issues raised in Chapter 5. Table 8.13 gives the distribution of households by size separately for the three areas-Nairobi, other towns, and rural, both for 1977-78 and 1986-88 when the two labor force surveys were conducted.

Table 8.13 Percentage Distribution of Households by HH Size

	1	*2*	*3*	*4*	*5*	*6*	*7*	*8*	*9 or more*
1977-78									
Nairobi	17.5	12.2	9.5	10.1	12.4	10.3	6.6	5.7	15.7
Other Towns	7.9	9.5	11.0	13.8	11.5	10.5	7.4	7.3	21.1
Rural	7.2	7.2	9.2	10.7	12.5	10.9	11.3	9.7	21.3
1986-8									
Nairobi	27.8	17.9	14.2	12.8	7.8	7.3	4.8	3.0	4.4
Other Towns	33.9	13.9	10.4	10.4	9.6	5.5	6.2	3.4	6.7
Rural	11.4	8.1	8.6	11.4	12.6	12.5	10.9	8.8	15.8

Source: Own tabulations from the Labor Force Survey tapes.

Two points stand out from the distributions. First, the relative importance of 1 and 2 member families in the urban areas, more so in other towns, compared to the rural sector at both dates. Secondly, there has been a rather striking increase in the proportion of such families in both Nairobi and other towns in the decade separating the two surveys. We conclude from this that the incidence of migrants living by themselves or with only a part of their family is important in the urban areas, and that its importance has increased substantially in the 1980s. It is, of course possible for the proportion of single migrants to increase if the rate of growth of migration into the urban areas has gone up in the 1980s. However, the available figures of the rate of growth of urban population does not suggest any such acceleration.[34] At the same time it will be recalled from Table 8.9 above that the proportion of urban workers who are natives or born in the town of the survey is very small. The more likely explanation is that the fall in urban real wages (which was documented above) has made it more difficult for new migrants to settle in town with their families in the last decade.

This decline in the size of households in urban areas does not necessarily mean an increase in the incidence of unstable short period migration. It is possible that workers are more inclined to leave their families in town even if they were committed to urban work. The data collected in the labor force surveys do not generally provide statistics, which can measure the incidence of temporary or circulatory migration. We might be able to draw some suggestive conclusions from the data on the period of residence in the urban areas collected from the migrants in the sample. The statistics are presented in Table 8.14.

[34]The World Development Report table on urbanization gives the annual rate of growth of urban population as 8.1 percent for 1965-80 and 8.2 percent for 1980-89. (WDR 1991, Table 31).

Table 8.14 Percentage Distribution of Adult-Age Migrants by Age-Group and Period of Residence

Age Group	*Period of Residence (Years)*						*Total*
	Less than 1 year	1-2	3-4	5-9	10-14	15+	
MALES: Nairobi							
15-19	26.6	21.5	3.8	17.7	20.3	10.1	100.0 (6.5)
20-24	18.8	33.5	20.5	16.1	5.4	5.8	100.0 (18.5)
25-29	6.9	10.2	20.4	47.3	10.2	5.1	100.0 (22.6)
30-34	2.2	2.7	4.9	38.4	34.6	17.3	100.0 (15.2)
35-40	0.7	4.0	4.0	14.5	37.5	39.5	100.0 (12.6)
40-50	1.0	3.1	4.2	12.4	10.4	68.9	100.0 (12.5)
50+	0.9	2.8	0.9	4.6	10.1	80.7	100.0 (15.9)
Total	7.4	11.5	10.6	24.8	17.1	28.5	100.0
MALES: Other Towns							
15-19	26.2	19.3	14.5	15.2	18.6	6.2	100.0 (10.0)
20-24	27.4	31.1	15.6	14.6	8.0	3.3	100.0 (14.7)
25-29	11.1	25.7	16.3	33.2	7.5	6.2	100.0 (21.2)
30-34	13.2	14.5	15.3	28.9	17.8	10.3	100.0 (16.7)
35-40	7.6	15.2	12.3	27.5	19.3	18.1	100.0 (11.8)
40-50	7.9	9.3	9.7	17.2	15.0	41.0	100.0 (15.7)
50+	10.0	2.9	2.1	8.6	12.9	63.6	100.0 (9.7)
Total	14.3	17.9	12.9	22.3	14.6	18.8	100.0

Source: Urban Labor Force Survey, 1986 Original Tabulations.

Although there is a sizeable proportion of migrants with less than 1 or 2 years of residence in the urban area, it should be remembered that the growth rates of the cities have been high — estimated to be in the order of

8 percent per annum for urban Kenya, as a whole so that at least 16 percent of those with less than 2 years residence could be fresh migrants who might indeed be settling down as stable migrants. It appears from the data that the 'other towns', which have as much as 40 percent or more of the total migrants with less than 2 years' residence have an important component of temporary migration.

We can go a little further by looking at the cross-tabulations of age groups by period of residence for the migrants in the two urban classifications. With a normal pattern of stable migration, a large proportion of the recent migrants (who generally come to the urban market at a young age) will settle in town. We therefore expect to see the percentage of migrants with a short period of residence to decline sharply with age. If the decline is not very marked we could infer that there is a strong presence of circular (or unstable) migrants. Indeed, if there is 'pure' circular migration there should be a large proportion of migrants with less than 1 or 2 years' residence in every age group up to the prime age of rural-urban migration. The data in Table 8.15 indicates that the 'other towns' with migrants with less than 2 years' residence is important (25 percent or more) for the age groups up to 35 years of age. Taken in conjunction with a much larger proportion of younger migrants than in Nairobi, this finding strongly suggests that short period migrants are an important part of the labor market scene in the 'other towns'. By contrast in Nairobi we find migrants with a short period of residence dropping off significantly after age 25 suggesting that circulatory migrants are no longer that important.

The implications of these findings for the comparison of earnings between the urban and the rural labor markets are the following. Short period circulatory migrants might be an important feature of the labor market in other towns, but are not very numerous in Nairobi. We should not, therefore, compare the actual earnings of workers in Nairobi with the supply price of individual migrants from rural areas to form a judgment if the urban-rural differential is too high, although this comparison may have some validity for a part of the labor market in the other towns. The decline in the average size of households in Nairobi is almost certainly due to the fall in urban wages over the last two decades forcing workers to leave their families behind in the rural areas. At the same time, since a larger proportion of the members residing in urban households are workers the observed income *per capita* or *per AEU* is inflated above the level which either the family would have if dependents living in rural areas were included, or what mature settled family in town would have. We need to approximate the supply price of family migrants or what a potentially settled family in the urban area would need to attract him to move from the rural labor market.

Let us now turn to a comparison of rural and urban incomes based on household surveys. This comparison is possible for the late eighties, using the Urban Labor Force Survey of 1986 and the Rural Labor Force Survey of 1988. The cost of living increase between the survey dates (using the Nairobi low income index it was around — (7.1 and 9.7 percent per annum for the December of 1986 and 1987 respectively).

Comparison of Rural and Urban Household Incomes

Figure 8.3 portrays the distribution of households by income per adult equivalent units (AEU) in the rural and urban areas and within the urban sector, in Nairobi and 'other towns'. (See notes to Table 8.15 for definitions used to calculate AEUs).

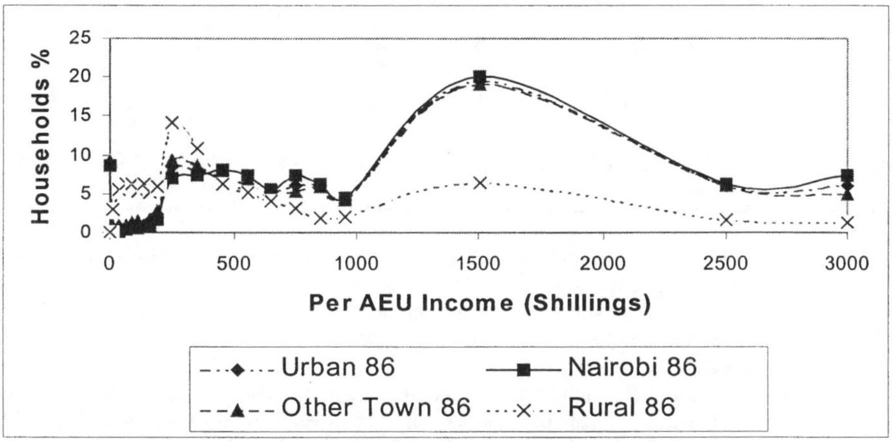

Figure 8.3 Income Distribution by Income Groups, Per AEU Household Monthly Income

The distributions for both the urban and rural areas are bimodal. But the higher mode for the urban sectors is much stronger with the percentage of households found in this income group being three times as much for the urban areas as for the rural ones. While this difference may partly reflect the realities of income distributions in the urban and rural areas, it is possible that a part of the difference might be due to the under-representation of large farms or estates. There is no indication in the published documents that this was indeed the case. We will, however, keep this possibility in mind and concentrate on the comparison of the lower half of the distributions as much as possible, since the latter will not be affected by the higher modes.

The basic data for the comparison of household incomes at the two dates for rural and urban areas, and for the latter separately for Nairobi and other towns were tabulated from the two labor force surveys. We computed summary statistics for mean, median and first quartile values, since we may be interested in comparing the incomes of the bottom end of the earnings distributions (in which case the Q1 measures will be appropriate). The urban/rural income ratios for each category are given in Table 8.15.

Table 8.15 Ratios of Household Income in Urban and Rural Areas

	Nairobi/Rural			*Other Towns/Rural*			*All Urban/Rural*		
	Mean	Median	Q1	Mean	Median	Q1	Mean	Median	Q1
Household Income	3.32	2.33	3.17	2.43	2.02	2.67	2.78	2.18	2.83
Per Capita Income	5.29	5.25	5.41	3.69	4.30	3.78	4.33	4.73	4.54
Per Earner Income	2.48	2.08	3.22	1.86	1.83	2.63	2.11	1.97	3.00
Per AEU Income	3.64	3.16	3.81	2.63	2.77	2.85	3.04	2.96	3.21

Notes:

(1) All households with zero income have been excluded. They are 8.90% of surveyed households in Nairobi and other towns, and 31.76% of households in rural area.

(2) Earners are defined as positive income household members in urban or rural areas. Their income sources are paid employment or self-employment or family business. Unpaid family worker is not considered as an earner.

(3) Adult equivalent unit for each household is calculate in the scale of 0.25 for below 6 years old, 0.5 for between 6 and 15 years old, and 1.0 for over 15 years old for urban area. The AEU of rural households is derived from the scale of 0.1 for below 10 years, 0.5 for between 10 and 15 years old, and 1.0 for ages over 15 years.

The Rural survey was done two years after the urban one. The cost-of-living index had increased by 15 percent over this period in Kenya. Assuming that the cost-of-living increase was the same for the rural and urban populations, the ratios of urban-to-rural incomes given in table 8.15 would have to be *increased* by 15 percent to get at the ratio in 1988 prices. Accepting the cost of living difference between urban and rural areas as reported by Collier and Lal to be 60 percent and also allowing for a price increase of around 15 percent between the urban and the rural surveys (1986 and 1988 respectively) we could attribute 45 percent of the difference in favor of the urban areas to be due to cost-of-living differences. The rural-urban income differential in real terms thus continued to be very high in the late eighties, confirming the conclusion of the previous section based on earnings of paid employees.

The rural-urban ratios in Table 8.15 refer to *all* workers in both areas — the formal as well as the informal. The following results are worthy of note:

- The difference in the income per earner for all the workers is significantly smaller than the difference in the average earnings of wage (formal sector) workers in agriculture and non which was studied earlier. This is partly because the rural-urban difference in earnings for the informal sector is smaller.
- The higher burden of dependency in rural areas is shown by the much larger difference when we compare income per capita or per adult equivalent unit rather than income per earner; and:
- For all measures the differentials are significantly smaller for 'other towns' than for Nairobi. In fact, for the 'other towns' income per earner is 50 percent higher than rural incomes in real terms.

Statistics for total household incomes are affected by a number of factors, which need to be disentangled. There are three major issues:

1. The summary measures are affected by the distribution of income in the two samples.
2. The income differences do not allow for differences in the human capital endowments of workers found in the rural and urban households of our samples. We would like to see how much of the observed difference is due to differences in the skill composition of workers.
3. The issues raised in the discussion above relating to migrant type and household composition need to be addressed.

On the second issue, we have already discussed in the previous section that this is possible to do only for individual wage employees — but data are insufficient for this purpose. We now discuss the other two issues in turn.

The Distribution of Income

The Lorenz curves for the distribution of income of households per AEU are graphed in Figure 8.4 for both rural and urban areas (the broken line refers to the rural sector).

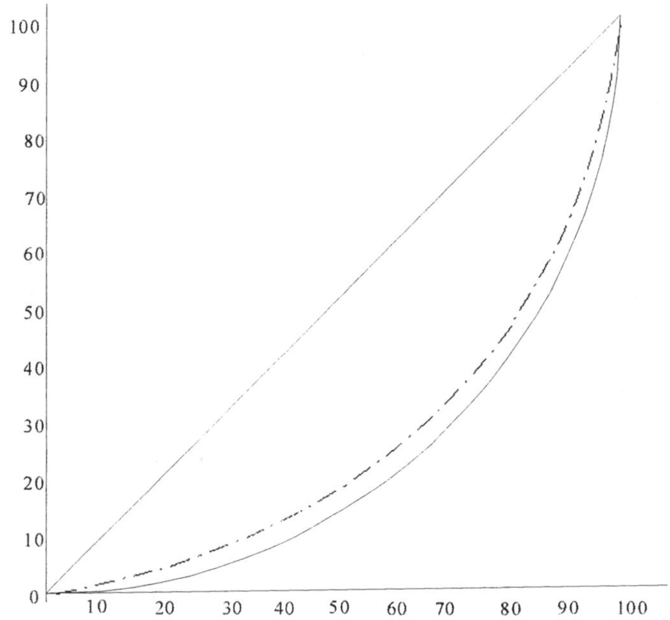

Figure 8.4 Lorenz Curves for Rural and Urban Incomes per AEU

The rural Lorenz curve lies well within the urban one, showing that, after taking into account the size of the households in terms of AEUs, income is less unequally distributed in the rural areas. This is partly due to the fact that the rural survey might have under-represented the large estates. The comparison of the frequency distributions of incomes per AEU in rural and urban areas given in Figure 8.4 strongly suggests that this might indeed have happened. The proportion of high-income groups is very much smaller in the rural survey. As is to be expected, a direct result of the difference between urban and rural samples is that measures of the rural-urban differentials given in Table 8.15 show smaller gaps when we compare median incomes rather than means. This is particularly evident in the Nairobi-Rural comparison. It is not possible to verify from the material at our disposal if this result — a relatively smaller presence of high-income households in rural areas — is a real phenomenon in the Kenyan economy or a quirk of the sample survey procedures. However, the result is of sufficient importance to merit further investigation.

While the income differential between Nairobi and the rural sector is reduced if we correct for the differences in income distribution by taking medians rather than means, the rural-urban gap seems to be the largest when we compare the first quartile (Q1) values of the different distributions. This result holds true for Nairobi as well as for 'other towns' when compared to the rural area. Evidently there is a much larger proportion of low income households in the rural compared to the urban sector. This result is again an important one, which merits further probing and verification from alternative sources. If true, it is a major part of the explanation for the persistence of rural-urban earnings gap in Kenya in spite of the positive growth in income per capita in the rural economy accompanied by the fall in real wages in the urban wage sector (see below for further discussion of this point). The rural land and labor markets have worked in such a way that a relatively large proportion of households have been left in the bottom quarter of the distribution even though the proportion of very high-income households is small. This hypothesis is consistent with the high rate of rural-to-urban migration, which has persisted in the last decade in spite of the fall in urban earnings.

Migrant Type, Household Composition and Life Cycle Effects

We are now ready to assess the implications of differences in family composition in the rural and urban areas for the rural-urban earnings gap. The summary table of ratios of household incomes (Table 8.15) itself reveals some important aspects of household composition in urban and rural areas. The urban household contains a larger proportion of earners to the total number of family members. Hence the difference in income *per capita* is much greater than the difference in income *per earner*. But the non-earners have a larger proportion of children in rural areas; hence the difference in income *per AEU* is smaller than the difference in income *per capita*. In each case the Nairobi-rural difference is larger than the 'Other towns'— Nairobi differentials.

The figures in Table 8.15 reflect income differentials as they are shaped by the existing distribution of households by their dependant-earner ratios in the town. However, as we have argued at length above, this existing pattern is heavily affected by (a) the prevalence of unstable migration, particularly in other towns, and (b) by families leaving some of their dependant family members in rural areas. This is clearly brought out by the statistics of the D/E ratio over the lifecycle of the average principal earner in the three labor markets given in Table 8.16.

None of these patterns correspond to the 'normal' or 'Western' pattern of D/E ratios by age of the household discussed above. The D/E ratio in the rural areas increases quite sharply with age as the number of dependents increase but does not reach its peak until the age-group 50-55, and falls only after the age 55. This reflects the prevalence of joint families in rural Kenya and the obligation of the principal earners to support aged dependents. In the urban areas (and more so in Nairobi) the D/E ratio lies all along below the age profile of the D/E ratio in the rural sector and increases less steeply. The relative absence of dependents from the urban households is evident from these data.

Table 8.16 Average Dependent/Earner Ratio of Households by Age Group of the Principal Earners

	Nairobi Dep/Earner Ratio Mean	Other Towns Dep/Earner Ratio Mean	Rural Area Dep/Earner Ratio Mean	All Dep/Earner Ratio Mean
20 <= AGE < 25	1.09	1.18	1.32	1.24
25 <= AGE < 30	1.06	1.03	1.51	1.31
30 <= AGE < 35	1.02	1.08	1.74	1.54
35 <= AGE < 40	1.04	1.11	2.21	1.95
40 <= AGE < 45	1.01	1.14	2.65	2.33
45 <= AGE < 50	1.04	1.25	2.59	2.34
50 <= AGE < 55	1.25	1.16	2.67	2.45
55 <= AGE	1.26	1.47	2.41	2.36
ALL	1.06	1.14	2.28	2.03

Note: Data for Nairobi and other towns is from 1986, for rural areas from 1988.

Three are two reasons why we need to correct for this lower burden of dependency in towns in estimating the rural-urban earnings gap. First, we do not have any data on dependents absent from the urban areas. Clearly this factor exaggerates the rural-urban difference in the welfare of households based on existing patterns. Secondly, we may be interested in the difference in income *per capita* which would exist, given existing earnings levels, if stable mature families settled in town with their dependents. This is the measure we need to examine if urban earnings are high enough to attract stable family migrants in the urban areas *à la* the Carpenter Commission.

There are two ways of getting at this measure of income difference with a 'corrected' figure of the D/E ratio. We could either use the D/E ratio of the rural sector, or derive a notion of the potential D/E ratio in town from an inspection of the actual distribution of households by size and earning strength. The median size of the household in rural Kenya, according to the 1988 Labor force survey, was 5. This was also the median size of the household in *urban* Kenya — both in Nairobi and other towns — in 1978 (see Table 8.17).

We find from the bivariate distribution of households by size and the number of earners (not shown) that in 1986, both in Nairobi and other towns, more than 20 percent of the households had 5 or more members and the modal earning strength of these households was unchanged at 1. We should then not be far wrong if we infer that the potential size of an urban household in Kenya was 5 in the late 1980s after allowing for missing members left in the villages and the incidence of circular migration. Thus, to see if the urban incomes are too high relative to rural earnings, for a mature stable family, we need to compare the household income in the two sectors using a household size of 5 for both sectors. If we accept this way of correcting for the lower observed D/E ratio in town without changing the existing difference in income per earner or per family, then the relevant comparison is between *family incomes* in the different sector.

From Table 8.15, the relevant ratios of urban to rural income are a little larger than 2 *at median values*. The ratios are somewhat larger and in the case of Nairobi a good deal larger (3.32) at *mean values* because of the more skewed distribution of income in the urban areas.

We have seen that about 45 percent of the difference in urban-rural income in the figures for the late 1980s could be due to cost of living difference. Thus, if we concentrate on the alternative income of a stable urban family- and specially if we look at median values — urban income in real terms is probably no more than 50-60 percent higher than the alternative rural income of such a family. Individual single migrants, who are employed at the same urban wage structure, enjoy a rent over their (lower) supply price. But as long as the incidence of circular migration is low, or alternatively we argue along with the Carpenter Commission that it is undesirable to have urban wages high enough only to attract single migrants — it is inappropriate to consider urban wages in relation to the supply price of unstable, single migrant.

Table 8.17 Summary Statistics of Household Size, Number of Earners, and Number of Workers — Positive-Incomed Households Only

	Household Size				*Number of Earners*				*Number of Workers*			
	Mean	Median	Mode	Q1	Mean	Median	Mode	Q1	Mean	Median	Mode	Q1
78 Urban - Nairobi	5.21	5	1	2	1.22	1	1	1	1.25	1	1	1
78 Urban-Other Towns	6.02	5	4	3	1.14	1	1	1	1.18	1	1	1
78 Urban - All	5.67	5	4	3	1.17	1	1	1	1.21	1	1	1
78 Rural	6.3	6	7	4	1.13	1	1	1	1.16	1	1	1
86 Urban - Nairobi	3.47	3	1	1	1.39	1	1	1	1.56	1	1	1
86 Urban-Other Towns	3.59	3	1	1	1.29	1	1	1	1.49	1	1	1
86 Urban - All	3.54	3	1	1	1.33	1	1	1	1.52	1	1	1
88 Rural	5.53	5	6	3	1.12	1	1	1	3.5	3	2	2

Note: The earner is defined as one who has a positive income, whereas the worker as one who has a positive economic working hours.
Source: LFS in 1977/78, 1986, and 1988/89, own calculation.

The Change in Household Composition in Urban Kenya between 1978 and 1986

We see in the data presented in Table 8.17 that there has been a sharp fall in the household size in the eight years between the two surveys. In 1978 the average household size was much the same in urban Kenya outside Nairobi as in the rural areas, and only slightly lower in Nairobi. The median household size in both Nairobi and other urban areas was 5, compared to 6 in the rural areas. In the 1986 survey the urban size has fallen drastically to 3, while the rural median size was now 5. The median number of earners in the urban household, however, remained unchanged at 1 suggesting a sharp fall in the dependant-earner ration in the urban sector.

Evidently, the urban labor market in Kenya in 1986 was no longer able to support a mature family in town easily. The fall in urban earnings documented above meant that the burden of dependency in urban households had to be reduced through a combination of two mechanisms: a larger incidence of single circulatory migrants, spending only a part of their working life in the urban labor market; and secondly, urban workers leaving a larger number of their dependents in the rural areas.

Although much reduced unadjusted figures of incomes per earner, the data still point to the existence of a sizeable gap in favor of the urban areas. Apart from data inaccuracies, we should point to two important considerations, which might be relevant for resolving this apparent inconsistency. First, the cost-of-living difference between rural and urban areas might have been underestimated. We have referred to above to an estimate made by COTU and reported by Collier and Lal suggesting a figure of 60 percent higher urban cost of living. However, while reporting this Collier and Lal write in the same paragraph: 'In 1949 prior to most institutional interventions, the mean non-agricultural African wage was 72 percent above that on the estates. Since urban employers were not charities, most of the differential presumably reflected cost of living difference.' We have, however, discussed in detail that at this date the urban non-agricultural wage was just sufficient to attract single, circulatory migrants. The cost of living difference between town and country for stable families could be expected to be substantially higher, for not only would housing cost significantly more, but the family migrant must also take into account the costs of illness, unemployment and old age — costs which are generally shared by the extended family in the rural setting, but which have to be borne by the migrant who settles permanently in town with his family.

A second reason why our estimate of the real difference in earnings between town and country for our family migrant might have been too high is because the costs of migration have not been included in the calculations. Migration studies have shown that, while for lone migrants the cost of transportation is predominant and tends to be generally low, more permanent migrants are faced with much larger costs associated with a change of residence. Such costs are high enough to require a relatively high investment so that migrants are generally unable to finance the move unless they already possess some assets. Thus longer-term migrants are more likely to come from rural income groups who are not at the bottom of the income distribution.[35]

Conclusions

At first sight we might be impressed by the surprising conclusion from the data on wage earners given in Table 8.12 that even after two decades of falling real wages in the urban labor market, there is a large wage gap between the rural and the urban areas, though it has declined a little from 4:1 to 3.4:1. This comparison, of course refers to wage labor in the formal sectors of both areas. But a detailed examination of household incomes from the Labor Surveys of 1986 Urban and 1988 Rural — in which the sampled households covered both the formal and the informal sectors — showed that income per adult equivalent unit was three times higher in the urban area. The current estimate suggests that the cost-of-living difference between town and country could account for only 45 percent.

We have argued at length in this section the importance of taking account of differences in household composition and the dependant-earner ratio in the rural and the urban areas, in coming to conclusions on the extent of the rural-urban earnings gap. This exercise is necessary because substantial differences exist in the D/E ratios between single migrants who stay in the urban labor market for short periods of time and more permanent family migrants. The analysis of the Household Survey data for 1986(urban) and 1988(rural) that the gap is exaggerated, because the median household size and the D/E ratio were much smaller in the urban areas at this date. When we correct for this difference the earnings level of a stable family in the urban labor market, at median values, would be *no* higher than 50 percent in real terms.

It was shown that there has been a marked fall in the household size and the D/E ratios between 1978 and 1986 (The earlier year is the date of

[35]For a survey of the literature on this point, and references see Mazumdar (1987).

the previous urban labor force survey). This implies that the relative fall in urban earnings over this period has meant that urban wages are no longer sufficient to attract mature families who settle in town. More accurate measurement of the COL difference between rural and urban areas, and of the costs of migration, would show that the 50 percent gap referred to above is exaggerated. Migrants who are able to reduce their D/E ratio in town either by staying in the urban market only temporarily or by leaving a proportion of their dependants in the rural areas (that is, in effect straddling the two sectors in their economic activity), however, stand to gain quite a bit by participating in the urban market. This, of course, explains the high rate of rural-to-urban migration.

Since the average income per capita has been increasing in Kenyan agriculture during the two decades, albeit slowly, the finding about the large rural-urban gap for single migrants at the end of our period raise important questions about the distribution of income in the rural sector. The concern is reinforced when it is noticed that the income gap is larger when it is measured at the first quartile level of the income distributions in the two areas, rather than at the median or mean levels. A part of the explanation could be that the sample surveys were less successful in covering the higher income households in the rural than in the urban areas. But in the absence of any documentary evidence to this effect, our working hypothesis must remain that factor markets in rural Kenya have worked in a way which has led to a relative deprivation of rural smallholder and labor families at the lower end of the income distribution. This point merits further exploration when more relevant data are available.

9 The Evolution of Labor Markets and the Rural-Urban Earnings Gap in Ghana

This chapter presents a case study of Ghana. The availability of the household surveys for three years spanning the years 1987-92 (called the Ghana Living Standard Survey — GLSS) enable us to examine the rural-urban earnings gap carefully.

As with the previous chapter on Kenya, we begin with a potted history of the evolution of government policies and the course of the Ghana's economy, with particular reference to the way the way earnings and employment of different groups were affected in the urban and rural labor markets. We consider developments during Ghana's economic decline in the seventies and the subsequent partial recovery after the structural adjustment program was initiated in 1983. After a brief look at the distribution of employment and earnings over different parts of the labor market in section 9.3, evidence on the rural-urban earnings gap is presented in 9.4 for different periods. It shows a markedly smaller differential in the Kenyan case even in the early sixties. The gap is demonstrated to have been even narrower in the post-adjustment period. The availability of the household survey data for the 1987-92 period enable us to probe in some detail the relative movements in household incomes, particularly at the lower end of the distribution, in important segments of the urban and rural labor markets, distinguishing between the formal and the informal sectors and between the capital city and other towns.

Economic Policies and Basic Trends in The Economy

Pre-1983

Ghana stands out among African countries as holding the unenviable record of decline from a very strong economy. Although it had one of the very highest per capita incomes in the continent in the early 1960s, by 1982 it was ranked twenty-first out of forty-four African countries (World Bank 1989, p.18). Although Ghana had its fair share of economic shocks in the form of oil price increase, and severe droughts in 1975-77 and again in 1981-83, the massive involvement of the State in economic affairs, its mismanagement, and excessive public spending clearly have been the root cause of the decline. Income per capita declined by 30 percent between 1970 and 1983, but the deterioration of the economy outside the peasant food-producing sector was much more destructive. Cocoa -the mainstay of Ghana's export earnings — had a production level in 1983 of just 28 percent of its level of 1965. This was the joint result of overtaxing of cocoa farmers and the massive overvaluation of the exchange rate. While Ghanaian cocoa producers received 15 to 40 percent of prevailing world prices, those in the competitor neighboring country Côte d'Ivoire received at least 66 percent. Thus production went up significantly in Côte d'Ivoire in the same period, and its share in the world market increased from 13 to 30 percent (World Bank 1994, p.156).

The overtaxing of cocoa farmers in Ghana eroded the revenue base as it depressed production and encouraged smuggling. In spite of falling revenues government spending increased unconstrained by budgetary considerations — quite a bit of it due to grants to public enterprises. At the peak of the fiscal imbalance in 1976 the budget deficit amounted to 11.3 percent of GDP. The inflation rate as a result went quickly from single to double and even triple digit levels — the average being 58 percent in the decade of 1972-82. The process of inflation eroded real wages in the formal sector, including the public sector. It had reached levels at which attempts to protect the real value of wages were quickly eroded by the consequent budget deficit and accelerated inflation. Government policy makers found it politically impossible to change the nominal exchange rate during the inflationary spiral. Instead the balance of payments deficits which the inflating real exchange rate caused were sought to be controlled by quantitative import restrictions. The shortage of essential intermediate goods dislocated production in non-agriculture and had a severe effect on the infrastructure. The public sector protected employment, but at the end of the period real wages of public employees were no more than 25 percent of their level around 1970. It is not hard to imagine the dive in efficiency of government services which this must have caused.

The Economic Recovery Program (ERP) and after

The program agreed to with international help in 1983 involved measures to stabilize the economy in the first place, followed by policies of structural reform on several fronts. A major effort was made on the exchange rate front leading to a massive devaluation as the black market premium on foreign exchange fell from 2000 percent in 1983-6 to 21 percent in 1987-91. It virtually disappeared in 1992-4. On the fiscal side a sharp increase in revenue as a result of a successful readjustment of its sources made it possible both to narrow the fiscal imbalance and raise the level of expenditure. The stabilization of the monetary base led to significant fall in the inflation rate.

The decline in the rate of increase of the consumer price level also saw a marked improvement of the internal terms of trade in favor of the rural sector — according to one source the ratio of the wholesale price index of manufactured goods to that of agriculture, forestry and fishing fell by more than 25 percent between 1983-6 and 1992-94 (World Bank 1995, p.16). The relative increase in the price of tradable — which in Ghana are mostly of rural origin — was one source of the shift. Other factors were the general rise in real consumption boosting the demand for food, and the erosion of scarcity prices for importables, including essential inputs for urban goods and services. It is also likely that the margin enjoyed by traders — particularly in the urban areas — had fallen with the stabilization of the economy.

The stabilization measures saw a remarkable turnaround in the economy. Overall, GDP growth rate increased from minus 1 percent to plus 5 percent in the first five years of the ERP. Total merchandise export grew at 22 percent per annum, with the traditional exports, logs and cocoa growing the fastest. Real wages recovered to some extent in the formal sector, as the rate of inflation fell. In the public sector some retrenchment allowed a greater part of the wage bill to be used to support recovery of real earnings.

The measures of structural adjustment of the economy seem to have been less successful. The public sector still dominates the formal labor market. Liberalization on the trade front has not led to the expected increase in manufacturing output. Public enterprises continue to be important and generally a drag on the efficient growth of the non-agricultural sector.

Recent Shocks

An adverse development has been the decline in Ghana's terms of trade since 1987. In 1994 it stood at a level more than 25 percent below that of 1987. It has been pointed out that the net aid flow has virtually been wiped out by the terms of trade loss (World Bank 1994, figure 4.1, p.155). Some authors have argued that the foreign aid flow has prevented depreciation of the Ghanaian currency in the foreign exchange market to reflect the terms of trade deterioration (Younger et al.). However, it should be remembered that that net foreign aid was less than 5 percent of Ghana's GDP, well below the average of 8 percent for sub-Saharan Africa (ibid, p.155).

More recently the fiscal situation has deteriorated. The fiscal shock of 1992 was triggered by a large across-the-board increase in wages for civil servants and was accentuated by a fall in tax revenue and a shortfall in foreign aid. The narrow fiscal accounts went from a surplus of 1.5 percent of GDP to a deficit of 4.8 percent in 1992 — reversing the improving trend of the last seven years. The attendant expansion of money supply triggered a reversal of inflation trend as well. After falling to 10 percent in 1992, the rate of inflation shot up to 15 percent in 1993 and 1994. The indirect impact on savings and investment seems to have been severe. The upward trend in gross private investment was interrupted in 1991 and could be directly related to the macro-economic instability. While public investment tried to make up for the shortfall, it could do so only at the cost of public dissaving, and at the same time private savings fell (World Bank 1995, pp7-9).

The Formal Sector

The Pre-ERP Period

Employment Ghana's employment in the formal sector has been dominated by the public sector for a long time, and it seems to be more true in the post ERP era. The employment series are summarized in Table 9.1 reproduced from ISSER 1995.

The major expansion in public sector employment took place before 1965. Over the next two decades the public sector increased its workforce by 40 percent — about the same relative increase as it had achieved in a single five-year period between 1960 and 1965. In the decade of 1965-75 the public sector employment increased at about the same rate as the private sector. Although the growth rate of employment in the formal sector had slowed down considerably, the public sector did not try to inflate it by over-zealous expansion. It was during the severe decline in formal employment during the crisis years of 1975-80 that the share of the public sector in formal employment increased significantly. Private formal employment fell drastically to a third of its level. Public employment also fell, but to a much smaller extent as the state tried to hold the line on formal employment. But in spite of this effort, total employment in the formal sector in 1980 was only three-quarters of the level of 1975, and the private sector share of formal employment reached its lowest level of 13.6 perecent.

Table 9.1 Formal Sector Employment, 1960-1991 ('000)

				Annual Change (%)		
Year	*Private Sector*	*Public Sector*	*All Sectors*	*All Sectors*	*Public*	*SOPSE (%)*
1960	149	184	333	-	-	44.7
1965	118	278	396	+3.8	+10.2	29.8
1970	110	288	398	+0.1	+0.7	27.6
1975	137	318	455	+2.9	+2.1	30.1
1980	46	291	337	-5.2	-1.7	13.6
1985	67	397	463	+7.5	+7.3	14.5
1986	66	347	414	-10.8	-12.6	15.9
1987	79	315	394	-4.8	-9.2	20.0
1988	55	252	307	-22.1	-20.0	17.9
1989	38	177	215	-30.0	-29.8	17.7
1990	40	189	229	+6.5	+6.8	17.5
1991*	31	136	186	-18.8	-17.5	16.1

Source: ISSER (1995), Table 9.4.
Notes: *Provisional, SOPSE= Share of private sector in total formal sector employment. Ghana ISSER 1994, Table 8.4, p. 139.

Wages The course of real earnings per worker employed in the formal sector is plotted in Figure 9.1 (reproduced from ISSER, 1995, Figure 9.2, p.159). The graph shows that the drastic decline in real wages took place in the decade of 1974-83. If the cost of living deflator is to be believed the level of real wages in 1983 was a mere 12 percent of its level in 1974 (ISSER, p.151). This decline in real wage was due to the failure of nominal wage increase to keep pace with the increasing rate of inflation. It was also the result of a deliberate policy of the government as the dominant employer to choose to reduce the wage bill, as much as it could, through wage decline rather than a reduction in employment. Between 1960 and 1985 while employment in the formal sector (with the public sector providing an increasing share) increased by 40 percent, real wage fell by more than 80 percent. Thus, in spite of the employment increase the wage bill fell pari passu with the decline in GDP per capita and government revenue, but clearly the employment situation would have been much worse if the government had opted in favor of protecting real wage rather than employment.

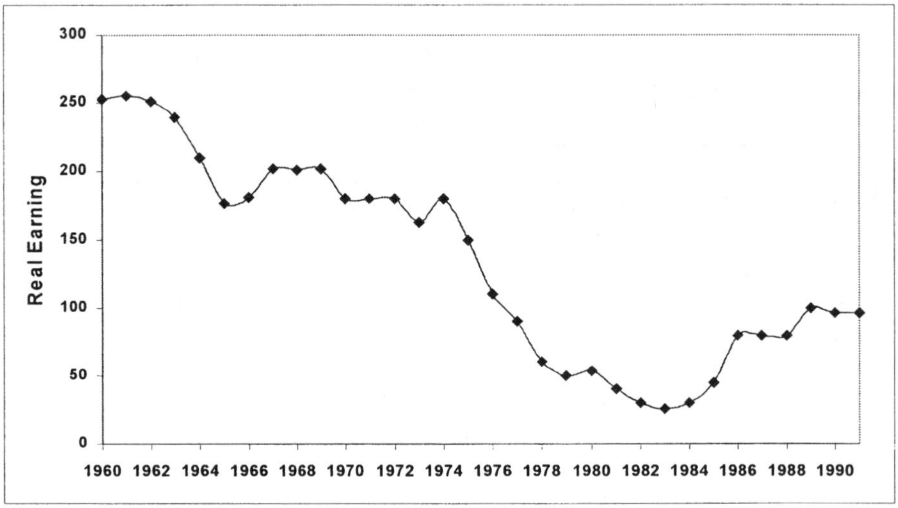

Figure 9.1 Average Real Wages of Formal Sector Workers, 1960-1991

Post-ERP Developments

The Public Sector In the years following the ERP there has been clearly an attempt to reverse the employment-real wage trade off implicit in the policies of the previous era. The government was persuaded to cut employment and increase the wage of the smaller workforce in the interests of efficiency. The public sector employment was cut by 60 percent between 1985 and 1991 (see Table 9.1 above). But at the same time real wage in the public sector went up by 170 percent over this period, including a major hike of 80 percent in 1992 (World Bank, 1994, Table 4.2, p.165). This put the public sector wage back to its 1970 level, but it was still only 72 percent of its peak in the early sixties.

The Private Sector

The recovery phase 1983-87 saw a significant increase of private sector employment, and a slower growth of public employment. The private share of formal employment (SOPSE) climbed to a level of 20 percent. But the figures bear adequate testimony to the story that whatever might have happened in the rural and the urban informal sectors, recovery in the formal wage sector has not been sustained. In the period 1987-91 private employment fell drastically. In fact in 1991 it was only 70 percent of its level in 1980. This time the public sector, under pressure from the adjustment program, offered only limited buffer for the decline in employment.

The setback after 1987 is evidently related to the trade liberalization measures, which were strengthened in the second phase of the program. This disappointing trend in employment is related to the fortunes of the Ghanaian private manufacturing sector in the post adjustment period. The initiatives supposed to have been created for private manufacturing were not nearly as strong as some might have predicted, and the response of the sector to such incentives as did emerge was sluggish.

The average real earnings in the private formal sector seem to have increased at the same rate as real wages in the public sector in the post-ERP period until 1988 (World Bank, ibid.). However, did private sector wages fall to as low levels as they did in the public sector in the years of accelerating inflation before the ERP? Unlike the public sector, the private employer could be expected not to let wages fall below a threshold, which would actually lead to a proportionately greater fall in efficiency than wages per worker. Nor is the latter obliged to follow a policy, which favors retention of employment more than falling wages. In fact, we have already seen that private formal employment fell sharply while the public sector workforce was expanding in the years prior to the ERP. Aggregate earnings data do suggest that in 1988, private sector average earnings were higher than those in the public sector: the private-public differential was 1.46. This differential in favor of the private sector seems to have been whittled down in the years after 1988 as public sector wages increased further. The overall private-public earnings ratio stood at 1.07 in 1991 (ISSER, Table 8.14, p.153). The massive wage increase of 80 percent in the public sector in 1992 must have pushed this ratio much further down although the data are not available for more recent years from this source.

It is, however, not enough to consider merely the difference in mean earnings between the public and private sectors, even if we are able to control for differences in the quality of labor to some extent. We need to know the distribution of earnings in different sectors of the economy, so that the relative position of workers in various parts of the distribution might be compared.

Distribution of Employment and Earnings in Different Sectors

The quantification of the different segments of the labor market in an economy like that of Ghana is complicated because of the prevalence of multiple occupations. The same household would be involved in more than one sector, according as different working members are involved in activities in different sectors, or the same individual earner divides his time between different activities. We have two options in classifying households by sector. If we want the households to be classified in mutually exclusive groups we can allocate each household to that sector from which it derives the largest portion of its income. Alternatively, a household could be allocated to a sector if any of its earning member reports his/her participation in that sector. If we go the latter route, the same household could be allocated to more than one sector of activity, and the sum of relative proportions would add up to more than 100 percent. In their classification of the Ghana labor market Appleton and Collier have adopted the second method. In the absence of other work attempting such classification, we summarize their results as giving a rough outline of the relative importance of the different types of income earners in the economy.

The authors analyzed the data available from the Social Dimensions of Adjustment Survey for 1988. They listed six socio-economic groups to which the households were assigned as follows;

- Households producing the exportable crop, cocoa (Cocoa);
- Households producing other agricultural goods — basically food (Food);
- Households with one or members who are retail or wholesale traders (Traders);
- Households with one or more members in wage employment producing non-traded goods and services — excluding traders and government services) (NTG);
- Households with one or more members in wage employment producing manufactured goods (Manu);
- Households with one or more members employed in providing government services (Gov).

The size of the groups and their mean and median incomes per capita are given in Table 9.2. As already explained the same household may belong to more than one group depending on the diversification of activities of their earning members. The figures are then not to be confused with earnings per worker in the different sectors.

Table 9.2 Distribution of Income by Socio-Economic Groups

Size of Groups	*Number in Sample*	*(%)*	*Mean pcy*	*Median pcy*	*S.D. pcy*	*Poor %*
Gov	1536	10.9	84,906	41,885	443,527	18.3
NTG	2064	14.6	44,977	34,237	44,030	26.6
Manu	575	4.2	43,751	36,598	37,255	25.2
Traders	5241	37.1	43,705	35,554	35,465	26.2
Cocoa	2227	15.8	52,210	39,460	64,605	21.0
Food	9166	54.9	45,122	31,916	1,182,18	32.7
Total	14130			46404	34289	151202

Notes: pcy= per capita income in cedis for Ghana. A Household is described as poor if it falls into the poorest 3 per capita income deciles.
Source: Table derived by Appleton and Collier and Collier from the SDA Survey of 1988.

The figure are of interest in giving an indication of broad differences between the income per capita of households in different groups after the Economic Recovery Program had gone some way. They will be referred to again below at appropriate points when we focus on the changing rural-urban income differences.

One point of general importance might be emphasized here. It is seen that the median incomes per capita are much closer together than the means. This implies that in some sectors there are considerably greater dispersion of incomes, with a lager proportion of households with relatively high incomes. This is particularly true of the government sector, and to a smaller extent the food sector. (The latter probably reflects regional diversity in the peasant sector in Ghana). However, focusing on differences in *median per capita income* the rather impressive conclusion emerges that the difference between different sectors — government-private, or agriculture-manufacturing or any other — is quite small, of the order of 30 percent or less.

The data in the table also gives an over-all picture of the distribution of labor among the classes of households distinguished by Appleton and Collier. It shows that although the government sector dominates the formal economy, its importance in the total employment scene as of 1988 was not that great. It was substantially smaller than the cocoa sector and considerably below the informal sector which was comprised of most of the households in NTG (wage employees producing non-traded goods) and services. The relative unimportance of the *private formal* sector is seen from the statistics that just 4.2 percent of households obtained their main income from wage employment in manufacturing — although a small proportion of those deriving their income from non-government services and trade would also be part of the private formal sector.

The relatively small role played by the public sector in direct employment in the total economy does not imply that government policies affecting the labor market are of a small order of importance. Because of the importance of public employment in the formal wage scoter of the economy, public sector wage and employment policies could be expected to have ripple effects on its private sub-sector. Extending our view to the rural private sector, government policy clearly has a direct effect on the earnings of labor in the exportable sector — cocoa. As an exportable, the domestic price of cocoa received by the producers is heavily dependent on the value of the exchange rate — which the government of Ghana has tried to influence over many years. Additionally, the active role of the government in the marketing of cocoa has meant that the margin of the selling price of cocoa going to the producers has been heavily influenced by the government's fiscal policy.

Apart from these direct effects on labor earnings, the indirect effect of government policies extends to practically all the socio-economic groups identified above. The peasant food producers respond to the rural-urban terms of trade and the availability of goods imported from the urban economy on which they can spend their cash earnings from their marketed surplus. These are heavily influenced by the state's exchange rate and trade policies. Besides, they will be affected by the state spending on infrastructure and subsidies on agricultural inputs. In the urban economy, investment and capacity utilization is heavily influenced by demand conditions on the one hand, and the supply of essential imported inputs on the other — both of which are conditioned by a whole spectrum of monetary, fiscal and state policies. The resultant course of productivity in manufacturing influences employment and wages in this sector. Finally, one of the major determinants of the incomes of traders is the rent created in the economy as a direct result of the gap between administered and market prices in the regulated economy.

Labor Absorption in Rural and Urban Areas

The data presented above does not distinguish employment in the rural and the urban areas. Another set of statistics are available from household surveys conducted in the post-adjustment period called the General

Household Sample Surveys (GLSS). GLSS1 was done in 1987-88, GLSS2 in 1988-89 and GLSS3 in 1991-2.

Table 9.3 gives the statistics of the changing absorption of labor over the period under consideration. Note that the sectoral classification given in this table is based on the main occupation of *individuals,* and not households as given in Table 9.2 above.

Table 9.3 Employment by Urban and Rural Sectors (Figures in percent)

	1987-88			*1988-89*			*1991-92*		
Sector	Rural	Urban	Total	Rural	Urban	Total	Rural	Urban	Total
Government	9.67	23.87	14.06	10.21	23.77	14.09	8.70	23.49	12.97
Private-formal	2.93	14.15	6.92	4.70	14.04	7.89	2.45	9.10	4.51
Private-informal	2.43	5.22	3.37	3.03	5.58	3.87	2.71	6.36	3.91
Self-employed agriculture	68.71	14.06	49.24	59.88	11.84	43.57	64.34	11.98	47.0
Self-employed business	15.92	39.17	21.54	21.93	42.39	28.80	20.41	43.24	27.46
Non-working	0.34	3.54	2.14	0.25	2.37	1.74	1.39	5.82	4.13
Total	100.0	100.0	100.0	100.0	100.0	100.0	100.0	100.0	100.0

Source: Canagarajah and Thomas; derived from GLSS 1, 2 and 3.

In 1987 the samples were distributed between urban and rural areas as follows: Urban 37.7 percent (the capital city Accra accounting for 10.6 percent and other towns 26.1) and 72.3 urban.[36] It will be seen no massive shifts in the pattern of employment took place between 1987 and 1991. The share of employment in self-employed agriculture, after a slight dip between 1987 and 1988, seems to have come back in a strong way, particularly in the rural areas. There has been some shrinkage in government employment, but the decline in its share is confined to the rural sector, and perhaps represents the massive reduction of employment in cocoa boards. The major change in shares is the decline in private formal (wage) employment in urban areas, which is balanced by the increase in the share of self-employed business and non-working. Evidently the latter two categories harbor a good deal of low-income labor in the urban economy.

---

[36]Computed by the author from the data tapes of the GLSS (Cf. Canagarajah and Mazumdar 1998, Table 3, p.8).

The Rural-Urban Earnings Gap and its Changes over Time

This section examines the trend in rural-urban income differences over a long period of time.

The Pre-Crisis Economy

Unlike East Africa Ghana was not distinguished by a spectacular rural-urban difference in income or labor earnings before the economy began its long slide downwards. An early report comes from Knight (1972) who presented data from a national sample survey of household expenditure survey conducted in different regions of Ghana in 1961-2. Some selected data from this source are given in Table 9.4. It is seen that consumption per household was highest in Accra — about a third higher than the hinterland rural areas. The rural-urban difference was somewhat lower when we look at smaller towns in the individual administrative regions and compare them with their rural hinterlands, and non-existent in the Volta and Western regions. The average size of households was lower in towns partly because of the greater proportion of single-member households in town. Thus, the level of urban consumption per capita exceeded the rural level by as much as one half. Part of this difference was, of course, accounted for the difference in the cost-of-living between town and country. Knight made an attempt to estimate the latter using the data from the sample survey, and estimated that the urban price level was 112 percent of the rural price level using rural weights, and 104 percent using urban weights (Knight, Table 4, p.209). Thus both the extent of the nominal income difference in favor of the urban sector, and of the cost-of-living difference were quite small in Ghana compared to what was prevalent in other parts of Africa. In Kenya, for example, the urban-rural differential was as high as 3:1, or even 4:1, and the cost-of-living was estimated to have been 60 percent higher (Chapter 8). There were two reasons for this difference. First, although we have mentioned that single member households were more important in the urban economy of Ghana, the urban labor market was never dominated by circulatory migrants with a high turnover of labor as in East Africa. Hence the massive increase in urban wages, which took place in East Africa in the sixties driven by the desire to change the urban system from a migratory to a stabilized one was never necessary in Ghana. Secondly, the urban centers in Ghana were clearly not so differentiated from the rural ones as in East Africa. But this relatively modest differential was enough to sustain a significant stream of rural-to-urban migration through the sixties. 'Between 1956 and 1967 modern sector non-agricultural employment grew on average by 3.3 percent per annum whereas urban population grew at more than twice this rate' (Knight, p.214).

Table 9.4 Expenditure of Urban and Rural Households 1961-62

Expenditure per household (NC per month)	*Urban*	*Rural*	*Urban*
All regions			
Consumption of own produce	2.6	8.5	31
Other expenditure	34.2	19.0	180
Total expenditure	36.8	27.4	134
By region			
Accra	46.3		
Ashanti	41.3	35.6	116
Brong Ahafo	42.5	30.7	138
Eastern	36.2	31.1	116
Northern	23.4	17.1	137
Volta	33.7	33.3	101
Western	27.9	26.5	105
Expenditure per capita (NC per month)	9.0	6.0	150
Average size of household	4.08	4.54	150
Percentage of single member households	22.3	13.4	

Source: P.T.F. Golding, 'An enquiry into household expenditure and consumption and sale of household produce in Ghana.' Economic Bulletin of Ghana, 1962, No. 4 Tables 6 and 7, Reproduced in Knight (1972).

Note: The data relate to a two-stage stratified sample of 990 households with income under NC100 per month.

The Course of Rural-Urban Earnings Differences During the Economic Decline

The decade spanning the years 1973 to 1983 saw, as already mentioned, one of the most spectacular declines in economic fortune that any country has known. All sectors of the economy shrank in real terms. The output in the cocoa sector declined as producer prices declined — fueled by both the decline in world prices, and the domestic policies of the State marketing Board. The producer price had reached a peak in 1956, but declined from a level of around 140 to less than 20 in 1983. Because of the long gestation period in the planting of cocoa trees, cocoa output did not start its downward course until after 1965, but then followed the price index down. The combined effect was that the index of cocoa income in 1983 stood at a level, which was one-seventh of the high point of 1960-61.

Cocoa, however, is only a part of the income of the rural peasants, and is moreover concentrate in the South of the country. How did the food sector behave during this period? Tabatabai has put together the record of eight major crops in terms of the annual growth rates of production, area and yield. His major conclusion is that there was hardly any statistically significant trend in yields, but production shrank with remarkable speed — cereals at an annual rate of 3.4 percent for cereals, and of 4.7 percent for starchy staples. Evidently this remarkable shrinkage of output was entirely due to a decline in acreage.

Tabatabai ascribes this decline in acreage — more pronounced in the South than in the Northern ecological region — to the large scale international migration of labor to neighboring countries which were experiencing a mini-boom triggered by the oil price increase. 'It has been estimated that between 1974-5 when the exodus began, and 1981 some 2 million Ghanaians had left for Nigeria and Côte-d'Ivoire alone.' (Tabatabai, p.718 quoting a UNICEF report). Since employment in the 'modern' or formal sector was maintained in the period under consideration (see above), much of the emigrant labor came from the traditional activities including agriculture. 'Even if only half of the reduction concerned the agricultural sector, the decline in the agricultural labor force would have been of the order of 15-20 percent between 1975 and the early eighties'. (Tabatabai, p.721). While this labor shortage accounts for a decline in food production in the decade, it also implies that the decline in the real income of food producers was not as much as the output figures might tend to suggest. Not only were there fewer people to share in the total output in the farm sector, the natives left behind enjoyed substantial income augmentation through the remittance of the emigrants.

Relative real incomes of different groups in the urban and rural labor markets were also changed by sharp relative movements in different price indices during the general inflationary period. In particular, although the statistical series are somewhat incomplete after 1977, 'the conclusion is inescapable that the underlying trend in real wholesale prices of food are at most steady, if not actually downward'. (Tabatabai, p.715; see p.714 for more details). The way the divergent movements in the different price series affected the relative real incomes of different groups can be seen in the trends in real returns calculated by Tabatabai in which he deflates the nominal returns of each group by the index of consumer prices most relevant to each. These are portrayed in Figure 9.2.

The course of real earnings of formal sector wage earners, as we have seen, mirrors the downward trend in the real wage of minimum wage earners, both of whom are to be found mostly in the urban areas. This is balanced by the increase in the real income of traders, many of whom are also found in the urban economy. The basic reasons for the increase in real earnings of traders over this period are two-fold: first, the deterioration of infrastructure meant that the cost of marketing went up; and secondly, the shortage of marketed goods — both imported and domestically produced — meant that important sources of 'rent' opened up for traders. Within the rural sector, cocoa farmers and the food producers in the South suffered relative to the farmers in the North.

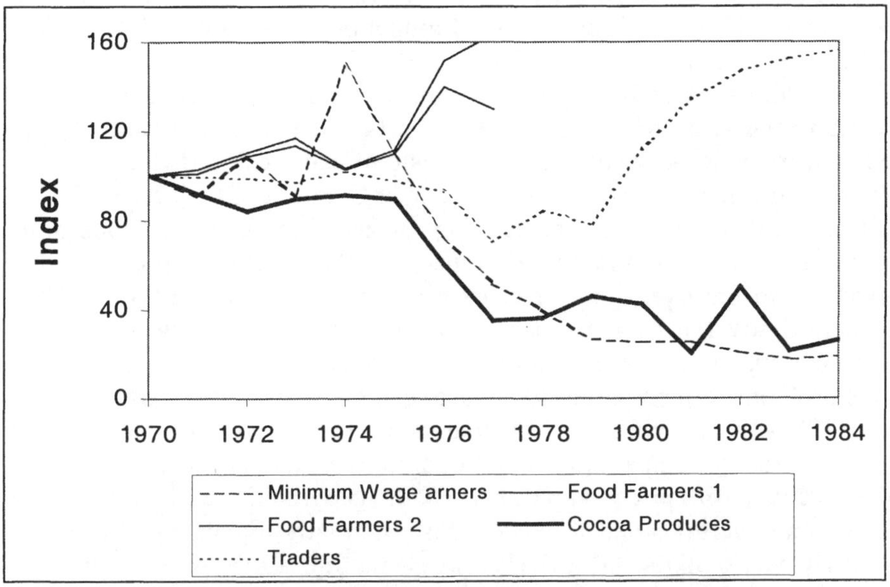

Figure 9.2 Trends in Real Returns, 1970-85 (1970=100)
Source: Tabatabai Figure 3. The data are presented in Tabatabai, Table 9.

Because of the mixed nature of the impact of the economic decline on different groups, it is difficult to be confident about the course of rural-urban income difference over this period. However, in so far as food producers are the most important part of the rural economy, and wage earners constitute a sizable section of the urban labor force, it is likely that real income per head, on the average, probably had declined in the urban areas relative to the rural, and indeed could have been lower in the former at the end of the period. Official Census data are consistent with this conclusion. They show that between the two Censuses of 1970 and 1984, urbanization had slowed down considerably, and the share of the three largest cities in total population had remained largely the same. (Tabatabai, Table 7, p.719).

The Rural-Urban Differential after the Recovery

The agricultural sector in Ghana suffered a dual shock in 1983, as the migrants to Nigeria were expelled back into the country, and the country experienced its worst drought in history. 'But once the returnees settled down in the rural areas and started farming activities, and when the rains also returned in 1984, the situation improved considerably. The index of food output per capita rose from 80.9 in 1983 to 114.6 in 1984, 105.7 in 1985 and 113.7 in 1986 (FAO Production Yearbook, 1987, p.47)' (Tabatabai, p.720).

With the successful implementation of the ERP the economy turned around in the years following 1983. Exports, cocoa output, manufacturing and non-tradable services all showed significant real growth. We have detailed information about relative incomes from the GLSS after 1987. It will be recalled that the dramatic improvement in economic conditions, which resulted from the initial impact of the Recovery program, had already been felt over the four years prior to the start of the GLSS. Thus, the period covered by these surveys do not convey what the rural-urban difference was like at the bottom of the economic decline. There are also some problems of comparability as between the three surveys over the five years 1987-91. A number of adjustments were required to ensure that they were reasonably comparable. 'In addition to the usual constructs needed to take account of price variations (both geographic and over time), adjustments were needed to correct for potentially higher recall errors in the early years of the GLSS' (World Bank, June1995, p. vi). Table 9.5 represents the figures worked out at the World Bank for urban and different rural areas in Ghana. It was generally felt that in these surveys the expenditure figures were more accurate than income figures.

The data reproduced shows that the expenditures level in 'other urban areas' were only slightly higher than in the rural districts. The level was generally higher in Accra, but the differential seems to have fallen significantly over the five-year period covered by the surveys. Comparing Accra with the lowest income rural region — the Savannah — the expenditure per capita was 93 percent higher in the former, but had fallen to 40 percent more in the 1991-2. The corresponding percentages for expenditure per adult equivalent units was 71 and 24.

Table 9.5 Total Expenditure in Different Areas

	Accra	*Other Urban*	*Rural Coastal*	*Rural Forest*	*Rural Savannah*
Per capita					
1987-8	314	217	176	179	162
1988-9	274	221	175	179	140
1991-2	260	228	225	213	185
Per AEU					
1987-8	458	320	299	299	268
1988-9	398	321	275	281	233
1991-2	376	343	334	333	304

Source: World Bank November 1995.
Note: Per capita figures have been adjusted for different recall error and seasonality. The figures for expenditure per adult equivalent units (AEU according to the Mclements scale) have been adjusted for recall errors. See the text of the source sighted for further details.

In any event these ranges of the rural-urban differential are a far cry from the differentials observed in Kenya in the late eighties (Chapter 8). The point underlines the finding already observed for the sixties, and could be due to the different type of rural-urban migration in West Africa compared to East African countries.

The result that the rural-urban differential seemed to be narrowing over the 1987-92 period is also noteworthy. It can be traced to the differential impact of structural adjustment programs, which improved incomes in rural areas rather more than in Accra and other larger urban locations. In recent work with the GLSS data, reproduced in the next section, attention is focused on the changes in the incidence of poverty. This concentrates attention on the lower end of the income distribution.

Decomposition of Changes in Poverty Incidence by Locality

The poverty line was defined as two-thirds of mean household expenditure *per capita*. The value of the line was expressed in constant May 1992 Accra prices, so that it takes account of differences in price levels, over time as well as spatially. The 'headcount ratio', which we will be analyzing is the proportion of total households in the area/sector concerned who are below the poverty line. Thus, the relative changes in the headcount ratios indicate the comparative movements of income at the lower end of the distribution. Overall, the incidence of poverty declined in Ghana in the period 1987-92, but the improvement only occurred in the rural areas and in the smaller towns, not in the capital city. According to the calculations by the World Bank (1995) the headcount ratio fell from 42 to 34 percent in rural areas, and from 33 to 28 percent in Other Towns, but increased in Accra from 9 to 23 percent. Doubts have been raised about the dramatic increase in Accra. But the ratio increased between the two subsequent surveys, 1988-9 and 1991-2 as well, albeit by a small margin. So it is likely that there has been a gradual increase in poverty incidence over the whole 5-year period, even if the headcount ratio was underestimated in the first survey. In each locality or sector the change in the headcount ratio would be affected by two factors; the change in the mean expenditure, and by any change in the distribution of income (expenditure) at the lower end. Besides, the overall change in the ratio for the economy as whole would also be dependent on the shifts in the population of households between the different segments studied.

Methodology

We can study empirically the extent of population shifts, changes in relative mean incomes, and in the distribution of income at the lower end all together by a decomposition analysis of poverty incidence. Let P_{0j} be poverty incidence (i.e. proportion of population under the poverty line) for a sub-group of a population, and P_{mj} be the mean expenditure per capita of that group, then the poverty incidence of the sub-group can be expressed as a decreasing function of mean expenditure per capita and an inequality measure:

$$P_{0j} = \frac{K_j}{P_{mj}}, \qquad (1)$$

where K_j is an inequality index at the lower end of distribution. A negative change in K_j would contribute to poverty reduction and a positive one would contribute to an increase in poverty. The opposite would obviously hold for mean expenditure per capita. The poverty incidence for the whole population is then just a weighted average of poverty incidence of all sub-groups:

$$\overline{P_0} = \sum_j S_j P_{0j} = \sum S_j \frac{K_j}{P_{mj}} \tag{2}$$

where $\overline{P_0}$ is weighted mean P_{0j} of all sub-groups, j is the index for sub-groups, such as localities or socio-economic groups, and S_j is the sub-group's share of population. The percent change in $\Delta\overline{P_0}$ can then be explained by the changes in population share S_j, in the change in inequality index and the mean expenditure (see appendix for details):

$$\Delta\overline{P_0} = \sum S_j \frac{P_{0j}}{\overline{P_0}} \{\Delta S_j + \Delta K_j - \Delta P_{mj}\} \tag{3}$$

where Δ represents percentage change. The first component shows how, other things being equal, movements of population between sub-groups affects the changes in poverty incidence. The second component quantifies the effect of a change in the degree of inequality within the sub-group. The third component, ΔP_{mi}, measures the impact on poverty of the change in the mean expenditure of a sub-group, j.

Results

Table 9.6 presents the decomposition of poverty incidence for Ghana into the changes of the components in equation (3) in each of three localities, both not weighted and weighted. (The weights are the terms outside the brackets in the equation 3 above). The table shows that there was a 15 percent decrease in poverty incidence between 1988 and 1992 for Ghana.[37] Figure 9.3 presents the contribution of the change in each component from

[37]The survey questionnaire of GLSS3 was changed from that of GLSS1 in some significant ways. The comparability of the 1988 and 1992 survey results have, therefore, been questioned in several studies (Coloumbe and Mackay 1995, Jones and Ye 1995, Demery and Mehra 1997). In Demery and Mehra's study, it is demonstrated that GLSS2 (1988-9) and GLSS3 (1991-2) are more comparable for expenditure analysis. The corrections on expenditure levels, however, do not affect distribution in any significant way. Sensitivity analysis was performed comparing GLSS2 and GLSS3 for all the exercises reported in the text. These produced results consistent with the comparison of GLSS1 and GLSS3. All the results are fully reported in Canagarajah, Mazumdar and Ye 1998.

each locality to the total poverty reduction in Ghana. In this 15 percent decrease, 70 percentage comes from the increase in mean expenditure per capita, P_{mi}, in Rural Areas (10.4, the weighted change, divided by 15). The improvement in inequality, K_j in rural areas also contributed substantially, over 30 percent, to the overall poverty deduction in Ghana. The changes in Accra pulled the other way. Mean expenditure (per capita) decreased by 17 percent in the capital city, and the degree of inequality also worsened significantly, contributing *negatively* to the poverty reduction in Ghana. However, 'other cities' showed significant improvement. There was a 9 percent increase in mean expenditure per capita, contributing 14 percent to the poverty reduction in Ghana (2.1, the weighted change, divided by 15). The inequality index also improved in Other Cities, contributing another 9 percent to the overall poverty reduction.

Table 9.6 Ghana: Decomposition of the Change in Poverty Incidence by Locality

	ΔS_j		$\Delta(K_j)$		$-\Delta P_{mj}$		$\Delta\overline{P}_0$
	Actual	Weighted	Actual	Weighted	Actual	Weighted	Total
Accra	-1.4	-0.03		2.9	17	0.3	
Other Cities	-3.7	-0.9	-4.4	-1.0	-9.0	-2.1	
Rural Areas	1.6	1.2	-6.8	-5.1	-14	-10.4	-15

Since the rural areas performed much better over the period 1988-92, both in terms of mean expenditure per capita and its distribution, it is not surprising to see from Table 9.6 that there was a significant redistribution of population from the urban to the rural areas. The shift, however, seems to have occurred more from Other Cities than from Accra, although the mean expenditure increased in the former and decreased in the latter. A couple of reasons could explain this. First, although expenditure decreased in Accra, it is still the region which has the highest mean expenditure per capita. Second, it is also possible that there is more integration between the economies of the rural areas and the Other Cities. The population in Accra might have been 'locked in' even though the living standards declined both absolutely and relatively.

The same exercise is applied to different localities separately — with decomposition of the locality-specific percentage change in P_0 into the components for three socio-economic groups. We want to examine how the incidence of low incomes has changed for the different socio-economic groups within each locality. Table 9.7 shows that the overall poverty incidence in Accra increased by 166 percent. There was a large contraction of the formal sector in the capital, compensated for by an increase in the informal sector. The mean expenditure decreased and the distribution of expenditure at the lower end also worsened substantially in both sub-sectors — much more so in the formal sector. It is this deterioration of the distribution which accounted for much of the decrease in living standards for the poor, and the increase in the incidence of poverty in Accra noticed earlier (see Figure 9.4).

In Other Cities poverty incidence decreased by 17 percent. The larger part (95 percent) of it came from an improvement in expenditure distribution at the lower end and an increase in mean expenditure for the Urban informal group. Again there was a shrinking Urban formal sector but a growing Urban informal sector. For Rural Areas, poverty incidence decreased by 19 percent, the largest decrease among all three localities. Much of this large part of decrease (67 percent) came from a 12 percent increase in mean expenditures at the farming sector and an improvement in expenditure distribution at the lower end in informal sector. In spite of an improvement in expenditure at the farming sector it lost some population over this period (see next paragraph for an explanation). The Informal sector in the rural areas absorbed both this loss and the labor that was shed by the formal sector. Fortunately for rural welfare, the informal sector in this area performed better than in Accra, registering both an increase in mean expenditure and an improvement in the inequality. Evidently labor was 'pulled' into the rural informal sector because of growing incomes.

Table 9.7 Ghana: Decomposition of Poverty Incidence, by Socioeconomic Groups

	ΔS_j		$\Delta(K_j)$		$-\Delta P_{mj}$		$\Delta\overline{P}_0$
Accra	Actual	Weighted	Actual	Weighted	Actual	Weighted	Total
Urban Formal	-20.6	-5.7	340	94.2	13.6	3.8	
Urban Informal*	24.40	17.6	46.9	33.9	18.7	13.5	166
Other Cities							
Urban Formal	-8.5	-2.1	-9.9	-2.4	-3.1	-0.8	
Urban Informal	5.6	3.0	-18.3	-9.7	-12.3	-6.5	
Farming	-0.6	-0.1	19.6	4.4	-14.9	-3.3	-17
Rural Areas							
Formal	-16.5	-1.4	9.3	0.8	-18.9	-1.6	
Informal	19.7	3.0	-25.6	-3.9	-17.2	-2.6	
Farming	-2.3	-1.7	-3.6	-2.7	-11.5	-8.8	-19

Note: Few farm households in Accra, are omitted due to the small size of the sample.

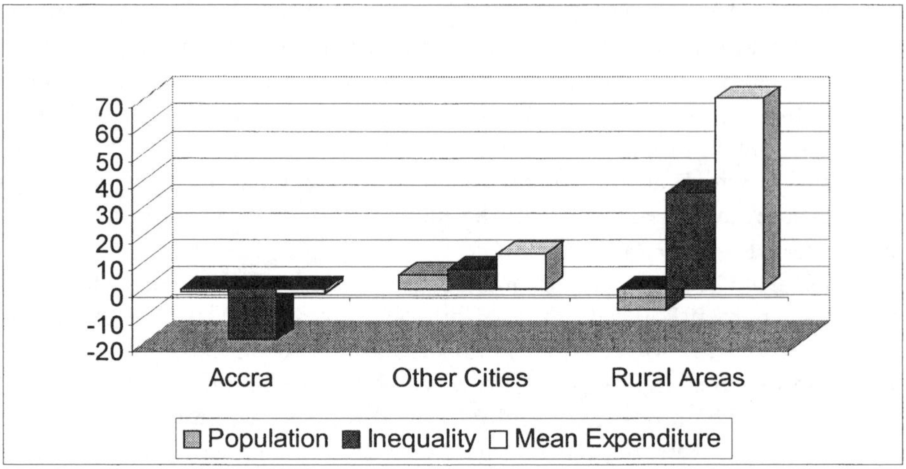

Figure 9.3 Contribution of Migration, Inequality, and Mean Expenditure to Poverty Increase in Ghana, GLSS1-GLSS3

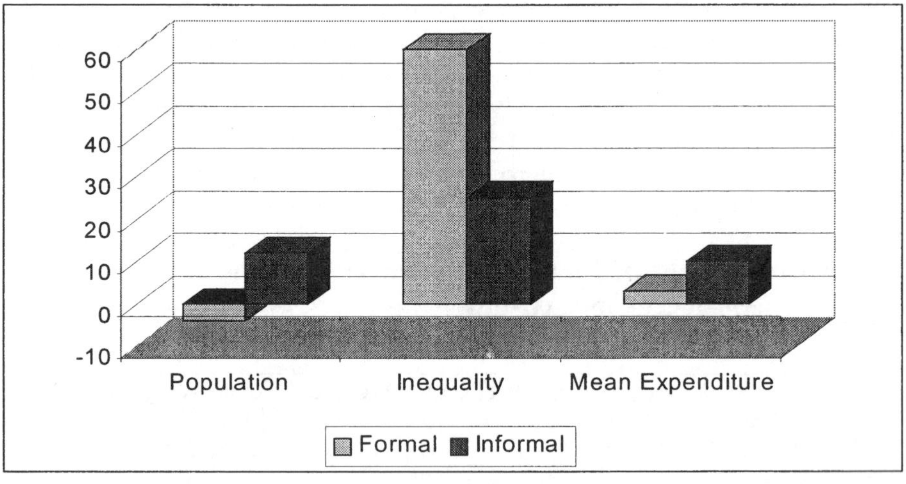

Figure 9.4 Contribution of Migration, Inequality, and Mean Expenditure to Poverty Reduction in Accra

The driving force behind the poverty reduction for Other Cities and Rural Areas are the improvement in inequality in informal sector and an increase in mean expenditure per capita in informal sector for Other Cities and in farming sector for the Rural Areas. Farming seems to be more important in the improvement in the Rural Areas and the informal sector in the Other Cities. However, it should be remembered that improvement in the farming group in the Rural Areas does not come necessarily or solely from an increase in agricultural output. The division of the population into the various socio-economic groups is based on the main occupation of the household head. In an economy in which multiple occupations of earners is the dominant mode, the increase in income could come partly from non-farm activities. The World Bank Report (1995) pointed out that informal employment activities cut across all sectors and essentially service-based. During 1988 to 1992, the proportion of rural self-employed working in the service sector increased from 54 to 62 percent, while the share of manufacturing employment — of the micro- and small-scale type declined from 37 to 31 percent. Table 9.8 gives the changes in the different sources of income for the households in the different localities. It will be seen that the share of income from non-farm activities — or the informal sector — increased rapidly in all localities at the expense of farming.[38]

Table 9.8 Income Shares by Locality (Share from Other Incomes Not Included)

	Agriculture	*Non-farm*	*Wage*
Accra			
1988		34.9	41.5
1992		41.1	42.2
% change		17.7	1.6
Other Cities			
1988	23.8	39.8	24.3
1992	15.6	48.8	24.4
% change	-34.2	22.7	0.2
Rural Areas			
1988	71.7	15.6	7.5
1992	57.4	27.9	9.0
% change	-20.0	78.7	20.7

Thus, to conclude, there is a marked difference in the way the proportion of low-income groups changed in Accra, on the one hand, and in the rural areas and other towns, on the other. Accra registered an increase in the incidence of poverty, but the other two registered a substantial decrease, thus bringing the headcount ratios much closer

[38]The GLSS data show that while expenditure declined in Accra, household income measures increased. We tend to accept the expenditure measures as more reliable, but still think hat the *shares* of total income from different sources in the total reported would be accurate. In any event the changes in shares are large as can be seen from Table 7.

together in the three areas. The informal sector, which expanded everywhere at the expense of the formal, contributed to the increase in poverty Accra, but helped the decrease elsewhere. The farming sector seems to have spearheaded the decline in rural poverty through an increase in mean incomes as well as better distribution. However, a larger proportion of the growing income of farming families came from the non-farm or informal activities. The growth of farm and non-farm income is in fact bound together in the process of economic development and growth.

Patterns of Migration between Rural and Urban Areas

We have seen above that rural-urban migration was an important part of the economic landscape of Ghana in the years before its decline. Beaudrey and Sowa have used the migration data available in the GLSS1, as well as other sources, to construct a table of net migration flows (i.e. inflow minus outflow) for different regions and periods. They are reproduced in Table 9.9 below.

Table 9.9 Net Migration Flows (Percent)

	(1) Up to 1970		*(2) Up to 1987*		*(3) 1982-87*	
Region	Destination	Origin	Destination	Origin	Destination	Origin
Western	21.1		74.0		39.0	
Central		22.4		11.0		6.8
Accra	46.5			15.0		57.6
Eastern		17.0		3.0	27.1	
Volta		28.9		31.0		15.3
Ashanti	12.3		13.0		13.6	
Northern- Upper		31.8	13.0		20.3	
Totals	100.0	100.0	100.0	100.0	100.0	100.0

Sources: (1) Ewusi (1984); (2) and (3): authors' calculations from the GLSS.

Column (1) of the table indicates that prior to 1970 46.5 percent of net migration was directed towards Accra. The next two columns show that the pattern of migration was completely reversed in the 1980s. Instead of being a region of net inflow, Accra has become the major source of out-migrants. Between 1982 and 1987, net migration out of Accra accounted for almost 60 percent of net outward migration in Ghana. The main destination migrants has become the Western region, which is the region of expanding cocoa production. For some purposes information on the volume and pattern of gross migration might be useful. Glewwe has produced data for such migration as took place over the last three years prior to the surveys of 1988-89 and 1991-92. These data are reproduced in Table 9.10 below.

While comparisons between the two surveys are somewhat hampered by the apparently more liberal definition of migration in 1988-89 survey, comparing the relative proportions among those who did migrate may still be possible. In both years there is very little migration from rural to urban areas — most migrants from rural areas went to other rural areas. What is even more interesting is that rather more than half of the migrants from urban areas went to the rural sector, and only a negligible fraction went to the capital city. Ghana had a remarkable experience among developing countries in actually showing 'deurbanization' in this period. Overall, the 1988-89 survey found that 63.7 percent of the population was rural, but in the 1991-92 survey this proportion had gone up to 65.2 percent.

The recent evidence on migration flows thus shows that, in the groups which are most generally prone to migrate, the income levels in town, in real terms are not perceived to be higher than in the rural areas. This is consistent with the finding reported in the last section that the incidence of poverty was declining in rural areas in the period considered but increasing in Accra.

Table 9.10 Migration between Urban and Rural Areas in Last Three Years, 1988-89 and 1990-91

	1988-89	*1990-91*
Did not migrate	78%	90.2%
Migrated from Rural areas	5.8%	3.9%
To Accra	0.4	0.2
To Other Urban areas	0.9	0.6
To Rural Areas	4.5	3.1
Migrated from Rural areas	14.5%	4.8%
To Accra	1.8	0.7
To Other Urban areas	3.6	1.6
To Rural Areas	9.2	2.5
Migrated from Rural areas	1.7%	1.1%
To Accra	0.5	0.5
To Other Urban areas	1.0	0.6

Source: Glewwe (1993), using data for GLSS 1 and GLSS3.

It should be noted, however, that the Extended Poverty Study of the

World Bank, while showing a decline in poverty in the rural areas, and an increase in the capital city, still maintained that in 1992 the absolute level of poverty was much higher in the rural areas. The poverty ratio was reported to be 23.0 percent in Accra, 27.7 percent in other urban areas, and varied from 28.6 percent to 38.3 percent in the different rural regions (World Bank June 1995, table 2.2, p.9). This can be reconciled with the changed flow of migration from urban to rural destinations if we accept the hypothesis advanced by the Harris-Todaro type of models that migrants respond much more to *expectations* of future income rather than *actual levels* of income. The falling poverty levels in localities outside Accra, and particularly the rural areas, might have provided a signal for conditions improving more strongly in the latter. Another hypothesis for which there is widespread support in many countries, and which can complement the first hypothesis, is that there are generally serious impediments to movement of labor due to economic or social barriers which prevent equalization of incomes in the bottom part of the distribution.

Conclusions

This case study of Ghana has taken us through the recent history of Ghana's economic decline and its moderate recovery after the post-1983 adjustment. The account paid particular attention to changes in employment and earnings in different sectors. The public sector seems to have played a dominant role — both in terms of state enterprises and government services — in the formal sector. It contributed the lion's share of the growth in employment in the formal sector in the sixties, and when it declined it did so at a slower rate than the private sector. There was clearly a policy of employment retention in this sector when wages declined drastically up to the adjustment period.

While public sector employment was reduced substantially in the period after adjustment, the formal private sector was sluggish in its recovery. In 1991, the fifth year into recovery, more than half the labor force *in the urban areas* was accounted for by the informal sector, while the formal private sector was under 10 percent.

The pattern of earnings among the various socio-economic groups in 1988 showed that the levels of per capita household income was not too much apart. Historical evidence also suggests that the rural-urban income difference was never very large in Ghana. The rural sector in Ghana has proved to be successful, not only in absorbing the addition to the labor force through natural growth, but also the large numbers expelled from neighboring Nigeria in 1983. The adjustment program helped significantly the recovery of agriculture. Thus, the rural-urban income gap, which was in any case small, has continued to shrink in the late eighties. Comparing household incomes in Accra with the rural region with the lowest income — the Savannah — expenditure per adult equivalent units was 71 percent higher in 1987-8 and only 24 percent higher in 1991-2. The difference in incomes between Accra and more prosperous rural regions were of course smaller and practically non-existent by 1991 (even if we did not make any allowance for the lower cost-of-living in rural areas).

More detailed analysis was done to study the changes in the incidence of poverty (low incomes) in different areas and the sectoral components contributing to it over the period 1987-91 when the impact of structural adjustment had time to work its way through. It was found that the poverty reduction in Ghana over the five-year period occurred mostly from the increase in mean income from rural Areas and other cities, as well as from an improvement in distribution in both regions. In Accra, not only mean expenditure experienced a big decrease, the inequality also worsened greatly. Evidently structural adjustment was successful in raising income and its distribution in the rural areas and other cities, where farming dominated and had a positive multiplier effect outside farming, but in Accra the contraction of the formal sector failed to produce compensating changes. Clearly, the tradable sector located in the capital did not respond to the adjustment policies as might have been expected from theory.

The relative improvement of incomes in areas outside Accra, particularly at the lower end of the distribution, has had an effect on the pattern of rural-urban flows. Ghana might be an unexpected case of reverse flow of new migrants from the capital city to other urban and rural areas. More case studies on internal migration in African countries are needed to see if the Ghana pattern is replicated in other cases.

Appendix to Chapter 9

Decomposition of poverty incidence

The poverty decomposition equation (4) $\Delta\overline{P}_0 = \sum \frac{P_{0j}}{\overline{P}_0}(\Delta P_{0j})$ is derived as following: Since

$$\overline{P}_0 = \sum_i S_i P_{0i} = \sum S_j \frac{K_j}{P_{mj}}, \tag{1}$$

(equation (2) in the text), the deferential of $\overline{P}_0$ is

$$\partial\, \overline{P}_0 = \sum \left(\frac{K_j}{P_{mj}}\right)\partial\, S_j + S_j\left[\frac{P_{mj}\partial\, K_j - K_j \partial\, P_{mj}}{P_{mj}^2}\right]$$

$$= \sum S_j P_{0j} \Delta S_j + S_j [P_{0j} \Delta K_j - P_{0j} \Delta P_{mj}] \tag{2}$$

$$\Delta\overline{P}_0 = \sum S_j \frac{P_{0j}}{\overline{P}_0}\{\Delta S_j + \Delta K_j + \Delta P_{mj}\} \tag{3}$$

10 The Evolution of Labor Markets and the Rural-Urban Earnings Gap in Other Countries

This chapter presents shorter studies of a few other countries in which household survey data on urban and rural areas were available. We have selected Zambia in East Africa and Sierra Leone and Côte d'Ivoire on the West to supplement the extensive discussion of Kenya and Ghana given in the previous chapters. It will be seen that the rural-to-urban migration patterns in Zambia are closer to those observed in Kenya, than those observed in the West African countries of Sierra Leone, and more importantly Cote d'Ivoire which are closer to the Ghana case — and the extent of the rural-urban earnings gap are closely related to these different patterns.

Zambia

We have already illustrated in Chapter 6 above how faulty concepts and data work could exaggerate the extent of the rural-urban wage gap. Zambia is rather an exceptional economy in Sub Saharan Africa. It is a mineral economy, dominated by one export i.e. copper, which accounted for 90 percent of total exports throughout the last two decades. It is also unique because of its high rate of urbanization, which is close to 50 percent. Although hard data on the structure of employment do not exist, an estimate for 1988 suggested that in spite of the high degree of urbanization, waged employment was not large. In the urban areas it amounted to about 20 percent of the labor force, and in the rural sector it was about 11 percent. These figures suggest the dominance of the rural sector by farmers, and the urban sector by the self-employed in the informal economy. (Odegaard 1988, quoted by Loxley 1990, p.15). The informal sector grew relative to the formal during the 1980s. In 1980 formal sector employment was almost

24 percent of the labor force, but this declined to under 10 percent by 1990 (World Bank 1993). There are also the unemployed and under-employed job seekers who make up a substantial part of the urban labor market During 1970-88 employment in the mining industry had been stable at around sixty thousand, or about one-sixth of the formal sector employment (Loxley, p.9).

As a result of the mineral domination, the share of agriculture in GDP has been small, around 13 percent in the seventies, two-thirds of which originated in the subsistence sector. There has been little export of agricultural products, except for a small amount of tobacco. The main function of the agricultural sector was to provide food surplus for the urban population. State policy has always been torn between the need to provide cheap food for the towns and to establish high producer prices to stimulate production as well as to reward the subsistence farmers. During the 1970s this contradiction was resolved by restricting producer price increases to less than the rate of inflation, in addition to subsidizing maize for the benefit of the urban consumer. A result of this policy was that the maize surplus did not keep pace with urbanization, and by 1980, 45 percent of the maize consumed off-farm was being imported from abroad (Loxley, p.18). This made the inflation rate in the economy very vulnerable to exchange rate changes.

The crisis in the Zambian economy started with a massive external shock in the form of a precipitous decline in the price of copper. The average prices in constant 1982 dollars as reported by the World Bank from information obtained at the London Metal exchange, are given below:

Table 10.1 Average Price of Copper, Constant (1982) Price, US Cent per lb

1965-69	*1970-74*	*1975-79*	*1980-84*	*1985-89*	*1990-91*
194	154	83	75	73	80

The unsustainable balance of payments deficit, which the massive TOT decline created could only be sustained with heavy borrowing, both external and internal. This led to the familiar vicious circle of inflation, further balance of payments crises and borrowing. Although the kwacha was depreciated continuously since the mid-seventies, because of the high rate of inflation, the currency succeeded in reducing its over-valuation only for a short period 1978-1984. (See Figure 2.9 in World Bank, 1992). At the end of our period in 1991 the black market premium was 70 percent, although less than the 180 percent reached at the end of the seventies.

Domestic production registered a downward trend as shortages developed, with the slashing of imports, and the decline in public services, investment and infrastructure.

Real GDP per capita in 1980 was 84 percent of the level of 1970 and by 1990 it had fallen to a level of only 65 percent. Per capita real consumption had fallen by less until 1975, as Zambia increased its share of consumption in GDP at the expense of investment, but in the second half of the eighties this trend reversed and in 1990 per capita consumption was one-third below the level of 1970 in real terms (World Bank, 1993, Table 1.1, p. 10).

The Trend in the Rural-Urban Wage Gap

The ratio of earnings of Zambian workers in non-agriculture when compared to those in (formal) agriculture are given in Table 10.1. This ratio appears to have been somewhat higher than 2.5 for much of the decade of the seventies (the highest value being attained in 1976 at 2.81). However, a decline in the next decade resulted in a value well below 2.0 by the mid eighties. Given the difference in the cost of living between town and country discussed in Chapter 6 above, this gap does not appear to be too large for a family with the same earning strength in the two locations — even when the gap was at its peak in the seventies; nor was it way out of line with the ratio for other African countries presented in Table 7.1 above.[39]

Table 10.2 Zambia: Ratio of Average Earnings of Zambian Employee in Different Sectors: 1970-86

	1970	*1972*	*1974*	*1976*	*1978*	*1980*	*1982*	*1985*	*1986*
All Sectors/Agr.	2.46	2.34	2.52	2.45	2.41	2.19	2.43	1.84	1.81
Mining/Agr.	4.43	3.69	3.82	4.16	3.49	3.22	3.23	NA	NA
Manufacturing/Agr.	2.30	2.36	2.41	2.81	2.60	2.05	2.06	NA	NA

Sources: 1970-83 from the World Bank (1993), Table 5, 1985-1986 from Loxlay table 4.7, p80.

The Course of Real Wages in the Formal Sector

The data presented by the World Bank (1993) show that real wages did not fall severely in sectors other than mining before 1980, in spite of the very

[39] Colclough (1989) also reported after considering the rural-urban earnings gap for a number of countries that it 'shared the median ranking with Costa Rica' in 1976. (p.23, and Appendix Table 1).

sharp decline in GNP per capita. This might have been due to the fact that the GDP per capita did not fall as much as GNP, which reflected the effect of the terms of trade decline. However, the situation seemed to have changed in the following years, particularly after 1980. Sharp declines in real wages were experienced in the first half of the eighties while real wages in 1991 were only 30 percent of the level of 1975, and the decline continued dramatically the next year with the continued hyper-inflation.

Two major policy shifts had an impact on the course of real wages. The first was the devaluation of the currency. A major instrument which had led to the relative protection of the real wage in Zambia was the exchange rate, which had shown a slight appreciation in the first half of the seventies, in spite of the decline in the terms of trade. After 1980 the exchange rate was allowed to drift downwards.[40] Since Zambia imported much of its consumption goods, the impact on domestic prices was substantial — the inflation rate doubling to 20 percent per annum in the late seventies and early eighties. It was therefore institutionally easier to achieve real wage declines in an inflationary situation.

Taking the lead in this process was the public sector. For example, 'between 1975 and 1980, workers in the public sector experienced a 16 percent decline in real earnings, ... whilst Zambian employees in the private sector were, on average, 14 percent better off over the period'. (Colclough, p.26).[41] After 1980, wages in all sectors fell in real terms as the inflationary process gathered momentum. The public sector's pay policy took the lead in tightening wage differentials. In real terms higher paid public servants in 1983 received only half of their actual salary of 1975, while the lowest paid employees lost about 10 percent over this period (Colclough, p.26 and Table 15).

After the introduction of a package of policy reforms under an agreement in 1985 with the IMF, Zambia witnessed an acceleration in the erosion of wages under its own reform programs. The package of policy reforms included, along with the standard liberalization measures, the introduction of foreign exchange auction, which led to an acceleration in the depreciation of the kwacha. The spurt in inflation, resulting from a

---

[40] Between 1980 and 1987 the kwacha was devalued by about 80 percent in nominal US$ terms. This exceeded the rate at which Zambia's inflation out-paced that of its trading partners so that the real effective rate was also devalued, by about 60 percent. ..In 1987 the kwacha was stabilized at a rate of K8 to the US dollar because policy makers felt that devaluation was itself helping to generate unacceptably high rates of inflation' (Loxley, pp.29-31). After the agreement with the Bank the kwacha was devalued further and in an explosive way.

[41] The dates were obtained from Meesook et al. (1986, Appendix Table 6.

combination of exchange rate depreciation and monetary undiscipline, led for the first time to a sharp fall in the real value of unskilled and minimum wages. The sharpness of the decline was one of the reasons why, as the government attempted to double the price of maize-meal as part of its commitment to the IMF, led to widespread riots in the copper belt. Coupled with other political protests the result was an abandonment of the reform program and a reversal to the 1987 system of fixed exchange rate and import controls.

Return to Adjustment and its Limited Impact

The new government, which came into being in October 1991, has embarked on a vigorous Structural Adjustment Program in collaboration with the World Bank. The long-term goal of the adjustment program is to reduce inflation and stabilize the economy with a view to stimulate growth, reduced poverty and improve the living standards of households. Since late 1991, the Government has accomplished an extraordinary turnaround in economic policy. In particular, the pace of liberalization has been impressive. Prices have been decontrolled and subsidies (over 10 percent of the budget a few years ago) eliminated; exchange rates and interest rates are market determined; licensing and other quantitative restrictions on imports and exports have been eliminated; and the tariff structure has been compressed and simplified. Parastatal monopolies have ended, marketing is being done by the private sector, and an ambitious privatization program is underway. This has been accompanied by tight monetary controls and overall improvements in fiscal policy. Financial sector reform has also taken place. Among other actions, the Government has made a commitment to reorient or liquidate the three state-owned institutions involved in term finance.

While most economic indicators continue to improve, the external financing gap is widening and overall growth has not yet resumed. Economic events in 1995 are illuminating in this respect. The first two months of 1995 were characterized by a promising surge in economic activity and a rise in business and consumer confidence. These positive developments were cut short, however, by several events, which adversely affected economic performance. First, investor confidence and the financial system were shaken by the insolvency, attempted Government bailout, and eventual closure of one of the country's largest commercial banks. Second, given Zambia's continued dependence on copper, declining production and revenues put a drag on overall economic performance. At the same time, agriculture, the sector which figures prominently in Zambia's growth prospects, performed poorly because of the failure of the harvest over the southern half of the country due to the premature end of the rains coupled with reduced plantings by farmers experiencing credit and cash flow difficulties.

Finally, a fiscal shortfall arose in the second quarter because of overspending on defense and salaries and benefits and lower than expected revenues from tax collection. Despite these difficulties, the Government regained control over the overall budget and the economic program remained basically on track. The events of 1995 and early 1996 illustrate the difficulties Zambia must confront in returning to a sustainable growth path. Despite the reforms, private sector investment has been hampered by high inflation and real interest rates. Concurrently, the prospects for agricultural growth, while promising, have been dimmed by several droughts. Investor confidence also continues to be shaken by periodic slips in fiscal performance, by the accelerating decline in revenues from the economy's mainstay, copper, and by the uncertainties and limitations brought on by the large external debt overhang and by the large external gap.

Incomes in the Rural Sector

Focusing now on rural incomes, policy shifts in recent years have clearly increased the income generated in this sector, compared to the urban economy. Although real average growth averaged only 2 percent a year between 1965 and 1971, it reached 7 percent in 1983-90 (World Bank 1993, p.21). The government's policy of moving towards food sufficiency was met with a good deal of success. At the same time important changes have taken place in the internal terms of trade of the agricultural sector. The barter terms of trade for agriculture, which had fallen by 20 percent between 1970 and 1975, reversed its trend in the early eighties. It increased by 25 percent between 1983 and 1987, but after that agricultural producer prices fell below the inflation rate and by 1990 the barter terms of trade had reverted to the 1970 level. However, after taking into account the increased production, the income terms of trade was at a level double that of 1970 (Loxley Table 4.6, p.79). It should not be perceived necessarily that the level of income of agricultural families had doubled as estimates show that only 25 percent of agricultural production was marketed. Furthermore, to the extent that rural households have their income augmented by off farm activities, and remittances from urban workers, the decline in urban earnings would have reduced the value of this component. It seems clear, however that the rural-urban gap has been compressed, if in fact income inequality within the rural sector had remained unchanged.

We do not have statistics for changing income inequality within the rural sector. However one important aspect of recent developments in the rural sector remains of particular relevance. Traditionally a clear regional bifurcation had developed in the Zambian agricultural economy between the prosperous line-of-rail (LOR) provinces and the others. A majority of the 'emerging' (2-10 hectares) farms-both large and medium size — were located in the LOR provinces, while in 1980, almost all subsistence farms were located in the non-LOR provinces. Almost all the workers in the formal agricultural sector, consisting of large estates, were also located in the LOR provinces. Their average earnings, although a quarter of the wages in the mines, were substantially above that of non-LOR farmers (Loxley, p.11). A development of major significance in the eighties was the production of the maize surplus — the major staple food of Zambia — had moved steadily away from the wealthier LOR provinces to the poorer outlying areas.[42] This trend clearly reduced the degree of rural inequality in Zambia.

The upshot of the discussion is that the rural-urban gap in earnings of workers fell significantly over the period of the wage decline in the eighties. However, recent droughts and the adverse impact on agricultural productivity might have hurt the rural sector in the first half of the nineties.

Comparison of Household Incomes in Rural and Urban Areas

Some data on household incomes by sector have become available from the sample surveys under the aegis of the World Bank — called the Priority Surveys and the Living Conditions Monitoring Surveys. The surveys were conducted in 1991, 1993 and 1996. Selected data on expenditure per adult equivalent units are presented in Table 10.3.

[42] Thus in 1978, the LOR provinces accounted for 80 percent of total maize procurement, whereas by 1986 this had fallen to 70 percent (Prices and Incomes Commission, March 1988) and by 1988 to 66 percent.' (Loxley,p.67).

Table 10.3 Selected Ratios of Expenditure per Adult Equivalent Unit

	1991	*1993*	*1996*
Ratio at median values			
Lusaka/Rural:	5.41	3.90	2.62
Other urban/Rural	3.26	3.10	1.99
All/Rural	2.06	1.54	1.34
Ratios at second deciles			
Lusaka/Rural	9.55	3.63	2.51
Other urban/Rural	4.14	3.70	2.15
All/Rural	1.91	1.36	1.23

Source: Own calculations from survey data.

The ratios from the survey of 1991 seems to give a grossly exaggerated idea of the rural-urban gap. It is almost certainly due to an underestimation of the incomes of rural households, particularly at the lower end of the distribution. This is apparent when we examine the expenditure ratios at the lower and upper end of the distributions in different sectors given in Table 10.4. It is clear by looking at the ratios for the rural distribution in the table that they are quite out of line with the respective value for 1993 and 1996. It shows that the median value is too high relative to the first decile, and so is the value of the 10th decile relative to the median. We should concentrate on the rural-urban differences for the 1993 and 1996 surveys to get a more accurate idea of household expenditure differences.

Table 10.4 Expenditure Ratios at Different Deciles

	1991			*1993*			*1996*		
	Lusaka	Urban	Rural	Lusaka	Urban	Rural	Lusaka	Urban	Rural
Deciles									
D5/D1	4.35	4.13	7.69	5.86	2.99	4.61	3.75	3.17	3.37
D5/D2	2.17	2.53	4.29	2.35	1.83	2.19	2.11	2.02	2.02
D10/D5	5.13	5.34	8.56	4.68	4.26	7.23	6.03	6.05	6.05

It seems that there has been a significant reduction in the rural-urban gap over the first half of the nineties, but even the values for 1993 show that the ratio of expenditure per AEU in the capital city and other urban areas *vis-a-vis* the rural areas were no higher than what was observed for Kenya (see Chapter 8 above). They are higher than the Ghana case, but it is likely that patterns of migration in terms of the prevalence of single or part-household rural-to-urban migrants in East Africa are different from in the

Western regions of the continent. It is probable that if we were able to do (which we were not) the type of analysis of the rural-urban income difference, taking account of differences in family composition, as in the case of Kenya, the gap would turn out to be practically non-existent.

Ogura did a survey of workers in the mining industry of urban Zambia in the late eighties. He found that even at this date most of the mining workers were migrants born in rural areas, the majority of them visited their village homes at least once a year, and most sent remittances home once or twice a year. His conclusion was:

> These figures show present-day migrants are far for being circulatory migrants. But they also show that the village remains the final place where migrants return to live...They have their own and or can find land to cultivate. They are partly modern workers, but at the same time they are partly peasants; thus they are not part of the proletariat. None of the miners in my samples intended to settle down in towns permanently. This might seem surprising at first, but it is not; for although miners are provided accommodations and good facilities, they cannot enjoy them after retirement (p.161).

If this was the situation in the mining industry where labor was most stabilized, other urban occupations, and particularly the large informal sector, must have been the repository of a large volume of unstable, circulatory migrants, whose household straddled the urban and the rural areas. A comparison of incomes per adult equivalent unit among the observed sample of households would thus exaggerate the gap in favor of the urban areas. The average urban household would have a lower burden of dependants because of the pattern of migration — as was discussed in detail in the Kenya case above.

The High Urban Wage Hypothesis — Was it a Myth?

We discussed in the introductory chapter to this part that Zambia had been singled out in the critique by foreign observers as the classic case of labor market distortion. The culprit was the mining industry, where trade union and post-independence state pressures kept wages at a highly inflated level — well above the supply price or alternative earnings of labor in the rural areas — and this high wage spread to other parts of the formal urban sector.

Did the mining sector present a special problem of an excessive wage gap? The data in Table 9.1 show that the average earnings of Zambian mining workers were indeed high i.e., more than 4.5 the agricultural earnings at the beginning of the seventies. However, the level of earnings did begin declining early in the decade. By 1983, this decline had fallen to a level of around three times the agricultural level — evidence of some degree by downward wage flexibility. Wages since then, of course, have shown a relentless downward trend.

But is there any reason to believe that high and rigid wages in the mining and in non-agriculture as whole in the sixties and seventies was a critical factor in the problems of the Zambian economy, which unfolded? Colclough (1989) looked at the level of wages in the non-agricultural sector of Zambia as compared with other countries, which included six African countries. His findings showed that in 1976 the average monthly earnings in the formal non-agricultural sector were two-to-three times the US dollar value of any of the other six sub-Saharan African countries included in the comparison (p. 23). He also noticed that in all the countries with similar or higher per capita income (in official US dollars) included in the sample, the ratio of non-agricultural wages to per capita income was highest for Zambia (Colclough, Appendix table 1, p.38). At the same time the ratio of non-agricultural to agricultural wages did not differ much from the ratios of other countries in the sample. All this led Colclough to conclude that it was not the wage gap in favor of non-agriculture, which was high in Zambia, but the level in the formal wage sector as a whole. What Colclough probably meant, although he did not spell it out, was that the currency was overvalued, in the sense that the official exchange rate was higher than the 'equilibrium' exchange rate. It seems plausible that because of the dominance of copper in the external trade account, Zambia might have indeed suffered from a variant of the 'Dutch Disease' following the upsurge in the price of copper in the late sixties. Since a great deal of Zambia's food were imported the overvalued exchange rate was crucial to the maintenance of a high real wage in the formal sector. The problem of the exchange rate might have been confused with that of high urban wages.

As we have seen the collapse of copper prices throughout the seventies made Zambia's external accounts vulnerable and the attempt to adjust to the declining terms of trade through adjustments in the exchange rate was very sluggish. Although there were a series of devaluations after 1975 these were not sufficient to compensate for the differential in the inflation rate between Zambia and her trading partners. Given the importance of imports in domestic consumption, a more active devaluation would probably have triggered an erosion of the real wage rate, which was not likely to affect the higher salaried workers. Nevertheless, the rigidity in the wage in dollar terms experienced through the seventies, did little to increase incentives to engage in non-mineral export production.

Another relevant point was the dependence of the industry for its skilled labor on a large number of expatriates whose earning far exceeded that of the native workers. Productivity and morale considerations could have prevented the lowering of the native workers' level of earnings in the mining sector. There has indeed been a slow response to incentives for skill development among Zambian workers, but this aspect of the low elasticity of supply of skilled workers is a different labor market problem from that of elevated and rigid wages.

It is possible that the exaggerated perception of the rural-urban wage-gap might have been blinded foreign advisers to donor agencies as to the consequences of the drastic fall in formal sector wages, for which the program was at least partially responsible — the absolute loss in welfare of the urban workers was striking.[43] Besides the program had little hope of succeeding since it hurt drastically the political consensus within the ruling party.

This evidence prompts one to agree with the judgment of long term observers of the African scene — Loxley and Colclough — that the attempt to accelerate the pace of change in policies witnessed in the early eighties was counter-productive and resulted only in unnecessary economic suffering. As Steel concludes: 'In retrospect, the pace of reforms exceeded what could be politically sustained, given resource constraints that prevented imports and domestic production from increasing fast enough to forestall inflationary pressures and rising inflation' (Steel, p.164).[44]

Sierra Leone

Evolution of the Economy

Sierra Leone's external trade was dominated by two mineral products — diamonds and iron ore. The share of diamonds, in total exports, peaked at around 65 percent in the middle seventies, although, in terms of the volume exported, the peak occurred earlier in the seventies. The mining sector contributed about 30 percent of GDP in 1970. Considering the existence of

[43] Loxley calculated the cost of a food budget of minimum standards suggested by the ILO/JASPA in 1980, covering the minimum nutritional requirements of a family of six- two adults and four children. 'Between 1980 and 1986 average formal sector earnings doubled; meanwhile the cost of the minimum food basket almost quadrupled' (Loxley, p.57). Real wages in the formal sector fell much more after 1986.

[44] Zambia returned to a more constructive relationship with the donor agencies in 1989. In the absence of detailed information on the post-adjustment period, no attempt has been made to bring the story up to date.

a large subsistence sector, it is understandable that mining dominated the monetized sector, contributing as much as 30 percent of GDP in 1970. The share of manufacturing in total GDP in 1970 was under 5 percent. The stagnation and decline of the mining sector after the early seventies marked a change in the fortunes of the economy. For about the first ten years after independence in 1963, Sierra Leone was considered one of the African success stories, with GDP growing at a rate of around 4 percent per annum. This growth trend seems to have halted due to the stagnation and decline — both in price and quantity — of the mining sector, in particular, diamonds. For example, in volume terms diamond production changed from growing at a rate of 6.6 percent per year in 1961-69 to declining at the rate of 14.5 percent in 1970-79.[45] At the same time the external terms of trade of the country — in spite of yearly fluctuations — had declined at an annual rate of 2.2 percent in the 20-year period 1966-86.[46] Sierra Leone, like a number of countries, was heavily dependant on the export of one or two commodities. When the international demand for such commodities declined followed by an increase in oil costs and interest payments, Sierra Leone was faced with this dismal picture of a declining long-term terms of trade.

During the first half of the eighties, the economic situation declined drastically. Budgetary revenues fell sharply — over 16 percent of GDP in 1980-81 to only 5.4 percent in 1985-86. There were both external and internal reasons for this severe reduction in the revenue base, e.g., the reduction in imports and official diamond sales reduced the tax base. Moreover, the collection efficiency of the government departments also eroded as declining efficiency in the public sector became an endemic problem. The proximate cause of the erosion of the morale and efficiency of the public sector was accelerating inflation which eroded the real purchasing power of the civil servants, even as the government tried to win domestic support by continuously expanding public employment. The government was therefore forced to cut expenditure drastically, but in spite of these cuts budget deficits did not fall as a percentage of GDP between 1980-81 and 1986-87, leading to accelerating inflation, which peaked at 170 percent in 1986-87. At the same time, the expenditure cuts were affecting capital expenditures disproportionately, causing serious decay in the economy's infrastructure.

---

[45] Kallon (1990), Table A5-8b.

[46] Kallon (1990) estimated the following equation from the World Tables, 1987.
log (terms of trade)= 4.946 - 0.022t (130.2) 6.6).
R^2= 0.076 (t-statistics in parenthesis).

The government made several attempts to restore macroeconomic stability with support from the IMF Extended Fund Facility in 1981-82 and a standby arrangement in 1984-5. However, these programs were cancelled before they had run their course because agreed targets could not be met and it was not until 1992 that relations with the multilateral agencies were fully restored. Throughout the 1980s, during the acrimonious dialogue with the Fund, several aspects of economic policies favored by the Fund were pursued with varying degrees of enthusiasm.

Two areas of policy in which multilateral concerns were most strongly focused were the exchange rate and agricultural price policies. Both types of price distortion were perceived as policies of 'urban bias' impoverishing the rural sector to favor the urban. As the World Bank report of 1993 stated: 'In order to protect, in particular, the urban groups from price increases for imports caused by a depreciating currency, the Government resorted to exchange rate controls' (p.2). Similarly the operations of the Sierra Leone Rice Corporation, which operated the marketing of rice — both domestic and imported — and the Produce Marketing Board (SLPMB) came under strong criticisms for setting producer prices too low, thereby taxing the rural sector in order that the urban sector might benefit.

Certain trends in the economy during its years of decline were certainly strong enough to suggest the 'urban bias'. A rapidly expanding parallel market in foreign exchange developed, often offering rates of at least four times that of the official rate. This type of over-valuation would favor importers more than exporters — and since a majority of importers are among some urban groups, an overvaluation of the currency could lead to 'an urban bias'. But as we shall see, one has to be careful when specifying the type of urban groups which is 'favored'.

Another result from the over-valuation was the rise of parallel markets in other traded goods. The traditional exports of diamond and other minerals declined, not just because of external market conditions, but also because of smuggling through unofficial channels as the official price fell drastically. The dampening effect of over-valuation on official exports of cocoa and coffee seems to have been reinforced by declining real procurement prices offered by the state monopolies. Increasingly larger proportions of these exports were alleged to have found their way into the parallel market. Sierra Leone has been a net importer of the major staple, rice, but while between 1961 and 1978, rice imports accounted for about 5 percent of total supply, during the next decade the percentage dropped below 10 percent in only two years; even though in several years the percentage was well above this level (Weeks 1992, Table 7.4, p.95). The trend, occurring in a period of falling per capita income, suggests significant decline in marketed surplus from the farm sector. Perhaps part of this decline was due to the disincentive effects of low real prices offered by the marketing board.

Attempts to correct the overvaluation of the exchange rate were not very successful for much of the decade of the eighties. Although the nominal exchange rate was changed in stages from 1.18 Leone to the dollar in 1980-81 to 5.20 Leone in 1985-6 the real effective exchange rate doubled, and the ratio of the parallel rate to the official peaked at 3.8 Leone (World Bank 1993, Table 9.1). The unsustainable balance of payments situation forced the government to accept the IMF conditionality in 1986. The set of conditions for the loan included, among other things, the provision of a 'clean float' of the exchange rate.[47] The immediate events following the clean float did not produce the stabilization hoped for the economy. The Leone sank from 5.7 on 27 June when the float was instituted to 30 to the dollar on 26 September (Weeks 1992, p.131). Inflation accelerated, leading to a spiral of devaluation and inflation, which threatened to spin out of control. A fixed rate was reimposed and IMF support was withdrawn, when the government, faced with massive inflation, was unable to respect the ceiling of monetary expansion. Economic and administrative institutions were, however, by this time too weak to support a fixed rate and rigid exchange control. It was reported that these control measures were by-passed by the majority of the business community. Since many exports shifted to unofficial channels, the pressure on the balance of payments continued and so did inflation.

Faced with acute economic instability, in early 1989, the government returned to the policy of liberalization in the foreign exchange and domestic trade areas. Relationship with the donor agencies was gradually mended, so that by the Spring of 1992 both the IMF and the Bank had returned to financial support of the economy. The World Bank reported that 'the structural reforms implemented by the government since 1989 are more far-reaching than the programs implemented by many other countries receiving support from the international community' (1993 p.6). It is too early to predict a successful turn around of the economy, though the rate of inflation and as of devaluation had declined markedly.

The Course of the Rural-Urban Wage Gap

How did the rural-urban earnings gap change during these difficult years of

---

[47] By a 'clean float' the Fund meant a process of exchange rate determination in which the government or central bank did not intervene at all.

spiraling inflation and difficult adjustment? In 1993, Weeks had compiled time series data purporting to show the change in the ratio of incomes of urban wage earners to those of rural farmers over an extended period of time. Weeks' Table is reproduced here as Table 10.5. His data show a startling decline in the relative earnings of urban wage earners — from a peak of 1.59 which the ratio attained in 1970-71, it declined precipitously to about a third in the mid-eighties. Several questions, however, remain about the accuracy of these figures, pertaining both to the *level* and the magnitude of the downward *trend* in the ratio.

First, on the sources of the data collected, Weeks comments: 'The figures incorporate an assumption that households do not have secondary sources of income. Thus, it is more precise to identify the calculations as farm income per household and wage income for a household with only one wage earner and no non-wage income'. With falling real wages in the formal sector, urban households with wage income, would increasingly diversify their sources of income, with some or all members of the household participating in income earning activity outside the formal wage sector. *Ipso facto* remittances which have been an important source of off-farm income of rural households must have fallen over time. Thus, the trend in the rural-urban ratio shown in Weeks' table cannot be used to demonstrate the course of the ratio of household income levels in the two sectors.

Secondly, some pertinent questions remain regarding the level of incomes of the groups being observed. It is likely that the urban group whose earnings are taken from special earnings surveys, conducted by the Ministry of Labor in Sierra Leone, could represent a subset of the urban population — excluding entrepreneurs and other high income groups.[48] The rural income level, on the other hand, is derived as average agricultural income of all farm households from the total income reported in the National accounts. Given the high degree of inequality in farm holdings — to which Weeks draws attention elsewhere in his study (1993, pp.16-21) — the mean income of all farm households would be well above the alternative earnings of groups seeking work as urban wage earners. The latter is best approximated by the first quartile, or at most the mode of the distribution of incomes of farm households.

Thirdly, Weeks has deflated both the urban wage and the farm income

[48] The results from the surveys carried out by the Central Statistical Office of Sierra Leone were reported to the ILO and published in their *YEARBOOK OF LABOR STATISTICS*. The following definition of the persons covered is found in their *Statistical Sources and Methods* (ILO, Volume 2,p.181): Working proprietors, wage earners, and salaried employees in establishments employing six or more persons.

series by the same cost-of-living series i.e., that pertaining to the working classes basket of consumption in Freetown, the capital city of Sierra Leone. Presumably, this series reflects the subsidized price of food grains in the city, but to the extent that this is so, it underestimates the extent to which the farm price index had increased over time. Thus the real value of farm production, and hence the relative real income per farmer, is overestimated.

Table 10.5 A Comparison of Farm Income and Wages and Related Magnitudes, 1963-87

			Ratio: Wage to Farm Income		*Real Income (1973=100)*		
	Farm family Income	Average Agr. Wage	Per family	Per capita	Farm	Wage	Cost of Living (Freetown)
	1	2	3	4	5	6	7
1963-64	257	188	0.73	0.97	103	73	58
1964-65	264	220	0.83	1.10	95	75	62
1965-66	269	237	0.88	1.17	92	95	63
1966-67	267	367	138	1.82	88	113	67
1967-68	263	379	1.44	1.91	83	107	68
1968-69	271	353	1.30	1.72	83	110	70
1969-70	267	415	1.55	2.06	80	116	75
1970-71	274	435	1.59	2.10	77	117	73
1971-72	286	441	1.54	2.04	82	114	80
1972-73	345	441	1.28	1.69	90	106	87
1973-74	413	456	1.10	1.46	100	100	100
1974-75	636	486	0.76	1.01	133	92	120
1975-76	738	537	0.73	0.96	129	86	140
1976-77	931	590	0.63	0.84	140	81	152
1977-78	995	601	0.60	0.80	138	76	167
1978-79	1146	627	0.55	0.72	144	73	192
1979-80	1185	702	0.59	0.78	130	78	217
1980-81	1308	926	0.71	0.94	127	77	268
1981-82	1842	940	0.51	0.68	144	67	340
1982-83	2222	1108	0.50	0.66	137	52	572
1983-84	2889	1142	0.40	0.52	106	35	955
1984-85	5247	1430	0.27	0.36	115	26	1685
1985-86	6833	1891	0.28	0.37	85	32	3048
1986-87		3318					
1987-88		5164					

Source: *Weeks (1993), Table II9, p.23.*

Nevertheless, while we can dispute the startling conclusion of the data in Table 10.4, in that urban wage levels had fallen so far below rural farm income, the two qualitative conclusions suggested by the figures are valid and important. The first is that the extent of the rural-urban earnings gap had been exaggerated; and secondly, there was a marked reduction of the differential over the last two decades.

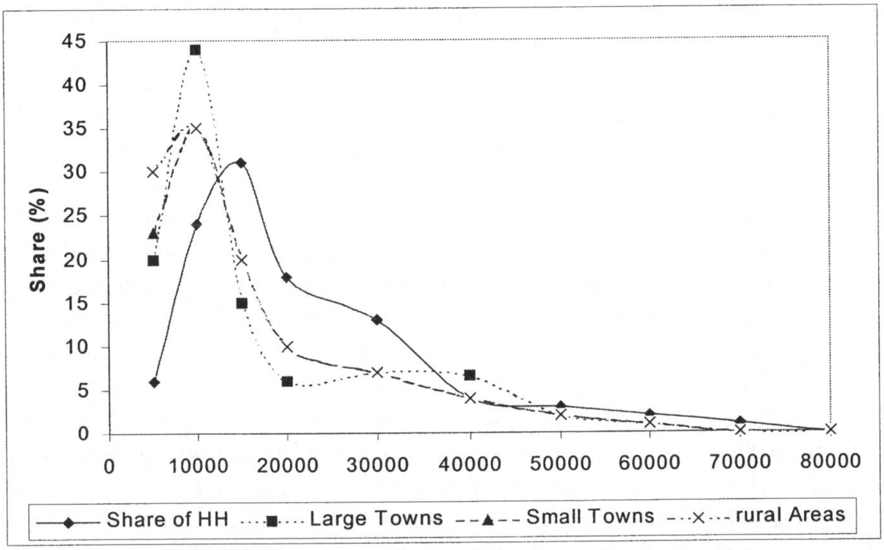

Figure 10.1 Distributions of Monthly Household Expenditure in Sierra Leone

World Bank (1993, Table 4.3, p.61) reports the distributions of monthly household expenditure for rural areas, small towns and large towns for 1989-90. These data came from a sample survey of households conducted by the Central Statistical Office. The distributions are graphed in Figure 10.1. It is seen that the distribution for large towns lies to the right of those for the rural areas — and the small towns. The modal value of household expenditure in large towns is 66 percent above that in either the small towns or the rural areas. While there is no suggestion from these data that urban earnings have fallen below rural incomes, the differential in 1992 could not be very large either in favor of large towns, since one can expect to see a higher cost of living in the latter (while in other countries have been measured to be in the range of 50-60 percent).

Côte d'Ivoire

Côte d'Ivoire is a recent settlement territory, populated by more than sixty different tribes. Migration of labor — both domestic and international — has been an important feature of the economy. There are important domestic flows of labor from north to south and from east to west. The north-south migration is a southern region's more developed economic state — and in particular the mythical power of attraction of the capital city, Abidjan. The movement from east to west is a 'frontier agriculture' phenomenon, labor opening up newly cleared forest land to grow coffee and cocoa.

International migration also has been a persistent phenomenon in Côte d'Ivoire, contributing significantly to its labor market scene. As the French colonial system seems to have paid less attention to the education of Ivorians, some skilled workers came from neighboring countries with better education to work for administration and other sectors. At the end of the fifties the vast majority of urban employment was in the hands of the French or non-Ivorian workers. At the same time a movement of *unskilled* African workers from Upper Volta (now Burkina Faso) was generated by the colonial government in the framework of the *Travail Obligatoire (forced labor)*. Hence, during the colonial era international migration of skilled and unskilled labor was prominent — the latter being numerically much more important.

After independence, only the migration of unskilled labor remained. Politically Ivorian reaction against the immigration of skilled African workers became strong. But the importance of continuing international migration is revealed by the fact that in 1978 the proportion of non-Ivorians was about 25.5 percent of the total workforce — vast majority of the newcomers came to the South, thus adding to the domestic migration stream in the same direction. The proportion of foreigners to the workforce seems to have increased somewhat by 1992. A country background study for the RPED surveys shows the foreign component being 60 percent in 1992.[49]

The large volume of international migration has two consequences for the economy: first, it is an important component of the fast population growth observed in Côte d'Ivoire, estimated to be accounting for 1 percent of each year's population growth (Berthelemy and Bourguignon, Chapter 1); secondly, it provided an elastic supply of low income workers which kept labor earnings down in the agricultural and informal sectors of the

---

[49] CERDI (1996), chart 3,12)

economy.

Despite an impressive urban growth, a large part of the Ivorian population lives in rural areas. The share of the urban population increased from 32 to 51 percent between 1960 and 1995. (Table 10.6)

Table 10.6 Population in Côte d'Ivoire

Years	*Growth Rate*	*% Urban*
1960	3.1	32.2
1970	3.7	33.8
1980	4.1	38.8
1990	3.7	47.4
1995	4.7	51.2

Source: World Bank 1980 and 1993.

The Macro-Economic Evolution

Côte d'Ivoire experienced its golden age of growth between 1965 and 1975. The rate of growth was an impressive 8 percent, based on an open economy both with respect to trade and capital flows. The impetus to the growth came from exports, first of coffee, cocoa and timber, and subsequently of some manufactured goods. Government policy wooed foreign capital investment and deviated from strict *laissez faire* to provide special incentives, including tax concessions, cheap credit and protection of the markets of foreign investors. By 1975 foreign investment accounted for a staggering 75 percent of total investment in industry (Mylteka 1984).

There was a major turn around in government policies between 1973 and 1975, as policies shifted to import substitution in industry with a large participation of the state in investment and operation of this sector. As it happened the shift in policy coincided with a boom in the coffee and cocoa markets internationally. The country's terms of trade increased from 96.7 in 1975 to 152.6 in 1977. The state marketing agency, controlling the export of the commodities, kept producer prices stable and accumulated large surplus for government revenue — amounting to 16 percent of GDP in 1977. The familiar story of misconception of the temporary boom as a permanent one followed, inducing the government to embark on an ambitious policy of investment under a regime of tariffs and quantitative restrictions.

The terms of trade decline after 1977 was sharp, reaching the level of 1975 early in the eighties. The post-boom low level of saving — the gross national saving in the country fell from 25 percent of GDP in 1977 to 6.8 percent in 1981 — combined with poor export performance to ensure that part of the continuing investment level had now to be financed through foreign borrowing, at the high interest rates of the early eighties. This was at the heart of the macro-economic imbalance which soon engulfed Côte d'Ivoire. The fiscal deficit, a rising real exchange rate and a serious balance of payments in the current account provided the familiar crisis which could be tackled only with serious measures of structural adjustment.

The period 1981-86 has been referred to as the period of partial adjustment (Demery 1994). Despite an apparent recovery in 1985-89 — the real GDP growth rate was about 2.2 percent during this period — the economy was unable to cope with a further decline in the terms of trade which began in 1987 (after a slight recovery in the previous three years) and continued till 1993. GDP growth was negative in most of this period. Given the substantial population growth the rate of decline in GDP per capita was impressive (Table 10.7). However, the GDP growth resumed following the devaluation of CFA franc in 1994.

An important issue for Côte d'Ivoire, apart from the usual macroeconomic imbalances, was the tying of the local currency to the French franc in the CFA zone. Since the country did not have a rate of inflation higher than its trading partners, the REER appreciation until 1993 seen in Table 10.7 was mainly due to the appreciation of the French franc relative to the dollar. The CFA franc was devalued in 1994 by 50 percent to ease the problems of recovery and led to an immediate fall in the REER.

The Evolution of the Structure of Employment and Labor Markets

It is not very difficult to infer from what has already been discussed above that the labor markets in Côte d'Ivoire has experienced a continuous pressure from the supply side of the market. The growth in population has been in excess of 3.5 percent over the entire period. Participation rates have been high and are higher on average for poor Ivorian households and in the rural areas. They have risen significantly in Abidjan as poverty levels have increased. Economic pressures have resulted in excess labor force participation by under age children in family farms and enterprises.

Table 10.7 Macroeconomic Indicators 1980-96

	1980-4	*1985-9*	*1990-7*	*1990*	*1991*	*1992*	*1993*	*1994*	*1995*	*1996*	*1997*
Real growth rates % p.a.											
GDP	1.0	2.2	2.4	-1.1	0.0	-0.2	-0.	2.0	8.0	5.8	6.0
GDP per capita	-2.7	-1.7	0.1	-4.83	-3.59	-3.51	-3.12	-0.95	5.21	3.15	3.49
Prices											
Annual Δ in CPI (%)	10.9	5.3	7.8	-0.64	1.58	4.22	2.55	32.27	7.65	3.49	3.02
REER (1990=100)	90.0	94.5	84.5	100	96.5	100.8	99.2	60.9	70.2	70.5	77.8

Source: African Development Indicators.

All major components of demand for goods and services — consumption, investment and exports — have contracted in real terms from 1985 to 1993, with a modest upturn in the very recent years of economic recovery. The period of decline necessarily translated into lower derived demand for labor. Estimates of employment from the Ministry of Employment quoted by the World Bank (1997, p.57) shows that employment in the formal sector shrank significantly — its share halved from 14 percent in 1980 to 11 percent in 1985 to 7 percent today. The agricultural sector also decreased its share — from 67 to 60 percent over this period. The bulk of the increase in employment thus took place in the informal sector.

What happened to labor earnings in the different sectors during this process of decline? In urban areas evidence from the *Banque des Donnes Financieres* is inconclusive, suggesting that real wages were maintained in the formal sector (World Bank 1997, p.58). Lavy and Newman (1989), however, have shown that at least in the eighties real wages did fall, after one controlled for the effects of changed average seniority of workers and the change in the average level of human capital. However, even in the analysis reported by Lavy and Newman the decline in wages do not appear to be as much as might be expected from an overview of the supply-and demand situation in the labor market.

Even though there was some downward rigidity of wages in the formal sector, the vast majority of job-seekers in the urban areas were absorbed in the informal sector where labor earnings are flexible. Incomes fell across sectors both in rural and urban areas. This can be seen from work that has been done on the incidence of poverty based on household surveys spanning the years 1985 to 1995. Table 10.8 reproduced the data on the percentage of households below the poverty line (defined as CFAF 75 Th. at 1985 prices).

Table 10.8 Incidence of Poverty by Region 1985-95

Poverty incidence(%)	*1985*	*1993*	*March-May 95*
Abidjan	0.7	4.8	20.2
Other towns	8.0	31.3	28.6
East Forest rural	15.2	37.3	41.0
Savannah rural	25.9	48.5	49.4
West Forest rural	1.6	35.6	50.1
All Côte d'Ivoire	11.1	32.3	36.8

Source: World Bank 1997, pp. 9,12.

It is clear that urban poverty, which was uncommon in secondary towns and almost non-existent in Abidjan in the eighties, has steadily emerged as an important phenomenon, showing the decline in incomes in the urban economy. The incidence of poverty has increased in the rural areas too, but since poverty was already present in a big way in 1985 in this sector, we can clearly infer from these data that incomes, particularly at the lower part of the distribution, has fallen faster in the urban areas. Recent policies including the devaluation of 1994 have at least permitted a stabilization, and possibly a small reversal of earlier trends in secondary towns, the incidence of poverty clearly rose in Abidjan between 1993 and 1995.

It is generally agreed that it is the decline of the formal sector, together with continued increase in the flow of job seekers in the urban areas that has contributed to the growth in urban poverty. The urban population of working age grew by over 70 percent in the decade 1985-95, while the demand for labor fell with the downward course of the economy. The difference in the degree of downward rigidity in labor earnings between the formal and the informal sectors is revealed by the difference in poverty incidence in 1995 (in percentage of total households) among different socio-economic groups as follows:[50]

Table 10.9 Incidence of Poverty among Different Socioeconomic Groups in 1995 (Percentage of Total Households)

Modern sector employee	*7.5*
Public sector employee	14.0
Informal sector employee	31.0
Self-employed in informal sector	29.3
Food crop producers	58.4

The Rural-Urban Earnings Gap

We can explore the nature of the rural-urban earnings gap in a little more detail from the analysis household surveys 1985-88, which were available to us. To put the conditions at this time in perspective, we note that the downward pressures on income was already under way though not quite as severe as in the nineties. The poverty incidence for the country as a whole increased from 11.1 to 17.8. Almost all of this increase was due to fall in incomes at the lower end of the distribution. Per capita consumption had

[50] The socio-economic groups have been classified by the occupation of the head of the household. The figures are from World Bank 1997, p.14.

declined by 16 percent between 1979 and 1985 and had been at this level over the 1985-89 period. However, the income share of the lowest quintile had jumped from 5.4 to 7.3 percent.

Table 10.10 presents the ratios of income in Abidjan and the rural areas, and Table 10.11 the ratios for other urban and rural.

Table 10.10 Ratios of Income of Abidjan to Rural Households

	Median		*1st Quartile*	
Category	1985	1988	1985	1988
Household Income	1.60	1.62	1.71	1.38
Per AEU Income	1.49	1.39	1.27	1.27
Per capita Income	1.71	1.54	1.51	1.43
Per Earner Income	1.70	1.83	1.73	1.88

Table 10.11 Ratios of Income of Other Urban to Rural Households

	Median		*1st Quartile*	
Category	1985	1988	1985	1988
Household Income	1.29	1.25	1.14	1.08
Per AEU Income	1.03	1.09	0.96	0.96
Per capita Income	1.19	1.14	1.05	1.11
Per earner Income	1.30	1.38	1.13	1.39

The data presented show rather a small income gap between Abidjan and the rural areas and even smaller gap between the other towns and the rural sector. Mostly the gap seems to be smaller for low-income households (as given by the first quartile values). Evidently, the labor mobility between rural and urban areas was sufficiently strong to keep income levels more or less at par particularly in other towns and villages. The Abidjan-rural differential might also be virtually non-existent in real terms, if we take account of cost-of-living difference (on which we have no information). The high incomes which might have been maintained in the protected formal sector had little effect on the population of urban areas as a whole. Lastly, there is no strong trend to show any significant change between 1985 and 1998.

An important point emerging from the table is that the income per adult equivalent unit shows smaller rural-urban difference than the per earner or per household difference. This is exactly the opposite of what was found in the Kenya case discussed in Chapter 8. Thus, while in Kenya the dependent-earner ratio is *smaller* in town showing the prevalence of single migrants or migrants with only part of their household in the urban areas, the Côte d'Ivoire case is exactly the opposite. It is the urban households, which have a higher burden of dependency. Clearly, migration is either of a more permanent type or the incidence of non-permanent migration (with smaller families) is equal or even somewhat more important in the rural areas. This is indeed not impossible when we recollect the point made above about the importance of labor migration from across the border is quite important in the rural economy of Côte d'Ivoire.

The data on the size of the household and its earning strength were analyzed to see which of the two alternatives seem more likely. The results are given in Table 10.12. It is clear from the data given in Table 10.12 that the incidence of non-permanent migration is of little importance either in the rural or the urban areas. The proportion of households with 1 or 2 members is quite small. In fact the distribution of households by size are very similar in all three areas, suggesting there is no differential impact of migration patterns. What is important in the rural-urban comparison is the larger proportion of workers in rural households. The burden of dependency is *lower* in the rural areas because of the greater participation of women and children in economic activity.

Table 10.12 Household Size and its Earning Strength by Area, 1988

Area	*Mean Size of household*	*Mean No. of workers*	*Distribution of HHs by size (%)*					*Distribution of HHs by No. of workers*					
			1	2-3	4-5	6-7	7+	0	1	2	3	4	5+
Abidjan	6.40	1.39	8	15	24	21	32	9	56	26	6	1	1
Other Towns	6.84	1.89	9	16	19	18	38	8	42	27	12	5	5
Rural areas	6.54	2.96	5	19	23	19	34	5	19	29	18	13	17

Source: Household Survey CILSS 1988, own calculations.

Conclusion to Part III

This part has presented five case studies — two detailed and three shorter accounts where the available data were limited — to provide some indication of the changing levels of labor earnings in different sectors of the economy. The motivation for the study was the hypothesis strongly maintained in the seventies that a large wage gap created in the post independence period in favor of the urban sector, though institutional intervention in the labor market, created severe labor market distortions and was a major cause for the decline of the economy witnessed since the mid-seventies.

The institutional intervention elevating wages in the urban economy could, of course, only occur in the formal sector of such economies. Our review of the evidence in all five countries brings out two points. First, the formal urban wage level has experienced a long-term decline, with the possible exception of Côte d'Ivoire (for which conclusive evidence either way is unavailable) — in some cases a precipitous one. Thus formal urban sector wages have not in any country shown a downward rigidity, even though, in most cases, it is the high rate of inflation which has been the mechanism which brought about the real wage decline. On this point, the evidence of the country case studies fully substantiate the finding drawn from statistics for a large number of countries reported by international agencies, and analyzed in Part II.

Secondly, the employment growth in the formal sector has been sluggish, and negative in some cases. However, increase in the urban labor force has been pronounced (with the sole exception of Ghana), most of the additional labor force being absorbed in the informal sector of the economy. The evidence from the detailed Kenya and Ghana case studies suggest that earnings in the urban informal sector have increased significantly relative to the formal, though in the case of Kenya formal sector earnings were still substantially higher than the urban informal (even when we control for measurable human capital factors) in the late eighties.

The rural-urban earnings gap thus have to be considered not just with reference to the urban formal sector, but for the urban economy as a whole in which the informal sector has been increasing its relative importance for at least three decades. We have used data from household surveys for all the five countries to throw some quantitative light on the rural-urban income differences taking all sectors into account. The major conclusion emerging from this review is that there is substantial difference in the nature of the observed gap between East African (Kenya and Zambia in this case) and West African countries (Ghana, Sierra Leone and Côte d'Ivoire). This difference, moreover, is related to the different patterns of rural-to-urban migration observed in these two regions.

In the East African countries there is a substantial migration of single male workers to the urban areas, and of migrants who divide their time between urban and rural areas with some members of the household left in the villages at any point in time. Thus, the urban economy contains a large number of households with a low dependent-earner ratio. The large rural-urban income gap observed per earner taking all households together can then be illusory, because it does not take account of the fact that a part of the burden of dependency of the average household found in the urban sector is not accounted for because it is left in the rural sector. Household surveys do not take account of the total household when it is split in this way between rural and urban areas. When we did a detailed examination of the urban-rural income gap for a potentially stable migrant who would have the normal dependent-urban ratio of a mature household in town, the apparent gap disappeared.

This pattern of rural-urban migration does not seem to be prevalent in West Africa. The Ghana and Côte d'Ivoire data suggest that the typical size of the household is the same in the two sectors, though the dependency ratio is *higher* in town, because typically there is less earning opportunity for some members in the urban sector e.g., women and children. Thus, the differential in income per earner in favor of the urban areas would be reduced if we consider income per adult equivalent unit — as was seen to be the case of Côte d'Ivoire.

The review of the available material on the rural-urban earnings gap in Africa suggests that, even when the gap was at its peak in the early seventies, its real magnitude, from the point of view of a labor system, was almost certainly exaggerated. The proximate reasons for this exaggeration was the misperception of commentators — like Turner — of the reasons for the rapid increase in formal sector wages in post-colonial African countries. It might have been more appropriate for such commentators to argue that the wage hikes needed to move from a migratory to a stable labor system had overshot its targets. However, there is no concrete argument, let alone evidence, put forward on this point.[51]

The major reason for the compression of the differential in the years since the seventies is that urban wages have been reduced in real terms by the inflationary process and inflationary price increases have only a limited effect on the welfare of small farmers who participate marginally in non-subsistence activities. The structural adjustment programs have also sought to increase the producer prices of farmers. Such efforts have succeeded to some extent. The Ghana case study shows that these measures have led to a significant fall in the incidence of poverty (low incomes) in the rural areas, and in secondary towns other than the capital city, while poverty seems to have increased in Accra. Ghana seems to be a unique case in our sample of countries where, consistent with the relative increase in incomes in the rural areas, there seems to have been a reverse movement of migrants from the capital city to other urban and the rural sector.

More detailed studies of internal migration flows in African countries are needed to see if the Ghana case is observed in other countries. It is perhaps more usual to equate the African stereotype with what was observed in Côte d'Ivoire in Chapter 10 — a continued movement of population to the capital city and other large conglomerates, despite falling incomes and rising incidence of poverty in these areas. We found that the difference in incomes at the median and at the 1st quartile between urban areas and the rural sector was minimal. It should be pointed out that this finding is not necessarily in conflict with the observed net flows of labor into the capital city. The differences in *marginal* income, or more likely the expectation of marginal income, which govern migration decisions, might still favor the capital city. In some cases such as Kenya, the distribution of income might be more unequal in the rural areas, and further absorption of labor in the low-income sector might be perceived to be difficult. Finally, we should reemphasize the point that in East Africa, in particular, a substantial portion of the rural-to-urban migration is that of circulatory flows. The urban informal sector offers an opportunity for temporary migrants to augment their total household income through participation in the urban informal sector for part of their working life.

---

[51] It is surprising to say the least that a Professor of Industrial Relations from Cambridge University should be so unaware of the recommendations of commissions of Enquiry appointed by his own country not more than perhaps 15 years ago.

Part IV:
Impact of Wage Decline

Introduction

Decline in average manufacturing wages documented in the Parts II and III have important potential consequences for the trends in labor productivity in this sector. It has been argued in Chapter 3 above that one of the major arguments for the wage hike in the immediate post-colonial years in sub-Saharan Africa was that the change in the labor system from the migratory to a more stabilized one inducing substantial increase in labor efficiency, so that wage costs per unit of output might not increase proportionately, and might even fall in the long run. It is possible that the persistent wage decline since the seventies might have worked in the other direction and reduced labor efficiency. If urban households have been forced by the decline in wages to revert, at least partly, to the old system of migratory labor — as indeed the Kenya case study suggests has happened — then we are back to the world of the Carpenter Commission and its concerns about the impact of labor instability on productivity. It can be hypothesized that inter-sectoral mobility and the transport system have developed so much in the years since the Carpenter Commission produced its report, that a household could cope with the falling formal sector wage by devoting more of the labor time of its members to different sectors of the economy. In this case the fall in wages will not lead to a significantly higher labor turnover and fall in productivity in the urban formal sector. But such thoughts remain at the moment as hypotheses. Case studies are needed to throw light on the impact of real wage decline on labor turnover and productivity, as well as on the labor market adjustments of households.

For a study of trends in productivity over time we need good time series data on labor, the capital stock and value added. One country, Kenya does have such data. This material enables us to consider the evolution of this sector over the seventies and the eighties for at lest one country. But before coming to this case study, we need to address one important issue about the impact of the decline on average real wage on the workers' standard of living. Decline in average real earnings is not the same thing as the decline in the real earnings of individual earnings. It is the latter, which is of relevance to the labor efficiency of the workers. The existence of some longitudinal series on the lifetime earnings of workers obtained through the workers' survey in the RPED data set enables us to address the question of the course of real earnings of individual workers over their career to date. The data are available for seven countries, including Kenya. We begin with this analysis in Chapter 11.

11 Change in Earnings over the Lifetime of Workers

This chapter analyzes the material contained in the RPED data sets on the lifetime change in earnings of the workers surveyed. Every worker interviewed was asked to recall the level of his initial earnings. The question was simply: 'What was your wage/salary when you started?' The question was about total earnings, not distinguishing between base wages and allowances. Also the way it was formulated, the initial earnings were those enjoyed when the worker joined the current firm, not his initial earnings in the industry or labor market concerned. Thus, when sorted by cohorts, the material gives an account of the change in earnings over the career of the worker in the firm concerned.

The material is valuable because it is very difficult to find longitudinal data on trends in wages in African manufacturing. The change in earnings of the sampled workers over their career in the firm goes some way towards filling this gap. The change reported would reflect two effects: (i) the trends in earnings in the economy as whole. These trends are to a high degree influenced by the trend in GDP, inflation rate, manufacturing output growth and so on; and (ii) the experience-earnings profile of the worker in the firm concerned, as influenced by his upward mobility within the firm, and also the firm-specific changes in the wage structure. There is no easy way of separating these two effects in the data set we have. However, we will try to shed some more light on the factors involved in the regression results reported later in the chapter.

Before proceeding to these results, we present the overall picture of trend in earnings, separating the sample by cohorts of employment in the current firm in each country. The data are given in Tables 11.1 for the whole sample, and for white and blue-collar occupations in the following two tables.

Table 11.1 Average Annual Percentage Changes in Real Wage

Cohort	*Cameroon*	*Côte d'Ivoire*	*Ghana*	*Kenya*	*Tanzania*	*Zambia*	*Zimbabwe*
Overall	-1.64 (1449)	-1.23 (1015)	1.25 (1228)	-3.66 (2300)	-2.76 (1079)	-10.71 (1930)	-0.12 (1614)
70-75	2.12 (66)	0.19 (61)	0.26 (61)	-1.77 (180)	-2.19 (681)	-1.95 (121)	5.24 (196)
76-80	0.97 (172)	-0.87 (140)	2.84 (120)	-1.88 (290)	-3.55 (1471)	-2.91 (178)	3.35 (327)
81-85	0.34 (487)	0.02 (152)	2.39 (174)	-1.97 (484)	-1.03 (209)	-3.56 (337)	1.28 (338)
86-90	1.21 (471)	-0.22 (272)	2.70 (512)	-4.84 (784)	-0.20 (384)	-7.59 (674)	-3.24 (520)
91-95	-7.14 (471)	-2.64 (408)	-1.73 (361)	-4.99 (562)	-7.71 (271)	-21.97 (620)	-4.54 (233)
90	1.20 (154)	-2.23 (58)	2.52 (127)	-7.09 (193)	-0.61 (104)	-12.73 (185)	-5.48 (139)
91	-0.31 (149)	-1.74 (74)	2.12 (153)	-8.52 (201)	-3.93 (121)	-20.39 (232)	-6.77 (145)
92	-4.76 (171)	-2.89 (86)	-1.50 (132)	-7.16 (181)	-8.62 (90)	-24.89 (199)	-2.10 (77)
93	-18.83 (114)	-3.52 (99)	-9.78 (76)	-1.90 (105)	-15.42 (49)	-20.87 (188)	7.78 (11)
94	-9.69 (37)	-3.88 (123)		5.40 (75)	-7.52 (11)	-	

Table 11.2 Average Annual Percentage Changes in Real Wage (Blue-Collar)

Cohort	*Cameroon*	*Côte d'Ivoire*	*Ghana*	*Kenya*	*Tanzania*	*Zambia*	*Zimbabwe*
Overall	-1.78 (776)	-1.26 (612)	0.58 (770)	-3.54 (1568)	-2.82 (491)	-12.05 (854)	-0.38 (1026)
70-75	0.66 (32)	0.48 (20)	-0.83 (27)	-1.92 (125)	-2.88 (29)	-3.08 (34)	5.33 (115)
76-80	0.63 (107)	-1.24 (93)	1.34 (63)	-2.20 (190)	-3.42 (66)	-2.45 (63)	2.05 (221)
81-85	-0.24 (107)	-0.59 (88)	1.20 (101)	-2.13 (343)	-0.90 (92)	-4.33 (122)	-0.01 (223)
86-90	1.84 (253)	-0.68 (172)	1.88 (346)	-5.05 (562)	0.01 (179)	-7.29 (318)	-3.53 (323)
91-95	-7.84 (244)	-2.09 (239)	-1.66 (233)	-4.04 (348)	-7.97 (125)	-22.65 (317)	-3.39 (144)
90	2.22 (8.3)	-2.59 (38)	1.98 (871)	-7.20 (115)	-0.01 (55)	-13.14 (90)	-5.64 (101)
91	-0.81 (83)	-0.57 (42)	2.47 (90)	-7.73 (110)	-4.50 (58)	-21.11 (109)	-5.59 (90)
92	-5.62 (79)	-3.74 (46)	-1.34 (96)	-671 (119)	-7.03 (41)	-25.93 (104)	-0.66 (46)
93	-18.4 (65)	-4.01 (59)	-10.24 (47)	-6.40 (71)	-18.20 (20)	-20.93 (103)	5.55 (8)
94	-11.6 (17)	-2.13 (71)		5.7 (48)	-12.82 (6)		

Table 11.3 Average Annual Percentage Changes in Real Wage (White-Collar)

Cohort	*Cameroon*	*Côte d'Ivoire*	*Ghana*	*Kenya*	*Tanzania*	*Zambia*	*Zimbabwe*
Overall	-1.48 (673)	-1.18 (403)	2.37 (458)	-3.90 (792)	-2.72 (588)	-9.65 (1076)	0.33 (588)
70-75	3.49 (34)	-0.06 (23)	1.13 (34)	-1.43 (55)	-1.67 (39)	-1.52 (87)	5.10 (81)
76-80	1.52 (65)	-0.13 (47)	4.49 (57)	-1.27 (100)	-3.65 (81)	-3.17 (115)	4.38 (106)
81-85	1.06 (113)	0.86 (64)	4.01 (73)	-1.59 (141)	-1.14 (117)	-3.03 (215)	3.79 (115)
86-90	0.53 (234)	0.59 (100)	4.42 (166)	-4.46 (282)	-0.05 (205)	-7.86 (356)	-2.78 (197)
91-95	-6.44 (227)	-3.43 (169)	-1.86 (128)	-6.53 (214)	-7.49 (146)	-21.25 (303)	-6.40 (89)
90	0.04 (71)	-1.56 (20)	3.70 (40)	-6.94 (78)	-1.22 (51)	-12.34 (95)	-5.04 (38)
91	0.31 (66)	-3.30 (32)	1.61 (63)	-9.48 (91)	-3.31 (63)	-19.75 (123)	-8.71 (55)
92	-4.02 (92)	-1.92 940)	-2.15 (36)	-8.02 (62)	-9.96 (49)	-23.76 (95)	-4.24 (31)
93	-19.41 (49)	-2.81 (40)	-9.05 (29)	-5.03 (34)	-13.5 (29)	-20.60 (85)	13.74 (3)
94	-8.09 (20)	-6.28 (52)		4.95 (27)	-1.17 (5)		

It is apparent that, for the entire period over which the cohorts can be traced in the data set, the rate of growth in real earnings has been mostly negative. The exceptions are Ghana and Zimbabwe. In Zimbabwe, the workers improved their earnings until the mid-eighties — more so, the white-collar employees — but suffered decline after then. For the whole period, Zimbabwe does register a mildly negative rate of growth of real earnings. Cameroon shares some of the characteristics of the sample for Zimbabwe, with the early cohorts (until, in fact, the most recent 91-95 one) showing positive growth rates. However, the decline in the last five years has been so large, and since a sizable proportion of workers started in these years, we have overall a negative trend in earnings. Ghana is exceptional in having an overall *positive* trend. Part of the explanation is the cycle of wage movements in the modern sector of Ghana over the years. Wages had collapsed in the decade of the seventies, and recovered significantly after the implementation of the adjustment program in 1983. Thus, many of the workers who had their first jobs in the firm in the years 1975 to the late eighties were starting at exceptionally low wages. In so far as the importance of these workers in the sample is significant, the overall growth rate of earnings turns out to be positive.

The last point brings into focus the importance of the wage history of the economy in determining growth of earnings of workers from a particular cohort. If the wage cycles have been strong, it would be a futile effort to identify economy wide 'trends' in wages. The 'cohort effect' would dominate the overall trend.

All the countries in the sample, in fact, show a worse trend in the performance of real wages in the post-1985 period. In the case of Tanzania and Zambia, the deterioration is remarkable. It seems clear that a major, if not the most important, cause of this deterioration was the much faster rate of price inflation which became important after the mid-eighties, particularly in the anglophone countries. This can be seen from the data presented in Table 11.4.

We have mentioned that the changes over time of the workers' earnings are partly the result of trends in the economy, and partly the returns to experience. In practice, it will be very difficult to distinguish the two in an economy characterized by highly fluctuating rates of inflation and real wage changes. Nevertheless, some attempt might be made to see the relative performance of different cohorts, after controlling for broad worker and firm characteristics. We estimated the determinants of wage growth in a regression model that included some of these characteristics as well as the cohort variable (as measured by dummies representing groups of starting dates in the firm). The results are presented in Table 11.5.

Table 11.4 Consumer Price Index (1990=100)

	Cameroon	*Côte d'Ivoire*	*Ghana*	*Kenya*	*Tanzania*	*Zambia*	*Zimbabwe*
1970	16.8	19.3	0.09	10.5	2	0.88	13.2
1971	17.5	19.2	0.1	10.9	2.1	0.93	13.6
1972	18.9	19.3	0.11	11.6	2.2	0.98	14
1973	20.8	21.5	0.13	12.7	2.5	1.1	14.4
1974	24.4	25.2	0.16	14.9	2.9	1.3	15.4
1975	27.7	28.1	0.21	17.8	3.7	1.2	16.9
1976	30.5	31.4	0.32	19.8	4	1.5	18.7
1977	35	40.1	0.7	22.7	4.4	1.8	20.7
1978	39.3	45.4	1.2	26.6	4.7	2.1	21.8
1979	41.9	52.8	1.9	28.7	5.3	2.3	25.8
1980	45.9	60.6	2.8	32.7	6.9	2.5	27.2
1981	50.8	65.9	6.1	36.5	8.7	2.9	30.8
1982	57.6	70.9	7.4	44	11.2	3.2	34
1983	67.1	74.9	16.5	49	14.3	3.9	41.9
1984	74.8	78.1	23.1	54	19.4	4.7	50.4
1985	81.1	79.5	25.43	61.1	25.9	6.2	54.6
1986	87.4	87.2	31.7	64	34.3	9.7	62.5
1987	98.9	93.3	44.3	68.9	44.6	14.3	70.3
1988	100.6	99.8	58.2	76.6	58.5	21.6	75.5
1989	98.9	100.8	72.9	86.5	73.6	48.3	85.2
1990	100	100	100	100	100	100	100
1991	100.1	101.7	118.1	119.8	128.7	197.6	123.3
1992	100	106	129.9	155.2	156.8	525.1	175.2
1993	96.8	108.3	162.3	226.3	196.4	1487.8	223.6
1994	130.8	136.5	202.7	292	263.4	2300.4	273.3
1995	149	156	353.4	294.3	335.7	3103.3	335.1

Source: World Bank World Tables.

The overall negative rate of growth in *all countries* is more clearly seen in the rather large constant terms. Generally earlier cohorts have done better, as shown by a larger positive value to offset partly the negative constant term. An exception like that of Ghana has already been discussed. This cohort effect partly reflects the return to experience.

Perhaps the most remarkable result of this set of regressions is the large and significant positive value of the ln (size) variable. In spite of the deteriorating wages, the differentials with respect to size of firms have not been squeezed, as one might have expected. Workers in larger firms fared better over time in their individual wage history. We do not know how much of this is due to the better performance of larger firms in terms of productivity (and wage growth) over time, and how much could be caused by higher returns to experience in large firms.

Table 11.5 Determinants of Average Real Wage Growth

	Cameroon	*Côte d' Ivoire*	*Ghana*	*Kenya*	*Tanzania*	*Zambia*	*Zimbabwe*
Constant	-10.30**	-7.19**	-8.25**	-1.28**	-3.67	-15.18**	-10.21**
Human Capital							
Female	-0.28	-0.34	-1.15	0.16	2.18*	0.51	0.56
Age	0.31	0.16	-0.003	-0.38**	-0.17	-0.37*	0.19
Age**2	-0.005**	-0.004	-0.001	0.003	0.001	0.002**	-0.003**
Education Years	-0.06	-0.06	0.33**	-0.06	0.04	-0.19	0.10
ln(Size)	0.25**	0.41**	0.86**	0.42**	0.39	1.13**	0.25*
Workers Category							
Management	1.09	1.16	-1.94	0.90	-2.70*	-0.35	0.36
Admin/Cleric	1.75	1.69**	-1.92	4.37**	-2.43	0.52	0.72
Commerce/Sales	1.39	0.98	-2.6	4.23**	-1.79	-1.04	0.78
Superior/Foremen	1.57	3.68**	-0.90	3.07**	-1.62*	0.37	2.39**
Maintenance	0.44	1.63	-0.87	3.14**	-1.33	0.51	2.24**
Production	1.42	1.08	-2.03	1.48**	-2.35*	-0.78	0.04
Starting Cohort							
71-75	6.3**	3.24**	4.21**	5.32**	6.99**	20.66**	9.39**
76-80	11.4**	2.66**	4.96**	4.92**	4.89**	19.14**	7.75**
81-85	4.55**	3.41**	3.11**	4.12**	5.96**	17.76**	4.93**
86-90	5.11**	2.91**	4.28**	1.22**	6.38**	13.63**	0.96
Number of Observations	1324	967	1058	2036	1017	1870	1464
Adjusted R^2	0.1438	0.0992	0.0954	0.0710	0.0993	0.3735	0.2245

12 The Impact of the Wage Decline on Competitiveness in African Manufacturing: A Case Study of Kenya

An important question on which answers are needed but not yet available, is what has been the impact of the fall in formal sector wage on labor productivity. If urban households have been forced by the decline in wages to revert, at least partly, to the old system of migratory labor, then we are back to the world of the Carpenter Commission and its concerns about the impact of labor instability on productivity. It is possible that the urban informal sector has developed so much in the years since the Carpenter Commission produced its report, that a household could cope with the falling formal sector wage by devoting more of the labor time of its members to the informal sector in the urban economy, rather than split its time between urban and rural areas. Alternatively, aspects of information systems might have improved so much that workers in the urban labor market could conveniently leave some members of the household in the rural areas, and work in urban jobs for long periods. In this case the fall in wages will not lead to a significantly higher incidence of circulatory migrants and high labor turnover in the urban formal sector. But such thoughts remain at the moment as hypotheses. Case studies are needed to throw light on the impact of real wage decline on labor turnover and productivity, as well as on the labor market adjustments of households.

This chapter seeks to provide a partial answer to this set of questions by examining the long-term series on productivity which are available for one country — Kenya. Two specific issues are singled out for analysis, partly because they are tractable from available statistical time-series. Our first topic is an exploration of the trends in productivity in the formal sector over the two decades of falling wages. A second topic of concern is the possible effects on the competitiveness of the tradable sector in Kenya. There might be an adverse trend in the competitiveness of this sector, not only because of a possible decline in labor productivity at a rate higher than the fall in wages, but also because of an adverse movement in the real exchange rate, when the real wage decline is being brought about by the rate of increase in prices exceeding the rate of increase of money wages.

A study of both these topics require quantitative information on trends in productivity, measured, for example, by value added per worker. Hence, the analysis is confined to the formal *manufacturing* sector of Kenya. Labor productivity in the public sector outside production is hard to define, and even in the private tertiary sector, it is difficult to obtain a reasonable measure of productivity separate from the earnings of labor in the absence of fairly detailed and difficult surveys of economic activity in this sector.

At first sight it might seem far fetched to postulate a wage-efficiency relationship in the private manufacturing sector, which admits of the possibility of wages falling below a threshold such that the reduction of wages could lead to a higher proportionate decreases in productivity so that we have an actual increase in wage cost. It might be argued that while this might easily happen in the public sector, specially in the a profit-maximizing private sector employer could hardly be expected to stick to wages so low — even if he initially stumbles below the threshold — that his wage costs actually increased. The answer to this critique is usually given in terms of external economy considerations. The efficiency performance level of an individual worker is heavily influenced by the work standards set by the general body of workers in that social network, and the boundaries of this network might extend well beyond the confines of an individual enterprise. Thus while raising wages above the threshold by all or a large group of employers might reduce wage costs, an increase of wages by a single employer might not be successful in eliciting a more than proportionate increase in productivity. This was indeed the rationale behind the use of minimum wages to create a stabilized labor force after independence.

Trends in Labor Productivity

Time series data on value added and labor are available for the formal manufacturing sector in Kenya for the period 1972-91. We can measure labor productivity by value added per worker. Labor productivity thus defined is a function of the use of both capital and labor. However, as a first step we can examine the change in the ratio of wage per worker to the value added per worker or the share of wages. The available time series shows that in the manufacturing sector the share of wages has fallen slightly over the 18-year period, from 41 percent in 1972 to 35 percent in 1990 and there have been no fluctuations in these statistics but only a very gentle decline (see Table 10.1). There is clearly nothing in these data to suggest that productivity of labor might have fallen *more than* wages. Indeed, since the share of labor share has been almost constant over this period, one might be tempted to suggest that real wages and real productivity of labor might have fallen at the same rate. But this is not the case because the ratio of the wage bill to value added has been calculated with both series valued at current prices. We have not considered any changes in the terms of trade between the commodity basket affecting workers and the manufacturers. If in fact value added is deflated by the manufacturing producer price index and the wage bill by the worker's cost of living index, the result shows that the share of labor in real terms has fallen substantially over time, showing that real productivity did not fall *pari passu* with real wages (see below, section on Uc). Thus far the data do not provide any evidence of the fall in wages having an impact on labor productivity.

The observed value of value added per worker over time is not a completely adequate statistic for measuring its efficiency, since other factors, principally capital, also affect labor productivity. It is indeed possible that the increase in labor productivity relative to wages might be due to a greater injection of capital, though — if it were true — such an increase in capital intensity, in a period of falling wages would require explanation. To check on this point we need to calculate the behavior of total factor productivity (TFP) over time.

Trends in Total Factor Productivity (TFP) in Manufacturing

The calculation of TFP is based on a comparison of the rate of growth of output to a weighted average of the rates of growth of the factors of production, generally limited to capital and labor. The weights applied are the shares of labor and capital on the assumption that profit maximizing employers equate wages to the marginal productivity of labor.[52] The difference in the rate of growth of output and what can be ascribed to the growth of inputs measures the growth rate of TFP. Although the assumptions are extreme and data limitations severe, broad changes can be discerned from the calculation of TFP growth.

[52] The theory is spelt out in the famous paper by Solow(1969).

Table 12.1 Time Series Data for Calculation of TFP Growth in Kenya, 1972-1990

	1972	*1973*	*1974*	*1975*	*1976*	*1977*	*1978*	*1979*	*1980*	*1981*	*1982*	*1983*	*1984*	*1985*	*1986*	*1987*	*1988*	*1989*	*1990*
GDP (mil.)	165.7	189.5	200.7	208.7	237.9	275.9	310.5	334.0	351.5	364.1	372.3	389.1	405.8	424.1	448.7	474.3	502.8	532.5	560.3
Labor (th.)	84.8	94.5	101.3	100.7	108.8	117.9	130.1	138.4	141.3	146.3	146.8	148.8	153.1	159.5	163.9	169.2	174.1	178.7	187.7
Capital (mil.)	603.3	701.5	796.6	844.8	888.6	942.4	1017.0	1109.8	1187.4	1232.9	1275.7	1274.2	1287.2	1284.7	1282.7	1299.7	1322.0	1365.3	1404.3
Real Wages (million.)	116.7	128.2	125.2	122.0	126.8	133.4	134.0	139.5	145.0	148.7	136.1	133.0	136.6	135.4	140.4	146.9	141.2	149.6	147.3
dGDP/GDP		0.14	0.06	0.04	0.14	0.16	0.13	0.08	0.05	0.04	0.02	0.05	0.04	0.05	0.06	0.06	0.06	0.06	0.05
dLab/Lab		0.11	0.07	-0.01	0.08	0.08	0.10	0.06	0.02	0.04	0.00	0.01	0.03	0.04	0.03	0.03	0.03	0.03	0.05
dCap/Cap		0.16	0.14	0.06	0.05	0.06	0.08	0.09	0.07	0.04	0.03	0.00	0.01	0.00	0.00	0.01	0.02	0.03	0.03
SL	0.41	0.40	0.37	0.40	0.40	0.38	0.37	0.36	0.36	0.37	0.37	0.37	0.37	0.36	0.34	0.36	0.34	0.35	0.35
SK	0.59	0.60	0.63	0.60	0.60	0.62	0.63	0.64	0.64	0.63	0.63	0.63	0.63	0.64	0.66	0.64	0.66	0.65	0.65

Note dGDP/GDP = change in GDP/GDP.
dLab/Lab = change in labor/labor.
dCap/Cap = change in capital/capital.
SL = share of labor in output.
SK = share of capital in output.

This has been estimated for the Kenyan manufacturing sector for the entire period 1972-90 and for the sub-periods of the 1970s an the 1980s separately. The data are presented in Table 10.2.[53]

Table 12.2 Total Factor Productivity (Manufacturing)

	1972-81	*1981-90*	*1972-90*
dY/Y	0.092	0.049	0.064
dL/L	0.061	0.028	0.040
dK/K	0.081	0.017	0.048
SL	0.390	0.360	0.380
SK	0.610	0.640	0.620
Trend Rates	1.94%	2.75%	2.49%

Note: dY/Y = change in output/output.
dL/L = change in labor/labor.
dK/K = change in capital/capital.
SL = share of labor in output.
SK = share of capital in output.

Source: The original data has been taken from 'Historical Economic Data for Kenya: 1972-1990.' Technical Paper 91-12, Long Range Planning Division.

It is seen that the growth rate in TFP has been positive throughout, and in fact has increased significantly in the 1980s. It appears that in spite of the slower rate of growth of employment in manufacturing in the eighties, and an even slower rate of growth of capital, output growth fell relatively less. A closer examination of the data shows that the crucial factor has been the better use of capital. While, growth rate of the partial productivity of labor (rate of growth of output *minus* the rate of growth of labor) *decreased* from 0.031 in the seventies to 0.021 in the eighties, the rate of growth of capital productivity *increased* dramatically from 0.011 to 0.032 — almost three times. TFP growth accordingly was quite impressive. The time series evidence is thus consistent with the conclusion that the falling wages might indeed have had some impact in the form of falling labor efficiency, but that this effect was more than offset by the pronounced increase in the efficient use of capital. It can be hypothesized that some of this increased efficiency is due to the favorable impact of the structural adjustment policies pursued in the decade of the eighties.

---

[53]The capital stock figures used by us are those calculated by Wilson, Barner and Milne.

Trends in Unit Labor Cost in Dollars (*Uc*)

We can now focus our attention on the issue of international competitiveness of Kenyan manufacturing sector. Initially, we would expect that the decline in real wages — taken in conjunction with the fact that there is only a moderate decline in labor productivity — should have led to a significant downward trend in unit labor costs. But there are two other factors, which enter into the *Uc*. Firstly, from the point of view of employers it is the product real wage, and not the consumption real wage, which matters. The two ratios might be changing at different rates if the index of producer prices moves differently from the consumer price index. Secondly, we ought to take into account the foreign exchange rate when assessing the cost of labor per unit of output in the international market. The different elements entering the picture can be assessed in our index of *Uc*.[54]

Determinants of Uc

Define the unit cost of labor in dollars, *Uc*, as

$$Uc = \frac{W}{V} \times \frac{1}{e} \qquad (1)$$

where, *W* denotes wages per worker, *V* denotes value added per worker, and *e* denotes the exchange rate (local currency per dollar).

The following relation can be derived from Equation 1:

$$\begin{aligned} Uc &= \dot{W} - \dot{V} - \dot{e} \\ &= (\dot{w} + \dot{P}c) - (\dot{v} + \dot{P}p) - \dot{e} \\ &= (\dot{w} - \dot{v} + \dot{P}c - \dot{P}p) - \dot{e} \end{aligned} \qquad (2)$$

where the dots represent proportionate rates of change. The additional variables are defined as follows: *w* is the real wage (in terms of consumer goods), v is an index of the physical productivity of labor, *Pc* is an index of the cost of living, and *Pp* is an index of prices of manufactured goods.

Equation 2 decomposes the percentage change in the unit cost into

[54]This index was used by the author in Mazumdar, (1993).

three elements: the wage-productivity gap, the shift in the ratio of consumer to producer prices; and the change in the nominal exchange rate.

The first term depends on the behavior of the labor market. The second is what is sometimes called the domestic real exchange rate (DRER) on the approximate fact that *Pc* is the price of non-traded goods and *Pp* is the price of traded goods.

The Domestic Real Exchange Rate and the Nominal Exchange Rate

Movements in DRER, are likely to be related to changes in e. Thus, when there is a devaluation of the currency, both *Pc* and *Pp* rises in the local currency. However, the price of traded goods is anchored in the world market setting, placing a limit on the extent to which *Pp* can rise in the domestic market. *Pc* depends much more on domestic fiscal and monetary policies and generally has a tendency to exceed increases in *Pp* in an inflationary situation fueled by the devaluation.

A second channel through which movements in *e* and DRER are related is through the familiar story of the 'Dutch-disease' class of models. Within tradable goods, commodities are distinguished from manufactured goods. The improvement of the terms of trade, leads to a balance of payments surplus on the current account, and, other things remaining unchanged, causes an appreciation of the exchange rate. At the same time the 'spending effect' induced by the boom of commodity prices in the private or the public sector or both-causes a relative increase in the price of non-tradable goods while, with unchanged world prices of manufactured goods, *Pp*, in domestic currency actually falls. Thus, there is a sharp increase of DRER together with *e*. The unit cost of labor increases both because of *e* and appreciation in the DRER, unless it is offset by a sufficient increase in the wage-productivity gap in the labor market. This course of events might be altered by changes in the capital account of the balance of payments.

The figures of annual percentage changes are given in Table 12.3.

Table 12.3 Percentage Changes in Unit Labor Cost in Dollars (Uc) — 1973-1990

	1973	*1974*	*1975*	*1976*	*1977*	*1978*	*1979*	*1980*	*1981*	*1982*	*1983*	*1984*	*1985*	*1986*	*1987*	*1988*	*1989*	*1990*
Wage Employees	11.4	7.3	-0.6	8	8.4	10.3	6.4	2.1	3.6	0.3	1.3	2.9	4.2	2.7	3.2	2.9	2.6	2.7
Wage bill (K £)	19.7	14.4	13.4	14.9	20	15.8	12.3	17.8	15.1	11.4	9.8	12.9	11.6	9.2	13.7	8	20.1	12.5
Money wage per worker	8.3	7.1	14	6.9	11.6	5.5	5.9	15.7	11.5	11.1	8.5	10	7.4	6.5	10.5	5.1	17.5	9.8
Weighted CPI (Nairobi)	9	17.9	15.6	10.6	14	15.4	7.9	13.4	12.2	21.7	12.3	10	12.5	5.3	8.7	12.3	13.4	15.7
Real wage (w)	-0.7	-10.8	-1.6	-3.7	-2.4	-9.9	-2	2.3	-0.7	-10.6	-3.8	0	-5.1	1.2	1.8	-7.2	4.1	-5.9
GDP at 1982 prices	14.4	5.9	4	14	16	12.5	7.6	5.2	3.6	2.2	4.5	4.3	4.5	5.8	5.7	6	5.9	5.2
Production (p)	3	-1.4	4.6	6	7.6	2.2	1.2	3.1	0	1.9	3.2	1.4	0.3	3.1	2.5	3.1	3.3	2.5
w - p	-3.7	-9.4	-6.2	-9.7	-10	-12.1	-3.2	-0.8	-0.7	-12.5	-7	-1.4	-5.4	-1.9	-0.7	-10.3	0.8	-8.4
Cost living (Pc)	9	17.9	15.6	10.6	14	15.4	7.9	13.4	12.2	21.7	12.3	10	12.5	5.3	8.7	12.3	13.4	15.7
GDP deflator (Pp)	7.3	17.9	2.3	-0.4	7.6	8.3	5.9	12.2	7.3	11	4.9	8.2	7.6	10.9	1.5	8.9	7.3	9.7
Pc - Pp	1.7	0	13.3	11	6.4	7.1	2	1.2	4.9	10.7	7.4	1.8	4.9	-5.6	7.2	3.4	6.1	6
Exchange rate (e)	-3.4	3.5	15.5	0.7	-4.4	-6.8	-1	3.3	35.9	23.7	8.4	14.4	3.2	-1.5	2.9	12.6	16.1	11.49
Unit labor cost (Uc)	1.4	-12.9	-8.4	0.6	0.8	1.8	-0.2	-2.9	-31.7	-25.5	-8	-14	-3.7	-6	3.6	-19.5	-9.2	-13.89

The objective of reducing the *Uc* for most years was achieved with the exception of the coffee boom period covering 1976-78. The somewhat continuous depreciation of the currency — excluding the coffee boom years — have been partly or occasionally more than compensated by the adverse movement of the DRER as the cost of living index rose faster than the index of producer prices. However, the downward movement of Uc was maintained because of the persisting real wage-productivity gap, which increased during the years of large devaluation (e.g. 1982). We can therefore conclude that the formal manufacturing labor market in Kenya has behaved in an extremely flexible way. A wage-spiral with continuous devaluation was avoided and a cut in real wages yearly was instrumental in offsetting the increase in DRER.

Given the long continuous decline in Uc one would expect to see the Kenyan manufacturing products being highly competitive internationally. However, we do not know how the value of Uc has changed over time for Kenya's competitors or trading partners in the last two decades: nor the initial value of Kenya's efficiency relative to her competitors at the beginning of our period.

It is, however, clear that one of the most disappointing part of the relatively poor performance of Kenyan manufacturing has been the export development, particularly if we leave out petroleum exports. Sharpley and Lewis studied the sources of manufacturing growth in Kenya for the seventies and the eighties. They concluded that export growth accounted for a little over 10 percent of output growth in manufacturing in the seventies, but this was largely due to the capital intensive sub-sector of petroleum-based products. In the period 1980-84, when the 'chemicals, rubber and petroleum' stagnated, the contribution of export growth to manufacturing output growth was a measly 1.75 percent. Evidently, the favorable unit cost trends in dollars had little impact on Kenya's export prospects. Such price trends could be a necessary but never a sufficient condition of export growth.

The Public Sector

So far we have discussed the changes in wages and productivity in the manufacturing sector — both in the public and private sectors in the formal economy. One of the major questions concerning the performance of the labor market in Kenya is the efficiency of the large public sector. It has often been suggested that this sector has been a sink of unproductive labor, thereby creating an inefficient allocation of labor. It is also thought to have contributed through its large wage bill, to the problem of unsustainable fiscal deficits, and accompanying macro-economic difficulties.

We have discussed in Chapter 8 above that real wages have been falling in the public sector at a rate somewhat higher than in the private sector, but employment growth has been faster than in the private sector. Since the rate of public employment growth has been higher than the absolute value of the rate of decline of real wages, the rate of growth of the wage bill has been positive — even though the growth rate has been low at less than 1 percent per annum, well below the rate of growth of GDP in real terms. Like many other African countries, Kenya has, over the two decades of the seventies and eighties, continued to slide down the wage-employment locus, ending up with a combination of higher employment and significantly lower wage, with the wage bill increasing slowly. The ratios of gross average earnings in the public and private sectors are given below:

Table 12.4 Ratio of Gross Earnings in the Public and Private Sectors

	1972-73	*1981-83*	*1988-90*
All Industries	1.45	1.25	1.10

These are gross averages and do not take account of differences in the measurable qualities of labor in the two sectors. Reference might be made here to Chapter 2 in Part I where we use RPED survey data to quantify the wage differentials between state-owned and private manufacturing firms in Kenya, net of the human capital factors and other significant determinants of earnings. The findings are that Kenya was unique among the seven African countries included in which state-owned manufacturing firms had 'net' average earnings substantially below private firms, although joint state-private firms had earnings on par with the latter. The coverage of the surveys is not comparable with the figures of the private-public differential given above, which pertain to all sectors, not just manufacturing. Further, they are for the period 1993-95. However, at least they underline the point emerging from the figures above that in Kenya the public sector wage premium had vanished by the beginning of the nineties.

While there is an apparent trend towards the equalization of the levels of earnings between the public and private sectors within the formal wage economy, it is impossible to gauge whether: (i) the total wage bill in the public sector is socially optimal; or (ii) the mix of employment and average wage which the public sector established at the end of the decade, is the best from the point of view of productive efficiency in this sector. It has sometimes been argued that wages may have fallen so low that efficiency of public employees was seriously impaired. Productivity in the public sector might be enhanced if, with the same size of the wage bill, a smaller number of people at higher wage were employed. Value added is not properly measured in much of the public activities, and even in those sub-sectors in which output could be measured at market prices, public sector enterprises often do not act as profit maximizing units. Hence, the wage-efficiency relationship, which could normally provide a floor to the wage level in private firms, would not operate in the public labor market.

Conclusions: Hypotheses about the Consequences of Wage Decline

Published statistics in the formal manufacturing sector help us to address a few policy issues pertaining to the impact of falling wages. But while we wait for other case studies like the Kenyan one reported in this chapter, our conclusions from these results must remain as tentative hypotheses.

The most direct question emanating from the experience of the long-run wage decline is: why has not the wage decline led to a much stronger increase in output and employment in the manufacturing sector, as labor costs fell? The first response might be the efficiency wage argument: that the real wage decline only resulted in fall in labor efficiency and productivity, and did not really achieve a fall in labor costs per unit of output. It seems that over the period studied Kenyan manufacturing has not suffered from this type of falling labor productivity. In fact, the trend rate in the 'wage-productivity gap' — the difference in the rates of growth of real wages and of real productivity has been negative and sizable. This is not due to the larger contribution of capital investment. In fact, the trend in total factor productivity has been significantly positive. Our analysis of the trends in unit labor costs showed that domestically the fall in the share of wages in real terms (an increase in the 'wage-gap') was only partially offset by the adverse movement of the domestic real exchange rate — the differential rate of increase of consumer prices over producer prices. There was thus a significant fall in unit labor costs in the domestic economy. The trends *vis-à vis* the external markets were even better, because of the persistent fall in the exchange rate over the two decades. This contributed importantly to the persistent improvement in Kenya's international competitiveness as measured by the unit cost of labor in dollars. We can address the query of the lack of strong increase in manufacturing output separately for the domestic and the external markets.

The Domestic Market

As far as the domestic economy is concerned we must recall the message of the old Kalecki-Keynes thesis that the wage is an element in demand, and not just costs. As real wages fell costs in manufacturing sector fell, but so did demand for the output of the sector. The question immediately arises in the African case: how could wage levels in a narrow sector like formal manufacturing constitute such an element of total demand for the output of the sector? The relevant issue would seem to be if the wage bill in the urban economy as whole fell, assuming that the demand for manufactured goods came mostly from the low income urban earners. We recall from Chapter 8 that while real wages in the formal sector fell over the eighties at the annual rate of 2 percent, employment, taking private and public sector together, increased at the rate of 4 percent, so that wage bill increased in the formal sector expanded at a rate of 2 percent. At the same time a larger proportion of labor was absorbed in the urban informal sector. Thus, taking the formal and informal sectors together, it is clear that the wage bill or total earnings of low income earners (if we want to include the self-employed in the informal sector in the calculation) did not fall, but in fact expanded at rather more than 2 percent per annum. What happened was that the wage or earnings per worker fell at a significant rate — not only because of the declining formal sector wage, but also because earnings per worker were generally lower in the informal sector. Now, it is reasonable to expect that as household incomes per earner or per capita fall in the low-income group, there will be shift of demand to goods and services produced by the informal sector. It has been seen in studies of small manufacturing enterprises that one of the ways in which small and micro firms compete with larger firms in the organized sector is by occupying the low end of the quality spectrum in a particular product line. In textiles for example micro firms specialize in producing coarse cloth which low income consumers can afford while larger firms in the formal sector, with more mechanized techniques, produce finer cloth for the middle classes (Mazumdar and Page, Chapter 13). In the service and repair sector, the informal sector meets an important need of low-income consumers for bulk-breaking, selling in small units, and prolonging the economic life of durable goods (Bauer and Yamey). Thus we can expect to see that with falling household incomes there would be a net shift of demand from the formal to the informal sector even if the aggregate wage bill were increasing.

The Export Sector

Turning now to the external sector, the future of African manufacturing exports has been much discussed in recent economic literature. There are two alternative views on the fundamental factors defining Africa's capability in manufactured exports. On the other hand, we have the hypothesis expounded by Adrian Wood and his co-authors, Kristi Berger and Jorg Mayer, which suggests that the abundance of natural resources (including land) and relative shortage of skilled labor tilt the comparative advantage against manufacturing in most African countries. Against this Bloom and Sachs have recently put forward strongly the opposite view that climate and topography make for low agricultural productivity even though the land-labor ratio is still relatively high in Africa — a situation rapidly being eroded by the high natural rate of growth of population. Thus, comparative advantage theory suggests that Africa should be a net importer of agricultural commodities (mainly foodstuffs), paid for by net exports of manufactures and services, and perhaps also by traditional resource exports which are endemic to the tropics. In supporting the Boom-Sachs position in this debate, Collier points out that Africa's decline has so reduced real income and wages that labor costs should be competitive. The Kenyan wage history in the formal sector, documented in this chapter and in chapter 8, supports the Collier point. Kenya's lack of competitiveness in the world export markets, even in light manufacturing, is then most likely due to the impact of policies rather than endowments.

According to some popular perceptions exchange rate and other macro-economic policies in Africa have succeeded in negating the potential advantage from declining wages by leading to a serious and continuing overvaluation of the currency. The case study of Kenya in this chapter decisively disproves this hypothesis. The causes of export sluggishness have then to be sought in other aspects of economic polices.

A relevant point to emphasize here is that while unit labor costs in dollar declined significantly over time, the costs of imported inputs and machinery increased all the time because of the constant depreciation of the currency. We cannot say, without a detailed study of African manufacturing, how far the increased costs of imported inputs canceled out the fall in unit labor costs. But it could be a critical factor in the overall change in competitiveness.

Other relevant factors impeding the expansion of external markets are infrastructure and marketing obstacles. It has already been remarked that the public sector had opted to trade off employment against wage per worker for the entire period of the two decades. There are strong reasons to suspect that this social and political solution might have caused serious loss in the quality of public sector services (including the provision of good infrastructure). Collier has listed four important constraints faced by African firms — high costs of power, high transaction costs, high costs of information and high level of risk — all of which have their roots in politics and policy (*ibid,* p.278). But as Bloom and Sachs conclude: 'Researchers have as yet undertaken very little systematic comparisons of African economies with other regions regarding factor costs, transport costs, tax arrangements, infrastructure availability, and the like. This basic fact finding should be made a high priority' (p.270).

Part V:
The Structure of Labor Markets in African Manufacturing

Introduction

Part V is meant to give a comparative account of employment and earnings in African manufacturing, based on the cross-section data available from the RPED surveys of firms and of a sample of workers employed by them. The data set allows us to use the characteristics of the workers along with the characteristics of the firms employed by them in our analysis of the determinants of the structure of employment and earnings. The survey design and methodology are discussed in the Appendix to this Part.

Chapter 13 is a detailed account of the structure of the labor force in the manufacturing firms — in terms of skill, types of units, sex etc. — and of the earnings of workers. We go on in Chapter 14 to analyze the determinants of earnings. It is seen that, apart from human capital factors, the size of the enterprise is a major determinant of earnings. Although the increase of wages with enterprise size is a worldwide phenomena, even in developed countries like the UK and the USA, the *quantitative dimensions* of this relationship is much larger in the African economies as in many other parts of the developing world. The factors causing this important and substantial relationship — which is found to exist even after many years of wage decline in some cases — merit detailed investigation. Chapter 15 presents a detailed examination of this relationship. The theoretical and empirical inquiry suggests several hypotheses, which seem to be supported by the data. This chapter should be viewed as a contribution to the bludgeoning literature on this problem.

For most of the analysis presented in this part the data for the three successive waves have been merged. Thus, the results are for the average for the three years taken together. The value figures, for example earnings, were suitably deflated by the price index appropriate to the series. A large number of regression results have been reported in this part. Unless, stated otherwise, a double star (**) denotes that the coefficient is significant at 1 percent level of probability, and a single star (*) at the 5 percent level.

13 The Structure of the Labor Force and of Earnings

The Structure of Labor Force

The RPED surveys have labor data, as already mentioned, in two parts. The management was asked some questions on the labor force in their establishments; and a sample of workers from each establishment in the units covered were provided answers relating to a set of issues relating to their working conditions. The latter sample is not a random one. Ten workers were covered from each of the roughly 200 firms interviewed according to their availability though an attempt was made to select workers proportional to the occupational categories. Thus while the workers' data set is more reliable for the information on earnings, we have to use the management questionnaire to throw light on some aspects of the structure of the labor force.

The Distribution of the Workers by Industry and Size of Enterprise

The distribution of the workforce in the firms surveyed is given in Tables 13.1 and 13.2 broken down by industry and enterprise size respectively. The classification of the groups is as follows: Micro- less than 10; small- 10-50; medium- 50-200; large- 200-500; very large- 500 plus.

This classification has been kept unchanged for all countries and throughout the analysis of the statistical material.

Table 13.1 Distribution of Employees by Sector (Percentages)

	Cameroon	*Côte d'Ivoire*	*Kenya*	*Ghana*	*Tanzania*	*Zambia*	*Zimbabwe*
Food	68.36	43.89	26.44	24.95	24.83	42.99	29.09
Metal	8.16	8.58	19.10	26.22	13.17	18.90	9.82
Textile	9.99	24.39	24.86	17.58	47.19	26.68	56.69
Wood	13.49	23.14	29.60	31.25	14.81	11.43	4.39

Table 13.2 Distribution of Employees by Firm Size (Percentages)

	Cameroon	*Côte d'Ivoire*	*Kenya*	*Ghana*	*Tanzania*	*Zambia*	*Zimbabwe*
Micro	1.24	1.14	1.86	3.56	2.55	1.55	0.54
Small	6.47	5.20	7.62	17.54	10.92	10.37	1.67
Medium	12.56	12.36	23.83	30.51	18.63	24.71	12.99
Large	13.2	16.05	21.39	32.49	11.29	22.34	17.70
Very Large	66.52	65.25	45.30	15.90	56.62	41.03	67.09

It should be remembered that these distributions are from the data collected by the questionnaire addressed to managers. Hence, they are based on the data typically available on the enterprise and its books. The survey aimed at a representative sampling of enterprises in the four main manufacturing sectors (industries). However, the number of large firms had a more than proportionate representation because it was felt necessary to have adequate numbers to ensure comparison with small firms. In addition, it should be emphasized that the survey was confined to the registered enterprises, and thus excludes much of the so-called informal sector, which is outside the legal framework of registration. This may explain the relatively small proportion of workers in micro enterprises.

Despite this caveat, the proportion of employment in small enterprises is quite surprising. Ghana is the only one of the seven countries in which there is a strong presence of small and medium enterprises, and this is also the country in which the distribution of employment by size approaches a 'normal' distribution. All the countries have size distribution skewed to large enterprises. This skewness is particularly pronounced in Zimbabwe and the two-francophone countries.

The Proportion of Regular Workers

It is well known that in many developing countries there is a practice of employing a substantial number of temporary workers along with a core of 'regulars'. The non-regulars might be casuals who are employed on a day-to-day basis, as conditions of demand fluctuations require. However, a large number of them are employed every day, but without the benefit of job security or other benefits. These 'temporaries' are the equivalent of non-tenured workers of the academic profession. The proportion of non-regulars is typically much higher in developing countries than in the advanced industrial countries.

It has sometimes been maintained that the substantial use of non-regular workers is the product of labor legislation, which legally enforces job security, and the payment of various kinds of non-wage benefits. However, studies of labor markets in developing countries showed that the practice existed in eras well before the coming of trade unions or government legislation. Mazumdar (1973) showed that the system of making extensive use of 'substitutes' was developed in the Indian Textile Industry in the early years of industrialization. He argued that there are at least three reasons for the development of a system the system making use of two types of labor. First, the system has its origin in the presence in the urban labor markets of two types of job seekers migrating from the rural areas: the temporary migrants wanting to spend only a limited amount of time in urban industry, whether for a part of the year or a part of their working life, and a more permanent job seeker wanting to follow a committed career in industry. The latter would be more productive but also will have a higher supply price. Management would prefer to use the stable type, as long as their higher productivity offsets the higher wage needed to attract them. However, such workers could also be expected to be in inelastic supply. Thus, it might be profitable to use the stable labor mixed in with a complement of temporary unstable labor — the exact proportion being determined at the point where the marginal cost of employing stable labor equaled the marginal gain in productivity by having more of such labor. Secondly, the use of temporary workers could serve as a useful method of screening and recruitment of labor with aptitude for sustained and disciplined industrial work. It offered management and labor foremen the opportunity of testing out potential workers and selecting a core with low turnover out of the floating mass of rural-to-urban migrants who turned up for jobs at the factory gate each morning. Thirdly, the use of temporary workers offered the opportunity for saving in wage bill by matching day-to-day fluctuations in demand for labor to the labor actually used and paid for on the day. Again, the use of temporary workers for this purpose alongside a permanent stable core avoids the problem of low productivity, which a purely casual labor system would entail.

There is thus substantial reasons for profit seeking employers to use a two-tier labor system, and such a system would be more prevalent the greater the incidence of temporary migrants in the labor market. Of course, labor legislation which comes later in the history of the labor market, as it did in Bombay, and increases the 'fixed costs' of employing permanent workers. It would also lead to another reason for the use of temporaries, and indeed would lead to an increase in the proportion of such labor employed. However, the authors of legislation, which increases the benefits for the permanent core generally, have been well aware of this problem, and seek to counter it by controlling the use of temporary workers. The most usual form is to put a limit on the period of time in which a given individual could be employed as a temporary worker — much like in an academic institution. Employers might be tempted to work around such legislation by employing new workers as temporaries, but this leads to falling productivity, which has to be balanced against the saving in wage bill.

The share of non-regular workers in the sample of firms in the RPED surveys is given in Tables 13.3 and 13.4 classified by size of enterprise and by sector (industry) respectively in the seven countries. Although such detailed data are not available for Indian manufacturing, Mazumdar's estimate was that in the Bombay Textile Labor market, the proportion of non-regulars was 25-30 percent of the total at the time of the introduction of comprehensive labor legislation around 1950. Judging by this standard the African picture is not that of excessively large use of non-regulars. Only Kenya and, to a lesser extent, Zimbabwe seem to have a proportion of non-regulars remotely approaching the historical case of the Indian Textile Industry.

Table 13.3 Average Share of Non-Regular Workers by Size

	Cameroon	*Côte d'Ivoire*	*Kenya*	*Ghana*	*Tanzania*	*Zambia*	*Zimbabwe*
Micro	0.15	0.06	0.37	0.12	0.09	0.12	0.25
Small	0.08	0.11	0.27	0.08	0.15	0.10	0.20
Medium	0.09	0.15	0.25	0.11	0.20	0.13	0.17
Large	0.12	0.06	0.29	0.08	0.08	0.09	0.14
Very Large	0.01	0.05	0.27	0.09	0.07	0.13	0.17
All	0.10	0.10	0.30	0.10	0.14	0.11	0.22

Table 13.4 Average Share of Non-Regular Workers by Sector

	Cameroon	*Côte d'Ivoire*	*Kenya*	*Ghana*	*Tanzania*	*Zambia*	*Zimbabwe*
Food	0.10	0.12	0.30	0.13	0.25	0.10	0.13
Metal	0.13	0.12	0.35	0.08	0.09	0.13	0.12
Textile	0.11	0.06	0.26	0.06	0.07	0.09	0.25
Wood	0.09	0.06	0.30	0.14	0.14	0.15	0.19

The difference between countries in the use of temporary workers is partly accounted for by the different pattern of rural-urban links in the economies of East and West Africa, which has been discussed in detail in Part III. It was seen that circulatory migrants (who alternate between rural and urban residence) and are by definition 'temporary' from the point of view of urban industry has been of much greater importance in East and Southern Africa than in the West). The migrant labor system was changed after independence by legislation and enhanced minimum wages. However, we know that there has been large erosion of real wages in the urban areas of these economies, leading to a partial reversal to the trend towards stabilization of labor with migrants settling permanently in town. Hence, this decline must have been at least partly responsible for the heavy dependence on temporary workers in the manufacturing sector of Kenya and Zimbabwe. Why is Tanzania an exception in East Africa? The difference might be due to the much more overtly socialistic pattern of the economy created in Tanzania for many years after independence. This implied more severe enforcement of labor legislation and a greater dominance of state enterprises in the manufacturing sector — both of which actively discouraged the use of temporary workers.

West Africa, by contrast, had a different pattern of rural-urban migration in which temporary migrants were much less important in the urban labor markets (see chapter 9 above for the Ghana case, and Chapter 10 for Cote d'Ivoire). Thus, all three West African countries in our sample make use of temporary workers only to a limited extent.

Distribution of Employees by Ownership Category

The relative importance of state, private and foreign ownership of manufacturing establishments in the RPED samples is shown in Table 13.5.

Table 13.5 Distribution of Employees by Ownership (Percentages)

	Cameroon	*Côte d'Ivoire*	*Kenya*	*Ghana*	*Tanzania*	*Zambia*	*Zimbabwe*
Private (Native)	18.44	8.09	67.82	44.46	29.62	44.94	36.24
Foreign	9.05	27.18	18.56	4.53	3.81	13.55	9.69
Private-Foreign		27.06		26.51			34.34
State	44.53	22.75	2.53	6.27	56.78	35.33	6.67
State-Private	27.98	14.92	11.10	18.23	9.80	6.18	12.97

The substantial importance of state ownership in Tanzanian manufacturing stands out from this table. Next in importance is Zambia, and, rather unexpectedly both the francophone countries in the surveys, especially if we take into account joint private-state ownership.

The importance of foreign ownership (whether purely foreign or jointly with native private owners) is striking in Côte d'Ivoire and Zimbabwe.

Occupational Distribution of the Workforce

It has sometimes been suggested that African manufacturing enterprises have an excessively high percentage of white collar workers in their labor force, and this is one of the reasons for their possible high cost of labor. It has been noted that the wage differential between white and blue collar workers is higher in African economies than in developed industrial countries — a finding that is in keeping with the economic theories of wage differentials (see the section on *Earnings Ladder by Occupation* later in this chapter). Therefore, if it is found that African manufacturing has a larger presence of white-collar workers, this could be because of political or sociological factors. A possible hypothesis is that kinship ties or the political influence of the educated forces employers to accommodate an unusually large proportion of white-collar job seekers. Alternatively, we could have an economic hypothesis postulating that, in spite of the higher wage differential, white-collar workers in Africa are relatively less productive than the blue collar ones, relative to the usual situation in developed countries. Secondly, the larger proportion of white-collar workers could be partly due to the inadequate development of infrastructure — for example, a shortage of service providers outside the firms to which various necessary functions could be contracted out.

The average share of blue-collar workers in total employment in the firms in our sample is given in Table 13.6. A quick glimpse of the data suggests that Tanzania seems to have a particularly low proportion of blue-collar workers- around 60 percent in all size groups, closely followed by Zambia. All the other countries have a larger proportion of such workers, in the 70-80 percent range. The data also have some suggestion that there is a tendency for larger firms to have a *larger* share of blue-collar workers. However, this size-related trend is really pronounced for one country — Ghana. Côte d'Ivoire might give a misleading visual picture because of the low value for the small percentage of micro enterprises.

Table 13.6 Average Share of Blue-Collar Workers

	Cameroon	*Côte d'Ivoire*	*Kenya*	*Ghana*	*Tanzania*	*Zambia*	*Zimbabwe*
Micro	0.68	0.35	0.67	0.38	0.56	0.58	0.70
Small	0.64	0.63	0.67	0.34	0.60	0.63	0.74
Medium	0.68	0.75	0.73	0.58	0.60	0.62	0.77
Large	0.81	0.68	0.79	0.70	0.59	0.66	0.76
Very Large	0.83	0.79	0.74	0.78	0.63	0.69	0.67

A regression of the pooled data might give a more satisfactory way of pinpointing the real differences.

Regression of the 'Blue Collar Share' Table 13.7 reports the results of an attempt to find the determinants of the blue-collar share using a regression analysis. Two specific patterns can be observed. First, the share of blue collar tends to increase with the size. This pattern is more transparent when one compares the larger negative coefficients for the micro and small firms (with the base being the very large firms). Second, firms in the food sector tend to use smaller share of blue-collar workers in all countries except for Ghana where they use significantly higher blue-collar workers.

Theoretically, the share of blue collars workers used in a firm should be a negative function of the relative wages of blue collar and white collars as higher relative wages tend to discourage firms from using blue collar workers. Unfortunately, the relevant wages at the firm level are not available except in few cases. We have approximated the relative wages using the workers questionnaire at the expense of losing many observations. The regressions of Table 13.7 were, then, repeated after adding the index for relative wages. The coefficient of relative wage was generally negative which is in line with the predictions of the theory; however it was insignificant except for the case of Zimbabwe.

Table 13.7 Determinants of Blue-Collar Share

	Cameroon	*Côte d'Ivoire*	*Ghana*	*Kenya*	*Tanzania*	*Zambia*	*Zimbabwe*
Constant	0.62**	1.04**	0.72**	0.85**	0.67**	0.75**	0.83**
Size							
Micro	0.02	-0.28**	0.01	-0.19**	-0.18	-0.21**	-0.09**
Small	-0.01	-0.10**	-0.12*	-0.06	-0.13	-0.24**	-0.06**
Medium	-0.03	-0.04	-0.23**	-0.14**	-0.09	-0.16**	-0.01
Large	0.09	-0.02	-0.04	-0.07	-0.08	-0.13**	0.02
Ownership							
Private (Native)	-0.05	-0.10	-0.08	-0.01	0.06	0.03	0.04
Foreign	-0.03	-0.13	-0.13	-0.03	0.07	-0.10	0.02
Private & Foreign	-0.02	-0.09	0.05	-0.07	0.02	-0.05	0.03
State	0.28	-0.41**	-0.11	-0.23	-0.03	-0.11	0.001
Sector							
Food	-0.06	-0.08*	0.17**	-0.06**	-0.15**	-0.07**	-0.09**
Metal	-0.03	-0.02	0.01	-0.03	0.03	-0.02	-0.08
Textile	0.05	-0.02	0.11**	0.02	0.10**	-0.03	0.01
No of Observations	204	136	446	562	348	494	387
Adjusted R^2	0.1178	0.3566	0.2615	0.0800	0.1333	0.0891	0.1910

Female Workers in Manufacturing

We next present data on the use of female workers in African manufacturing as revealed by the RPED surveys. We can underline the obvious fact emerging from these data about the low utilization of female workers in African manufacturing outside the informal sector. The results are particularly striking for the food and textile sectors, which in many countries are dominated by female workers. A noteworthy but perhaps anticipated exception seems to be Ghana. As is to be expected, smaller firms generally make more use of female labor. The only exception would seem to be Tanzania. In general, large firms could be expected to have more rigid labor deployment with less flexible work patterns. Thus given the high fertility rate in Africa female labor would be at a disadvantage in trying to combine factory work with household tasks. Perhaps this factor is important in explaining the small proportion of females in African factories compared to the informal sector.

Table 13.8 Average Share of Female Workers by Firm Size

	Cameroon	*Côte d'Ivoire*	*Kenya*	*Ghana*	*Tanzania*	*Zambia*	*Zimbabwe*
Micro	0.11	0.19	0.19	0.39	0.12	0.14	0.43
Small	0.10	0.08	0.14	0.20	0.11	0.13	0.33
Medium	0.06	0.07	0.13	0.13	0.19	0.11	0.11
Large	0.03	0.10	0.09	0.12	0.22	0.06	0.11
Very Large	0.03	0.02	0.25	0.18	0.27	0.09	0.07
All	0.09	0.11	0.16	0.26	0.14	0.12	0.14

Table 13.9 Average Share of Female Workers by Sector

	Cameroon	*Côte d'Ivoire*	*Kenya*	*Ghana*	*Tanzania*	*Zambia*	*Zimbabwe*
Food	0.07	0.11	0.20	0.53	0.16	0.11	0.37
Metal	0.05	0.07	0.12	0.07	0.08	0.06	0.07
Textile	0.09	0.24	0.28	0.41	0.25	0.24	0.06
Wood	0.13	0.04	0.06	0.10	0.10	0.05	0.15

The Structure of Earnings

We now turn to an overview of the structure of earnings in the manufacturing industries as revealed by the RPED survey in the seven countries. Since individual earnings (wages plus allowances) are available only from the workers' questionnaire, we depart from the previous section in using the data thrown up by this part of the survey, rather than the management questionnaire. It should be recalled that the selection of workers was *not* done with a careful random sampling procedure from the books of the firm. Rather 'the sample was drawn according to occupational categories in proportion to each occupation's weight in the firm's total labor force' (see Appendix to this Part). It is likely that biases from a strictly random sampling were introduced in this process, since the worker more easily available to the interviewer had a greater chance of being selected. This, for example, is apparent in the distribution of the workforce by educational attainment. (The analysis from this point on is confined to the sample of *regular* workers).

Distribution of Regular Workers by Educational Levels

Table 13.10 gives the distribution of workers by education in the seven countries.

Table 13.10 Distribution of Regular Workers by Level of Education

	Cameroon	*Côte d'Ivoire*	*Kenya*	*Ghana*	*Tanzania*	*Zambia*	*Zimbabwe*
None	2.86	7.70	6.34	11.41	4.79	1.83	2.21
Primary	19.93	27.03	37.81	1.88	29.29	22.09	42.20
Secondary	40.58	54.33	41.31	57.13	30.93	48.44	52.65
Vocational	10.20	5.16	4.31	13.42	6.53	14.26	1.21
Technopol	15.71	3.24	6.78	15.86	11.70	10.21	0.68
University	10.72	2.54	2.54	0.56	6.70	3.17	1.05

Note: Include complete and incomplete education level.

The largest group of workers in all the countries is one with secondary education. Workers with only primary education are almost as prominent in Kenya and Tanzania, but the modal groups in all the other countries are those with a level of secondary education. Ghana seems to be very peculiar in having an extremely small presence of workers with primary education.

The Earnings Ladder by Occupation

An important element in the analysis of individual earnings is the pattern of occupational differentials in the economy. No doubt, the extent of the differentials is shaped partly by economic, i.e., supply-and demand, forces. However, there are institutional and even political factors shaping these differentials, particularly in economies like the African ones where public sector employment is of much importance. The picture emerging from the RPED data set is given in Table 13.11 and 13.12, separately for males and females.

It is seen that African countries differ enormously in the extent of the occupational differentials. For males, the highest differentials are found in the Southern African countries, Zimbabwe, and Zambia, while the lowest exist in Tanzania and Ghana. This is true whether we look at the managerial or the administrative/clerical groups. This finding is clearly in keeping with other information we have about the Southern African countries. Zimbabwe, as we have seen, has the most marked distribution of employment skewed to the very large firms. It is an economy with a strong influence of racial segmentation. Both factors would tend to increase the premium in earnings enjoyed by white-collar employees. Zambia also had some touches of this type of 'top-heavy' manufacturing sector because of the strong influence of the once prosperous mining sector. What is surprising is that the relentless decline in average earnings and GDP per capita, particularly in Zambia, had failed to erode the occupational wage differential to levels seen in Tanzania and similar African countries.

Table 13.11 Index of Earning of Regular Workers by Occupation (Male)

	Cameroon	*Côte d'Ivoire*	*Kenya*	*Ghana*	*Tanzania*	*Zambia*	*Zimbabwe*
Management	380	321	400	302	227	437	850
Admin/Clerical	192	196	221	154	155	253	278
Commerce/Sale	127	163	110	132	146	163	202
Super/Foreman	170	193	190	165	152	173	204
Support	81	96	90	123	109	108	96
Maintenance	105	174	115	120	115	126	128
Production	100	100	100	100	100	100	100

Table 13.12 Index of Earning of Regular Workers by Occupation (Female)

	Cameroon	*Côte d'Ivoire*	*Kenya*	*Ghana*	*Tanzania*	*Zambia*	*Zimbabwe*
Management	357	566	581	303	302	380	399
Admin/Clerical	124	199	189	204	156	202	366
Commerce/Sale	124	155	184	113	110	119	117
Super/Foreman	288		283	181	141	231	182
Support	86	226	190	140	123	124	110
Maintenance	92		94	104	201	127	112
Production	100	100	100	100	100	100	100

In a prolonged period of declining earnings, as most of the African economies in our sample have witnessed, there is general tendency for the lower paid workers to suffer less for both economic and socio-political reasons. Tanzania, of course, is the classic example where the political system went to great lengths to protect the less privileged workers. Thus, the finding that the occupational wage differentials were the lowest in this country fits in with what is generally known about recent African economic history. The rather low levels of the differential seen for Ghana could be a reflection of the bias in the sample already noted, showing a very small representation of workers with only primary education.

It would appear from Table 13.11 that the two francophone countries and Kenya represent the 'normal' pattern of occupational wage differentials in Africa, with the workers in the premium white collar grade earning *four times* the average of the production workers.

Turning to Table 13.12, depicting the differentials for women workers, it should be noted that the numbers in the top 'management' grade are typically small, and hence we should not consider the indices for this group to imply too much. However, looking at the indices for the administrative/clerical grades only may conclude that they do not appear to be systematically different from the respective differentials for men workers.

Evidence from Other Studies

We try to place the pattern of occupational wage differentials in the RPED countries against a wider perspective of the African and international picture. Mazumdar (1994) used the data on earnings by occupations for a large number of countries collected by the ILO on a regular basis each year.

The ILO has been sending out formatted questionnaires to member countries each year asking them to report both the minimum and average earnings of workers in a long list of designated occupations. The list has increased in length from time to time, but is seen to have remained reasonably stable for a number of years at a stretch. The returns are edited and we are supplied with a liberal amount of footnotes which document what type of wage is being reported — whether minimum or average or a range; for males or females or both; time-rated or piece rated etc. It is thus possible to identify occupational wages, on a reasonably comparable basis for a number of countries. The returns are published in special issues of the ILO Bulletin each year in October, and are identified as the data from the 'October Survey'. Because of the nature of the survey, it is quite clear that the data are collected from registered establishments, i.e., the information relates to the 'formal' sectors of the labor market.

Despite some limitations of the data[55] this wealth of material can be used to provide some indications of the extent of occupational wage differentials in Africa compared to the advanced countries. This is done for 1991 in Table 13.13.

Table 13.13 Occupational Wage Differentials in Africa, United States and United Kingdom by Sector (1991)

Sector	Worker	Africa 1990-91 (Average)	United States 1991	United Kingdom 1991
Mining	Miner	95.34		115.83
Industry	Unskilled	55.65	73.28	
	Semi-Skilled	79.90	63.31	78.86
	Skilled**	100.00	100.00	100.00
Construction	Unskilled	62.94	79.55	69.79
	Skilled	96.03	107.24	92.52
Distr. & Trans.	Unskilled	83.40	62.18	46.92
	Salesperson	82.74	73.73	65.25
	Skilled	116.68	97.54	82.58
White Collar	Clerical (Low)	147.11	78.58	86.27
	Technical (Middle)	210.44	137.03	108.28
	Professional (High)	296.47	196.19	192.42
Public	Unskilled	73.19		77.04
Administration	Clerical	105.42	97.59	92.34
	Executive	205.93	153.95	97.36

Note: The data presented for Africa are simple averages of the respective statistics of the following countries: Algeria, Benin, Burkina Faso, Burundi, Cameroon, Cent. Afr. Rep., Chad, Côte d'Ivoire, Gabon, Mali, Mauritius, Rwanda, Seychelles, Sierra Leone, Tunisia, and Zambia. It should also be further noted that data were not available for all of these in some of the occupations given in the table.

** 100=Base

Source: October Survey of the ILO.

[55]The basic problem with using the 'October Survey' is the question if Labor Offices across the world have interpreted the occupational categories in a meaningful way for us to make either inter-temporal or inter-regional comparisons of occupational wage differentials. The confidence of the unit responsible for collecting these data on this point rests on two arguments: first, the number of occupations is quite large so that averages for particular categories, say arranged by skill-groups would most likely iron out misreported or extravagant numbers. Secondly, since the same type of information has been asked for over a long period of time, reporting authorities tend to acquire familiarity with the procedures and sources.

The material is more extensive in its coverage than the RPED dataset. Sectors other than manufacturing are also included. It is given here because readers might interest in the broader perspective

The major points, which emerge from the tables, are the following:

- The skilled-unskilled differential within industry and in the construction sector in Africa is wider than in the U.S.A. or the U.K. However, the differential between skilled and semi-skilled workers is lower in Africa. Both these results can be explained in terms of Reder's substitutability hypothesis (Reder 1955). African economies, with a shortage of skills, are able to adjust downward the skill content required in the highly skilled occupations. However, since a minimum of skills is needed for industrial work, a large gap in skills exists between operatives and unskilled laborers. With the shortage of skills going down to the operative's level, the substitutability of unskilled labor for all labor with some skill is smaller in Africa, but the substitutability of semi-skilled for skilled labor in the sectors remains high.
- It is sometimes maintained that the distributive sector is the soft under-belly for the labor market where wages for unskilled or low-skill labor is allowed to fall to levels below those maintained in industry and construction by institutional or efficiency-wage factors. Our data show that this hypothesis is borne out in the U.S.A. and the U.K. (at least in 1991), but not in Africa. It should, however, be remembered that more of the employed in the tertiary sector in Africa are found in the informal sector, which is not covered in this wage survey.
- A major difference between Africa and the developed countries is revealed in the ratio of wages of white collar to blue collar workers. In Africa, the premium above skilled industrial work is high for even low and middle levels of white collar work (outside public administration), but not so in the U.S.A. or the U.K. The premium seems to have fallen sharply in the latter half of the eighties, but was still well above that for the developed countries. This result is, of course, what is expected from the general shortage of educated labor in Africa.
- The major differences on this point between the private and the public sectors in Africa are also seen in the tables. Public sector wages for middle and higher level white-collar workers are lower than in the private sector in Africa as well as in the developed countries. However, the margin of the difference tends to be much larger in Africa.

Evidently, the wage decline in many African countries in the last decade has taken a toll on the public sector white-collar workers disproportionately.

How do the results from the RPED survey look against the background of this discussion of African occupational wage differential from the ILO surveys? A direct comparison is not possible because in the RPED data the base is all production workers — not *skilled* workers in industry as in Table 13.13. In addition, the ILO survey did not include returns from Zimbabwe where the occupational differentials were found the highest. However, the comparatively high differential in favor of white-collar workers, much higher than in the advanced countries, is confirmed by the RPED data for manufacturing enterprises alone.

The Distribution of Earnings in the Seven Countries: An Overview

In this section, we look at the inequality in the distribution of earnings as has been revealed by the RPED data set for the seven countries. This overview is preliminary to the study of the determinants of earnings in the next chapter.

The summary statistics most widely used to measure the inequality of the distribution is the Gini coefficient. This statistic is, however, a measure pertaining to the entire distribution, and does not give us much idea of the nature of the distribution at the lower and the upper end respectively. For this purpose we present the ratio P25/Median (the ratio of the earnings at the first quartile of the distribution to the median) to indicate the degree of inequality in the bottom half of the distribution; and the ratio P75/median to be a proxy for inequality in the top half. Finally, the ratio P10/P90 is a useful measure to indicate the distance in the levels of earnings between the bottom and the top earners in the distribution.

Table 13.14 Measures of Earning Inequality

	Cameroon	*Côte d'Ivoire*	*Ghana*	*Kenya*	*Tanzania*	*Zambia*	*Zimbabwe*
Gini Coefficient	0.4621	0.5092	0.4196	0.4406	0.4528	0.5020	0.5382
CV	109	167	124	122	147	145	143
P1/P90	0.02	0.06	0.06	0.11	0.02	0.07	0.04
P25/Median	0.62	0.68	0.7	0.67	0.66	0.68	0.73
P75/Median	1.83	1.75	1.56	1.54	1.58	1.77	1.9

Note: CV stands for coefficient of variation.

Of the seven countries, Zambia and Zimbabwe are the two with the greatest inequality of earnings (though in the case of Zambia the Gini measure of inequality might have been exaggerated by data errors, as revealed by the exceptionally high coefficient of variation). This finding about the Southern African countries is consistent with what we have found about occupational differentials earlier. Contrary to expectations it is Ghana and not Tanzania, which shows the lowest degree of inequality. However, we have already drawn attention of the under-representation of workers with primary education in the Ghana sample and this might have resulted in being partly responsible for the low Gini coefficient in this country.

Turning to the information on the distribution at the lower and the higher end, it is seen that the high degree of inequality in Zambia and Zimbabwe can be traced to the high earnings above the median as indicated by the relatively large P75/Median ratios for these countries. The two francophone countries also have P75/Median ratios — higher than the other three Anglophone countries, Ghana, Kenya and Tanzania. This is reflected in their Gini coefficients being higher, but not as high as Zambia and Zimbabwe.

Additional information on the differences in the degree of inequality might be obtained by looking separately at the blue and the white-collar workers.

Table 13.15 Measures of Earning Inequality (Blue-Collars)

	Cameroon	*Côte d'Ivoire*	*Ghana*	*Kenya*	*Tanzania*	*Zambia*	*Zimbabwe*
Gini Coefficient	0.3942	0.4026	0.3654	0.3207	0.3610	0.3682	0.3938
CV	96	137	127	84	108	121	122
P1/P90	0.08	0.10	0.09	0.16	0.15	0.14	0.05
P25/Median	0.67	0.76	0.7	0.73	0.69	0.72	0.83
P75/Median	1.59	1.53	1.43	1.38	1.48	1.42	1.38

Note: CV stands for Coefficient of variation.

Table 13.16 Measures of Earning Inequality (White-Collars)

	Cameroon	*Côte d'Ivoire*	*Ghana*	*Kenya*	*Tanzania*	*Zambia*	*Zimbabwe*
Gini Coefficient	0.4445	0.5143	0.4047	0.4689	0.4836	0.4925	0.4967
CV	96	149	106	110	146	127	106
P1/P90	0.1	0.05	0.08	0.07	0.08	0.05	0.04
P25/Median	0.57	0.58	0.69	0.6	0.65	0.6	0.6
P75/Median	1.85	1.75	1.65	1.68	1.59	1.89	2.21

Note: CV stands for Coefficient of variation.

The higher degree of inequality noted above for Zambia and Zimbabwe are seen to hold separately for the two groups of workers. Generally, in all the countries of the sample inequality can be expected to be higher for the white than the blue-collar workers. This is seen clearly if we compare the values of the P25/median and the P75/median for the two groups in each country. These ratios also show that at the upper half of the distributions, it is the earnings differentials for white-collar workers that make Zambia and Zimbabwe more unequal than the other Anglophone countries. We can also see from a comparison of the values of the P75/median ratio that the two francophone countries have a more unequal distribution of earnings for blue collar workers than the Southern African countries, but less so as far as the white-collar are concerned.

How Does Earnings Inequality Look Compared to Developed Countries?

In conclusion, it might be interesting to make a quick comparison with some readily available data that exists for advanced countries. The comparison is not exact. Gottschalk and Smeeding present some data on earnings inequality for selected developed countries around 1990. They refer to full time regular males with 'full year jobs', and in all occupations. Thus, unlike the RPED sample, they include non-manufacturing. Secondly, the RPED data discussed above include female workers, though the proportion of such workers, as we have seen, is small. Nonetheless, some interest attaches to the following numbers of the P10/P90 ratios given by Gottschalk and Smeeding. The data are presented in *ascending* order of inequality:

Table 13.17 Spread of Earnings in Selected Developed Countries

Country (date)	*Ratio of P10 to P90*
Netherlands (1987)	0.42
Germany (1984)	0.40
Australia (1989/90)	0.36
United Kingdom (1986)	0.32
Sweden (1992)	0.29
Canada (1987)	0.22
United States (1991)	0.18

Source: Gottschalk and Smeeding, Figure 1, p.644.

The comparison shows the very much larger degree of inequality that exists among African workers, even if we consider the most unequal of the sample of developed countries — which happened to be in North America. No doubt, the degree of inequality discussed above in Africa is increased by the inclusion of female workers in our sample. But as against this, it is very likely that the inequality measure for our sample in Africa is dampened considerably by the exclusion of workers in non-manufacturing, particularly in the tertiary, agricultural and the informal sectors generally. It seems clear that the underestimation of earnings inequality in the African scene because of the latter would be vastly more than the overestimation due to the former.

14 Determinants of Earnings of Manufacturing Workers

In this chapter, we present the results of standard earnings functions. The functions were estimated for each country after deflating the earnings of each year by the consumer price index (so that our observations are earnings at prices of the base year 1992), and then pooling the data for all the years. The results are given in the series of tables in Appendix 1 to this chapter, and the notes in Appendix 2 describe the variables and the specific problems (if any) for them in the country concerned. The dependant variable is the log of monthly earnings per worker (including allowances were available). The mean values of the variables used are set out in the first table of Appendix 1.

The Returns to Education

The basic earnings function treats education in two ways: as a continuous variable in years: and as a set of dummies. The education systems differ rather significantly from country to country, which make the task of coming up with a unified approach rather difficult. The following issues regarding systems of education, years of education, and the corresponding dummies are noteworthy:

For Kenya, Zambia, and Zimbabwe, years of education are calculated by assuming 7 years for Primary, 6 years for Secondary, and 6 Years for University. For Cameroon and Côte d'Ivoire, 6 years for Primary, 3 years for Middle, 4 years for secondary, 1 year for Lycee, 2 years for Lycee Technique, and 4 years for University are added. For Ghana and Tanzania, 6 years for Primary, 3 years for Middle, 4 years for Secondary, 1 year for Vocational, 2 years for Professional and Polytechnic, and 4 years for University are added. If the education of each level is not completed, where applicable, the corresponding years of education are added instead of the above-mentioned numbers.

The dummies for the education groups are created using Zimbabwe as the standard. Six levels of education (None, Primary, Secondary,

Vocational, Techno pol, and University) are distinguished. For some countries, namely, Cameroon, Côte d'Ivoire, Ghana, and Tanzania, levels of education are reported in much more detail. For instance instead of secondary education as in most countries, Ghana has middle school, and secondary school. In these cases, to preserve the standard only the six education levels are used.

Vocational education and Technopol education corresponds to some supplementary education. In some countries like Zimbabwe, one cannot distinguish if those with vocational education or Technopol education have formal education in terms of Primary or Secondary education. In those cases, to calculate years of education, Vocational and Technopol education are considered equivalent to Secondary education. In other countries like Ghana, it is possible to calculate the formal education that may accompany vocational or Technopol education. In these cases, one year for vocational and two years for Technopol education are added to the corresponding years of formal education.

In each equation, we control for the wave of the survey, sex, and the industry in which the worker is currently employed. Furthermore, since the size of the establishment (the plant in which the worker is interviewed) is such a consistently important variable in any of the functions estimated (see below) it is included in all the basic earnings functions.

- Table 14.1 shows that the return to Schooling (measured in years) has the lowest value of 5 percent per year in Tanzania and the highest of 14 percent in Zimbabwe. Both these limits are consistent with what has been already noted above about the distribution of employment by enterprise size and the spread of occupational earnings differentials in these countries.

Table 14.1 Rates of Return to Years of Schooling (Per Annum)

Cameroon	*Côte d'Ivoire*	*Ghana*	*Kenya*	*Tanzania*	*Zambia*	*Zimbabwe*
0.07	0.07	0.06	0.07	0.05	0.11	0.14

Source: Appendix Table 2.

- The earnings functions were also estimated with broad groups of educational levels as dummies. The coefficients of the education dummies were used to calculate the *incremental* proportionate increases in earnings corresponding to successively higher levels. The results are presented in Table 14.2. It should be noted that the levels do not represent different stages of *completed* education. As Velenchik (1994) reports for Zimbabwe: 'The dummy variables ... represent the highest level of academic education achieved, with additional dummies indicating whether the individual also attained vocational or technical school. Thus, Primary = 1 means that the last year of academic schooling the individual achieved was a primary grade. Primary =1 does not imply that the individual completed primary school. Secondary and University are constructed the same way.'

Table 14.2 Incremental (Marginal) Returns for Different Education Levels (1), (Log Differences in the Coefficients of the Successive Levels of Education)

Country	*Primary*	*Secondary*	*Vocational*	*Technopol*	*University*
Cameroon	0.07*	0.25	0.26	0.32	0.51
Côte d'Ivoire	0.28	0.36	0.86	0.55	-0.15
Ghana	0.11*	0.18	0.24	0.31	0.48
Kenya	-0.07*	0.30	0.10	0.20	0.55
Tanzania	-0.27	0.32*	-0.05*	0.24	0.37
Zambia	-0.20	0.39	0.26	0.27	0.84
Zimbabwe	0.18*	0.67	0.39	0.97	0.11

Source: Appendix Table 5. *Not significant.

The results strongly suggest increasing returns to the successive levels of education. Furthermore, returns to primary education are not significantly different from zero in *any of the anglophone countries* (with those in Zambia being perversely negative). Does the quality of education in the *francophone* countries ensure that primary education does bring in significantly positive returns although they are lower than for the higher levels? It is quite striking that for *all* countries there is a clear tendency for the premiums to increase as we go up the hierarchy. We will return to these important conclusions when we discuss the evidence from other data sets and other sectors below.

Differences in education levels across countries: One difficulty with this unified approach of introducing education dummies is the fact that existing differences in education standards make the comparison difficult. The prime example of this difficulty is the grouping of Middle school education and Secondary education into a single dummy for countries like Cameroon, Côte d'Ivoire, Ghana, and Tanzania where the education system allows for further decomposition. To shed some light on the importance of this issue, we have re-estimated the earning functions for these countries after adding one more education dummy, Middle. The corresponding incremental rates of returns to education are provided in the following table:

Table 14.3 Incremental (Marginal) Returns for Different Education Levels (2) (Log Differences in the Coefficients of the Successive Levels of Education)

Country	*Primary*	*Middle*	*Secondary*	*Vocational*	*Technopol*	*University*
Cameroon	NS	0.23	0.06	0.25	0.33	0.54
Côte d'Ivoire	0.28	0.23	0.35	0.64	0.48	-0.11
Ghana	NS	0.09	0.36	-0.03	0.30	0.48
Tanzania	NS	0.23	0.15	NS	0.02	0.44

The difference is especially important for Ghana where a large percentage of workers (51 percent) have Middle school education. In this country the incremental returns to vocational education almost disappear in favor of incremental returns to secondary education. Also worthy of note is the result that the negative return to primary education in Tanzania now disappears and the middle schools are seen to bring in a substantial increment to earnings.

Blue and White-Collar Occupations

In the results given so far, we have lumped all occupations together. It might be worthwhile looking separately at blue and white-collar workers because in developing countries these groups are often non-competing, coming from different social strata. Special interest attaches to the question if the increasing returns to education observed for all workers together holds separately for the blue collar workers, and if the strong increasing returns really come from the pattern of earnings of the white collar grades. The full results are given in the Appendix.

As is to be expected, the rate of return to years of schooling when we did not distinguish between different levels is lower for the blue-collar. This difference ranges between 2 and 5 percent for the sample of our countries, as against between 5 and 17 percent for the white-collar. The ranking of the countries by the size of the returns stays more or less the same whether we consider the blue-collar and while-collar separately, or both groups together.

Turning now to the results when we treat the education variables with dummies representing levels, the coefficients are presented separately for the blue and the white-collar workers in Table 14.4. Clearly, more interest attaches to the returns to education below the university (college) level where the sample for blue-collar workers are likely to be small (The coefficients for primary are omitted because they are mostly not significant).

Table 14.4 Coefficients of Education Dummies for Blue and White-Collar Workers

Level and Category	*Cameroon*	*Côte d'Ivoire*	*Ghana*	*Kenya*	*Tanzania*	*Zambia*	*Zimbabwe*
Secondary							
White	0.46	0.96	NS	NS	NS	0.19	1.58
Blue	0.28	0.46	0.22	0.18	0.06	NS	0.29
Vocational							
White	0.75	1.67	NS	0.23	NS	0.42	2.00
Blue	0.35	1.12	0.50	0.36	NS	0.40	0.65
Technical							
White	1.01	2.03	0.62	0.56	0.23	0.68	2.57
Blue	0.80	2.23	0.58	0.25	NS	0.55	NS

Source: Appendix Table 23, 24.

Comparison with Results from other Studies in Sub-Saharan Africa

The major conclusion from the estimation of the earnings functions from the RPED data sets reported above is the convex nature of the functions for all countries, even when we separate the samples into two classes of occupations. This finding contradicts the received view propagated by Psacharopoulos (1994) among others. In a popular paper summarizing his previous work (1985, Table 1, and Figure 1, pp 586-87), Psacharopoulos wrote that the 'table maintained the earlier well documented declining rate of return pattern by level of education' (p.585). The sources of Psacharapoulos's reported results are diverse. They have been culled from the work of different researchers employing different types of analysis to different types of data sets. In most cases, it is not possible to go back to the original analysis to see if they are compatible with the present data sets. In any event, the majority of these studies are quite old. Nevertheless, Psacharapoulos's presentation has established a 'norm' for the whole world, which the evidence surely is not able to bear. In a very recent study, for example Gallup (1994) found that in Malaysia, for all three races separately — Malays, Chinese, and Indian — the rates of return to education increased systematically from primary through secondary to the tertiary level. Gallup was induced to remark, citing Psacharapoulos that the

Malaysian situation was 'unusual' compared to other countries.

Admittedly, the rates of returns given in Tables 14.2 and 14.3 are for several years of education for each level in question. But since the number of years are larger for primary and become smaller as we go to higher levels, the returns per year would increase even more than shown as we go up the educational ladder.

Secondly, the coefficients reported measure returns to education only on the assumption that the worker would have earned a sum equal to the amount estimated at each level, if he had chosen to work in the labor market rather than increase his human capital. For primary school participants this might be an overestimate of the foregone earnings if they participate only partly in the labor market when they do not go to school. For the higher levels we have to similarly devalue the costs of education in so far as unemployment for these educational groups is quite high in African economies. Thus while the absolute rates of return are overestimated by taking the uncorrected values of the coefficients of the earnings functions, the relative differences for the three levels, after correcting for non-participation and unemployment, are not obvious.

Thirdly, the social costs clearly increase with the level of education, as far as higher education in African countries is heavily subsidized. The social rates of return cold then be increasing at a faster rate than the private returns for higher levels of education. (It will be recalled that Psacharopoulos suggested that the social rate declined linearly with higher levels, 1985, Figure 1, p.587).

A more detailed critique of the Psacharopoulos's thesis is to be found in Bennell (1996). He goes through a systematic review of the individual studies, which were used by Psacharopoulos for his aggregate generalizations. He finds that they are so flawed in data quality and methodologies used that 'they should be discarded altogether in any serious discussion of education investment priorities both for the continent as whole and for individual countries'. Moreover, Bennell makes the point that, while most of these studies date back from the seventies and the early eighties, labor market conditions have changed severely in the last two decades. We would like to know the results from more recent studies. In particular, it would be very interesting to compare the RPED results, which are confined to the formal manufacturing sector, with others in the same countries which deal more broadly with at least the employees in the urban labor market as a whole.

Kenya

For Kenya it is possible to compare the results obtained from the data set on manufacturing enterprises with results on returns to education obtained from the Labor Force Surveys in 1977-8 and in1986 which cover all sectors of the economy. The relevant statistics, extracted from Mazumdar (1993), are given in Table 14.5. Although more levels of education are considered in the analysis of the Labor Force Survey than in the earnings functions from the enterprise surveys, it is clear that the marginal private returns to education (gross) increased with successive levels of education in the Kenyan urban economy, particularly for the wage employees. It is also apparent from a comparison of the statistics in Tables 14.3 and 14.5 that the return to education have fallen significantly between the mid-eighties and the mid nineties, if in fact the patterns of earnings in manufacturing are comparable to those in the urban labor market as a whole.

Table 14.5 Earnings Function for Urban Men: Kenya (Incremental Coefficients of Education Dummies)

Years of Education (Base = No education)	*1977-8 (All *)*	*1986 (All *)*	*1986 (Employees Only)*
1 – 4 Years Primary	0.19	0.03	0.12
5 – 8 " "	0.12	0.33	0.25
1 – 2 Secondary	0.31	0.19	0.14
3 – 4 " "	0.59	0.40	0.27
5 – 6 " "	0.36	0.50	0.43
University	0.42	0.50	0.74

Source: 1977-8 Bigsten, Table IV.9, P. 85 1986 Urban Labor Survey. Own Computations. The full results are given in Mazumdar (1993), Table A III.3.

Ghana

Results from the analysis of the Socio-economic household surveys (LSMS surveys) are available for Ghana for dates nearer to the RPED surveys. Canagarajah and Mazumdar provide an overall picture of the relationship of earnings to education in the market for wage employees only, i.e., excluding the self-employed but without distinguishing between the private and public sectors. The estimated earnings functions are for two dates — 1987-88 and 1991-92. These were the years of recovery after the Structural Adjustment programs had been established in Ghana. The period saw a strengthening of the labor market and real wages made some recovery after falling precipitously between 1974 and 1984 (see Chapter 9, Part III). The results of the earnings functions show some interesting points of comparison with the RPED results for manufacturing employees discussed above.

The first OLS equation estimated the earnings function with education years measured continuously as in Table 14.1 above. The coefficient for years of schooling was 0.035 for 1987-8 and 0.061 for 1991-2. The latter figure is quite close to the value from the RPED surveys of Table 14.1.

Secondly, educational levels were treated as dummy variable, although the categories are not identical to those available from the RPED data set. However, some categories are directly comparable. We find that in both the years of the Socio-economic surveys, the return to primary education is not significant. This result agrees with the RPED estimation. It is an important part of the educated labor market scene, which will be commented on further below.

The incremental coefficients (showing the percentage increase in earnings relative to the previous stage) for middle, secondary and higher are 0.09, 0.19, and 0.60 for 1987 respectively and 0.40, 0.35 and 0.41 for 1991. We see that in 1987 the returns to post-primary stages show increasing returns to schooling, as in the RPED estimates, with large percentage gains only occurring at the level higher than secondary. However, by 1991 the labor market had changed to a condition in which all the stages of education beyond the primary offered equal percentage increase in earnings.

Returns to Education in Public and Private Sectors An important difference between the RPED and the GLSS samples is, of course that the latter included the non-manufacturing sectors, and particularly the services sector in which government employment predominates, more so for the more educated workers. Could it be that a narrowing of wage differentials in the public sector was the proximate cause of the equalization of returns for stages of education beyond the primary — which is observed in the GLSS sample and not the RPED one in the nineties? There are two reasons why the squeezing of wage differentials would be felt more in the public services. First, the structural adjustment program was very strong in its support of reduction of the public sector wage bill. We have seen in discussions in earlier chapters that the State in Ghana, and elsewhere in Africa, responded to this demand by leaning towards the option of real wage decline rather than slashing employment. The across-the-board public sector wage increase of mid-1992 would not have time to have been reflected in the GLSS sample. Secondly, public manufacturing enterprises which are included in the RPED sample, along with private firms, could be expected to pay some attention to the quality of workers, more so than the administrative sector where output is difficult to define. In a period in which the quality of education is declining the observed return to education could be expected to fall more significantly in the public service sector.

The importance of the change in the labor market in the public sector can be assessed from some other results presented in Canagarajah and Mazumdar (section 5.3). They consider the labor market all together, including the self-employed, the private sector employees, and those employed in the public sector. We can estimate separate earnings functions for these three categories, but the resulting estimates might be biased because we are not allowing for the selectivity factors which govern the allocation of the workers to the three types of employment.

The authors propose a model in which parents' occupational and educational backgrounds affect the individual's relative employment opportunity in the three different types of job. The selection equation is a multinomial logit estimate of sectoral choice in which the explanatory variables are education and age of the individual, as well as the parental background factors, and regions of the country. The equation applied to the 1991-2 GLSS data set provided estimates of the expected sign for almost all the variables. Thus middle school and above education helped job seekers enter the wage sector as opposed to self-employment, as did different kinds of diplomas and certificates from training. Using Accra as a benchmark, residence in other regions decreased the probability of entering the public sector, but increased the probability of self-employment.

Family background had a small but significant effect on the job seekers' sectoral choice. In particular, the parents' while-collar occupation — clerical, professional or managerial — increased the probability of public employment. When the earnings function was estimated correcting for the selectivity bias, none of the parental variables were significant in this equation. What is of more interest for the present discussion is that the returns to years of schooling were quite different from the uncorrected version of the earnings function, as follows:

The important result is that, after correcting for selectivity, the rate of return per year of schooling is found to be much higher in private employment. This is consistent with the changes in wage structure in Ghana discussed above. The recovery of the economy in the few years preceding 1991-2 had increased the importance of human capital in the market for wage labor in the private sector. At the same time the squeezing of wage differentials due to the factors discussed in the public sector had reduced the returns to education, particularly at the higher levels (see Canagarajah and Thomas 1997 and Dar *et al* 1997).

Table 14.6 Coefficients of Years of Schooling in Earnings Function: Ghana 1991-2

	Self-employed	*Private employee*	*Public employee*
OLS estimate	0.028	0.040	0.039
Estimate in equation with correction	0.030	0.067	0.017

Source: Canagarajah and Mazumdar, Table 5.3. All the coefficients are highly significant.

It is thus seen that the result mentioned earlier showing a marked increase in the rate of return to education over-all in the wage labor market between 1987 and 1991 is entirely due to the changes in the labor market for privately owned enterprises. At the latter date, education at all levels above the primary was being rewarded equally, not just the highest level. This result might be an indication that the labor market was by 1991 recovering to the point of being sensitive to the acquisition of human capital.

Quality of Schooling

Glewwe (1996) made a direct attempt at incorporating the quality of schooling in the estimation of the returns to education for the GLSS Survey of 1988-89. No such exercise could be attempted for the later years because of the absence of special data, which were available for 1988-89 only. It is nevertheless important to refer to this work for the light it throws on the importance of quality of education in assessing the overall returns to education. Glewee's standard OLS estimates yielded the result that the coefficient of 'years of schooling' were practically identical — 0.0751 for the public employees and 0.0738 for private wage earners. (Remember, this is the period earlier than the one referred to in Table 14.6 above for 1991-2. Structural adjustment policies had a few more years to affect the labor market by then). But when selectivity of workers entering the two sectors were allowed for through two selection equations determining the choice between wage work and other work, and also between government wage and private wage employment, there were dramatic changes in the return to education. Two alternative methods of estimation yielded the identical result — that 'in the government sector the returns to education drop to about 4-6 percent, and in the private sector they appear to be zero' (p.274).

Commenting on the result Glewwe wrote that it is difficult to believe that education had no impact on earnings unless one got a government job — that there were no returns to education in private wage employment.

Rather, Glewwe suggests one got this result because the quality of schooling had dropped so much in Ghana at this date, that 'years by education' by themselves did not produce significant earnings increment. The variation in the quality of schooling were probably more important than those in the *quantity* of schooling. In the absence of any variable capturing the quality of schooling in the earning function, one was left with a non-significant coefficient for the education variable.

It has been known for sometime from detailed analysis done in Latin America that when school quality varies widely across time and space, years of schooling may be a very imperfect indicator of human capital attained (Behrman and Birdsall; Harbison and Hamushek). The general model, which emerges from these discussions, is that the impact of education on earnings is best captured in a two-equation system. The first equation traces the determinants of earnings to human capital attainment, not years of schooling. The second equation attempts to estimate the level of human capital attainment as a function of both quantity and quality of schooling. Algebraically the two equations are as follows:

(1) $\ln W = g(H, E, A)$ where W is wage, H a measure of human capital attained, E is experience, and A individual ability unrelated to H;
(2) $H = h(S, Q, A, B)$ where S is years of schooling (quantity), Q is quality of schooling and B is family background.

In this model, the impact of schooling on earnings is spelled out as working indirectly through an enhancement of human capital attained, along with other factors. The total effect of schooling years on earnings can be determined by combining the partial derivatives from the two equations:

(3) $d \ln W / dS = d \ln W / dH \times dH/dS$

To implement this model empirically, we need a measure of H, human capital attained. Glewwe in the work on the 1988-89 LSMS Survey for Ghana uses scores of 'cognitive skills' available in the data set. The survey data contained the results of three tests of 'cognitive skills' applied to a sub-sample of individuals in the 9-55 age category. These covered abstract reasoning (Raven's Colored Progressive Matrices), mathematics, and reading (English) comprehension. The last two are used as measures of H, and the first as a measure of A in equation (1).

Turning to equation (2) above, in the absence of direct data, which might measure school quality, Glewwe tries to control for variation in school quality by specifying interaction terms between years in school and the geographic region and age variables. 'The former should control for variation in school quality across regions and the latter across age cohorts' (p. 278).

In his estimation of equation (1), Glewwe finds that in the private sector, reading skills have a significant impact on earnings, while in the public sector the mathematics score has a strong positive effect. Turning to the results of equation (2), 'years of schooling alone is insignificant, but when interacted with age, Raven's score and regional dummy variables, it has a strongly significant quadratic impact on reading and mathematics scores, the impact being stronger for those with higher school attainment' (p.380). These results, showing the significance of the interaction terms, reveal that schooling years work in conjunction with other factors. The interaction with Raven's score shows that more talented individuals benefit more from school years — as judged by the labor market. The interaction with age captures the secular decline in the quality of education. Persons who attended school many years ago were able to enhance their earnings per year of schooling more than recent cohorts were. The result that the regional dummies, which are insignificant in themselves, show strong and significant variation in the attainment of reading and mathematical skills across regions, when interacted with years of schooling, point to the importance of regional difference in the quality of schools.

The total effect of education on earnings was calculated from these estimated equations as shown in equation (3). The rate of return to school years, calculated at the mean value of both schooling and Raven's score was higher in the public but no longer zero in the private sector. In the former, they ranged between 5.4% and 6.2%, and in the latter between 3.4 and 6.3. As already noted, the rates of return rise with age, and are higher in Accra reflecting the higher school quality in the capital city at all age groups.

The discussion in this sub-section has relevance to the result in the RPED analysis mentioned above that, when dummy variables for educational levels were used, the earnings function in Ghana showed that returns to primary education were zero, although they were large for further levels. It is very likely that this is also a 'quality of education' effect. The quality of primary education in Ghana had been degraded much more than for other levels, so that the market no longer attached any value to primary education only. The fact that erosion of quality is relatively less at higher levels in education probably reflects the fact that a grade of education involving large numbers and widespread resources is likely to deteriorate more with the decline in public salaries, administration and general infrastructure.

Zambia

Some work on the returns to education in Zambia has been done by Nielsen and Nielsen (2001) using data from the Priority Survey II for 1993 (a sample survey of households in all areas of the country conducted by the Central Statistical Office in association with the World Bank). A total of 55,000 individuals were covered, but the authors excluded people older than 17 years, and also disregarded individuals for whom essential variables were missing, leaving them with a sample of about 26.000 individuals, one-third coming from the rural areas, and two-thirds from the urban. 'The sample is stratified, and therefore weights are part of the data set.' The statistical analysis seeks to estimate the determinants of total income, including the returns from activities as a self-employed worker (but consumed own produce is excluded since it is computed only at the household level. The analysis is done separately for men and women, and for urban and rural areas. For each category the authors distinguished the formal and the informal (residual) sectors, the former defined as the public sector (including parastatals) and enterprises having more than 5 workers. Two sets of regressions were run: an OLS estimate with two levels of education (primary and more than primary), and several other variables including experience; household variables like head, married or living in large household; industrial sector and region dummies. The other set of regressions used a 'full model' which allowed for the decision to participate, and to choose the formal or the informal sector in the urban economy, and paid employment or self-employment in the rural. The most striking result of these regressions were that return to primary education is close to zero in the urban areas, but clearly larger than zero in rural areas. The returns to post-secondary education are higher in the urban areas, but comparing the OLS with the full model, there is an interesting suggestion that as far as urban men are considered post-primary education plays its determining role more in allocation males to more lucrative sectors than in increasing income in the urban market per se. In fact, after allowing for selectivity in employment decisions, there is a significant extra return to education for urban residents who are employed in the informal sector.

The Zambia results draw attention to a distinction between the urban and rural labor markets in sub-Saharan, as far as the returns to education are concerned. The zero or close to zero return to primary education in urban areas might be due to the low quality of schooling noticed in the studies cited above. Nielsen and Nielsen write: 'Because a large part of the rural residents have no education at all, having some education probably works as a signal for some underlying favorable unobservable characteristics. For instance, parents may choose to let the brightest children attend to school; therefore, having completed some schooling is correlated with "being bright" although children may not learn much in primary school.' The existence of increasing returns to education with post-primary education in the urban, and not in the rural areas, might be due to the greater availability in the former of sub-sectors of the labor market which reward education.

Earnings and the Size of the Enterprise

We now turn to a discussion of the other factors found important in the determination of earnings in the estimated earnings functions. The single most important factor affecting earnings after education and after experience, is the size of the enterprise in which the worker was employed. In our analysis, we measure the Size by the total number of *regular* workers. As can be seen from the Table 2 of Appendix 1 to this chapter, the size factor is important in itself as an explanation of earnings. However, the value of the coefficient is reduced somewhat when we introduce human capital factors in the function and control for industry. The elasticity of earnings with respect to enterprise size is as given in Table 14.7.

Table 14.7 Coefficients of Log of Size in the Earning Function

Variable	*Cameroon*	*Côte d'Ivoire*	*Ghana*	*Kenya*	*Tanzania*	*Zambia*	*Zimbabwe*
Log Size	0.22	0.15	0.14	0.12	0.10	0.17	0.20

Source: Table 3 Appendix.

The overall elasticity hides the relative changes of the size coefficient in different parts of the distribution. It might be more interesting to look at the coefficients of the size dummies as given in Table 14.8.

Table 14.8 Coefficients of Size Dummies in the Earning Function

Variable	*Cameroon*	*Côte d'Ivoire*	*Ghana*	*Kenya*	*Tanzania*	*Zambia*	*Zimbabwe*
Micro	-0.49	-0.44	-0.42	-0.29	-0.14	-0.19	-0.73
Small	-0.32	NS	-0.16	-0.29	-0.11	-0.14	-0.22
Large	0.25	NS	0.25	NS	NS	0.38	0.15
V. Large	0.42	0.28	NS	0.13	0.27	0.44	0.47

Source: Table 6 Appendix. The coefficients give the relative change by size-groups with respect to the Medium sized firms.

Note that the estimated equations for this set of results included a dummy for location distinguishing the capital city from other areas. It was significant for all the countries except Zimbabwe.

The difference in earnings levels between the smallest and the largest establishments, after controlling for other factors, is largest for Zimbabwe, followed by Cameroon and Zambia. This finding is in accordance with earlier observations about the more unequally distributed structure of manufacturing in the two Southern African countries in our sample. The large size related wage differential in the francophone country, Cameroon, is also consistent with expectations, but Côte d'Ivoire result negates any generalization for this group of countries.

When we separate the blue and white-collar workers, the size effect is found stronger for the white-collar as is to be expected. Administrative and managerial staffs in particular enjoy a larger size-related wage premium. However, the difference is not spectacularly large. In Zimbabwe, for example, the size elasticity of earnings was 0.17 for blue collar and 0.20 for while collar workers. The spread of earnings (net) from the micro to the very large firms was ln 0.96 for the blue-collar and ln 1.20 for the white-collar workers (Tables 9-10 Appendix).

Size of the enterprise is an important determinant of the level of earnings in many developing countries. Generally, the extent of the wage differential due to this factor is well above that in developed countries (see Chapter 15). To place the results from the African in perspective, we can compare them with those obtained by Mazumdar in two studies of the urban labor market in Asia in the late seventies. Table 14.9 brings together the relevant statistics for manual workers in the African and Asian labor markets:[56]

Table 14.9 Spread in the log of Earnings from the Lowest to the Highest Size Groups

Category	*Cameroon*	*Côte d'Iv.*	*Ghana*	*Kenya*	*Tanzania*	*Zambia*	*Zimbabwe*	*Bombay 1979*	*Malaysia 1975*
Manual	0.86	0.45	0.63	0.32	0.16	0.69	0.95	0.67	0.23
Non-Manual	0.79	1.02	0.49	0.60	0.50	0.62	1.20	NA	0.47

Source: Tables 9-10 Appendix; Mazumdar (1984) and (1981) for Bombay and Malaysia respectively.

The striking conclusion which emerges from this table is that even after the lapse of 15 years or more of downward pressure on wages in the African economy, which could have been expected to work towards the squeezing of earnings differentials, the magnitude of the size related differentials in Africa were much higher than what was observed in Malaysia in 1975 (with the sole exception of Tanzania), and in five of the seven countries, on the same level as or higher than Bombay.

We shall attempt a detailed analysis of size-related differentials in the next chapter. At the end of the analysis, some suggestions will be made as to why these differentials tend to be generally higher in developing countries.

Earnings Differentials by Ownership Category

We want to know if categories of firms belonging to the private, foreign or state sectors or under joint ownership lead to different levels of earnings for workers — after we have controlled for the other significant factors affecting earnings. A set of 'ownership' dummies, giving the different types available for all countries in the survey data, were added to the regression of Appendix Table 6. The coefficients of this set of dummies are reproduced in Table 14.10.

[56]The analysis for Bombay and Malaysia employed the statistical form of multivariate analysis called the Multiple Classification Analysis (MCA). This technique transforms a multiple regression model into deviations of the grand mean for the whole sample. Thus, the values of the 'spread' are comparable to the African regression results. There are, however, some but not important differences in the explanatory variables used.

Table 14.10 Coefficients of Ownership Dummies in Extended Earnings Regression

	Cameroon	*Côte d'Ivoire*	*Ghana*	*Kenya*	*Tanzania*	*Zambia*	*Zimbabwe*
Foreign	0.25**	0.29**	0.24	0.22**	-0.15	0.28**	0.38**
Private-Foreign	0.05	0.31**	0.16**	0.08*	0.03	0.20**	0.19**
State-Private	0.16**	0.11	0.40**	-0.16	0.37*	0.34**	0.13
State	-0.16	0.77**	0.03	-0.72**	-0.09	0.21**	0.57**
N	1712	1250	1613	2405	1246	2169	1907
Adj.-R^2	0.5171	0.4725	0.2271	0.3498	0.2847	0.3625	0.3880

It is remarkable that in most countries foreign or state ownership, even when it is jointly with the private sector, produces a significant, and often large, addition to earnings. The only exceptions are the foreign sector in Tanzania, and the State sector in Kenya.

It is possible that the ownership dummies will be picking up some of the effects of the other variables in the regressions. In particular, there might indeed be some correlation with size of enterprise. To check on this we present in Table 14.11 changes in the coefficients of the size dummies when the ownership variables are added to the regression model.

The changes in the coefficients of the size dummies are in the expected direction. When we introduce ownership, the difference in the earnings coefficients of small and large firms is reduced. The coefficients of micro and small firms *increase,* while those of large and very large firms *decrease.* Generally, the effect although quite perceptible is not substantial — generally of the order of 10 percent, which implies that the relative earnings difference between the micro and the very large firms are reduced by around a fifth when we consider ownership along with size in the regression model. The exception might be Ghana where the relative change is quite large.

Table 14.11 Changes in the Coefficient of the Size Dummies because of Adding Ownership Dummies

	Cameroon	*Côte d'Ivoire*	*Ghana*	*Kenya*	*Tanzania*	*Zambia*	*Zimbabwe*
Micro	0.0097	0.0266	0.0515	0.0519	-0.0794	0.0306	0.0427
Small	0.0886	-0.0278	0.0016	0.0236	-0.0683	0.0513	0.0355
Large	-0.0640	-0.1119	-0.1134	0.0031	0.0397	-0.0875	-0.0473
Very Large	-0.0169	-0.0823	-0.1695	0.617	-0.0403	-0.1044	-0.0707

Finally, it has sometimes been suggested that foreign or state owned firms have a larger premium for white collar workers, and in fact the observed premium for these types of firms really reflect the higher wage structure for the salaried staff, as opposed to the production workers. To check on this hypothesis we added ownership dummies to the separate regressions for blue and white collar workers of Appendix Tables 9 and 10. The results are reported in the Appendix tables 11 and 12. An inspection of these tables suggest that the premium for foreign and state does seem to be somewhat larger for white collar workers in most of the countries, but not uniformly so. Except for Cote d'Ivoire, Kenya and Zimbabwe, the differences are not that great. Blue collar workers also enjoy a significant premium in most cases when state or foreign ownership is involved.

Decomposition of the Sources of Earnings Difference between Foreign and Other Firms

We need to shed some light on the factors causing the higher earnings in foreign-owned firms. It might be because of labor with superior endowments employed in such farms, or it might be more due to the higher returns to the worker endowments in foreign firms. The 'Oaxaca' decomposition procedure enables us to estimate quantitatively the portion of the difference due to difference in endowments from the part due to different returns. The algebra of the methodology is given in Appendix 3 to this chapter. Briefly, we estimate separate earnings functions for two groups of firms: the foreign defined as all firms with more than 10 percent foreign assets; and all the others lumped together as non-foreign. We can then estimate predicted earnings from the two regression equations evaluating the explanatory variables in each of the equations at the mean values of the 'endowments' or 'characteristics' of the foreign firms, but using the separate estimated coefficients in the two equations. This hypothetical earnings difference is what would have prevailed if the characteristics of the workers in both types of firms were held constant. It thus represents the difference in earnings due entirely to difference in rewards or returns to the characteristics of workers, and could be called the 'discriminatory' pay advantage of foreign firms. The rest of the overall earnings difference is attributable to difference in endowments of workers.

The share of each group of factors in the earnings difference can be gleaned from the figures in Table 14.12. Tanzania is one country in which workers in foreign firms get less pay, but the magnitude of the difference is small. In all other countries, where the premium in favor of foreign firms is substantial, the larger part of the differential is attributable to 'better' endowments of workers in foreign firms. The only exception is Côte d'Ivoire where only a third of the rather large differential is accounted for by endowment differences. In Kenya, the relative importance of endowments and rewards is more or less the same.

Table 14.12 Decomposition (log Percentage Points) of the Foreign-Domestic Pay Gap by Rewards and Endowments

	Cameroon	*Côte d'Ivoire*	*Ghana*	*Kenya*	*Tanzania*	*Zambia*	*Zimbabwe*	*Average*
Endowment	24.12	13.88	14.82	15.39	-2.82	30.02	40.90	19.47
Rewards	5.80	26.67	10.79	16.28	-1.53	21.93	13.73	14.24
Total	29.92	40.55	25.61	31.67	-4.35	51.95	54.63	33.71

Tables 14.13 and 14.14 give a quantitative assessment of the relative importance of different factors in accounting for the pay advantage in favor of foreign-owned firms. A look at the two tables together suggests two factors, which are of the greatest importance, age, and size of the firm, with education also being important, but running a distant third. For all countries taken together, and also for those, which show the largest foreign-domestic wage gap, workers in foreign firms are not only older, but also their earnings higher because the age-earnings profile is substantially steeper. Foreign firms are larger in size, but the pay advantage associated with this is dampened because the elasticity of earnings with size is lower in such firms.

Table 14.13 Contribution (log Percentage Points) of Selected Variables to the Discriminatory Foreign Ownership Pay Advantage

	Cameroon	*Côte d'Ivoire*	*Ghana*	*Kenya*	*Tanzania*	*Zambia*	*Zimbabwe*	*Average*
Male	12.02	6.49	0.43	-20.95	0.58	-6.85	-8.16	-2.35
Age	84.28	-41.45	4.29	62.78	68.99	-1.81	129.42	43.79
Education	-3.88	2.13	11.19	24.24	10.63	-10.49	32.52	9.48
Tenure	2.46	2.40	1.41	-2.30	-0.86	2.34	-5.57	-0.02
Sise	-33.17	-35.44	-6.45	7.49	9.79	-29.24	-49.14	-19.45
Category	-26.55	15.08	18.51	4.94	-7.57	17.59	7.27	4.18
Subtotal	35.16	-50.79	29.38	76.20	81.56	-28.46	106.34	35.63
Constant	-29.36	77.46	-18.59	-59.92	-83.09	50.39	-92.61	-22.25
Total	5.80	26.67	10.79	16.28	-1.53	21.93	13.73	13.38

Note: The return is computed at average values of workers in foreign firms and indicates the premium (discount) paid to them at these mean values.

Table 14.14 Contribution (log Percentage Points) of Selected Variables to the Non-Discriminatory Foreign Ownership Pay Advantage

	Cameroon	*Côte d'Ivoire*	*Ghana*	*Kenya*	*Tanzania*	*Zambia*	*Zimbabwe*	*Average*
Male	0.14	0.36	0.63	-0.17	0.41	0.18	0.86	0.34
Age	8.75	3.66	3.13	2.40	2.33	3.42	4.51	4.03
Education	-0.14	2.64	2.65	1.79	-1.06	3.72	1.65	1.61
Tenure	2.56	0.66	0.55	-0.08	-0.19	-0.79	0.67	0.48
Size	11.06	6.23	7.41	5.89	-1.12	15.40	19.86	9.25
Category	1.75	0.33	0.45	5.56	-3.19	8.09	13.35	3.76
Total	24.12	13.88	14.82	15.39	-2.82	30.02	40.90	19.47

Earnings Difference by Sex

We followed the same 'Oaxaca decomposition' procedure to study the causes behind the difference in earnings of two other types of groups — male and female workers. Earnings functions were fitted separately for males and females in the RPED sample. These were used to decompose the difference in earnings predicted by the functions into two sources: due to differences in the characteristics of the workers and second, due to returns to the characteristics. The difference in predicted earnings, evaluating the regression variables at the male means, gives the effect of rewards or discriminatory wage patterns, while the rest of the difference is due to differences in 'endowments' of male and female workers.

The male pay advantage in the sample countries is non-existent or very small in three countries — the two francophone countries and Zambia. Of these only in Zambia both the endowment and reward structures seem to be very similar for males and females such that the difference in the wage gap caused by these two groups of factors are of small magnitudes. In the two francophone-countries, on the other hand, the two groups have sizable effects, but largely cancel each other out, pulling in opposite directions. Both in Cameroon and Côte d'Ivoire, the characteristics or endowments of the employed female workers are overall superior so that there should have been an earnings gap *in favor of the females* if the wage structure had been the same. However, the coefficients of the earnings function are of lower value for the females. Thus, the effect due to differential rewards favoring the male workers wiped out the endowment effect (Table 14.15).

Table 14.15 Log Percentage Points of the Male-Female Pay Gap by Rewards and Endowments

	Cameroon	*Côte d'Ivoire*	*Ghana*	*Kenya*	*Tanzania*	*Zambia*	*Zimbabwe*	*Average*
ENDOWMENT	-18.27	-24.98	1.83	-12.87	13.97	-2.73	2.39	-6.6
REWARDS	19.46	24.13	24.35	17.09	8.44	0.78	22.00	17.4
TOTAL	1.19	-0.85	26.18	4.22	22.41	-1.95	24.39	10.8

There are three countries in the RPED sample in which the earnings gap in favor of males is large — around 25 percent. They are Ghana, Tanzania, and Zimbabwe. In all these three countries, the endowment and the reward effects worked in the *same direction,* favoring males. However, in these cases and in the overall average for all countries, the quantitative impact of differences in rewards was substantially higher than that of differences in endowments.

There is thus clear evidence of discriminatory structures of earnings biasing the wage gap towards males in all the countries, with the possible exception of Zambia. Moreover, a glance at the table will show that the discrimination is of substantial magnitude. The pay gap in favor of males would have been much larger except for the unexpected situation in Cameroon, Côte d'Ivoire, and Kenya where the female workers seemed to have better endowments.

It might be of interest to compare the situation just described in the African countries with results we have for other regions of the world. Psacharopoulos and Tzannatos (1992) have employed the same methodology to the male-female earnings difference in Latin America, although the type of data used is rather different. It refers to employment in the formal sector as a whole, and not just formal manufacturing. Psacharopouls and Tzannatos concluded that 'sex wage differences in Latin America are by comparison to other regions small'. The unweighted average of female relative pay comes to about 70-75 percent — women workers even in many industrialized countries are still short of this figure in terms of average remuneration in the labor market' (p.199). It would appear from our results in Table 14.16 that the sex wage difference in African manufacturing is even lower than this level, although in Ghana, Tanzania and Zimbabwe it approaches it.

Turning to the sources of the difference, the Latin American experience is different from the African. Overall, in terms of the simple regional average, endowments of females in Latin America were less than those of males. Difference in endowments accounted for 22 percent of the wage gap, while in Africa difference in endowments actually favored females and served to wipe out some of the effect of a discriminatory reward structure. Even in the three countries — Ghana, Tanzania, and Zimbabwe — where difference in endowments put the females at a disadvantage, the contribution of this factor was smaller than that of discrimination.

We now present results giving the *components* of the differences in rewards to worker characteristics in Table 14.16.

Table 14.16 Contribution (log Percentage Points) of Selected Variables to the Discriminatory Male Pay Advantage

	Cameroon	*Côte d'Ivoire*	*Ghana*	*Kenya*	*Tanzania*	*Zambia*	*Zimbabwe*	*Average*
Age	6.08	65.17	183.76	19.42	-23.59	-116.22	125.56	37.17
Education	4.02	-19.51	-11.45	10.89	-11.84	-50.86	16.38	-8.91
Tenure	2.69	-10.37	-10.58	0.00	-0.17	-2.01	8.64	-1.69
Size	-26.84	-16.71	-3.69	-24.74	11.52	-23.61	-35.28	-17.05
Category	-16.39	2.20	-9.77	-2.04	-7.06	16.07	2.29	-2.1
Subtotal	-30.44	20.78	148.27	3.53	-31.14	-176.63	117.59	7.42
Constant	65.56	3.35	-123.92	13.56	45.11	177.41	-95.59	12.21
Total	19.46	24.13	24.35	17.09	13.97	0.78	22.00	17.4

Note: The return is computed at male average values and indicates the premium (discount) paid to the male at the mean values.

It has already been explained that the components of the pay gap attributable to differences in rewards are worked out from the differences in the coefficients of the variables entering the earnings function (holding the endowments constant). Countries differ on the role of individual variables making it difficult to summarize the points that emerge. Overall and individually for four of the seven countries, the role of the coefficient of age works strongly in favor of male workers. The age-earnings profile is steeper for males, and is one of the major reasons for the pay gap observed. Surprisingly for some, the coefficients of education and of firm size seem in most cases to favor *female* workers. The higher returns to women with more education and those working in larger firms probably reflect the scarcity of supply of workers who are acceptable to management to fill these positions: the results should not be interpreted to suggest relative scarcity of such workers in the market per se. The values of the constant term in the results presented in Table 14.16 should be noted. Overall and for five of the seven countries the value is positive, and quite a large negative value for some. Two countries, Ghana and Zimbabwe, have a negative constant term, and quite a large negative value at that. The constant term can be interpreted as the 'pure premium' enjoyed by males independent of the rewards to specific worker characteristics determining wages. In the Latin American study referred to above the value of this term was large and positive (*ibid,* table 6.3, p. 191). Thus the African scenario does not seem to be any different from the Latin American one — the exceptions being Ghana and Zimbabwe.

Other Studies of the Gender Gap in Africa

The RPED data generally show a limited amount of gender differential, but of course it is confined to the formal manufacturing sector. Work on pay differential between men and women in other sectors of the economy is very scarce in Africa. Recently Appleton, Hoddinott and Krishnan have tried to fill the gap by using household survey data from three countries. Unfortunately, only one of these three overlap with our RPED countries, Cote d'Ivoire, the other two being, Ethiopia and Uganda. The Ethiopian survey refers to youths only in the age group 15-30 for 1990, the Uganda and Cote d'Ivoire surveys are for a broader age group 15-59. The survey for Uganda is the Integrated Survey of 1992, and the Cote d'Ivoire ones are the Living Standard Measurement Surveys of 1985, 1986 and 1987 which have been used in Part III of the book. In all three cases the analysis is restricted to *urban residents* only to ensure comparability.

Appleton et al find that in all three countries male wages exceed those of females, but in Cote d'Ivoire the differential is negligible at 3 percent (a finding reinforcing our conclusion from the RPED survey). In Ethiopia males earned approximately one-quarter more, and in Uganda the differential is about one-third. The authors note at the beginning of the exercise that the gender gap is heavily influence by the public-private sector differentials. The public sector has a much higher wage structure as is to be expected, since much of private employment in the urban economy is in the informal sector (The difference with the RPED sample with its preponderance of *formal* manufacturing, both private and public should be noted). One important fact for the discussion in hand is that in all three countries women are more likely than men to be employed in the public sector, and since the public sector has the higher wage structure, gender difference in earnings is likely to be more muted than otherwise. It should be noted, however, that Uganda, which has the highest gender differential of the three, the public sector premium, is the lowest, 5 percent for men and 12 percent for women. In the other two countries average wages were two-thirds higher in the public sector.

Appleton et *al*. are able to carry their analysis into considerable detail extending the methodology of the Oxaca decomposition employed in this chapter. The Oxaca procedure, although standard, had to be used exclusively in this chapter for reasons of space, has the potential for creating index number problems if in fact using the male earnings function for both sets of regressions produce different results from the set using the female earnings function (see the Appendix). One extension of the procedure suggested by Neumark is to use a non-discriminatory or pooled wage structure, consisting of the weighted average of the male and female ones. Appleton *et al.* employ this extension to the analysis, and also consider a model that allows for the difference in the pay structures between the public and private sectors for the two gender groups. The index number problem of the Oxaca procedures was encountered slightly in the Uganda case but not in the other two countries.

In the country common both to the RPED and the Household Survey samples, Cote d'Ivoire, while the overall gender differential turns out to be small for both samples, the reasons for the net outcome are different. In the RPED data set the substantial male advantage in rewards were compensated by the unexpectedly better endowments for the females. In the LSMS sample we have the more 'normal' outcome with males having the better endowment, but it was somewhat compensated by lesser rewards — the latter clearly due to the larger proportion of females in the public sector. In Uganda and Ethiopia the substantial pay advantage of males is largely due to the reward structure favoring them — and this in spite of the fact that females are represented disproportionately in the high-paying public sector. In fact, the overrepresentation of females in the public sector makes the discrimination against females less burdensome. Appleton et al calculate that in Ethiopia and Cote d'Ivoire, the gender gaps would be 17 percent and 20 percent greater if men and women were equally allocated across the public and private sectors. In Uganda sectoral location matters less because of the smaller wage gap in favor of the pubic sector; the relevant percentage is of the order of 5.

There is thus evidence of significant evidence of discrimination in the pay structure in the three African countries studied, but unlike the stereotype image of the informal-formal dichotomy of urban labor markets, female workers are 'protected' somewhat by better access to the public sector. This unusual finding needs further probing and research. Appleton *et al.* provide a partial answer in their extended analysis. 'It is not that the women employees' observable characteristics are more conducive to public sector employment. Indeed, the reverse is true in all three countries. Instead, it is because — given their characteristics — women are more likely to be in the public sector. It is unclear to what extent it reflects discrimination or choice. The public sector may adopt less discriminatory hiring than the private sector. Alternatively the occupations to which girls commonly aspire may be more concentrated in the public sector than those that are aspired to by boys. For example, a number of studies of African school children have found girls' career aspirations to be highly concentrated only in a few occupations — notably teaching and nursing, both of which are in the public sector. By contrast, there is more variation in the range of occupations aspired to by boys.'(*ibid,* pp 300-01, Table 4).

Appendix 1

Table 14A.1 Mean of the Variables Used in the Regression Analysis

	Cameroon	*Côte d'Ivoire*	*Ghana*	*Kenya*	*Tanzania*	*Zambia*	*Zimbabwe*
Ln(Real Earning)	11.10	11.39	10.28	8.02	9.96	10.10	6.57
Real Earning	94,486	137,409	39,398	4,204	20,745	20,745	1,171
Wave (2)	0.33	-	0.28	0.34	0.31	0.37	0.29
Wave (3)	0.23	0.57	0.45	0.28	0.13	0.30	
Male	0.86	0.90	0.81	0.88	0.78	0.81	0.83
Experience in Years	15.34	18.12	16.75	17.83	16.01	16.56	19.88
Education in Years	10.72	7.08	10.68	9.13	10.13	12.18	8.43
Distribution by Education							
Primary	0.20	0.28	0.04	0.38	0.39	0.22	0.42
Middle School	0.12	0.33	0.51	0.19			
Secondary School	0.29	0.19	0.16	0.12			
Total Secondary = Middle +Secondary	0.41	0.52	0.66	0.41	0.31	0.48	0.53
Vocational	0.10	0.05	0.10	0.05	0.07	0.14	0.01
Technopol	0.16	0.03	0.11	0.07	0.12	0.11	0.01
University	0.11	0.02	0.004	0.04	0.07	0.03	0.01
Distribution by Sector							
Food	0.27	0.26	0.28	0.24	0.20	0.33	0.26
Wood	0.27	0.26	0.32	0.32	0.26	0.16	0.13
Textile	0.22	0.11	0.12	0.19	0.27	0.26	0.42
Metals	0.24	0.36	0.28	0.23	0.27	0.25	0.19
Distribution by Size							
Micro	0.20	0.13	0.14	0.12	0.17	0.13	0.14
Small	0.39	0.41	0.45	0.32	0.37	0.35	0.18
Large	0.09	0.08	0.10	0.11	0.07	0.10	0.18
Very Large	0.04	0.09	0.02	0.05	0.12	0.10	0.15
Ln(Size)	3.64	3.943	3.759	3.98	3.88	4.004	4.534
Size in Number of Workers	134.97	174.19	92.24	152.01	188.14	146.23	308.82
Location(Capital)	0.68	0.88	0.61	0.71	0.39	0.44	0.56
Blue Collar	0.53	0.65	0.66	0.71	0.39	0.44	0.56

Table 14A.2 Earning Functions (1)

	Cameroon	*Côte d'Ivoire*	*Ghana*	*Kenya*	*Tanzania*	*Zambia*	*Zimbabwe*
Constant	10.23**	10.36 **	9.34 **	7.27**	8.85**	9.26**	5.32**
Wave 2	-0.28 **	0.12**	0.08	-0.05	0.15**	-0.13**	-0.01
Wave 3	-0.27**		0.01	0.25**	0.49**	-0.10*	
Male	0.06	0.03	0.21**	0.03	0.27**	-0.02	0.11**
Lsize	0.27 **	0.24 **	0.20**	0.17**	0.14**	0.23**	0.25**
N	1921	1301	1667	2470	1310	2398	1953
Aadj. R^2	0.2634	0.1707	0.1348	0.1384	0.1317	0.1482	0.1834

Table 14A.3 Earning Functions (2)

	Cameroon	*Côte d'Ivoire*	*Ghana*	*Kenya*	*Tanzania*	*Zambia*	*Zimbabwe*
Constant	9.68**	9.68**	8.69**	6.70**	8.36**	8.08**	3.78**
Wave 2	-0.31**	0.23**	0.01	-0.13**	0.17**	0.03	-0.03
Wave 3	-0.28**		-0.05	0.27**	0.62**	0.04	
Male	0.07**	0.06	0.15**	0.03	0.19**	-0.04	0.14 **
Lsize	0.22**	0.15**	0.14**	0.12**	0.10**	0.17**	0.20**
Experience	0.01**	0.04**	0.03**	0.02**	0.02**	0.03**	0.06**
Exp2	-.00002**	-.0002**	-.0004**	-.0002**	-.0002**	-.0003**	-.0007**
Education	0.07**	0.09**	0.06**	0.07**	0.05**	0.11**	0.14**
Food	-0.26**	-0.09	0.01	-0.23**	0.02	-0.32**	-0.15**
Wood	-0.21**	-0.07	0.03	-0.15**	-0.06	-0.28**	-0.34**
Textile	-0.17**	-0.30**	-0.11*	-0.29**	-0.05	-0.35**	-0.28**
N	1865	1299	1637	2404	1276	2385	1919
Adj. R^2	0.4079	0.3699	0.2564	0.2781	0.2187	0.2832	0.3743

Table 14A.4 Earning Functions (3)

	Cameroon	*Côte d'Ivoire*	*Ghana*	*Kenya*	*Tanzania*	*Zambia*	*Zimbabwe*
Constant	7.33**	9.22**	7.75**	6.30**	7.72**	6.70**	2.88**
Wave 2	-0.29**	0.22**	0.13**	-0.12**	0.12**	-0.005	-0.01
Wave 3	-0.30**		-0.0003	0.27**	0.53**	-0.002	
Male	0.003	0.07	0.14**	0.005	0.13**	-0.09*	0.11**
Lsize	0.17**	0.13**	0.13**	0.12**	0.09**	0.15**	0.19**
Aage	0.09**	0.036**	0.06**	0.3**	0.04**	0.08**	0.08**
Aage2	-.0009**	-.0002	-.0006**	-.0001	-.0002**	-.0008**	-.0007**
Tenure	0.005*	0.008**	0.006**	-0.004	-0.005	-0.005	0.003
Education	0.06**	0.06**	0.05**	0.06**	0.04**	0.09**	0.13**
Food	-0.22**	-0.10**	0.02	-0.23**	0.03	-0.29**	-0.17**
Wood	-0.16**	-0.05	-0.05	-0.26**	-0.06	-0.29**	-0.35**
Textile	-0.16**	-0.26**	-0.13	-0.12**	-0.04	-0.36**	-0.26**
N	1865	1301	1576	2418	1234	2259	1820
Adj. R^2	0.4847	0.3725	0.2616	0.2773	0.2368	0.2894	0.3500

Table 14A.5 Earning Functions (4)

	Cameroon	*Côte d'Ivoire*	*Ghana*	*Kenya*	*Tanzania*	*Zambia*	*Zimbabwe*
Constant	9.84**	9.75**	9.02**	7.06**	8.91**	9.19**	4.38**
Wave 2	-0.32**	0.14**	-0.02	0.02	0.21**	-0.007	-0.01
Wave 3	-0.33**		-0.07	0.34**	0.58**	-0.05	
Male	-0.08*	0.007**	0.13**	0.04	0.18**	0.10	0.15**
Lsize	0.19**	0.14**	0.16**	0.12**	0.088*	0.14**	0.20**
Experience	0.02**	0.04**	0.02**	0.02**	0.03**	0.025**	0.06**
Exp2	-.00002	-.0003**	-.0003**	-.0002	-.0004**	-.0003**	-.0008**
Primary	0.09	0.28**	0.12	-0.03	-0.27	-0.18**	0.22
Secondary	0.34**	0.64**	0.30**	0.25**	0.07	0.19**	0.88**
Voc	0.60**	1.50**	0.52**	0.35**	-0.10	0.47**	1.32**
Technopol	0.92**	2.05**	0.83**	0.55**	0.23**	0.74**	2.20**
University	1.43**	1.90**	1.31**	1.11**	0.61**	1.54**	2.34**
Food	-0.22**	-0.11	-0.001	-0.19**	-0.02	-0.29**	-0.18**
Wood	-0.16**	-0.09**	0.01	-0.12**	-0.06	-0.28**	-0.36**
Textile	-0.12**	-0.32**	-0.01*	-0.29**	-0.04	-0.26**	-0.31**
N	1865	1299	1644	2405	1297	2385	1925
Adj. R^2	0.4825	0.4477	0.2257	0.3079	0.2528	0.3428	0.3676

Table 14A.6 Earning Functions (5)

	Cameroon	*Côte d'Ivoire*	*Ghana*	*Kenya*	*Tanzania*	*Zambia*	*Zimbabwe*
Constant	10.62**	10.12**	9.65**	7.45**	9.19**	9.66**	5.4**
Wave 2	-0.32**	0.16**	-0.02	0.04	0.23**	-0.002	-0.02
Wave 3	-0.29**		-0.07*	0.35**	0.61**	-0.03	
Male	0.08	-0.03	0.14**	0.07	0.18**	0.02	0.14**
Experience	0.02**	0.04**	0.02**	0.02**	0.03**	0.03**	0.06**
Exp2	-.00002**	-.0004**	-.0003**	-.0002**	-.0004**	-.0003**	-.0008**
Primary	0.07	0.29**	0.11	-0.07	-0.27**	-0.20**	0.18
Secondary	0.32**	0.60**	0.29**	0.23**	0.05	0.19**	0.85**
Voc	0.57**	1.51**	0.53**	0.33**	-0.05	0.45**	1.24**
Technopol	0.90**	2.01**	0.84**	0.53**	0.24**	0.72**	2.21**
University	1.44**	1.99**	1.32**	1.08**	0.61**	1.56**	2.32**
Food	-0.18**	-0.10*	0.02	-0.13**	0.03	-0.29**	-0.19**
Wood	-0.16**	-0.05	0.06	-0.09**	-0.06	-0.34**	-0.40**
Textile	-0.12**	-0.29**	-0.09	-0.28**	-0.05	-0.26**	-0.30**
Micro	-0.49**	-0.44**	-0.42**	-0.29**	-0.14*	-0.19**	-0.73**
Small	-0.32**	-0.04	-0.16**	-0.29**	-0.11**	-0.14**	-0.22**
Large	0.25**	0.06	0.25**	0.03	-0.01	0.38**	0.15**
Very Large	0.42**	0.28**	-0.01	0.13**	0.27**	0.44**	0.47**
Location	0.14**	0.21**	0.07**	0.25**	0.17**	0.12**	0.05
N	1865	1248	1644	2405	1297	2385	1925
Adj. R^2	0.4789	0.4480	0.2169	0.3368	0.2727	0.3495	0.3738

Table 14A.7 Earning Functions (Female)

	Cameroon	*Côte d'Ivoire*	*Ghana*	*Kenya*	*Tanzania*	*Zambia*	*Zimbabwe*
Constant	11.12**	10.30**	10.49**	7.55**	8.99**	9.94**	6.94**
Wave 2	-0.28**	0.17**	-0.08	0.008	0.26**	-0.01	-0.06
Wave 3	-0.19		-0.14	0.48**	0.87**	-0.05	
Experience	0.02**	0.014	0.002	0.03	0.05**	0.04**	0.04**
Exp2	-.00002**	-0.025	-.0001	-.0006	-0.001*	-.0005**	-.0006*
Primary	-0.44	-0.03	-0.15	-0.13	-0.19	-0.37*	-0.87
Secondary	-0.22	0.54	0.22	0.21	0.05	-0.08	-0.20
Voc	0.18	1.23	0.63**	0.18	0.17	0.20	0.47
Technopol	0.35	2.74**	0.80**	0.62**	0.25*	0.26*	0.95
University	0.99**			0.89**	0.68**	1.20**	1.08
Food	-0.09	-0.27*	-0.18	-0.20*	0.08	-0.36**	-0.22
Wood	-0.21	0.19	-0.26	-0.02	0.08	-0.42**	-0.14
Textile	-0.22	-0.70**	-0.10	-0.51**	0.0003	-0.42**	-0.40**
Micro	-0.48**	-0.30	-0.80**	-0.39**	-0.09	-0.37**	-1.10**
Small	-0.40**	0.04	-0.45**	-0.46**	-0.22**	-0.11	-0.34**
Large	0.25	0.32	-0.24	0.07	-0.31**	0.41**	0.17
Very Large	0.52**	0.75**	0.15	0.37*	0.22	0.52**	0.38**
Location	0.08	0.32	-0.11	0.35**	0.13	0.14*	-0.08
N	260	123	307	302	278	446	337
Adj. R^2	0.5499	0.5611	0.2275	0.3986	0.3197	0.3856	0.4534

Table 14A.8 Earning Functions (Male)

	Cameroon	*Côte d'Ivoire*	*Ghana*	*Kenya*	*Tanzania*	*Zambia*	*Zimbabwe*
Constant	10.35**	10.04**	9.64**	7.45**	9.40**	9.60**	5.29**
Wave 2	-0.33**	0.17**	-0.02	0.04	0.22	-0.01	-0.01
Wave 3	-0.30**		-0.06	0.33\41**	0.55**	-0.03	
Experience	0.05**	0.05**	0.03**	0.02**	0.02**	0.03**	0.07**
Exp2	-.0006**	-.0005**	-.0004**	-.0002**	-.0003**	-.0003**	-.0009**
Primary	0.10	0.25**	0.10	-0.05	-0.27**	-0.13	0.25
Secondary	0.38**	0.65**	0.27**	0.23**	0.07	0.27**	0.92**
Voc	0.64**	1.52**	0.38*	0.37**	-0.08	0.53**	1.19**
Technopol	1.01**	2.00**	0.80**	0.53**	0.26**	0.84**	2.48**
University	1.58**	2.00**	1.26**	1.11**	0.62**	1.66**	2.49**
Food	-0.19**	-0.08	0.08	-0.10**	0.02	-0.28**	-0.17**
Wood	-0.13**	-0.07	0.07	-0.08**	-0.07	-0.34**	-0.42**
Textile	-0.11**	-0.22**	-0.12**	-0.26**	-0.03	-0.21**	-0.27**
Micro	-0.41**	-0.44**	-0.33**	-0.25**	-0.11	-0.12	-0.57*
Small	-0.27**	-0.05	-0.11**	-0.26**	-0.18**	-0.13**	-0.18**
Large	-0.22**	0.06	0.35**	0.02	0.02	0.37**	0.15**
Very Large	0.36**	0.21**	0.006	0.10	0.28**	0.42**	0.47**
Location	0.13**	0.20**	0.12**	0.25**	0.18**	0.13**	0.09**
N	1604	1124	1336	2102	1018	1938	1587
Adj. R^2	0.4970	0.4418	0.2227	0.3341	0.2464	0.3489	0.3564

Table 14A.9 Earning Functions (Blue-Collar, 1)

	Cameroon	*Côte d'Ivoire*	*Ghana*	*Kenya*	*Tanzania*	*Zambia*	*Zimbabwe*
Constant	10.18**	10.07**	9.61**	7.22**	9.18**	9.57**	5.72**
Wave 2	-0.31**	0.17**	0.05	0.04	0.18**	-0.10*	0.03
Wave 3	-0.27**		0.01	0.37**	0.49**	0.03	
Male	0.28**	0.26**	0.14*	0.22*	0.13	0.11	0.29**
Experience	0.04**	0.03**	0.02**	0.014**	0.02**	0.01**	0.03**
Exp2	-.0005**	-.0002**	-.0002	-.0001**	-.0004**	-.0001*	-.0005**
Primary	0.08	0.26*	0.09	0.03	-0.16	-0.06	0.06
Secondary	0.28**	0.48**	0.21**	0.16**	0.04*	0.10	0.29**
Voc	0.36**	1.06**	0.50**	0.36*	-0.09	0.37**	0.56**
Technopol	0.81**	2.21**	0.59**	0.24**	0.12	0.49**	0.79
University	1.43**	1.80**		0.41*	0.56**	2.08**	2.31**
Food	-0.11*	-0.02	-0.04	-0.16*	-0.12**	-0.31**	-0.19**
Wood	-0.17*	-0.09	-0.08	-0.11*	-0.09*	-0.34**	-0.46**
Textile	-0.10**	-0.21**	-0.05	-0.26**	0.05	-0.20**	-0.33**
Micro	-0.38**	-0.46**	-0.38**	-0.22**	-0.16*	-0.07	-0.59**
Small	-0.20**	-0.05	-0.11*	-0.21**	-0.12	-0.11*	-0.14**
Large	-0.01	-0.06	0.25**	0.10*	0.03	0.39**	0.10*
Very Large	0.48**	0.07	-0.03	0.06	0.13	0.58**	0.36**
Location	0.07	0.14*	0.04	0.25**	0.08	0.16**	0.13**
N	993	757	954	1562	594	1089	1203
Adj. R^2	0.3940	0.3395	0.1589	0.3166	0.11254	0.2456	0.3388

Table 14A.10 Earning Functions (Blue-Collar, 2)

	Cameroon	*Côte d'Ivoire*	*Ghana*	*Kenya*	*Tanzania*	*Zambia*	*Zimbabwe*
Foreign	0.27**	0.26**	0.13	0.11**	-0.25*	0.36**	0.29**
Private-Foreign	0.03	0.20**	0.18**	0.03	-0.07	0.07	0.05
State-Private	0.08	-0.20	0.57**	-0.36**	0.52**	0.23	0.04
State		1.17*	0.21**	-0.99**	0.02	0.29**	0.57**
N	910	757	932	1562	571	965	1195
Adj. R^2	0.4317	0.3689	0.1831	0.3284	0.1455	0.2735	0.3507

Note: Coefficients of ownership variables added to the regression model of Table 9.

Table 14A.11 Earning Functions (White-Collar, 1)

	Cameroon	*Côte d'Ivoire*	*Ghana*	*Kenya*	*Tanzania*	*Zambia*	*Zimbabwe*
Constant	10.58**	9.95**	9.72**	7.63**	9.32**	9.76**	5.10**
Wave 2	-0.32**	0.13**	-0.02	0.007	0.28**	0.05	-0.05
Wave 3	-0.29**		0.01	0.37*	0.68**	-0.11	
Male	0.10*	-0.09	0.22**	0.15	0.26**	0.11*	0.04
Experience	-0.03**	0.04**	0.03**	0.03**	0.03**	0.03**	0.06**
Exp2	-.00003**	-.0004**	-.001**	-.0004**	-.0004**	-.0004**	-.0008**
Primary	0.09	0.51*	-0.07	-0.31*	-0.40**	-0.29**	0.59
Secondary	0.42**	0.99**	0.16**	0.11	-0.05	0.18	1.49**
Voc	0.70**	1.70**	0.20**	0.25**	-0.12	0.41**	1.91**
Technopol	0.95**	2.04**	0.60**	0.53**	0.25**	0.68**	2.50**
University	1.44**	2.25**	0.97**	0.96**	0.43**	1.41**	2.50**
Food	-0.23**	-0.25**	0.06	-0.12**	0.06	-0.30**	-0.22**
Wood	-0.14**	-0.05	-0.01	-0.03	-0.07	-0.33**	-0.22*
Textile	-0.12	-0.31**	-0.16	-0.29**	-0.17**	-0.29**	-0.17*
Micro	-0.45**	-0.51**	-0.33**	-0.30**	-0.09	-0.22*	-0.81*
Small	-0.43**	-0.07	-0.24**	-0.33**	0.13*	-0.10	-0.30**
Large	0.23**	0.09	0.17**	-0.12**	-0.27**	0.37**	0.24**
Very Large	0.34**	0.49**	0.04	0.07	0.34**	0.40**	0.39**
Location	0.20**	0.27**	0.15**	0.27**	0.23**	0.08	0.002
N	871	492	689	842	702	1295	721
Adj. R^2	0.5036	0.4683	0.1944	0.3311	0.3347	0.3203	0.3675

Table 14A.12 Earning Functions (White-Collar, 2)

	Cameroon	*Côte d'Ivoire*	*Ghana*	*Kenya*	*Tanzania*	*Zambia*	*Zimbabwe*
Foreign	0.20**	0.33**	0.21	0.31**	-0.09	0.19**	0.38**
Private-Foreign	0.11	0.42**	0.15*	0.08	0.15	0.22**	0.21**
State-Private	0.28**	0.23	0.18	-0.18	0.27	0.35**	0.08
State	-0.11	0.65**	-0.18*	-0.27	-0.12	0.13	0.64*
N	801	492	680	842	677	1203	711
Adj. R^2	0.5294	0.4926	0.2062	0.3454	0.3457	0.3250	0.3797

Note: Coefficients of the ownership values added to the regression model Table 10.

Appendix 2

General Notes

- Only Full time workers are considered.
- Apprentices are deleted from the data set.
- The size dummies in the regressions correspond to:

MICRO: total number of workers for the firm less than or equal to 10
SMALL: total number of workers for the firm less than or equal to 50 but greater than 10
MEDIUM: total number of workers for the firm less than or equal to 200 but greater than 50
LARGE: total number of workers for the firm less than or equal to 500 but greater than 200
VLARGE: total number of workers for the firm over 500

- Blue-collar workers correspond to those engaged in production or maintenance, the rest are white collar.
- A single asterisk denotes that the coefficient is significant at the 5 percent level of probability, and the double asterisk indicates significance at the 1 percent level.

Country Specific Notes

Cameroon

- Since in the first wave the benefits are not reported in the workers data set, and the firm data set cannot be used to approximate the benefits, the dependant variable is wages rather than earnings.
- Workers with real wage over 1,000,000 and fewer than 1,000 are considered outliers and hence dropped from the analysis.

Côte d'Ivoire

- Since in the first wave the benefits are not reported in the workers data set, and the firm data set cannot be used to approximate the benefits, earnings are replaced with wages.
- Workers with real wage under 1,000 are considered outliers and hence

dropped from the analysis.

Ghana

- Since for the first wave the benefits are not reported in the workers data set, they are approximated using the average benefits per category as reported in the firm's data set.
- Workers with real wage over 1,000,000 and fewer than 100 are considered outliers and hence dropped from the analysis.

Kenya

- Since for the first wave the benefits are not reported in the workers data set, they are approximated using the average benefits per category as reported in the firm's data set.
- Workers with real wage over 40,000 are considered outliers and hence dropped from the analysis.

Tanzania

- Since for the first wave the benefits are not reported in the workers data set, a very rough method is used to approximate the benefits from the firm data set. This approximation is made necessary since the benefits are not reported in the firm data set by category and unlike other countries where the regressions with the log wage and log earning as the dependent variable did not show a significant qualitative difference, in Tanzania the these two functions materially differ. In addition to this approximation, all the functions are estimated after adding a union dummy. This union dummy is added to reflect part of the error in our approximation. We chose the union dummy, since it was significantly negative when we ran the regressions using the log wage as the dependent variable whereas it was insignificant when we ran the regressions with the log earning as the dependent variable for both the second and the third wave. This implies that a sizable portion of the unionized workers compensation comes through benefits.
- Workers with real wage over 1,000,000 and fewer than 1,000 are considered outliers and hence dropped from the analysis.

Zambia

- Since for the first wave the benefits are not reported in the workers data set, they are approximated using the average benefits per category as reported in the firm's data set.
- Workers with real wage over 1,000,000 and in the Management category are considered outliers and hence dropped from the analysis.

Zimbabwe

- Since for the first wave the benefits are not reported in the workers data set, they are approximated using the average benefits per category as reported in the firm's data set.
- Workers with real wage over 1,000,000 and fewer than 1000 are considered outliers and hence dropped from the analysis.

Appendix 3

The decomposition of earning difference between two groups used in this chapter (Foreign and Private: and Male and Female) follows the methodology of Oxaaca(1973). The decomposition of the earning differential between (a) male and female, and (b) domestic firms versus firms with foreign ownership was done by estimating the earning equation for (a) male and female workers, (b) domestic and foreign firms separately. In general, the earning functions will take the following specialized format:

$$\ln(W_i) = C_i + f(X_i)\beta_i + e_i \qquad (1)$$

Where (a) i = male or female (b) i = domestic or foreign firms. X represents all the variables that affect the earning, β are the corresponding parameters and F is the functional form. Then the difference between the log earning for (a) male and female, (b) foreign and domestic firms will give us percentage difference between their corresponding earnings. For instance, for the case of male versus female we have,

$$\ln(W_m) - \ln(W_f) = \ln(1 + (W_m - W_f)/W_f)$$
$$= (W_m - W_f)/W_f \qquad (2)$$

In which *m* and *f* stand for male and female. This implies that the difference in the logarithms of male and female earning is equal to the percentage difference of male to female earning. Then, the right hand side will give us the decomposition of the earning differential to its components i.e.

$$\ln(W_m) - \ln(W_f) = (C_m - C_f) + [f(X_m)\beta_m - f(X_f)\beta_f] \qquad (3)$$

Where the first bracket refers to the difference in the constant term and the second bracket refers to the difference in the other variables.

Rearranging the equation will lead to,

$$\ln(W_m) - \ln(W_f) = [(C_m - C_f) + f(X_m)(\beta_m - \beta_f) + [(f(X_m) - f(X_f))\beta_f] \tag{4}$$

This gives the decomposition of the earning differential into its two components. Clearly, this decomposition depends on the values of the variables used in the earning function. A standard approach is to evaluate the decomposition at the average values. This means that for the purpose of this decomposition, W and X are the average values.

By looking at (4), the percentage change in the earning can be seen to come from two possible sources. First, the differential rewards to male and female (foreign and domestic) characteristics (β_m-β_f) in the labor market including the difference in the constant term and, second, the difference in the quantities of these characteristics ($f(X_m)$-$f(X_f)$). In this framework, the earning differential attributed to the endowment can be considered non-discriminatory whereas the portion of the earning differential, which is due to differences in the values of the coefficients, is discriminatory.

We have a choice, however, about what average W and X to adopt — pertaining to which of the two groups. Two versions of the decomposition are provided in (4). The results might not be equal in practice, in which case we have an index number problem. For example, in the male-female decomposition, the first version in (4) evaluates the decomposition of the earning differential if (m) is paid as (f), whereas the latter decomposes the earning differential if (m) is paid as (f). In practice, it is not certain if decomposition based on (m) means produces higher or lower estimate than that produced by (f) means. It all depends on the relative shape of the two earning functions. However, both decompositions have produced similar results in many recent applied studies and in the current application.

15 Wage Difference by Size of Firm: An Extended Analysis

Introduction

We saw in the last chapter that the size of the enterprise was an important determinant of the level of earnings, after controlling for measurable human capital factors. This result is in keeping with other studies of wage labor markets in developing countries. The positive relationship between enterprise size and wage levels has also been noted to have been a feature of labor markets in advanced industrialized countries; but the quantitative dimensions of the size related difference are altogether different in developing countries. Idson and Feaster (1990) arranged the US census of Population data into fives size groups: 1-24 workers, 25-99, 100-499, 500-999, 1000 and more. The size effect of earnings for the four larger groups relative to the smallest was (in percentages) 7.9, 16.4, 19.8, 23.8 respectively. In the analysis of earnings from the RPED data set reported in the last chapter the size groups were slightly different: Micro 1-10, small 10-50, medium 50-200, large 200-500, very large 500 and more. However, even a cursory look at the magnitudes is enough to convince anyone that the wage differentials found in African countries is several times that reported for the United States. The log difference in earnings of the very large compared to the micro ranged from a low of 0.41 or 0.42 for Tanzania and Kenya to a high of 1.20 for Zimbabwe and 0.92 for Cameroon. It should also be remembered that the earnings-differences for the African countries quoted, unlike the US example, was net of human capital factors (sex, education, experience, industry and location). Similarly, very large differentials in earnings by size groups have been found in other parts of the developing world. The Bombay labor market study reported by Mazumdar (1984) found the spread of earnings from the smallest to the largest size-groups, with roughly the same type of categories, to be 0.67 for manual male workers, after controlling for the human capital differences. (Cf. also Manning for Indonesia 1979; Schaffner for Peru 1994).[57] The size-related differential has also been of markedly large magnitude in Japan during its process of industrialization (Yosuba 1976).

In the African economies studied, as in developed countries, wages and labor productivity increase with firm size, but in keeping with the evidence sighted above, both wages and labor productivity increase much more with firm size in Africa. This can be seen from data assembled together in the table 15.1.

In the United States, both wage and output elasticities with respect to plant size seem to have doubled in the eighties, but are generally nowhere near the magnitudes observed in the African economies. The evidence suggests that there are important differences in the economic landscape of developed and less developed economies, which produce such huge differences in wage levels by size in the latter. We think immediately of the less homogeneous quality of labor (not captured by measurable human capital factors) and the larger dispersion of techniques of production in the less developed countries, which causes a much larger increase in labor productivity in bigger establishments with more modern technologies.

The purpose of this chapter is to present a systematic discussion of the factors involving differences in labor quality and production techniques which might impinge on the wage differential over and above the human capital factors. We attempt to incorporate some of these influences in models, which can be estimated quantitatively. Although several key assumptions have to be made at different stages to enable us to implement the models, it is hoped that the decomposition of the different effects accounting for the size related differential gives some idea of the relative importance of the various influences at work.

---

[57]Velenchik (1997) gives a convenient summary of the results from some of these studies (p.313). Note that these wage differences exist for different classes of establishments *within* the formal sector. The difference in earnings between the formal and *the informal* sectors are even lager.

Table 15.1 The Elasticity of Earnings and Productivity in African Countries and in the United States

Elasticity	*Cameroon*	*Côte d'Ivoire*	*Ghana*	*Kenya*	*Tanzania*	*Zambia*	*Zimbabwe*	*US 1977*	*US 1987*	*US 1992*
Earnings	0.27	0.24	0.20	0.17	0.14	0.23	0.25	0.035	0.078	0.075
Productivity	0.36	0.54	0.33	0.32	0.09	0.20	0.25	0.086	0.144	0.172

Source: The elasticities for the African countries are calculated from the RPED data set, regressing the log of average monthly earnings and value added per worker on log size. The United States statistics are taken from Oi (1999). The original sources are from the Censuses of Manufacture. Earnings are payroll per hour productivity is output (shipments) per hour (See Oi, p.106).

The chapter follows with five sections. The second section discusses the sources of wage differential that are not captured by observed human capital variables. The third section attempts to quantitatively estimate contribution of these factors for a sample of four African countries, namely Ghana, Kenya, Zambia, and Zimbabwe. Building on the findings of the third section, the fourth section attempts to determine the relative importance in this relationship of the models of efficiency-wage of rent sharing. The final section concludes.

Factors Affecting the Enterprise Wage Differential

Neoclassical labor economics predicts that in a profit maximizing environment workers are paid the value of their marginal product, which is equated with their supply price. Since the individual enterprise in a large labor market is a price taker as far as labor is concerned, the supply price of labor to enterprises of different sizes will vary only in so far as it differs in skills. The labor market literature has traditionally measured skill differences in terms of human capital factors such as experience, education and tenure. Theoretically, if workers are paid their marginal product these human capital factors should fully explain the wage differentials.

If there remain significant parts of the differential to be explained over and above these basic human capital factors, we have to look to other influences. These factors can be classified into three main categories: those specific to workers; those specific to the production process; and those specific to the environment the production process takes place. Clearly, these three categories in many cases cannot be separated empirically.

Worker Specific Factors

The worker-specific factors are those components of labor quality that are not captured by the conventional factors intended to define human capital. Clearly 'good' workers co-exist with 'not so good' workers in a given supply of labor of equivalent endowment of measurable human capital. However, additional pieces of argument are required to maintain the that the demand for 'good' workers increase with enterprise size, so that larger enterprises are willing to offer a higher wage in order to increase the *proportion* of 'good workers' in their labor force. An enterprise paying a relatively higher wage has the possibility of both having a larger proportion of 'good' workers applying for jobs, and of retaining a larger proportion of such workers. However, why should larger firms be interested in following this root more than small firms?

One relevant factor in this regard is capital-specific skills. Capital-skill complementarity can result in workers with the same experience, education, and tenure being more productive in the production process that require higher capital intensity. Since bigger firms are more likely to utilize higher capital-intensive production process, the positive relation between the firm size and wage differential might be plausibly attributed to capital-specific skills. Hamermesh(1980) argues in favor of this alternative while other studies that relate wage differential to firm size test such plausible causes by using longitudinal data. The argument is simple. If there is capital specific skill that causes the wage differential, the same workers, after accounting for their human capital, should not be paid differently in different periods even if the firm size changes or they move on to a bigger firm. Brown and Medoff(1989) is a prime example of this approach.[58]

Firm Specific Factors

Firm specific factors cover a wide range of explanations for size-related wage differentials. However, they all share the fact that they do not reflect human capital effects and therefore may be regarded as an extra payment beyond what is justified by marginal productivity. Unionized firms, as has been argued and tested empirically, pay more not because their workers are more productive but to satisfy a negotiation process. State owned firms and those having foreign ownership may pay differently simply because of the preferences of their owners (or their sensitivity to public perception). Also, firms that are more profitable may share part of their profit with the workers as a part of a process that is known as rent-sharing in macroeconomics. In view of this, a positive relation between the firm size and wage differential might be attributed to the fact that bigger firms are more profitable. There are three sources of a larger share of rent in bigger firms. First is the existence of economies of scale. The second is the greater market power of larger firms who are able to charge monopoly prices in the product market. The third is the increase in capital intensity (capital-labor ratio) with enterprise size. The last factor might need some explanation. It

---

[58]Brown and Medoff found that the size-wage differential observed with cross sectional data is reduced by 45 percent by estimating the earnings function with fixed individual effects over a 5-year period 1973-77. 'But the fixed-effect estimates of the size-wage effect (remain) large in practical terms: if a typical worker went from an establishment with employment one standard deviation below average to an establishment with one standard deviation above average, the employee would enjoy a wage increase of 8-12 percent, about as large as the union-nonunion differential in these data' (p.1038).

can be seen from the Appendix Table 15A.1 that capital intensity does increase with firm size. But is there any reason why firms with higher capital intensity have a larger share of profits or rent? If competitive conditions prevail both capital and labor are paid according to their marginal products, and there is no rent or surplus left for the larger capital-intensive firms after allowing for normal profit, in the absence of increasing returns to scale. But segmentation in capital markets might vitiate this competitive outcome. Capital market segmentation implies that larger firms have access to capital at more favorable terms.

In addition to what has been known as *profit-sharing*, one may discuss another class of factors affecting the level of wages which has been much discussed in the literature. The *efficiency-wage* hypothesis argues that a higher wage induces greater efficiency from the worker. Hence, as long as the increase in the supply of units of labor, measured in standard efficiency units, increases proportionately more than the wage per worker, it would reduce wage costs for the employer if he meets his demand for labor units by increasing wages rather than hiring extra labor at the going wage rate. In effect, if this mechanism holds, a profit maximizing employer would set the wage at the point where the cost of a standard efficiency unit of labor is minimized., even if there is a pool of labor wanting to be employed at a lower wage per worker. This point of a 'wage floor' is established where the elasticity of the supply of effort with respect to the wage per worker changes from being more than unity to less than unity.

The basis for the postulated relationship between wages and the worker's efficiency has been detailed in the literature. Explanations include better nutrition, incentive and morale factors, and a range of labor market variables like size of good quality applicants, labor turnover rate, cost of shirking etc. (for reviews see Velenchik 1997; Akerloff and Yellen). The wage-efficiency relationship could be observed in firms of any size group. But it has been maintained that it would be more important in larger enterprises, that is to say, the minimum wage-cost point would be established at a higher level, the larger the size of the enterprise. The more important points supporting this hypothesis include:

- The cost of supervision increases with employment size. Hence, larger firms, at the margin, would meet more of their labor requirements by increasing wages rather than by hiring more workers.
- Larger firms have more expensive machinery and a higher capital-labor ratio. Thus, the cost of labor turnover for them — in terms of output loss when a worker leaves and a new recruit has to be trained — is higher than for smaller firms. Hence, they will be willing to offer a

higher wage to reduce the turnover rate.

- Since larger firms generally have more complex, multi-stage production processes, the costs of ''shirking' and the resultant stoppages in production would be much higher for the bigger enterprise.
- If the quality of labor needed increases with the size and value of the capital equipment, larger enterprises would be offering a higher wage to attract a pool of applicants in which workers of potential quality are better represented.

Clearly these two sources of wage differential discussed above, namely profit sharing and efficiency-wage, are difficult to separate. Both indicate a positive correlation between productivity and earning. In the profit sharing framework this correlation runs from productivity to wage whereas the in the efficiency-wage hypothesis the causality is reversed. Although theoretically appealing, this difference, specifically in a cross-section framework, does not provide enough information to differentiate between these two sources of potential wage differential. A more elaborate discussion of these issues will follow in a later section when we analyze the efficiency-wage models in detail.

Direct Effect of Firm Size

Aside from the worker and firm specific factors, the firm or establishment size might directly lead to high wages because of organizational reasons. This effect can be considered as a pure size effect not related to the workers' quality or production characteristics. The argument here rests on the organization theory of the firm. The relevant point for our purposes is that the workforce is organized in hierarchical way with different grades of labor, and for the hierarchy to work bureaucratically the different grades have to be differentiated from one another by perceptible differentials in pay scales. Larger firms need a larger bureaucracy with many more grades, and will consequently end up with a higher level of average wage.

Another somewhat different argument has to do with skill formation internal to the firm. A great deal of high wage labor, with skills specific to the production process of the plant, is produced with in-house training. The hypothesis that the cost of producing 'superior' labor within the enterprise increases with the *volume* of superior labor needed in large enterprises yields the wage-size relationship directly. This is not an unreasonable hypothesis if the production function of 'superior' labor includes some relatively fixed factor of production, specific to the enterprise, which cannot be increased at unchanged cost at the same rate as the total volume of employment. Management or supervisory labor could indeed be such a factor of production.

It should be evident that this direct effect of firm size on wages would be empirically indistinguishable from that part of the efficiency wage hypothesis which makes the efficiency wage relationship a function of the monitoring cost of labor (see above).

Separating the Direct and Indirect Effects of Firm Size on Wages

If wages, establishment size and labor productivity were perfectly correlated, then the direct size effect could not be empirically separated from any of the other factors mentioned: unobserved labor quality (related to capital intensity), profit sharing and efficiency wage. The data on the correlation coefficients given in the Appendix Table 15A.2 show that the correlation between these variables, although mostly significant, are not uniformly high. This leaves scope for the empirical work to try and disentangle the direct effects of size from those of the other factors.

Valenchik (1997) addresses the problem of size-wage relationship in one of the RPED countries, Zimbabwe. She uses different measures for profitability including profit per worker, value added per worker and sales per worker to test the rent sharing models. These variables are added one at a time to an earnings function which includes the usual labor quality (human capital) variables as well as industry and occupation controls. She concludes: "while there is a positive coefficient on all of the rent proxies, indicating that rent sharing is a component of the wage setting process, the size coefficients are actually larger in the specifications including the rent proxies". Thus, in her analysis, while rent or profit sharing is significant in wage formation, it does not work through the size effect. Her analysis is subject to a number of criticisms. First, in common with all single equation approaches, the simultaneity bias could be serious. The author herself recognizes that "profits per worker are clearly function of wages, and therefore endogenous with respect to wage decision" (*ibid*, p.333), but maintains that value added and sales per worker do not suffer from this problem. Second, the equation might be miss-specified because the profit variable (along with value added and sales) is entered as natural numbers while the earnings function is specified as log-linear one, in which all other variables apart from dummies are in log values. She is forced to do that because there are a large number of firms with negative profits. Third, the inclusion of non-profitable firms is contrary to the spirit of the rent-sharing hypothesis. It implies that these firms will pay their workers less than their marginal product (or alternative earnings of the embodied human capital) or in other words will share their losses with their workers. In addition to this, the inclusion of numerous firm specific dummies is counter-productive since those dummies might be picking up some of the productivity effect.

Teal (1996) tests the evidence of profit sharing in Ghana, also using parts of the RPED data sets. He also explicitly incorporates measures of profitability in his earning functions. But Teal recognizes the problem of simultaneous bias, and uses instrumental variables to estimate the earning function.[59] However, having decided to include both profitable and non-profitable firms, he is forced to use profit per worker as levels in an earning function which is by design a log liner function. This makes his analysis in favor of profit sharing vulnerable in two main ways, first, his earning function is clearly miss-specified; second, the problem mentioned earlier about firms sharing their losses with the workers, and hence driving down wages below alternative earning remain.

In fact, the problem of unprofitable firms in the African context, revealed by the RPED surveys, is more serious than either author realizes. In the developed country context, it is unusual to find a large fraction of firms to show negative accounting profit (value added *minus* wages) except in a business cycle context. In the four RPED countries considered here, Zimbabwe had the lowest percentage of the firms with negative profits at 15 percent, while for the other three this percentage ranged between 22 and 27 percent (see Tables 1 and 12 below). The institutional conditions in sub-Saharan Africa, with its heavy state subsidization of the formal sector and imperfect bankruptcy laws, clearly are factors in the continued existence of firms with negative profits. It is not realistic to hypothesize that under these conditions workers in loss-making firms to accept a wage below their alternative earnings in the hope that it is transitory condition produced by the business cycle, as the Teal-Valenchik formulation would need to assert to justify the specification of their earnings function.

Unless a separate analysis is provided which includes only profitable firms and that corrects for the miss-specification, Teal's results should be considered with caution. In fact, we have repeated his analysis using our dataset for Ghana for the profitable firms and found little support for the profit sharing hypothesis in the single equation approach for this subset of

[59] The instruments are foreign borrowing per employee and the share of intermediate input costs in total cost. Teal (p.969, last paragraph) explains why an exogenous shock, operating on these variables, could be expected to affect profits but not wages directly.

firms. We can only conclude that the positive and significant coefficient for the profit variable is due to the mixing together of the unprofitable and the profitable firms. The variance in the data for the accounting firms is high, as could be expected in firm surveys of this type. While the data are strong enough to pick up the differences between broad classes of firms, e.g., the profitable and the unprofitable, they do not establish significant inter-firm differences within the profitable group.

The models embodying the hypotheses of capital-specific skills, profit sharing and efficiency wage outlined above, have some elements in common but also some differences in terms of their empirical testing. All of them imply an interaction between the production process and the determination of workers' earnings. They thus involve a simultaneous estimation of the production and earnings functions. However, while the workers' skills, augmenting the production function, imply that the predicted wage from the earnings function enters directly as a variable in the production function, in the efficiency wage model, it is the premium over predicated wage or the 'residual' of the earnings function which will enter as an augmenting factor in the production function. This distinction will hopefully become clearer when we set out the formal models for the empirical implementation in the following sections.

In what follows we work with two different models. In the first model in the section which follows immediately, the levels of earnings and value added are determined simultaneously through the specified earnings and production functions. We are able to separate the direct effect of firm-size on earnings from that part due to the impact of the production function. In the second model discussed in section after the next one, the *residuals* from the earnings function interact with the production function with a view to determine the relative importance of the direction of causation — from 'relative' earnings to value added suggesting efficiency wage effects, and the other way suggesting profit sharing.

Size, Human Capital and Profit Sharing

Economic theory suggests a plausible positive relation between wages and productivity stemming from wages, since higher wages imply higher skills, which in turn tend to increase productivity. On the other side of the interrelationship, productivity or value added per worker affects the level of wages through two distinct routes: first, the higher productivity of the firm, as explained in the last section, could increase rents per worker either because of economies of scale or higher capital intensity, which could augment wages through the profit sharing mechanism. Secondly, the higher productivity might partly reflect the capital-specific and unobserved skills of labor used, and the latter would lead to a higher demand price and hence average wage of the workers.

This interrelationship implies that the earnings and production functions can only be estimated within a simultaneous system of equations. These can be written as follows:

$$\ln(W_i) = \alpha_1 + f(X_{1i}) + \beta_1 \ln(\frac{Y_i}{L_i}) + \gamma_1 \ln(L_i) + \varepsilon_{1i}$$
$$\ln(\frac{Y_i}{L_i}) = \alpha_2 + g(X_{2i}) + \beta_2 \ln(\frac{K_i}{L_i}) + \gamma_2 \ln(L_i) + \eta_2 \ln(W_i) + \varepsilon_{2i} \quad (1)$$

The following points about this system need to be stressed:

- The vectors X_{1i} and X_{2i} represent variables which enter one or other of the two functions to be estimated exclusively — the former variables such as capital utilization which affect only the production (value added per worker) equation; the latter measured human capital variables which influence earnings.
- The employment size variable ln(*L*) enter both the earnings and the production functions, but it has different interpretations in the two equations. In the earnings function the coefficient of this variable (γ_1) measures what we have called the effect of 'organizational factors' on earnings (see above). On the other hand the coefficient in the production function — ln(L)'s coefficient(γ_2) — measures the impact of economies of scale.

This model allows explicitly for the decomposition of the size effect in the earning function into a direct effect not attributed to the production process, labeled as an organizational effect, an indirect effect through returns to scale, and a productivity effect as higher capital labor ratio may lead to higher productivity (rents) and higher wages. However, as stated earlier, the size and production factors, particularly the latter, might merely capture unobserved human capital effects. This means that any argument for or against the profit sharing or capital specific factors is inconclusive. In other words these two factors in the framework of the model are not identifiable, although the decomposition of the size effect into its components is still achievable.

Profitable and Unprofitable Firms

One way to identify if higher productivity, as associated with higher capital intensity and the scale factor, might affect earnings is to repeat the estimation for firms with different degrees of profitability. The analysis makes sense only if we assume (to be verified in the empirical work reported below) that the unprofitable firms are not solely concentrated in the smaller size groups and if the capital intensity varies sufficiently for unprofitable firms as well as profitable firms. If one estimates the simultaneous system for two sub-groups, one exhibiting stronger profitability and the other weaker, the coefficient of size should not differ since theoretically it captures the organizational structure that is not correlated with the production process or profitability. However, the coefficient of productivity in the earning functions in the two sub-samples may be expected to be different depending on the relative strength of the two effects — unobserved quality of labor and profit sharing.

If the relevant coefficients in the two groups are not significantly different from each other, we can reasonably argue that profit sharing is *not* a serious influence in the outcome. Any significant positive value of the coefficient of productivity in the earnings function could then be ascribed to 'unobserved quality' of labor associated with capital intensity.

Obviously, this conclusion relies heavily on the two assumptions made earlier that the profitability is not just a function of enterprise size and that the capital labor ratio for both profitable and non-profitable firms exhibits similar variation.

Empirical Results

Table 15.2 presents the estimated single equation function for four countries. The human capital components are those used frequently in the empirical analysis including experience and education. The effect of wave is discounted in all estimations. We have also estimated the equations after controlling for the workers' categories (occupational groups). However the results did not change qualitatively. The size effect although significant varies for different countries with a minimum of 0.114 and a maximum of 0.185. The inclusion of category dummies reduces the size effect for all countries. We have also tried adding some other variables such as tenure and union; however the overall results with respect to the size variable and its decomposition as well as the interaction between the productivity and earnings remained unchanged.

As discussed earlier, the size effect in the earning function is misspecified since the size in the simple equation estimation is picking up all firm specific effects including those related to organization, structure, and production process. To decompose the size effect we re-estimate the earning function in a simultaneous equation setup. The results appear in Table 15.3. The size effect is reduced except for Kenya and the reduction in the size effect is more significant for those countries where the feedback from the production process is most significant. For Kenya where the production process does not seem to add much to the explanation of the earning function, the coefficient of size remains unchanged.

Table 15.2 Estimation of the Earning Function

	Ghana	*Kenya*	*Zambia*	*Zimbabwe*
Constant	8.82 (105.09)	6.793 (98.75)	7.67 (67.46)	3.65 (36.47)
Experience	0.03 (5.16)	0.022 (7.85)	0.03 (7.61)	0.06 (11.05)
Experience**2	-0.0005 (-3.08)	-0.0001 (-2.56)	-0.0004 (-5.05)	-0.0007 (-7.02)
Education in Years	0.06 (13.74)	0.075 (18.60)	0.12 (16.21)	0.14 (20.92)
Sex Dummy (Female)	-0.21 (-4.48)	-0.06 (-1.64)	-0.015 (-0.32)	-0.14 (-3.22)
Ln(Size)	0.1214 (8.09)	0.1135 (10.52)	0.159 (11.61)	0.185 (16.04)
Number of Observations	1204	2278	1440	1760
Adjusted R^2	0.2766	0.2238	0.2402	0.3634

Table 15.3 Estimation of the Earnings Function and the Production Function Simultaneously

	Ghana	*Kenya*	*Zambia*	*Zimbabwe*
Earnings Function				
Constant	6.522 (15.56)	6.147 (16.46)	6.46 (11.17)	1.812 (6.06)
Experience	0.029 (4.96)	0.022 (7.23)	0.030 (7.44)	0.055 (11.04)
Experience**2	-0.0004 (-3.17)	-0.0001 (-2.80)	-0.0004 (-5.03)	-0.0007 (-6.57)
Education in Years	0.048 (11.10)	0.073 (16.34)	0.120 (15.25)	0.130 (19.94)
Sex Dummy	0.204 (4.56)	0.064 (1.50)	0.015 (0.32)	0.046 (1.04)
Ln(L)	0.095 (5.37)	0.1157 (9.88)	0.137 (7.87)	0.132 (10.05)
Ln(Y/L)	0.179 (5.37)	0.059 (1.72)	0.094 (1.96)	0.215 (6.47)
Adjusted R^2	0.2930	0.2318	0.3105	0.3767
Production Function				
Constant	8.285 (8.57)	4.800 (7.79)	5.535 (8.14)	4.922 (18.55)
Ln(K/L)	0.299 (16.04)	0.268 (18.13)	0.317 (15.98)	0.400 (24.61)
Ln(L)	0.016 (0.58)	-0.002 (0.11)	0.104 (4.48)	0.048 (2.90)
Ln(Wage)	0.103 (0.92)	0.456 (5.41)	0.309 (4.28)	0.150 (2.92)
Number of Observations	1204	2198	1440	1723
Adjusted R^2	0.3593	0.2497	0.3069	0.4089

Table 15.4 Estimation of the Earning Function and the Production Function Simultaneously (Firm Averages)

	Ghana	*Kenya*	*Zambia*	*Zimbabwe*
Earning Function				
Constant	5.876 (6.33)	6.359 (6.64)	6.779 (7.12)	1.329 (2.48)
Experience	0.049 (2.21)	0.007 (0.60)	0.010 (1.22)	0.044 (1.93)
Experience**2	-0.001 (-2.04)	0.0005 (2.35)	-0.0002 (-1.63)	-0.0004 (-0.65)
Education in Years	0.046 (3.20)	0.095 (6.20)	0.66 (2.65)	0.158 (6.54)
Sex Dummy	0.396 (3.10)	0.208 (1.50)	0.143 (1.10)	0.024 (0.18)
Ln(L)	0.101 (2.95)	0.101 (6.23)	0.175 (6.15)	0.189 (8.30)
Ln(Y/L)	0.212 (2.79)	-0.009 (-0.10)	0.134 (1.57)	0.247 (3.60)
Adjusted R^2	0.3055	0.3357	0.3451	0.6194
Production Function				
Constant	10.68 (3.80)	6.22 (3.81)	-0.98 (-0.27)	3.714 (4.26)
Ln(K/L)	0.340 (6.46)	0.218 (6.18)	0.292 (5.50)	0.354 (7.53)
Ln(L)	0.022 (0.30)	0.051 (0.84)	-0.109 (-1.03)	-0.047 (-0.82)
Ln(Wage)	-0.190 (-0.56)	0.315 (1.43)	1.045 (1.33)	0.466 (2.44)
Number of Observations	249	390	295	253
Adjusted R^2	0.3425	0.2097	0.2643	0.4492

One technical problem with this analysis is the fact that the dimensions of the data sets used for workers and firms are different. More specifically, the worker data set normally contains more than one observation per firm, which will lead to a non-diagonal residual variance covariance matrix. These will make the statistical inference unreliable. We have tried to resolve this technical difficulty by estimating the system on firm average variables. Table 15.4 presents the estimated system using firm averages for the relevant variables. The results, overall, do not change materially and are still in accordance with the prediction of the theory. The coefficient of size is higher for Zambia and Zimbabwe whereas it remains unchanged for Ghana and Kenya.

The reduced form of the earnings equation of the system (1) can be used to decompose the *total* size effect into its three components: the direct size effect; the impact of the production process emanating from the scale effect; and the production effect captured by the capital intensity variable. Tables 15.5 and 15.6 illustrate the decomposition of the size effect into the three components. Except for Kenya, a sizable share of the size effect is attributed to the production process and is captured by capital intensity and scale effect. For instance, in the case of Zimbabwe about 25 percent of the total size effect is associated with the production process including 0.21 percent capital intensity and 5 percent scale effect. Ghana and Zambia also have substantial impact of the production function on earnings — 18 and 11 percent respectively. Only in the case of Kenya, the production process does not seem to be contributing to the explanation of the earning function and hence almost the entire size effect can be attributed to direct size effect or as defined earlier the organizational effect.

Table 15.5 Decomposition of the Elasticity of Earning with Respect to Size of the Firm

	Ghana	*Kenya*	*Zambia*	*Zimbabwe*
Direct Size Effect	0.097	0.1189	0.141	0.137
Indirect Size Effect				
Scale Effect	0.003	-0.005	0.010	0.010
Capital Intensity	0.0214	-0.010	0.008	0.038
Total	0.1214	0.1135	0.159	0.185

Note: Total elasticity is the elasticity of earning with respect to size in the single equation estimation as in Table 1. The decomposition was achieved by decomposing this elasticity to its components in the reduced form of the simultaneous equations.

Table 15.6 Percentage of Total Elasticity of Earning with Respect to the Size of the Firm

	Ghana	*Kenya*	*Zambia*	*Zimbabwe*
Direct Size Effect	0.82%	0.99%	0.89%	0.74%
Indirect Size Effect				
Scale Effect	0.03%	0.01%	0.07%	0.05
Capital Intensity	0.15%	0.00%	0.05%	0.21%
Total	100%	100%	100%	100%

Note: See Table 5.

The explanation of inter-country differences is outside the scope of the paper. But it is clear from a cursory look at the data that the structure of industry in terms of establishment size do seem to play a significant role. Looking at the distribution of value added by size groups of establishments, Zimbabwe has the one most skewed to the right, with the 'very large' (more than 500 workers) accounting for nearly 86 percent of the total. The corresponding percentage for Kenya, at the other extreme, was 48, with the percentages for Ghana and Zambia being 58 and 66 respectively. At the same the higher capital use per worker in the very large firms did not produce any decline in capital productivity in the countries with more skewed distribution as compared to Kenya. The value added-capital ratio in the very large firms was 0.75 for Zimbabwe, 0.78 for Zambia, 0.77 for Ghana — and only 0.48 for Kenya. The higher capital productivity in the large firms in countries other than Kenya translated itself into the higher elasticity of earnings with respect to size attributable to the production process.

As we indicated earlier, the capital intensity component might actually be capital-specific skills not accounted for by the standard human capital indicators. Alternatively, it might represent a rent sharing effect on earnings. One of way of distinguishing between the two alternative paths of interaction is to divide the sample between profitable and unprofitable firms. If rent sharing were the principal causal factor we should find a clear difference in the impact of the production function on earnings between the two sub-samples.

We choose the first quartile of the distribution of profit per worker as the upper bound of non-profitable firms and the rest of the distribution account for the profitable firms. We have also tried negative and positive profit as a measure of profitability. The results in general remain the same; however since for some countries the sample of firms with negative profit is quite small, we preferred to use the first quartile as our cut-off point.

This argument based on the differentiation between the two sub-samples requires that the distribution of non-profitable firms is not concentrated in the smaller size-groups. Also the capital intensity for the non-profitable firms should exhibit enough variation to ensure that the possible relation between higher capital intensity and higher labor quality is captured.

Table 15.7 presents the distribution of firms by size for the 'unprofitable' sub-group, while Table 15.8 gives a summary of the distribution by capital intensity overall and for both the sub-groups. Table 15.7 clearly demonstrates that the distribution of the non-profitable firms does not show a concentration in small size-group although a mild skewness toward smaller firms can be observed. Table 15.8 shows that non-profitable firms have a wide spectrum of capital intensity. In general, one may certainly argue that mean capital intensity, as expected, is larger for profitable firms. However, the requirement of our analysis is focused on the variation of capital intensity and not on its average value. The coefficient of the variation does not show a specific pattern and indeed one may find that it is higher for non-profitable firms. This finding paves the ground for our final analysis, which is the determination of the productivity variable in the earning function. With profitability not a direct function of size, and with the capital intensity showing wide variation for both profitable and non-profitable firms, the revealed difference in the way the production process affects the earning function of profitable and non-profitable firms cannot be due to variation in size or capital intensity and hence can not be attributed to capital specific skills or unobserved human capital.

Table 15.7 Distribution of the Lowest Quartile Profitable Workers (Firms) by Size

	Ghana	*Kenya*	*Zambia*	*Zimbabwe*
Micro	15.8 (13.9)	29.0 (28.9)	25.7 (28.8)	34.7 (33.3)
Small	22.9 (24.8)	23.5 (23.1)	26.3 (29.9)	28.4 (34.4)
Medium	20.4 (22.0)	25.3 (25.0)	24.9 (23.6)	26.4 (25.8)
Large	36.1 (31.3)	17.0 (20.6)	16.7 (19.0)	17.2 (16.0)
Very Large	28.6 (33.3)	33.3 (37.5)	15.5 (18.8)	27.2 (24.2)

Table 15.8 Distribution of Capital Intensity by Profitability

	Ghana	*Kenya*	*Zambia*	*Zimbabwe*
All Firms				
Mean	13.49	11.93	13.93	10.08
Variance	4.28	2.89	1.72	1.85
90% (10%)	16.05 (10.68)	14.03 (9.79)	15.70 (12.12)	11.80 (8.39)
CV	15.33	14.26	9.42	13.49
Profitable Firms				
Mean	14.02	13.44	12.06	10.12
Variance	1.74	3.99	2.77	1.68
90% (10%)	15.87 (12.33)	15.05 (10.73)	14.12 (10.08)	11.90 (8.55)
CV	9.42	14.86	13.81	12.70
Unprofitable Firms				
Mean	13.65	13.65	11.53	9.70
Variance	1.58	5.37	3.07	2.18
90% (10%)	15.14 (11.88)	16.50 (10.09)	13.79 (9.19)	11.20 (7.69)
CV	9.22	16.98	15.20	15.24

Note: CV stands for Coefficient of variation.

Tables 15.9 and 15.10 repeat the same estimation for the profitable and non-profitable firms. As discussed earlier, we expect the size effect not to differ significantly for the profitable and non-profitable firms whereas we expect the production effect to be different. This expectation is confirmed nicely for two countries: Zimbabwe and Zambia. The direct size effect remains practically the same for both cases whereas the production process seems to be contributing to the determination of the earning only for the sub-sample of the profitable firms. This finding strongly enhances our belief that the inclusion of the productivity variable in the earning function captures the impact of profit sharing on earnings rather than that of unobserved human capital.

Table 15.9 Estimation of the Earning Function and the Production Function Simultaneously, Profitable Firms

	Ghana	*Kenya*	*Zambia*	*Zimbabwe*
Earning Function				
Constant	5.557 (9.46)	5.683 (12.11)	6.050 (9.41)	1.293 (2.78)
Experience	0.034 (5.07)	0.027 (7.38)	0.029 (6.55)	0.056 (9.36)
Experience**2	-0.0005 (-3.07)	-0.0002 (-2.74)	-0.0003 (-4.52)	-0.0007 (-5.39)
Education in Years	0.049 (9.76)	0.078 (15.25)	0.123 (13.68)	0.131 (16.86)
Sex Dummy	0.179 (3.56)	0.082 (1.62)	0.006 (0.11)	0.021 (0.38)
Ln(L)	0.101 (5.18)	0.096 (7.20)	0.146 (7.72)	0.124 (6.75)
Ln(Y/L)	0.242 (5.30)	0.070 (1.70)	0.120 (2.34)	0.268 (5.24)
Adjusted R^2	0.3277	0.2346	0.3222	0.3686
Production Function				
Constant	9.233 (9.21)	5.403 (9.18)	6.371 (9.01)	5.972 (21.70)
Ln(K/L)	0.260 (12.20)	0.285 (16.80)	0.339 (15.72)	0.326 (18.49)
Ln(L)	0.079 (2.35)	-0.033 (-1.53)	0.087 (3.476)	0.121 (6.92)
Ln(Wage)	0.068 (0.57)	0.417 (5.22)	0.217 (2.82)	0.071 (1.33)
Number of Observations	930	1685	1102	1293
Adjusted R^2	0.3197	0.2319	0.3254	0.4240

Table 15.10 Estimation of the Earnings Function and the Production Function Simultaneously, Unprofitable Firms

	Ghana	*Kenya*	*Zambia*	*Zimbabwe*
Earnings Function				
Constant	8.028 (14.67)	7.289 (4.06)	8.551 (4.69)	2.651 (6.82)
Experience	0.008 (0.71)	0.008 (1.41)	0.042 (3.34)	0.056 (6.11)
Experience**2	-0.001 (-0.48)	0.0003 (0.50)	-0.0006 (-2.12)	-0.0007 (-3.97)
Education in Years	0.039 (4.74)	0.053 (5.45)	0.121 (6.17)	0.127 (10.26)
Sex Dummy	0.206 (2.07)	-0.025 (-0.31)	0.064 (0.608)	0.093 (1.30)
Ln(L)	0.026 (0.91)	0.200 (5.73)	0.122 (2.56)	0.125 (5.98)
Ln(Y/L)	0.112 (2.26)	-0.063 (-0.35)	-0.074 (-0.45)	0.130 (3.02)
Adjusted R^2	0.1945	0.2333	0.2407	0.3779
Production Function				
Constant	4.312 (1.64)	6.489 (3.75)	3.912 (2.31)	2.179 (3.49)
Ln(K/L)	0.366 (10.63)	0.097 (4.02)	0.227 (4.98)	0.510 (15.49)
Ln(L)	-0.035 (-0.80)	0.092 (1.48)	0.126 (2.50)	-0.140 (-3.95)
Ln(Wage)	0.328 (1.14)	0.363 (1.53)	0.546 (3.32)	0.496 (4.25)
Number of Observations	273	512	337	429
Adjusted R^2	0.5941	0.1400	0.2143	0.4479

The evidence for Ghana and Kenya is rather mixed. While for Kenya the productivity factor is not significant for either the profitable or the non-profitable firms, in the case Ghana, for profitable firms the production process seems to be contributing significantly more to the determination of earnings. However, the direct size effect seems to be different for profitable and non-profitable firms, a finding that questions one of the presumptions of the profit sharing effect. Despite this, in the repeat of our analysis using data of firm averages (Tables 15.11 and 15.12), this problem was resolved.

Table 15.11 Estimation of the Earning Function and the Production Function Simultaneously, Profitable (Firm Averages)

	Ghana	*Kenya*	*Zambia*	*Zimbabwe*
Earning Function				
Constant	5.117 (4.33)	6.065 (4.23)	5.490 (5.47)	0.508 (0.57)
Experience	0.060 (2.23)	0.068 (2.62)	0.0009 (0.10)	0.009 (0.30)
Experience**2	-0.002 (-2.00)	-0.001 (-1.69)	-0.0001 (-0.73)	0.0006 (0.81)
Education in Years	0.047 (2.71)	0.093 (4.62)	0.075 (2.75)	0.130 (4.20)
Sex Dummy	0.364 (2.41)	0.156 (0.84)	0.207 (1.39)	-0.033 (-0.18)
Ln(L)	0.084 (1.96)	0.111 (3.74)	0.183 (6.08)	0.187 (5.86)
Ln(Y/L)	0.261 (2.76)	-0.006 (-0.05)	0.221 (2.72)	0.381 (3.48)
Adjusted R^2	0.3107	0.3009	0.4141	0.5834
Production Function				
Constant	13.57 (3.84)	3.438 (1.87)	4.03 (1.24)	5.621 (5.63)
Ln(K/L)	0.350 (5.25)	0.174 (4.34)	0.341 (5.78)	0.315 (5.40)
Ln(L)	0.106 (1.20)	-0.044 (-0.70)	-0.021 (-0.21)	0.049 (0.74)
Ln(Earning)	-0.409 (-1.17)	0.814 (3.23)	0.475 (1.21)	0.212 (0.92)
Number of Observations	196	293	216	189
Adjusted R^2	0.3242	0.2011	0.3375	0.4276

Table 15.12 Estimation of the Earning Function and the Production Function Simultaneously, Unprofitable (Firm Averages)

	Ghana	*Kenya*	*Zambia*	*Zimbabwe*
Earning Function				
Constant	7.603 (6.05)	8.518 (3.19)	11.47 (2.86)	2.115 (3.61)
Experience	0.019 (0.45)	-0.033 (-1.72)	0.075 (1.81)	0.125 (3.98)
Experience**2	-0.0007 (-0.62)	0.001 (3.87)	-0.0009 (-1.00)	-0.002 (-3.11)
Education in Years	0.050 (1.98)	0.073 (2.60)	0.151 (1.21)	0.200 (4.89)
Sex Dummy	0.488 (2.05)	-0.022 (-0.09)	0.133 (0.37)	0.015 (0.09)
Ln(L)	0.096 (1.68)	0.287 (3.73)	0.123 (1.45)	0.138 (4.00)
Ln(Y/L)	0.113 (0.88)	-0.174 (-0.68)	-0.354 (-0.78)	0.077 (1.02)
Adjusted R^2	0.2322	0.4677	0.095	0.7123
Production Function				
Constant	2.021 (0.351)	7.989 (3.60)	-7.238 (-0.89)	0.671 (0.40)
Ln(K/L)	0.320 (3.85)	0.142 (2.34)	0.294 (2.20)	0.449 (5.58)
Ln(L)	-0.091 (-0.67)	0.170 (1.67)	-0.146 (-0.78)	-0.194 (-1.88)
Ln(Earning)	0.640 (0.95)	0.067 (0.24)	1.634 (0.75)	0.814 (2.60)
Number of Observations	52	96	78	63
Adjusted R^2	0.4343	0.1365	0.0970	0.4690

Efficiency-Wage Models versus Profit Sharing

Efficiency wage models in their most general formulation would apply to firms of any size. Models as proposed by Shapiro and Stiglitz (1984) build on the presumption that higher wages prevent individuals from shirking and motivates them to work harder. This presumption leads to a reduced form solution for which the productivity is a positive function of wages and unemployment, since higher relative wages as well as higher unemployment increases the cost of shirking. This reduced form, in the context of the Solow implicit production function can be written as:

$$F(Y,K,L,w,U)=0 \tag{2}$$

Here Y is production, K and L are capital and labor, w is the efficiency-wage and U is the unemployment rate. Levine(1992) building on Solow (1979) demonstrates that for a production function that depends only on labor and capital, if wages enter the production function as a labor-augmenting factor, then the reduced form will be equation(2) without the unemployment rate. More specifically, he assumes constant returns to scale Cobb-Douglas production function with labor augmenting technology. In other words, this production function includes effective labor instead of physical labor;

$$Y_i=(e^{\eta}L_i)^{\alpha}K_i^{1-\beta}f_i\varepsilon_i \tag{3}$$

in which (*f*) represents a firm specific productivity factor that is invariant over the time and (η) represents the labor augmenting efficiency factor or in other words the elasticity of effective-labor with respect to labor efficiency. A simple re-organization of the first-order condition will lead to the inclusion of the wage in the production function with a parameter that under special conditions will equal the parameter of labor, or in log terms,

$$\ln(Y_i)=A+a\ln(w_i)+a\ln(L_i)+(1-a)\ln(K_i)+\varepsilon_i \tag{4}$$

This implies that, a firm finding it profitable to increase its labor component which will increase its wage bill by 1% has two options: hiring 1% more workers or inducing more efficient work by increasing wages by 1%. At the optimum, these two strategies must be equally profitable. Thus, the elasticity of output with respect to wages equals the elasticity of output with respect to labor. Levine uses firm wages relative to wages of the firm's nearest three competitors for (w) as a measure of the wage premium.

Under certain conditions, the implicit production function of equation (2) can be approximated with a translog function in which production is the dependent variable and specifically includes the usual factor inputs as well as measures of the 'wage premium'. Using this idea, Huang *et al.* (1998) formulate the reduced form and derive testable predictions. In their analysis, Huang *et al.* argue that the implicit production function should include human capital in addition to the wage premium; a higher human capital leads to higher productivity. They estimate the log of earnings as a function of measurable human capital including tenure, education, and percentage of female workers. The residual from this regression is the wage premium paid by a firm and is not associated with human capital whereas the predicted value is the return to human capital. This differentiation enables them to examine if the higher productivity is associated with higher human capital or higher wage premium or both and if these two effects are separable. They obtained some encouraging results. They found that for two-digit manufacturing industries in the United States over the period 1968 to 1991, wage premia and higher unemployment rates raise productivity and that wage premia and the human capital components of the observed wage cannot be aggregated into a single human capital index. Thus, they concluded that the effect of these two factors were separable.

Efficiency-wage models are similar to models of profit sharing in predicting a positive relation between excess wage and productivity. The direction of causation is different. However, this difference is unidentifiable in a reduced form framework. Economists have used different model-specific properties to identify these two alternative models. Among the most popular is the use of union as an identifier. Profit-sharing models predict that unionized firms should be more prone to profit sharing whereas efficiency-wage models predict the reverse. This stylized fact can be used to identify these two alternatives by estimating the models for these two sub-samples separately. Despite this, the literature is still to a large extent silent as to whether an observed positive relation between excess wage and productivity can be attributed to profit sharing or efficiency-wage.

Table 15.13 provides the single equation estimation of the efficiency-wage model in which the wage premium is the residual from the estimated earnings function using the observed human capital variables. In other words, borrowing from Huang *et al.* (1998), the wage differential not accounted for by the human capital variables is called the wage premium

— and this premium is then included as a variable in the production function. This table demonstrates that the conventional model of efficiency-wage finds support from the data in all four countries. However, as we indicated earlier, the unidentifiability of the two alternative explanations, efficiency-wage and profit sharing, makes it difficult to attribute the observed positive relation between the wage premium and productivity to one or the other of these factors. We have re-estimated the model after crossing a dummy for the unionized firms with the coefficient of the wage premium. The results, as expected, are not convincing either way.

Table 15.13 Test of the Efficiency-Wage Models Using the Reduced form Model

	Ghana	*Kenya*	*Zambia*	*Zimbabwe*
Constant	9.263 (20.67)	8.208 (43.61)	8.320 (13.96)	6.248 (15.33)
Ln(K/L)	0.310 (8.90)	0.277 (19.01)	0.342 (7.60)	0.383 (9,61)
Ln(L)	-0.013 (-0.249)	0.037 (1.91)	0.093 (2.34)	0.006 (0.15)
Ln(Wage Premium)	0.221 (1.89)	0.373 (2.92)	0.348 (3.62)	0.396 (3.90)
Number of observations	249	390	295	253
Adjusted R^2	0.3627	0.2456	0.2980	0.4537

In the absence of sufficient time series data, one alternative is to estimate the equation for the wage premium and the production equation simultaneously; however this alternative may suffer from an argument that the wage premium might not be identified. To resolve this issue, we assume that the wage premium has two main components; one attributed to the workers' category (of occupations) and the other is the efficiency-wage or profit-sharing component. This allows us to identify the wage premium by category and since category is presumably unconnected with the production process, the equation for the wage premium as well as the production function will be identified. In Table 15.14 we re-estimate Table 15.13 after accounting for workers' category. The coefficients of the wage premium in this Table correspond closely to those of Table 15.13, providing further evidence that the correlation between productivity and workers' category is rather weak.

Table 15.14 Test of the Efficiency-Wage Models Using Reduced form Model (Fixed Workers Category)

	Ghana	*Kenya*	*Zambia*	*Zimbabwe*
Constant	9.400 (20.56)	8.550 (20.86)	8.928 (12.91)	6.358 (15.91)
Ln(K/L)	0.305 (8.71)	0.228 (6.40)	0.346 (7.69)	0.32 (9.10)
Ln(L)	-0.030 (-0.56)	0.080 (2.03)	0.100 (2.55)	0.0002 (0.043)
Ln(Wage Premium)	0.240 (2.25)	0.286 (2.79)	0.404 (3.77)	0.570 (4.00)
Number of observations	249	390	295	253
Adjusted R^2	0.3665	0.2141	0.3006	0.4732

The results of the estimation of the simultaneous equation are presented in Table 15.15. The model exhibits a positive and significant feedback from the production process to the wage premium for both Ghana and Zimbabwe whereas for Kenya there is a significant feedback from the wage premium to the production process; and for Zambia the results are inconclusive although it favors a positive feedback from the wage premium to the production process.

Table 15.15 Test of the Efficiency-Wage Models Using Simultaneous System

	Ghana	*Kenya*	*Zambia*	*Zimbabwe*
Wage Premium				
Ln(L)	0.085 (2.46)	0.132 (5.96)	0.104 (3.85)	0.120 (6.00)
Ln (Y/L)	0.178 (3.12)	0.028 (0.34)	0.023 (0.30)	0.223 (4.65)
Adjusted R^2	0.1061	0.1741	0.2074	0.5342
Production Function				
Constant	10.07 (11.90)	8.68 (19.91)	8.37 (13.51)	5.871 (11.87)
Ln(K/L)	0.269 (5.21)	0.236 (6.30)	0.341 (7.51)	0.401 (9.30)
Ln(L)	-0.091 (-1.10)	-0.001 (-0.01)	0.083 (1.63)	0.045 (0.98)
Ln(Wage Premium)	0.878 (1.38)	0.851 (2.23)	0.430 (1.53)	0.15 (0.74)
Number of Observations	249	390	295	254
Adjusted R^2	0.3299	0.1962	0.2791	0.4302

This simultaneous method allows us to differentiate if a positive relation between the production process and the unexplained human capital (wage premium) as found in the last section is due to profit sharing and/or efficiency wage contribution. The results clearly demonstrate that for the case of Zimbabwe and Ghana, the wage premium has a non-significant impact on the production function, whereas productivity is a main contributor to the wage premium. This implies that the profit sharing hypothesis is clearly a better choice for these countries in the attempt to account for the unexplained components of earnings. For Kenya the efficiency wage theorem provides a better explanation; the wage premium contributes significantly to productivity whereas productivity does not explain the premium. The question for Zambia remains unanswered although efficiency wage models might find more support.

Conclusion

Previous studies of the effect of enterprise on earnings have suffered from biases resulting from single equation estimates of the earnings function. Such approaches ignore the interdependence between the determinants of earnings and production. The earnings function impacts on productivity through the skills of the labor employed. The latter could be made up of measured human capital or unobserved labor quality. Similarly the production function has an impact on earnings through two distinct sources: first, the unobserved quality of labor is likely to be correlated with the capital intensity of the processes used in production, and secondly, there might be sharing of abnormal profits (or rent) with the workers.

The analysis of this chapter explicitly took account of this interdependence, which allowed us to investigate this two-way relationship quantitatively, and break down the impact of enterprise size on earnings into its various components. A direct effect of firm size was found to be dominant: it represents organization factors related to the bureaucratic hierarchy of the firm's labor force as well as the monitoring costs of producing and managing the internally formed skilled labor force. There was a significant element of indirect size effects emanating from the production function — more important in some countries than in others. We also sought to determine if unobserved skill or profit sharing was the dominant factor in the influence of the production function on earnings. By distinguishing the sub-samples of 'profitable' and 'non-profitable' firms we concluded that profit sharing indeed was the determining factor.

This conclusion still left open the possibility that 'efficiency wage' effects might be the alternative to profit sharing. This issue was explored, again within a simultaneous equation framework, in the last section. It seems that for three of the four countries the results lean towards the profit sharing alternative.

The overall message of this extended analysis is to suggest that the production process is indeed a key to the understanding of wage differentials. Indeed this might be the crucial point explaining the frequently observed fact that the enterprise size effect seems to be so much more significant and quantitatively important in developing countries than in the advanced industrialized countries. Even if we confine our attention to the so-called 'formal' sector in African manufacturing (as the RPED surveys do), the dispersion in production techniques could be expected to be much wider in Africa and other developing countries. Future work on this range of issue might fruitfully pay more attention to the analysis of production as a significant input into the study of earnings differences.

Appendix

Table 15A.1 Descriptive Statistics

	Micro	*Small*	*Medium*	*Large*	*Very Large*	*Overall*
Ghana						
WL/Y	0.25	0.31	0.38	0.25	0.05	0.29
K/Y	1.17	2.28	2.88	3.96	2.16	2.02
K*/Y	0.02	0.16	0.22	0.12	0.13	0.11
K/L (relative average)	0.69	0.81	1.43	3.29	2.67	1.00
R/Y	.	.	.	.	.	.
Sample Size	126	142	55	20	4	347
Kenya						
WL/Y	0.66	0.22	0.42	0.15	0.17	0.42
K/Y	1.90	2.26	1.91	2.75	2.29	2.08
K*/Y	0.18	0.20	0.26	0.27	0.23	0.42
K/L (relative average)	0.32	1.11	1.51	1.99	1.14	1.00
R/Y	0.03	0.05	0.05	0.07	0.10	0.08
Sample Size	174	141	138	42	16	511
Zambia						
WL/Y	0.49	0.33	0.58	0.27	0.23	0.43
K/Y	2.22	3.11	3.06	2.47	1.49	2.67
K*/Y	0.06	0.17	0.29	0.28	0.22	0.16
K/L (relative average)	0.97	0.83	1.03	1.70	1.61	1.00
R/Y	0.03	0.07	0.12	0.09	0.11	0.07
Sample Size	140	147	82	24	17	418
Zimbabwe						
WL/Y	0.56	0.59	0.42	0.35	0.33	0.44
K/Y	0.91	2.01	2.03	1.85	1.91	1.77
K*/Y	0.11	0.48	0.42	0.50	0.50	0.39
K/L (relative average)	0.28	0.54	0.98	1.32	1.74	1.00
R/Y	0.03	0.06	0.06	0.17	0.15	0.09
Sample Size	55	39	101	57	42	294

Note: Y: value added, K; value of replacement capital, W: average wage: L: total number of workers, K*: value of the working capital (inventory and work in progress). R: value of total interest paid by the firm.

Table 15A.2 Pearson Coefficient of Correlation

	Ghana	*Kenya*	*Zimbabwe*
Correlation with Size of the Firm			
1. Wages	0.08866**	0.08954**	0.19152**
2. Benefits	0.14229**	0.02576	0.18536**
3. Value added per Worker	0.16497**	-0.04694	0.13374**
Correlation with Value added per Worker			
1. Wages	0.18416**	0.02730**	0.20040**
2. Benefits	0.15871**	0.06691**	0.06656**

Appendix to Part V

The Regional Program on Enterprise Development (RPED) is a multiyear survey of the manufacturing sector in eight African countries: Cameroon, Côte d'Ivoire, Ghana, Kenya, Burundi, Tanzania, Zambia and Zimbabwe. The RPED has been organized by the Africa Regional Technical Department of the World Bank, and has been funded by a number of European and the Canadian governments. The RPED Surveys have been designed to collect information on the performance of the manufacturing sector in the (post-) structural adjustment period in the various countries, and they have generated a unique data set containing a wealth of firm-level information comparable across the eight African countries surveyed. The survey generated very detailed firm-level information on a wide range of firm behavior aspects. One of the modules was a set of questions addressed to employers on labor. The topics covered included — employment, labor force structure and characteristics paid compensation and benefits, level of unionization, employee turnover etc. The questionnaires also included a survey for a sample of each firm's employees, who were asked about their starting and current wages, occupation, union status, education, tenure, apprenticeship history, layoff experience, and also some very limited demographic information.

While most of the data refer to the current year, recall questions were asked for some of variables. For instance, employment and sales data were collected for some selected dates in the past.

The sample design and selection of firms followed the same format in all the countries though the details might have differed slightly from country to country. It was carried out in three waves, in successive years in the period 1991-95, the actual years of survey varying slightly from country to country. We can illustrate the procedure by the way it was actually implemented in the case of one country — Zimbabwe.

The Selection of the Sample

The RPED industrial surveys for Zimbabwe[60] were conducted during the

[60]This section draws heavily from Chapter 2 of *Industrial Change in Africa* edited by Gunning and Oostendrop (mimeo, May 1999).

Winter in June-July 1993, 1994, and 1995, and used a sample of manufacturing firms in four sectors: food processing, textile and garments (including leather and footwear), woodworking and furniture, and metalworking. The sub-sectors were defined in terms of ISIC codes:

Table VA.1 ISIC Codes

	ISIC Codes
Food processing	3111 – 3139
Textile, garments, leather and footwear	3211 – 3240
Woodworking and furniture	3311 – 3329
Metalworking	3811 – 3824

A broad definition of 'manufacturing' was used. Any kind of processing of raw materials or intermediates was accepted. Millers, butchers, bottlers, spinners and weavers were all included. However, neither tobacco processing nor electronics was included.

For a firm to be included in the sample it should employ at least five employees (including owner-managers) and be in a position to make its own investment decisions (i.e. it should not be a totally dependent subsidiary and it should have separate accounts). The former restriction excludes many existing firms from the survey. Mead et al. (1993), on the basis of a very large-scale survey, estimated that there were approximately 15,000 small-scale enterprises in Zimbabwe. The vast majority of these were tiny enterprises, typically one or two person 'firms' engaged in production at home, e.g. in crocheting. Most of the entrepreneurial decisions on which the survey focuses do not arise in such activities so that it was decided to impose a minimum size.

The sample includes both registered formal sector enterprises and unregistered informal ones. From the Central Statistical Office (CSO) a list of registered (formal sector) firms could be obtained. This list has been used for firms with 50 employees or more, which virtually guarantees that the coverage of the CSO list is complete. Smaller firms are included on the CSO list (since many of them are registered) but here the CSO cannot possibly cover all firms. For these smaller firms use was made of the Gemini survey of small-scale and micro firms (most of them in the informal sector) held in August 1991 (Mead et al. 1993).

The GEMINI survey was conducted in randomly selected areas throughout Zimbabwe, using stratified cluster sampling. The enumerated clusters (areas) were selected on the basis of the 1982 population census, but with a certain distribution over four urban and four rural strata. The survey covered only enterprises with 50 or fewer employees (including the proprietor(s)), marketing at least 50 percent of their product and engaged in an economic activity other than agriculture or primary product production. The survey covered over 15,000 households and shops, and 5,575 micro and small enterprises were identified. For these 5,575 firms the number of employees is known. Although 60% of the enterprises were engaged in manufacturing activities, the number fitting our definition of a firm turned out to be small. Of the 5,575 firms only 561 employed at least five employees and of these only about a third (182) were engaged in manufacturing. When confining ourselves to the four selected sub-sectors this number falls to 107. These firms were included in our sampling frame.

In order to combine the CSO and the GEMINI lists, blow-up factors were applied to the GEMINI firms, corresponding to the sampling fractions. The CSO list was then used for firms with more than 50 employees and the GEMINI list for enterprises with 50 or fewer (but at least five) employees. GEMINI did not distinguish formal and informal firms. The CSO list, however, contains only formal enterprises. Therefore we have implicitly assumed that there are no informal enterprises with more than 50 employees.

The sampling procedure gave each worker the same probability of being chosen. This was achieved by drawing randomly from the list of workers where each firm is represented by the actual number of workers times the blow-up factor. Selection was done by taking fixed steps from a random starting value (fixed interval sampling). Although drawing firms, the sampling criterion was to give equal probability to each worker of being drawn. Thus, in fact, a worker was drawn and then the corresponding firm was selected.

The selected sample consisted of 133 firms from the CSO list and 67 from GEMINI, distributed over the four sub-sectors. In case a selected firm was unwilling to cooperate or could not be found, the most suitable replacement was selected.

In total 205 firms were interviewed in the first round (1993), 107 of which were in the original sample. Four firms were rejected (two from the original sample). Three because the interview was incomplete, and one because the information given seemed highly unreliable. Therefore, the final response rate turned out to be 52.2 percent.

In the first and second rounds of the Survey (June-July 1993 and 1994) a maximum of 10 workers were interviewed in each firm (fewer than 10 workers in firms with less than 10 employees). The fact that not all workers were interviewed in firms with more than 10 workers implies that workers in large firms are underrepresented in the sample. Each firm was asked to indicate how many workers it employed in each of 10 broad occupational categories: management, administration and clerical, technical (primarily engineers and scientists), sales, equipment maintenance and repair, factory supervisors and foremen, skilled production workers, semi-skilled and unskilled production, support staff (janitors, night watchmen, canteen staff), and apprentices. The sample was drawn according to these occupational categories in proportion to their representation in the firm's total labor force.

In the second round only the workers were interviewed which were also in the first round sample. While the first round yielded responses of 1,717 workers in all 201 firms, only 637 workers in 116 firms were interviewed in the second round. No workers were interviewed in the third round. The relatively small number of employees interviewed in the second round compared to the first round is due to a number of reasons: (1) recording worker's names was not a uniform practice in the early part of the first-round, so the workers from some firms could not be identified and included in the second round, (2) some workers were no longer working at the firm or unavailable for a second interview, and (3) the firm was not interviewed in the second round because of non-response.

Attrition and Selection of Replacements

As noted, the first round yielded complete interviews for 201 firms. During the second round of the Zimbabwe surveys in June-July 1994, these firms were contacted again for a follow-up interview. Ten firms that were successfully interviewed in 1993 could not be interviewed again in 1994. In three cases this was because the firm went bankrupt, in one case the firm's owner was seriously ill and unable to do business, in another case the firm was in the process of moving to other premises, and in one case the firms' books were not available. The other four firms refused to participate in the survey mainly for reasons of time. The sample's attrition rate between 1993 and 1994 was therefore 5 percent.

During the second round of interviews in June-July 1994, 12 additional firms were interviewed to make up for the 10 firms, which could not be interviewed again, as well as for 2 firms, which had temporarily stopped their production. The replacement firms were selected from the same sector as the firm to be replaced, and of roughly similar size in terms of employment.

The total sample size for the 1994 survey was therefore 203: 191 of the original firms, plus twelve replacements for firms that could not be re-interviewed or that had temporarily stopped producing. For one of these

203 firms, we have only been able to re-interview some of its last years workers from the previous year. This leaves a sample of 202 firms in 1994 with information about other issues than workers.

During the third, and last, round of the Zimbabwe surveys in June-July 1995, each of the 203 interviewed firms of the previous year was contacted for another interview, of which eleven firms could not be interviewed again. Five of these firms went bankrupt or closed down for lack of perspective. Three firms had been taken over by other firms or were in the middle of a merger, and three others refused to be interviewed again for reasons of time. This means that the sample attrition rate between 1994 and 1995 was also (about) 5 percent.

Because no replacement firms were selected for this year's survey, the total sample for 1995 consists of 192 firms. In four cases the interviews could be completed only partially, because of an inability or refusal to provide financial data. Nevertheless, because these interviews contain other valuable information, they are included in the final sample.

It is noticeable that the number of firms which went out of business in the course of the year was very low for the periods 1993-94 and 1994-95 (1.5 percent and 2.5 percent respectively). Furthermore, the sector distribution of non-response firms mirrors the sector distribution of all firms interviewed in 1993 (Table 11.2): non-response had no effect on the sectoral distribution of the sample.

Table VA.2 Sector Distribution of All Firms in 1993 and Non-Response Firms in 1994 and 1995 (Percentage)

	All 1993	*1994*	*Non-Response*
Food	24	20	18
Wood	13	30	9
Textile	44	30	55
Metal	18	20	18

In this part we will use four size classes (in terms of employment): 10 or less ('small'), from 11 up to 100 ('medium'), from 101 up to 250 ('large'), and more than 250 ('very large'). Table 11.3 reports the frequency of firms by size class and sector for the initial 1993 sample. Size is measured as the employment at the time of the interview in 1993.

When classified according to size, the firms are roughly equally distributed over the chosen categories: 40 firms employ less than 10 employees, 66 firms between 10 and 100, 47 firms between 100 and 250 workers, and 48 employ more than 250 people.

Table VA.3 Selected Firms by Size (Employment) and Sector (Unweighted Sample)

Size	*Food*	*Wood*	*Textile*	*Metal*	*Total*
<= 10	8	6	17	9	40
11 - 100	14	9	29	14	66
101 – 250	10	7	21	9	47
> 250	17	4	22	5	48
Total	49	26	89	37	201

Because the sample was selected by drawing workers rather than firms, Table 11.3 does not reflect the distribution of firms in the population — larger firms are over-represented. In Table 11.4 we therefore present the frequency of firms if we give an equal probability to each firm to be in the sample by reweighting the actual sample.

Table VA.4 Selected Firms by Size (Employment) and Sector (Weighted Sample)

Size	*Food*	*Wood*	*Textile*	*Metal*	*Total*
<= 10	47	15	40	19	121
11 – 100	8	5	55	4	72
101 – 250	1	1	2	1	5
> 250	1	0	2	0	3
Total	57	21	99	24	201

We observe that sector totals have not changed much, but size classes change dramatically. Most firms in Zimbabwe are small firms (10 or fewer employees), with the exception of the textile sector where a majority of the firms is medium-sized (between 11 and 100 employees). So, if we had drawn our sample on the basis of equal probability per firm, the number of small firms would probably have tripled. However, because we are interested in firms across the entire size distribution, the sample procedure of giving equal probability per employee was chosen to have a sufficient number of large and very large firms in the sample.

Finally, we look at the location of the sample firms (Table 11.5). Of the 201 firms visited in 1993, 110 firms were located in Harare, 56 in Bulawayo and 35 in regional centers and growth points. When ranked according to size, we observe that the small and medium sized firms were mostly concentrated in the regions.

Table VA.5 Size Distribution of Firms by Location (Unweighted Sample)

	Employment				
Location	5-10	11-100	101-250	> 250	Total
Harare	17	33	29	31	110
Bulawayo	8	22	15	11	56
Other	15	11	3	6	35
Total	40	66	47	48	201

Note: Differences between the column totals and the row totals are due to rounding.

To complete the comparison we also show the weighted sample by location, ranked according to size. As small firms are typically located outside the two large cities, giving more weight to them results in a larger number in the other regions. Of the 201 firms 57 would then be located in Harare, 32 in Bulawayo and 112 in regional centers and growth points.

Table VA.6 Size Distribution of Firms by Location (Weighted Sample)

	Employment				
Location	1-10	11-100	101-250	> 250	Total
Harare	38	15	2	2	57
Bulawayo	17	13	1	1	32
Other	66	45	0	1	112
Total	121	73	3	4	201

'Urban' was defined as a town with an estimated 1982 population of more than 20,000. The urban strata distinguished were: high density areas, low density areas, commercial districts and industrial areas. The four rural strata were: smaller towns, growth points, district councils and rural councils.

GEMINI used estimated growth rates of the population of the eight strata (and the whole of Zimbabwe), based on growth prior to 1982, to get estimates of the population per stratum in 1991. The population per stratum was divided by average household size to get the number of households per stratum. This number of households was then used to calculate the fraction of enumerated households. The inverse of this fraction was used as the blow-up factor.

This procedure of drawing a worker and then selecting the corresponding firm leads to firms being selected more than once. The step size in the interval selection procedure was adjusted in such a way that finally 200 firms were selected. It may be noted that firms with more employees than the step size are always in the sample. The same applies for GEMINI firms if the product of employment size and blow-up factor is larger than the step size.

The Selection of the Sample of Workers

As mentioned the data-set included a sample of workers interviewed in each firm, who were administered the labor questionnaire. A maximum of ten workers were interviewed in each firm (fewer than ten in smaller firms). The sample was drawn according to occupational categories in proportion to each occupation's weight in the firm's total labor force.

Part VI: Conclusions

16 Conclusions

The book has taken us through a large body of labor marker data on different aspects of wages and employment during the period of African decline in the twenty five years between the early seventies and the mid-nineties. The self-employed predominate in the laborforce of sub-Saharan Africa. This is the principal mode of employment in farming, in off-farm employment and in the urban informal sector. Wage employees constitute a small part of the total workforce, and, apart from a very limited presence as casual labor or as employees in micro-enterprises, belong to the formal sector of these economies. The average for a number of economies of SSA reported in Table 1.8 is 12 percent for the early nineties, though the proportion could be quite high in a few countries. The formal sector, however, exerts a disproportionate influence on the course of the African economies, partly because its share of GDP and more so its share of the monetized part of the GDP is much greater than its share of employment, and secondly, because the impulses and signals emanating from this sector are often the determining factors in the trends in the rest of the economy.

Much of the formal sector employment is located in the urban areas. Evidence is produced in Chapter 1 that the rate of urbanization in the period of our study has been very high, the urban population growing at more than twice the rate of the average in the countries concerned. Employment in the formal sector, while not stagnant, has not grown at anything like this rate, so that much of the rural-to-urban migrants have been absorbed in the urban informal sector. In a few countries like Ethiopia, where the informal sector is underdeveloped they have swelled the rate of open unemployment.

Some commentators have contributed to the popular view that the formal sector in SSA has been subjected to a widespread set of institutional influences which have a led to an inflexible labor market. Indeed, labor market rigidity in this sector has often been considred to be a major problem hampering development of the formal sector and, because of it, the economy as s whole. The study, therefore, begins with an evaluation of the most important institutional factors affecting the formal labor market. The evidence on the widespread decline of the level of real earnings in the formal sector, as well as of lifetime real earnings in the sector, documented in previous chapters, cast doubts on the importance of institutional factors causing wage rigidity in this sector. Chapter 2 supplements aggregate evidence on real minimum wages and public sector wages with responses from employers about their perception of labor market regulations. These responses were to parts of the questionnaire addressed to the employers of the sampled firms in the RPED surveys. The regulations considered related to (I) minimum wages (ii) restrictions on laying off permanent workers; (iii) limits on hiring of temporary or casual workers and (iv) permission required for hiring foreign workers. The tabulations of the answers in Chapter 2 enabled us to conclude that, as was to be expected from the evidence on wage decline, the effect of minimum wages was perceived to be the least burdensome for the employers, most of them in all countries saying that a slight reduction in minimum wages would have no effect on the decision to hire more workers. The restrictions on hiring and firing did have some impact on employers in some countries. Severity of existing regulations was considered to be an obstacle to temporary layoffs as well as to more hiring of permanent workers in Zambia and Zimbabwe in particular. In general, however, the responses of employers confirm that labor market regulations rank low in the list of obstacles to enterprise development compared to other factors, e.g., problems of finance and infrastructure. This conclusion is consistent with the finding of Part III that detailed analysis shows that the inter sectoral wage gap as between the urban formal, urban informal and the rural sectors are much less than what a cursory look at incomes per earner would suggest.

We have used the data collected by international organizations like the ILO and the UNIDO on the basis of returns submitted by national governments. Most of these data refer to the formal manufacturing sector. This material has been supplemented by the data set generated by sample surveys of manufacturing in seven countries organized by the Regional Program on Enterprise Development (RPED) of the World Bank in the mid-nineties. The sample is comprehensive in the sense of including micro, small and large firms, though it excludes household enterprises which employ one or only one or two paid employees. For sectors outside the formal manufacturing we depend on household sample surveys which have been conducted in a number of African countries, and on a variety of national data sources.

Wage and Employment Trends in Formal Manufacturing

The ILO and the UNIDO data-sets, studied in Part II, present the general picture of the course of earnings in the formal sector over the last three decades. After a burst of rapid real wage increases in the sixties, largely induced by government wage policies, wages have shown a persistent declining trend over the quarter of a century ending in the mid nineties.

The data from the international bodies give us the opportunity of placing the African experience in manufacturing wages in the context of the trends in other regions of the world. Latin America and the Caribbean (LAC) is the other region which includes a number of counties which have had a negative, sometimes severely negative, growth of real wages. But the mean negative trend was lower than in sub-Saharan Africa (SSA).[61] Secondly, the ILO data for recent years show that in the nineties the average growth rate of the LAC sample has recovered to positive values, but have become more negative for the SSA countries (Table 4.3 above). The Asia region, as is well known, had a strong positive growth rate of real wages in the seventies and the eighties, and has continued to be positive in the first half of the nineties, though with a lower trend value.

Our regression analysis of changes in average wages from a limited sample of countries in the different regions suggests that failure to compensate for inflationary increases in prices was the proximate cause and the mechanism of bringing about real wage decline (Table 4.1). This is what distinguished the experience of Africa over the last two decades from that of either Latin America or Asia. It was interesting to see that in the cross country experience the influence of per capita GDP growth on wage changes over time was not statistically significant for Africa (unlike the other regions). It seems almost that, alone in the world economy, the SSA region in the formal manufacturing sector experienced real wage trends which were divorced from trends in the supply price of labor (as approximated by the GDP per capita), but behaved autonomously within the sector — declining because of uncompensated inflationary trends.

The rate of inflation is, however, only a proximate cause of real wage changes, though it must be admitted that it serves the function of a useful machinery for real wage reduction. With stable prices it must have been more difficult for to bring about real wage reduction by cutting money wages. A more fundamental reason for wage reduction has to be sought in the factors affecting the growth of the real wage bill, and the way the latter is divided between employment increase and wage increase.

A simple decomposition model was developed in Chapter 5 of Part II

---

[61]The best summary measure for regions is probably the weighted average of the countries included in the exercise reported in table 4.6 above. The negative trends for LAC in both decades were lower than those for SSA.

which helped us to assess quantitatively the importance of four factors affecting the trend in real wages. These are: (i) the rate of growth of production or value added; (ii) the trend in the share of wages in value added: (iii) the way the resultant increase in wage bill is shared between wage increase and employment increase; and (iv) a price effect arising from the differential movements of the index of consumer prices and producer prices — a higher trend rate of the former causing a 'leakage' from the increase in the *real* value of the wage bill. The time series available for different regions were studied for two separate periods 1971-80 and 1981-92, after aggregating the country series into regional series with appropriate weighted averages. The differences between the regions are illuminating, as is the special characteristic of the Sub-Saharan region revealed by this comparative exercise. It is seen that, contrary to popular expectations, the negative trend in real earnings per worker (wages) in African manufacturing, was not due to a particularly low rate of growth of value added. The latter, although well below the trend growth of East Asia, and marginally below that LAC, was higher than the growth rate of OECD in both periods. The wage bill in African manufacturing did grow at a lower rate than value added in both periods, but the fall in the share of wages was not dramatic, and was less than the fall in the OECD region in the eighties, where real wages grew at a respectable rate. The more important reason for the declining trend in wages in SSA was the fact that this region chose to take the available wage bill increase more in the form of employment increase than wage increase. This is a function of labor market institutions which favored the interests of 'outsiders' by providing employment to a larger pool of job seekers, rather than serving the interest of 'insiders' who are already in employment. The SSA region, in this respect was at the opposite end of the spectrum of employment-wage growth trade-off than the OECD countries. The OECD as a whole preferred to realize its gains in output over time in the form of real wage enhancement rather than employment growth. In fact the results show that the real wage growth in OECD was high enough — given the modest output growth — to actually result in a declining trend in employment in both periods. This story is again consistent with much discussion of the power of the 'insiders' in OECD industrial firms. East Asia is revealed to have been in between these two regions — dividing the wage bill growth equally between wage and employment growth, while LAC was closer to the SSA region in favoring employment. This experience of massive decline in real wage has been noted for many individual countries in Africa, as has been the phenomenon of 'labor retention' on the part of African employers in the formal sector. A large proportion of manufacturing enterprises in the large-scale (as opposed to the informal) manufacturing sector have been state-owned or joint State-private ventures. The pressure to provide employment in this sector has been strong, and has increased as the decline in the economy shrank earnings and employment opportunities in other sectors. Another factor responsible for the African type of labor market outcome is the fact that, as will be evident from the discussion in Chapter 5 (Part II) in particular, a large fall in wages reduces the supply of units of work (of standard efficiency) per worker. This necessitates hiring of more workers to maintain the same level of labor input. Although the UNIDO data set for SSA is imperfect, and the number of countries which could be included in the sample is small, the over-all pattern is consistent with the conclusions of other case studies, including those reported in Part III.

A secondary reason for the negative real wage trend in SSA is that the second period, in particular, saw a significant negative price effect with consumer prices increasing at a faster rate than producer prices. In the seventies SSA shared with LAC the dubious distinction of having the lowest growth rates of manufacturing output in the world. The negative 'price effect', however was much less than in LAC. Nevertheless, net of the price effect the wage bill in real terms grew at a rate barely exceeding 1 percent per annum. Yet employment growth was at a substantial rate of over 4.4 percent. The only way the manufacturing sector of this region could accommodate this rate of employment growth was by a massive decline in real wage at the rate of 3.4 percent per annum. In the next decade, the manufacturing sector of SSA seemed to have recovered a lot, registering a rate of growth of output averaging 4.4 percent per annum over the period. But unfortunately the negative trends in the price effect nullified much of this enhanced growth. Net of the price effect output growth could not sustain the combined wage and employment growth at any higher level. Thus as employment growth continued unabated at over 4 percent per annum, the SSA region as a whole experienced a decline in real wage at a rate even greater than what was witnessed in the previous decade.

Labor Markets Outside Formal Manufacturing

While Part II of the book is concerned mostly with wage and employment trends in the modern (formal) manufacturing sector, Part III broadens the perspective to take account of other sectors of the economy — the fast-growing urban informal sector and the rural sector in which self-employed labor predominates. In general, formal statistics on earnings are not regularly collected for this sector. Household surveys have, however, become available for a number of countries, and in some cases such surveys have been conducted at two or more dates over time. Part III uses this body of material to throw light on the course of earnings in the non-formal sectors. We are able to report on detailed study of two countries — one in East Africa, Kenya, and the other in the West, Ghana. Shorter studies have been done on three other countries, distributed between East and West Africa.

Many African economies have seen a high rate of urbanization in the last thirty years or more, but a larger of the increased flow of labor fed by rural-to-urban migrants have been absorbed in the urban informal sector. The Kenya study has provided much needed empirical material on the characteristics of employment and earning in this sub-sector. The earnings distribution of the workers participating in this sector is very widely spread — with a sizable proportion earning more than even the upper tail of the formal sector wage earners. Because of this phenomenon the Urban Labor Force survey of 1986 showed that the *mean* earnings of the male self-employed was 50 percent higher than the mean of formal sector wages in non-agriculture. But the urban informal sector contains a large pool of low income groups. The decomposition analysis of the difference in earnings between the employees (mostly formal) and the self-employed (mostly informal) showed that after controlling for difference in the characteristics of the two groups, *male* employees in 1986 earned double the amount of the self-employed, but the *female employees* had a slightly lower level of earnings.

An attempt was made to piece together various sources of data to see if we can discern possible trends in the differential between formal sector wage earnings and the earnings in the informal sector. Our conclusion was that, looking at the bottom half of the distribution for the informal sector, the formal-informal differential almost certainly fell significantly in the period 1977-86 for which data existed. The ratio of *mean* formal wages to the *median* earnings of the self-employed (Business heads) in the 1977 survey was around 3:1, while in the 1986 Urban Labor Force Survey it had fallen to 2:1. The shrinking of the formal-informal differential is one way in which the urban economy coped with the declining earnings and massive rural-to-urban migration.

The other important aspect of inter-sectoral earnings difference is the gap between rural and urban incomes. Since the larger part of the employment in the rural areas is in non-wage employment the study of rural-urban earnings difference has to depend on statistics of income from all sources, not just wages. Such data are available only from socio-economic household surveys. The analysis of Part III is thus limited to the case studies of those countries for which household survey data were available. The traditional picture of the African economy, popularized by the Harris-Todaro model, is that urban wages have been pushed up by institutional forces well above rural incomes, and that this earnings gap has been at the heart of the continuing rural-to-urban migration. They are attracted to the urban sector in the expectation of landing in the high wage formal sector, but most of them have to settle for a place in the informal urban sector with a lower (and presumably falling) earnings level. The evidence presented about the declining formal wage and the narrowing earnings gap between the formal and the informal sectors have already undermined the traditional model in important ways. Deeper analysis of the rural-urban earnings gap reveal that the Harris-Todaro view of the migration process has to be modified to take account of different types of rural-to-urban migrants. There seems to be an important difference in patterns of migration in East and West Africa. In countries like Kenya and Zambia in the East, circulatory migrants of single males, or of part of the complete household, form an important component of the migratory process. The presence of such migrants in the urban areas gives a misleading picture of high incomes per earner observed in this sector, because it does not allow for the fact that the urban earners need to support the dependents left in the villages, or that the dependent-earner ratio of more permanent settled households in town would be potentially much larger than what is observed in the surveyed sample. The detailed analysis for Kenya showed that by 1986 urban households had adjusted to falling incomes during the previous decade by reducing the average size of the household present in the urban areas. If we made allowance for this, the earnings per capita or per adult equivalent unit for mature households would be only about 50 percent higher in the urban areas (at the median values of the distributions), and not the 200 or 300 percent difference suggested by the uncorrected data.

In the West African cases studied — Ghana and Cote d'Ivoire in particular — the size and composition of households in the rural and urban economies do not show the marked difference observed in Kenya. This suggests that circulatory or temporary migrants are not a dominant part of the rural-to-urban migration in this region. The difference in the pattern needs more investigation. The importance of international migration — going to the rural as much as the urban areas — might be one of the reasons for the difference. Unlike Kenya and Zambia, the difference in income per earner between rural and households in the West African countries studied was not large in the mid-nineties. In fact in Ghana the differential was slight even in the sixties, suggesting that incomes must have fallen at the same rate in the urban and the rural sectors during the period of Ghana's economic decline. Structural adjustment programs, initiated in 1983, seem to have improved the incomes in the rural sector and in the smaller towns, more than in the capital city in the late eighties. There is some evidence of reverse movement of labor from Accra to the rural economy after this in response to the relative income changes.

A different scenario of relentless migration of labor towards the capital city in spite of falling incomes is given in the case study of Cote d'Ivoire. By the end of the eighties income levels in rural areas, small towns and in Abidjan were more or less in equilibrium, with income per capita as well as income per earner being at more or less the same levels. There was moreover no difference in family size in the different areas suggesting that migration to all areas (fed partly by cross border streams) was of the permanent family type. At the same time, incomes fell at a faster rate in Abidjan. Even if there might have been some downward rigidity in formal sector wages in this area, the Harris-Todaro mechanism was weak, since most of the migrants were being absorbed in the urban informal sector. The continued migration to the capital city, with falling incomes and rising poverty levels in the latter, is compatible with the finding that incomes had reached similar levels in different areas by the end of the eighties, only on the hypothesis that *marginal income — or the expectation of it —* was lower in rural areas and small towns.

Life-time Trend in Earnings

The questionnaire addressed to the sample of workers in the RPED surveys asked questions on the wage history of the workers. Although based on recollection, the material makes available for the first time data on the changes in earnings of workers over their career in the firm in which they were employed at the time of the survey. The retrospective data give the trends in earnings which is the combined result of the returns to experience and the changes in the market wage rates over time. This body of data are analyzed in Chapter 11 of Part IV, which is devoted to assessing the impact of the decline of average wages in manufacturing, documented in Part II. The material adds importantly to the results on wage trends discussed in Part II.

The cohort of workers cover the period from 1970 to 1994. They were grouped in five-yearly intervals. The data confirm the findings of Part I about the generally declining trend in real wages in the African formal sector. All the countries in the RPED surveys show an overall negative trend, taking all cohorts together, with the sole exception of Ghana. Some of them like Kenya and Tanzania had average negative growth rates in excess of 2.5 percent per annum, while Zambia had an astonishing average rate of decline in excess of 10 percent. Zimbabwe, and to a lesser extent, Cameroon had positive growth rate of wages for the cohorts of the seventies and the early eighties, but for both countries there are strongly declining trends after that. The exceptional case of Ghana is explained by its macro-economic history. As can be seen from the case study presented in Chapter 9 wages had collapsed in the decade of the seventies, so the majority of those hired after 1975 had started at exceptionally low wages, and shared in the partial restoration of wage levels after the adjustment of the eighties. More recently, however, in the nineties, the wage trends have again been downward.

It is seen that all seven countries registered dramatic wage declines for the most recent cohorts. Apart from the weaker experience effect on wages of recently employed workers, a new burst of inflation in the nineties have led to a further decline in real wages. The negative trend in *individual* earnings is more serious than that in average wages discussed in Part II, because we can generally expect workers to progress along the wage ladder as their tenure in the firm increases.

The regression analysis of wage trends given in Chapter 11 yielded an important result that, apart from the cohort effects, the average annual growth rate of real wage was positively and significantly related to the log of firm size in every country other than Tanzania. In spite of the wage decline workers in larger firms have fared much better over time than the workers in smaller firms. Possible explanations include higher productivity growth in larger firms, which get translated to higher wages; and the bigger retention of experienced workers in larger firms together with higher returns to experience in such firms. In any event this important effect has no doubt caused a higher degree of wage inequality as real wages declined over all.

Impact of Falling Wages on Labor Productivity

One of the major impulses promoting the high wage policy in the formal sector in Africa of the sixties (documented Part III above) was the consideration that there was a need to augment labor efficiency by switching from the migratory to the stable labor system. The obverse of this concern is that the falling wages of the next three decades might have adversely affected labor productivity. Data on this topic are very difficult to get. The existence of time series for formal manufacturing over the period

1971-91 for one country, Kenya, prompted us to have a look at some aspects of this question in Chapter 12. The analysis decisively rejected any notion of falling productivity. The trend rate of growth of real wages was well below that of labor productivity over this period showing that the share of wages in value added *in real terms* fell continuously. This was, however, not due to higher capital intensity and diminishing returns to capital. Although over the whole period the rate of increase of capital was slightly higher, the growth in total factor productivity was high at nearly 2.5 percent per annum. The continuous lag in real wage growth behind the growth of real productivity tended to produce a persistent 'real wage gap' (in terms of the model of Chapter 11, equation 1) which led to a fall in unit labor costs (Uc) in most periods (except the coffee boom years of the late seventies). In an inflationary economy like Kenya, movements in the real domestic exchange rate tended to offset this decline as consumer prices increased faster than producer prices. But the continuous devaluation of the Kenyan shilling compensated for this adverse effect, so that Uc in dollars fell continuously. The Kenyan evidence thus does not reveal any adverse effect of the real wage decline on costs in manufacturing. Rather it contributed to the general flexibility of factor markets in increasing the competitiveness of Kenyan manufacturing both in the domestic and the external markets. The reasons for the failure of exports to respond positively to the increase in competitiveness in prices have to be sought elsewhere.

The Structure of the Labor Force and its Earnings in Manufacturing

The availability of the survey data from the Research Program in Enterprise Development (RPED) enabled us to look closely at the structure of the laborforce and earnings within the manufacturing sector in several African countries. These were sample surveys of a cross-section of firms, ranging from the micro to the very large, and also surveyed a sample of employees in each firm. It is thus possible to use this unique data set to study the labor variables as related to the characteristics of different groups of firms. The period of the surveys is generally 1992-95, after the wage decline over the past quarter of a century, and after some of the economies had adopted structural adjustment programs.

The presence of the state is important in African manufacturing, though in most countries the joint venture with partial state participation predominates. Taking the two categories together, the proportion of the total employed in such enterprises ranged from a low of 14 percent in

Kenya to 70 percent in Cameroon and Tanzania. Many developing countries make use of temporary or casual labor along with 'regulars' in their manufacturing enterprises. It saves the firms in benefit payments and it is also a very useful system of recruitment and selection of suitable labor out of a heterogeneous mass. In the Indian textile industry around 25 percent of the complement of labor has been of the 'casual' type. Surprisingly, in the seven countries studied only Kenya and to lesser extent Zimbabwe have use of non-regular workers of this magnitude: for all other countries the proportion of such labor is around 10 percent.

Another complaint about African firms has been that the use of white-collar workers has been excessive, adding to the labor costs of industry, particularly in the state sector. Our analysis of the data showed that, controlling for ownership and other relevant variables, the proportion of the blue-collar share generally increase with the size groups of firms. This is understandable because there is a minimum number of management, administrative and clerical personnel are needed in a firm of any size, and the family workers of small firms, who might be classified as white collar, generally perform multiple jobs. A quick glance at our tables organizing this set of data shows that only Tanzania seems to have a particularly high share of white collar workers in the larger firms — around 40 percent, the other countries hovering around 20-30 percent, which does not seem to be excessive. Female workers are a distinct minority in the manufacturing labor force in Africa: Ghana has the largest proportion in our sample at 26 percent, the others in the range of 10-16 percent. The regular workforce is surprisingly well educated. The proportion with secondary education (including vocational) or more was in the 60-75 percent range.

A great deal of analysis was devoted to the structure of earnings and its determinants. The RPED data set provides for the first time comparable material from seven African countries, and we can supplement this material from other sources like the ILO. Our detailed survey in Chapter 13 shows that there are important differences in occupational differences between countries in Africa. Zambia and Zimbabwe have the largest occupational differentials, with Tanzania showing the least. The other countries — including the two francophone countries have moderate differentials. Overall, the differentials among *production (blue-collar)* workers in Africa are not excessive compared to Western countries like the US and the UK: the skilled-unskilled differential among such workers is larger in Africa, but the semi-skilled-unskilled differential is lower. The major difference is seen in the extent of differential between white and blue collar workers which is much higher in Africa — though not by the nineties among public service employees, who took the brunt of the declining formal sector wage in Africa. Readers would probably be more interested in the degree of inequality of the wage distribution as a whole than in the difference in earnings per worker by occupation. The former includes the distribution of employment among categories of wage groups. Although not strictly comparable (coming from different sources, as discussed in the text), the material enables us to see the wage-earners in the seven African countries in relation to each other as well as to some advanced countries of the world. It appears that among the advanced countries North America has the highest inequality among wage earners: the ratio of the first decile to the ninth decile of the earnings distribution (P10/P90) is 0.18 for the USA and 0.22 for Canada. The European countries generally have much lower degrees of in equality in the range of 0.30-0.40. Our sample of African countries has significantly more unequal distribution than even the USA.

The discussions in Chapters 14 and 15 carry us through various factors causing the wage inequality. An important factor, of course, is the impact of education on earnings. The evidence from the RPED studies show that the return to schooling is high — very high at 11 and 14 percent per year of schooling in Zambia and Zimbabwe, but generally in the 5-7 percent range for the other five countries. There is clear evidence of *increasing returns* to successive levels of education, contradicting the views of writers like Psacharapoulos who might have used older or inadequate data. This important result was confirmed by data covering sectors other than manufacturing obtained from household surveys in a few countries. It was suggested on the basis of a detailed study of Ghana that one reason for the phenomenon of increasing returns to educational levels is the deterioration in the quality of education over time. This deterioration has gone so far that in several countries the market does not attach any premium to primary education at all.

Other important factors contributing to earnings differentials are ownership category and size of establishment. It is remarkable that in most countries foreign or state ownership, even when it is jointly with the private sector, adds significantly to earnings, after we have controlled for other factors in the earnings function. The only exceptions are the foreign sector in Tanzania and the State sector in Kenya. Ownership category is somewhat correlated with firm (enterprise) size, but the analysis shows that they exert separate and significant influence on earnings.

One of the most important factors contributing to wage inequality is the difference in wage levels by the size of the enterprise. Careful study of the wage data in the RPED countries showed that the wage-size relationship exists in an important way after we have controlled for observed quality of labor and other firm characteristics like ownership category. In the African economies studied, as in developed countries, wages and labor productivity increase with firm size, but consistent with the evidence available for other developing countries, both wages and labor productivity increase much more with firm size in Africa. In the United States, both wage and output elasticities with respect to plant size seem to have doubled in the eighties, but are generally nowhere near the magnitudes observed in the African economies.

The evidence suggests that there are important differences in the economic landscape of developed and less developed economies, which produce such huge differences in wage levels by size in the latter. We think immediately of the less homogeneous quality of labor (not captured by measurable human capital factors) and the larger dispersion of techniques of production in the less developed countries which causes a much larger increase in labor productivity in bigger establishments with more modern technologies. The existence of marked difference in unobserved labor quality in the pool of job-seekers means that various strands of the efficiency-wage models are particularly strong in the African economies: labor efficiency responds strongly to wage increase up to a certain point. At the same time, more mechanized techniques of production produce high labor productivity and profits which tend to be shared among workers for morale and other factors stressed in rent sharing models. The work reported in Chapter 15 above tried to sort out the relative importance of these different factors within an econometric framework. Since these factors work together, their relative strength can only be studied in a system of simultaneous equations and it can be identified by evaluating the strength of the direction of causation — the one running from wages to productivity as suggested by the efficiency wage models, and the other running from productivity to wages as stressed by the rent sharing models. Although they are difficult to disentangle, our econometric model goes some way towards sorting out the various factors. We conclude that the preponderance of evidence is that the profit-sharing influence is the stronger one in several of the economies studied.

Bibliography

Akerlof, G. A. and Yellen, J. L. ed. (1986), *Efficiency Wage Models of the Labor Market*, Cambridge, Cambridge University.

Alderman, Harold, Sudarshan Canagarajah and Stephen Younger (1994), 'A comparison of Ghanaian civil servants' earnings before and after retrenchment'. *Working Paper of the Cornell Food and Nutrition Policy Program # 64*. Ithaca, NY.

Amsden, Alice (1990), 'South Korea's Record Wage Rates: Labor in Late Industrialization', *Industrial Relations*, 29,1.

Appleton, Simon and Collier, Paul (1990),'Agriculture and the Macro-economy: consequences of negative external shocks in Ghana and Côte d'Ivoire, 1978-87', *World Employment Program Working Paper #10-6/WP 103,* ILO, Geneva.

Appleton, S., Hoddinott, J. and Krishnan, P. (1999), 'The Gender Wage Gap in Three African Countries', *Economic Development and Cultural Change,* 47 (2), pp. 289-312.

Arrighi, Giovanni and Saul, J (1968),'Socialism and Economic Development in Tropical Africa', *Journal of Modern African Studies*, 6, 2.

Behrman, J. and Birdsall, N. (1983), 'The Quality of Schooling: Quantity Alone is Misleading', *American Economic Review,* 73 (5), pp. 926-946.

Bennell, P. (1996), 'Rates of Return to Education: does the Conventional Pattern Prevail in sub-Saharan Africa?' *World Development,* 24 (1), pp. 183-199.

Berthelemy, J.C. and Bouguignon, F. (1996), *'Growth and Crisis in Cote d'Ivoire',* The World Bank, Washington DC.

Bauer, P.T. and Yamey, B. S. (1951), 'Economic Progress and Occupational Distribution', *Economic Journal,* 61 (December).

Bloom, David E., and Sachs, Jeffrey (1998), 'Geography, Demography and Economic Growth in Africa', *Brookings papers in Economic Activity,* 2, pp. 207-295.

Brown, C. and Medoff, J. (1989), 'The employer Size Wage Effect', *Journal of Political Economy*, 97, pp. 1027-1059.

Canagarajah, Sudarshan and Saji, Thomas (1996), *'Ghana's Labor Market 1897-92'*. Processed. Africa Region, World Bank, Washington DC.

Canagarajah, Sudarshan and Mazumdar, Dipak (1997), *'Employment, Labor Markets and Poverty in Ghana: a Study of Changes during recovery and Decline*', Policy Research Working paper, 1845, World Bank, Washington DC.

Canagarajah, S., Mazumdar, Dipak and Ye, Xiao (1998), 'The Structure and Determinants of Inequality and Poverty reduction in Ghana, 1988-92', *Policy Research Working Paper,* October, Africa Region, World Bank, Washington D.C.

Colclough, Christopher (1989), *'The Labor Market and Economic Stabilization in Zambia*', World Bank Working Papers, Policy Planning and Research, # WPS 222, Washington.

Collier, Paul & Lal, Deepak (1986), *'Labor and Poverty in Kenya 1900-1980*', Clarendon Press, Oxford.

Collier, Paul (1998), 'Comment' on Bloom and Sachs (1998), *Brookings Papers on Economic Activity,* 2, pp. 274-281.

Collier, Paul (1999), 'Explaining African Economic Performance', *Journal of Economic Literature,* XXXVII (March), pp. 64-111.

Commander, Simon and Uzag, Cecilia (1994), 'What seems right and what seems wrong with Ghanaian labor markets', *The Economic Bulletin of Ghana*, 1, 129-141.

Coulombe, Harold and Mckay, Andrew (1995), '*An Assessment of Trends in Poverty in Ghana, 1988-92*', World Bank, Washington D.C., Mimeo, May.

Dabelan, Andrew, Mengistae, Taye and Dorte Verner (2001*), Employment and Wages during the Reform Period in Sub-Saharan Africa: A Synthesis,* Mimeo, World Bank, March.

Dar, A., Tzannatos, Z., Canagarajah, S. and Thomas, S. (1997), '*Ghana: Earnings and Inequality in 1987-8 and 1991-2.*' Processed, Africa Region, World Bank, Washington DC.

de Merode, Louis (1992), 'Implementing Civil Service Pay and Employment Reform in Africa: The Experiences of Ghana, the Gambia and Ghana' *Draft,* World Bank, Washington D.C.

Demery, Lionel, and Mehra, Kalpaha (1997), '*Measuring Poverty Over Time: Dealing With Uncooperative Data in Ghana*', World Bank, Mimeo, 1997.

Ewusi, K. (1984), 'The Dimensions and Characteristics of Rural Poverty in Ghana' *Technical Publications* No. 43, Institute of Statistical, Social and Economic Research, Lagon, Ghana.

Fallon, Peter R. (1985), '*The Labor Market in Kenya: Recent Evidence*', Mimeo, World Bank, October.

Glewwe, Paul (1996), 'The Relevance of Standard Estimates of Rates of of Return to Schooling for Education Policy: A Critical Assessment', *Journal of Development Economics,* Vol. 5, pp. 267-290.

Gottschalk, Peter and Smeeding T.M. (1997), 'Cross-National Comparisons of Earnings and Income Inequality', *Journal of Economic Literature*, 35, 633-687.

Grossan, Boris, (1953), '*Industrial Efficiency and the Urban African*', Africa, , pp. 143f.

Hammermesh, Daniel S., (1980), 'Commentary' in *The Economics of Firm Size, Market Structure, and Social Performance*', edited by J. J. Seigfried, Washington, Federal Trade Commission.

Harbison, R. and Hamushek, E. (1992), *Educational Performance of the Poor: Lessons from Rural North-East Brazil,* Oxford University Press.

Heller, Peter and Tate A (1983), 'Government Employment and Pay: Some International Comparisons', *International Monetary Fund Occasional Paper* 24, Washington DC.

House, Ikira and McCornick. [see Dabalan].

House, William J. (1981), 'Nairobi's Informal Sector: An Explanatory Study' in Killick, Anthony C. (ed.) *Papers on the Economy of Kenya,*Heinemann, London.

House, W. J. (1984), 'Nairobi's Informal Sector: Dynamic Entrepreneurs or Surplus Labor?', *Economic Development and Cultural Change,* January.

Huang T-L, Hallam, A., Orazem P. F. and Paterno, E. (1998), '*Empirical Tests of Efficiency Wage Models*', 65, pp. 125-143.

Idson, T. and Feaster, D. (1990), 'A Selectivity Model of Employer Size Wage Differentials', *Journal of Labor Economics*, 8, pp. 99-122.

Institute of Social and Economic Research (ISSER) (1995), '*The State of the Ghanaian Economy*', in 1994. University of Ghana, Accra.

International Labor Organization (ILO) '*Yearbook of Labor Statistics*', Annual. Geneva.

International Labor Organization. (1972), '*Employment, Income and Equality: A strategy for increasing productive employment in Kenya*', Geneva.

_______ (1975), '*Report to the Government of Zambia on incomes, wages and prices in Zambia*', policy and machinery, Turner Zambia Report 1, Geneva.

_______ (1978), '*Second Report to the Government of Zambia on incomes, wages and prices*', policy and machinery, Turner Zambia Report 2, Geneva.

Jamel, Vali and Weeks, John (1993), '*Africa Misunderstood or Whatever Happened to the Rural-Urban Wage Gap*', McMillan for the ILO, London.

Karp-Todaro, Ealine (1991), 'Les Fonds d'Emploi—Sont-ils Efficaces', *Draft Report,* Socio-economique de la Dire/ FNE, Senegal.

Kenya (1954), '*Report on the Committee on African Wages'*, Government Printer, Nairobi (Carpenter Committee).

Kenya Ministry of Planning and National Development (1991), '*Historical Economic Data for Kenya*', 1972-90. Technical Paper 91-92.

Kilby, P. (1969), *Industrialization in an Open Economy,* Cambridge University Press, London.

Kingsbury, David S. (1992), 'Compensatory Social Programs and Structural Adjustments: A Review of Experience', *Draft Report,* Development Policy Alternatives Inc., Bethesda, Maryland.

Knight, John B (1972),'*Rural-urban Income comparisons and Migration in Ghana*', Bulletin of Oxford University Institute of Economics and Statistics, 34,2.

Knight John B. and Sabot, R. H. (1978), 'Educational Expansion, Government policy and Wage Compression', *Journal of Development Economics.*

Knight, John B. and Sabot, Richard, H. (1990), '*Education, Productivity and Inequality: The East African Natural Experiment*', Oxford.

Lavy, V., and Newman, J.L. (1989), 'Wage Rigidity: Micro and Macro Evidence on Labor Market Evidence in the Modern Sector', *World Bank Economic Review*, 3, 97-117.

Leechoor, Chad. (1994), 'Ghana: frontrunner in adjustment', Chapter 4 *in Adjustment in Africa; Lessons from country experiences*, edited by Ishrat Husain and Rashid Faruque, World Bank, Washington DC.

Levine, D.L. (1992), 'Can Wage Increases Pay for Themselves? Test with a Production Function', *Economic Journal*, 102, pp. 1102-1115.

Leys, Colin (1971), 'Political perspectives' in Dudley Seers and Leonard Joy (eds.). *Development in a Divided World.*, Penguin, London.

Lindauer, David (1991), 'Parastatal pay policy in Africa', *World Development*, 19 (7), 831-838.

Lindauer, David and Sabot R.H. (1983), 'The Prove-Public Wage Differential in a Poor Urban Economy', *Journal of Development Economics* 12 (1/2), 137-152.

Lindauer, David, Meesook, O. and Suebsaeng, P. (1988), 'Government wage Policy in Africa: some Findings and Policy Issues', *World Bank Research Observer*, 3(1), 1-25.

Little, I.M.D., Page, John M., and Mazumdar, Dipak (1987), *Small Manufacturing Enterprises: A Compartive Study of Indian and Other Economies,* Oxford University Press for the World Bank, Washington D.C.

Loxley , John (1990), '*Rural Labor Markets in an Adjusting Mineral Economy: Zambia*', ILO World Employment Program.

Mazumdar, Dipak (1959), 'Underemployment in agriculture and the industrial wage rate,' *Economica*, 26, 107, 328-340

Mazumdar, Dipak (1973), 'Labour supply in early industrialization: the case of the textile industry', *Economic History Review* (1973) 26 477-496. World Bank Reprint Series, no. 79.

Mazumdar, Dipak (1981), '*The Urban Labor Market and Income Distribution: a Case Study of Malaysia*', Oxford: Oxford University Press, 1981, A World Bank Research Publication.

Mazumdar, Dipak (1983) 'The rural-urban wage gap, migration and the working of urban labor markets: an interpretation based on a study of the workers of Bombay city', *Indian Economic Review*, 18, 169-198. *World Bank Reprint Series*, no 300.

Mazumdar, Dipak (1987), 'Rural-Urban Migration in Developing Countries', in Mills, Edwin S. (ed) *Handbook of Regional and Urban Economics,* Vol II, Ch. 28, pp. 1097-1128, Elsevir Science Publishers B.V.

Mazumdar, Dipak (1993a), 'Labor Markets and Adjustment in Open Asian Economies, The Republic of Korea and Malaysia', *World Bank Economic Review*, 7, 1, 349-380.

Mazumdar, Dipak (1993b), '*Wages and Employment in Kenya. Processed*', Africa Region Chief Economist's Office, The World Bank, Washington DC.

Mazumdar, Dipak (1994), '*Wages in Africa*', Draft, Office of the Chief Economist for Africa, The World Bank, February 1994.

Mazumdar, Dipak (2001), '*Labor Markets and Adjustment in Open Asian Economies: Korea and Malaysia, World Bank Economic Review*, forthcoming, September.

Meesook, Oy, et al. (1986), '*Wage Policy and the Structure of wages and Employment in Zambia*', CPD Discussion Paper # 1986-1. World Bank, Washington DC.

Mengistae, Taye (1998), 'Wage Rates and Job Queues: Does the Public Sector Overpay in Ethiopia?' *Working Papers,* WPS/ 98-20, Center for African Economies, Oxford.

Mills, B. and Sahn, D. (1993), 'Is there Life after Public Service: the Fate of Retrenched Workers in Conarkey, Guinea', *Working Paper,* No. 42, Cornell Food and Nutrition Policy Program, Ithaka, New York.

Mills, B. and Sahn, D. (1995), 'Reducing the Size of the Public Sector Workforce: Institutional Constraints and Human Consequences in Guinea', *Journal of Development Studies,* 31 (4), pp. 505-28.

Milne, William, J. (1993), '*Labor Markets in an Era of Adjustment: Kenya*' forthcoming in a volume to be published by the Economic Development Institute, World Bank, 1993.

Myint, H. (1964), '*The Economics of Developing Countries'*, Hutchinson, London.

Mylteka, C. (1984), 'Foreign Capital and Textile Industry', in Delgado C. et Zartman (eds.) *The Political Economy of Ivory Coast*, Praeger, New York.

Natal University (1950), '*The African Factory Worker*', Oxford.

Nielsen, Helena S. and Westergard-Nielsen, Niels (2001), 'Returns to Schooling in Less Developed Countries: New Evidence from Zambia', *Economic Development and Cultural Change,* 49(2), pp. 365-394.

Oaxaca, R. (1973), 'Male-female wage differentials in urban labor markets', *International Economic Review*, 14, 3, 693-709.

Ogura, Mitsuo (1991), 'Rural-Urban Migration in Zambia and Migrant Ties to Home Villages', *The Developing Economies*, XXIX-2,145-165. Tokyo.

Psacharapoulos, Soerge, Tzannatos Z. (1992), '*Women's Pay and Employment in Latin America*', World Bank, Washington DC.

Reder, M.W. (1955), 'The Theory of Occupational Wage Differentials', *American Economic Review,* 44, pp. 833-52.

Rempel, H. and House, W. J. (1978), '*The Kenya Employment Problem: An Analysis of the Modern Sector Labor Market',* Oxford University Press, Nairobi.

RPED, (1996), '*Cote d'Ivoire: An Agricultural Export-led Growth with Low Industrialization*', Country Background Papers. March, Washington DC.

Sahn, David E (1992),' Public Expenditures in Sub-Saharan Africa during a Period of Economic Reforms', *World Development*, 20 (5), 673-693.

Sahn, David E., Dorosh, P. and Younger, S. (1994), 'Economic Reform in Africa: A foundation for Poverty Alleviation', *Draft Prepared for the Special Program of Assistant Donor's Meeting* (September), Cornell University Food and Nutrition Policy Program, Ithaca, New York.

Schaffner, J. (1994), 'Larger Employer Wage Premium in Peru', Mimeo, Stanford University.

Shapiro, C. and Stiglitz, J. E. (1984), 'Equilibrium Unemployment as a Worker Discipline Device', *America Economic Review*, 74, pp. 433-444.

Sharpley, Jennifer and Lewis, Stephen (1990), 'Kenya: Manufacturing sector to the mid-1980s' in Roger C. Riddle (ed), *Manufacturing Africa*, James Curry, London and Heinemann, Portsmouth, N.H.

Smith, A.D. (ed.) (1969), '*Wage Policy Issues in Economic Development*', Macmillan, London.

Solow, Robert M. (1957), '*Technical Changes and Aggregate Production Function*', *Review of Economic and Statistics*, August.

Solow, Robert M. (1979), 'Another Possible Source of Wage Stickiness', *Journal of Macroeconomics*.

Squire, Lynn and Suthiwar-Narueput S. (1992), 'The Impact of Labor Market Regulations', *World Bank Economic Review*, 11 (1), 119-143.

Standing, Guy and Tokman, Victor (1991), '*Towards Social Adjustment: Labor Market Issues in Structural Adjustment*', ILO, Geneva.

Stewart, Frances (1972), 'Choice of Technique in Developing Countries', *Journal of Development Studies*, 9, 1.

Tabatabai, Hamid (1988), 'Agricultural decline and access to food in Ghana', *International Labor Review*, 127, 6, 703-734.

Teal, Francis (1996), 'The Size and Sources of Economic Rents in a developing Country Manufacturing Labour Market', *The Economic Journal*, 106, pp. 963-946.

Thias, Hans Heinrich and Carnoy, Martin (1972), '*Cost-Benefit Analysis in Education: A Case Study of Kenya*', Johns Hopkins, Baltimore.

University of Natal (1950), *The African Factory Worker,* Durban.

Van der Gaarg J. and Vijverberg W. (1988), 'A Switching regression Model for Wage Determinants in Public and private Sectors of a Developing Country', *Review of Economics and Statistics*, 70, 2, 244-52.

Valenchik A. D. (1997), 'Government Intervention, Efficiency Wages, and the Employer Size Wage Effect in Zimbabwe', *Journal of Development Economics*, 53, pp. 305-338.

Weeks, John (1990), 'Structural Adjustment and Rural Labor Markets in Sierra Leone', *World Employment Program Working Paper,* ILO, Geneva.

Wood, Anthony (1997), 'Openness and Wage Inequality in Developing Countries: the Latin American Challenge to East Asian Conventional Wisdom', *World Bank Economic Review,* 11 (1), pp. 33-57.

Wood, Adrian and Berge, Kristi (1997), Exporting Manufactures, Human Resources, Natural Resources and Trade Policy', *Journal of Development Studies,* 34(1), pp.35-59.

Wood, Anthony and Mayer, Jorg (1999), '*Africa's Export Structure in Comparative Perspective*', Economic Development and Regional Dynamics in Africa: Lessons from the East Asian Experience series, United Nations Commission on Trade and Development, New York.

World Bank (1983), '*World Bank Tables* ', Johns Hopkins for the IBRD, Baltimore.

World Bank (1985), '*Ghana: Growth, Private Sector and Poverty Reduction*', World Bank, Washington DC.

World Bank (1989), '*Ghana: Structural Adjustment for Growth*', Western Africa Department, Washington DC.

World Bank (1993a), '*Sierra Leone: Policies for Sustained Economic Growth and Poverty Alleviation*', Report 11371-SL. Africa Region, May. Washington DC.

World Bank (1993b), '*Zambia: Prospects for Sustainable and Equitable Growth*', Country Economic Report, Washington DC.

World Bank (1993c) '*Adjustment in Africa: Reforms, Results and the Road Ahead*',

Washington DC.

World Bank (1994), '*Ghana: Economic Memorandum*', Washington DC.

World Bank (1995a), '*Ghana: Growth, Private Sector and Poverty Reduction*', Washington DC.

World Bank (1995b), '*Ghana: Poverty Past, Present and Future*', Report no. 14504-GH, June .

World Bank (1997), '*Poverty in Cote d'Ivoire: A Framework for Action*', Report no. 156-40-IVC. June, Washington DC.

World Bank, (1999), '*African Development Indicators*', Washington DC.

Younger, Stephen D. (1991), '*Aid and the Dutch disease: Macro-economic management when everybody loves you*', Cornell University Food and Nutrition Program, Working Paper #17, Ithaca, NY.

Younger, S. (1996), 'Labor Market Consequences of retrenchment of Civil Servants in Ghana in Sahn, D.E. (ed) *Economic Reform and the Poor in Africa,* Clarendon, Oxford.

Index